The Herbfarm Cookbook

Jerry Traunfeld

*Botanical Watercolors of Herbs
by Louise Smith*

Illustrations by Elayne Sears

Color Photographs by Jonelle Weaver

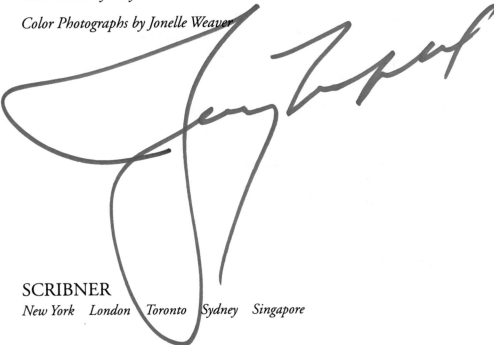

SCRIBNER
New York   London   Toronto   Sydney   Singapore

Scribner
1230 Avenue of the Americas
New York, NY 10020

Scribner and design are trademarks of Macmillan Library Reference USA, Inc.,
used under license by Simon & Schuster, the publisher of this work.

Designed by Virginia Hand
Set in Adobe Garamond

Manufactured in the United States of America

10 9

Library of Congress Cataloging-in-Publication Data
Traunfeld, Jerry, date.
The Herbfarm cookbook / Jerry Traunfeld ;
botanical watercolors of herbs by Louise Smith ; line drawings by Elayne Sears.
p. cm.
Includes bibliographical references and index.
1. Cookery (Herbs) 2. Herbfarm Restaurant (Fall City, Wash.) I. Title.
TX819.H4 T72 2000
641.6'57—dc21   99-056990

ISBN 0-684-83976-8

To my parents,
Poppy and Irving

CONTENTS

INTRODUCTION

When I first learned to cook, at age eleven, my mother kept herbs in jars, alphabetically arranged on a shelf. I was taught to apportion these dusty-smelling powders and flakes with the precision of a chemist—one teaspoon of oregano in the tomato sauce, one-quarter teaspoon of tarragon in the vegetable soup, one-half teaspoon of sage with the chicken—as if alchemy would occur when a recipe's formula was followed perfectly. It never occurred to me then that we could grow all these herbs in our backyard, and I had no idea how they looked or smelled before they were dried, processed, and packaged. At the time, the only fresh herb in the supermarket was parsley.

Now fresh herbs are everywhere. More often than not the word "fresh" precedes thyme, tarragon, or basil in recipes we see in print. Freshly cut sprigs of all common herbs are available year-round in supermarkets across the nation. Farmers' markets are flooded with lush bunches of locally grown herbs, and garden centers and specialty nurseries are packed with potted herbs from angelica to verbena. More and more backyards have oregano and dill planted next to the tomatoes, and pots of chives and rosemary are replacing the petunias on the patio or terrace. This availability is making a fundamental change in the way we cook.

The flavor of a fresh herb has little in common with what comes in a jar. Taste a few flakes of dry tarragon and they will seem little more than mild and musty. Then taste a leaf of fresh tarragon, just picked from the garden; it will be sweet and peppery and fill your mouth with a punchy anise flavor underscored with green savoriness. Stir a coarsely chopped spoonful of the fresh leaves into a braising pan of chicken and its flavor will permeate the juices and flavor the chicken itself. Next, compare a spoonful of dried basil with a bunch of fresh Genovese basil from the farmers' market. The flakes are insipid and lifeless, but the complex layering of mint, clove, anise, and cinnamon scents that waft from the fresh sprigs is so enticing you'll want to bury yourself in them. Pound the leaves in a mortar with garlic, pine nuts, olive oil, and Parmigiano-Reggiano, and you'll have fragrant, unctuous pesto, the nonpareil pasta sauce.

Fresh herbs offer an astounding palette of vibrant and glorious tastes, but their delights go beyond the flavors they lend to food. For a cook, there is joy in simply handling fresh herbs in the kitchen. Who can resist stroking the proud sticky needles of rosemary, rubbing a plush sage leaf, or crushing a crinkled leaf of verdant mint between their fingers? When you strip the fragrant leaves off sweet marjoram or tuck a few sprigs of shrubby thyme in a simmering stew, you feel connected to the soil and the season, no matter where your kitchen is.

I have the opportunity all chefs dream of. As chef of The Herbfarm Restaurant in the lush, rainy foothills of the Cascade Mountains, I design nine-course menus for an intimate dining room surrounded by acres of kitchen gardens. If I need a bunch of chives, a bucket of chervil, or a leaf of rose geranium, I pick it right outside. Over the course of my nine years at The Herbfarm and many years of herb gardening in my own backyard in Seattle, I've come to know each herb as an old friend, and they have offered me endless inspiration. I've written this book to share what I have learned about these soul-stirring ingredients with those who love to cook at home.

CHAPTER 1

Soups

If you're learning to cook with fresh herbs, you'll do well by starting with soups, for in a soup everything is told in a single spoonful. Each style—cream of vegetable, bisque, hearty bean, consommé, or chowder—is a framework, and each addition to the soup pot builds another layer of flavor. Some flavors will jump to the forefront and some will provide support behind, but in a great soup, they'll find perfect balance and highlight the essence of the main ingredients. The collection of recipes in this chapter represent not only a wide range of soup styles but also varied techniques for incorporating the herbs, from simply chopping them and adding them to the pot, to puréeing and infusing. Here's the perfect opportunity to discover how each herb's personality can mingle, lend an accent, or take center stage.

Chicken Stock

Makes 4 quarts

Every chef has a slightly different idea about how to make basic chicken stock, but all agree on a few basic principles. First, don't add more water than is needed to cover the chicken and vegetables. The smaller the pieces of chicken, the less volume they'll take up in the pot, the less water needed to cover them, and the stronger the stock. If the stock comes out too strong, you can always dilute it with water. Second, start with cold water—as it heats it will gently pull the impurities from the bones. Third, keep the stock at the gentlest simmer and don't disturb it. If you boil it rapidly or stir it up, you'll end up with cloudy stock. You needn't be obsessive about skimming, but it's important to remove the impurities as it comes to a boil, and then a couple of more times in the following thirty minutes as the fat rises.

Stock making is the one area of cooking where I use a light touch with herbs. The end product should be full of chicken flavor but neutral in every other respect, so that it doesn't add unwanted flavors to a dish. Stock is an ingredient, not a finished soup. The classic "flavor packet" for simmering in stocks is called a bouquet garni. It varies slightly depending on the cook but usually has thyme sprigs, parsley stems, and bay leaves. The ingredients can be tied with a string, wrapped in a leek leaf or celery ribs and tied, or put in a cheesecloth bag. If you're in a hurry, you can toss them in without bundling.

If your family eats chicken often and you cut up the birds yourself, you might have a freezer full of carcasses for your stock; otherwise, you'll have to buy chicken parts. Backs, wings, and necks are a good choice if they're available. Since whole chickens are comparatively inexpensive, I usually buy two or three birds, remove the breast meat to freeze individually for other recipes, and cut up all the rest of the chicken for the stock.

> *6 pounds chicken parts or bones, or 2 whole chickens with breast meat*
>   *removed, each cut into 6 pieces*
> *About 4 quarts cold water*
> *1 small bunch parsley stems*
> *4 4-inch sprigs fresh or dried thyme*
> *2 fresh bay laurel leaves, or 1 dried*
> *1 onion, quartered with peel*
> *1 carrot, peeled and cut into 1-inch pieces*
> *2 ribs celery, cut into 1-inch pieces*

1. Stock. Put the chicken parts in an 8-quart or larger stockpot and add enough cold water to cover. Bring the stock to a simmer over medium heat, then reduce the heat to maintain a very gentle simmer. Using a ladle, skim off any fat or impurities that rise to the surface. Simmer for 30 minutes, skimming several more times.

2. Aromatics. Tie the parsley, thyme, and bay leaves together with cotton string to make a bouquet garni. Add it to the pot along with the vegetables. Continue to cook the stock uncovered at the lowest simmer for 2 to 3 more hours, skimming from time to time if needed.

3. Straining and storing. Pour the stock through a large colander placed over another large pot or a very large bowl. Discard the solids. If you wish to use the stock right away, let it settle for about 5 minutes, then skim off all the fat with a ladle. Otherwise refrigerate the stock uncovered and later remove the congealed fat with a large spoon. Store the stock covered in the refrigerator for up to 3 days or freeze it in small batches for later use.

A Note on Canned Stocks

All good cooks know that homemade stocks have a great deal more flavor and body than canned ones. But even the most conscientious cooks will sometimes find themselves in need of a ready-made substitute and, apart from expensive frozen stocks found in some high-end markets, canned stock is the best alternative.

Ordinary supermarket brands of stock have an enormous amount of salt added—1,000 milligrams or nearly ½ teaspoon per cup—and most contain MSG. Lower sodium versions are now available with one-third less salt, but you're still left with about 650 milligrams or over ¼ teaspoon per cup. A soup with 4 cups reduced-sodium stock will have over 1 teaspoon of salt, more than some recipes require in the first place. An alternative is to search out the no-salt-added stocks that are sold in some supermarkets and natural food stores; these contain about 50 milligrams of sodium per cup. Otherwise, anytime you cook with a salted stock, don't add any of the salt that the recipe calls for until you taste and determine whether or not it's needed.

Golden Vegetable Stock

Makes 4 quarts

A dish made with vegetable stock is never going to taste the same as one with a meat stock, but skillful vegetarian cooking never tries to imitate meat flavors. Instead, it strives to highlight the qualities inherent in ingredients grown from the soil.

The goal in making good vegetable stock is to produce an aromatic liquid with a deep neutral flavor that won't throw off the balance of the dishes in which it's used. I always like to include mushrooms, either fresh button or dried porcini, because they have a savory quality that adds a much needed depth of flavor. Also I try not to use too many onions or carrots, which make the stock overly sweet. It's best to use a wide variety of vegetables. Feel free to vary this recipe to accommodate what you have in your refrigerator. By no means add anything on the far side of fresh, but a vegetable stock can make use of odds and ends like mushroom stems, fennel stalks, leek greens, celery leaves, and parsley stems. Just don't add too much of any one ingredient.

This is an all-purpose stock. Use it in vegetable soups or risotto when you need a light-bodied stock that has some depth of flavor.

1 large leek
1 medium onion, coarsely chopped
1 medium carrot, coarsely chopped
2 ribs celery, coarsely chopped
1 wedge green cabbage (about ⅛ medium head), coarsely chopped
1 medium turnip, coarsely chopped
6 large white button mushrooms, coarsely chopped, or 6 ounces
  mushroom stems
Stalks from 1 fennel bulb, coarsely chopped
2 cloves garlic, smashed
1 medium bunch parsley, or stems from 1 large bunch
6 4-inch sprigs fresh English or lemon thyme
4 fresh bay laurel leaves, or 2 dried
4 quarts cold water

1. Stock. Slice the leeks lengthwise in half, keeping the roots attached so that the layers will not fall apart, and wash thoroughly. Coarsely chop both the green and white parts. Put the leek and all the remaining ingredients in a 6-quart or larger stockpot. Bring the stock to a boil over medium heat, then reduce the heat, cover, and cook at the gentlest simmer for 1 hour.

2. **Finishing the stock.** Strain the stock through a colander and press down on the solids to extract as much liquid as possible. The stock will keep for 1 week covered in the refrigerator, or it can be frozen in small batches for up to 3 months.

A Note About Salt

All the recipes in this book call for ordinary table salt unless otherwise specified, but there are several other types of salt available to home cooks, and each gives slightly different results. Kosher salt has large coarse crystals that melt quickly. Many cooks prefer the feel of kosher salt, and I like it for seasoning leafy salads and for sprinkling meats and fish. When substituting kosher salt for table salt, remember that kosher salt is fluffier and lighter. One teaspoon of table salt is equal to 1¼ to 1⅓ teaspoons of kosher salt.

Sea salt is a favorite of mine for its wonderfully complex flavor. Fine sea salt can be substituted for table salt in any of the recipes in this book. Teaspoon for teaspoon it usually has the same sodium content as table salt, but it seems to taste saltier. Begin with a pinch less of sea salt than the recipe calls for, then taste the dish and add more if you like.

Puréeing Soup

Puréed soups are not only elegant but often the fastest to prepare. Since everything is whizzed together at the end, careful chopping of the ingredients is not necessary, and when you add herbs, you simply need to strip them off the stem. Always add herbs with soft leaves at the end of the cooking process to retain the most flavor.

The consistency of a puréed soup can be velvety smooth to coarse and chunky—the choice is up to the cook. Smooth soups have a creamy feel in the mouth and a refined style; they tend to work best as a first course. Textured soups are more exuberant and are often more satisfying to build a meal around.

The tool used to purée the soup has much to do with the final result. For a soup that is absolutely smooth and fine, a blender is essential. When I was growing up, there was a blender in every kitchen, but in the last decade or two they were upstaged by food processors. Both are useful, but blenders do a much better job of liquefying. If you've sent your blender to the secondhand store or sold it in a garage sale, it's worth purchasing a replacement. Use caution when blending hot soup. Never fill the blender container more than half full and hold the lid down with a dry towel to ensure it doesn't fly up. Begin puréeing on the lowest speed, then gradually increase to high. When the soup is smooth, switch to low speed before turning the machine off to prevent the soup from burping up. To blend well, the soup must be thin enough to form a vortex when the machine is running. If the soup seems to be moving only in the bottom portion of the container, add more liquid.

For a soup with texture, a food processor allows you to have more control of the soup's consistency. Don't fill the bowl more than half full. Pulse briefly for a rough purée; for a finer texture, run the machine continuously until the consistency suits you.

A handheld immersion blender is another option for puréeing soups. Large and powerful versions of these gadgets have been used in restaurants for years, but recently a smaller, less powerful home model has become popular. It's handy for a variety of tasks, but when you purée soup with it, be sure the ingredients are very soft. It will not produce results nearly as smooth as a blender, or even a food processor, but for rough purées it's convenient because you use it right in the soup pot.

The low-tech alternative to these appliances is a food mill—the hand-cranked machine that passes food through a screen with a rotating scraper. Like the immersion blender, this tool works best if the ingredients are very soft, for it will only pass ingredients that can be easily pressed through the holes of its screen. Unless herb leaves are finely chopped with a knife before they're added, they'll probably be removed during the process. This works to your advantage if you want to infuse the soup with an herb's flavor rather than blend the herb into it. If you steep whole sprigs in the soup pot to release their flavor, they'll be left behind when the soup passes through the mill.

Spring Sorrel and Chive Soup

4 to 6 servings

Sorrel and chives are herbs that vanish in the herb garden through the winter but burst into growth early in the spring. One is tart, the other oniony, and they are natural partners in this verdant soup. Usually when making sorrel soup, the herb is cooked in the pot, but my version is different. I start with a base of vegetable or chicken stock flavored with onion and mushroom and lightly thickened with rice. Just before serving I combine the sorrel with chives in a blender, pour the hot soup over them, and purée them together. What emerges is a bright green soup exploding with fresh lemony flavor.

You can prepare the soup base up to the point that it is ready to be puréed with the herbs as much as 2 days ahead of time, and store it covered in the refrigerator. Reheat and purée it with the leaves at the last minute. Frozen in small batches, this soup base can provide you with nearly instant herb soups at any time. All that's needed is the blending in of a few handfuls of herbs and greens from the garden. Any leftover herbed soup can be reheated the next day—the color will fade but the flavor will still be strong.

> *2 tablespoons unsalted butter*
> *1 medium onion (about 8 ounces), coarsely chopped*
> *4 cups homemade (page 12) or canned low-sodium chicken stock, or*
>   *Golden Vegetable Stock (page 14)*
> *8 ounces white button mushrooms, sliced*
> *2 tablespoons long-grain white rice*
> *About 1 teaspoon salt, less if using canned stock*
> *4 ounces sorrel leaves (1 large bunch), washed and spun dry*
> *1 cup coarsely snipped chives (1 ounce)*
> *Freshly ground black pepper*
> *Garnish: very thinly sliced sorrel*
> *Optional garnish: crème fraîche or sour cream, and heavy cream*

1. Soup base. Melt the butter in a medium (3-quart) saucepan over medium heat. Add the onion and cook, stirring often, until softened but not browned, about 6 minutes. Add the stock, mushrooms, rice, and salt (omit if using canned stock) and bring to a boil. Reduce the heat, cover, and simmer until the rice is very soft, about 30 minutes.

2. Finishing the soup. Pull the thick center vein from each sorrel leaf by folding each leaf in half and holding it as you pull down on the stem. You should end up with a little more than 2 cups of firmly packed leaves. Put half of the sorrel and half of the chives in the container of an electric blender (you can use a food processor instead, but the soup will not be as smooth). Pour half of the boiling-hot soup over the greens and cover. Hold the lid down with a dry towel and turn the blender on at low speed so that the soup doesn't splash up, then gradually increase the speed to high and blend until very smooth. Pour the puréed soup into a second saucepan and repeat with the remaining greens and soup. When all of the soup is puréed, stir it over medium heat until it almost comes to a simmer; don't let it boil or the color will turn drab. Taste and season with pepper and additional salt if needed. Ladle the soup into warmed bowls and place a small mound of sorrel strips in the middle of each serving.

3. Optional garnish. If you wish to garnish with cream, vigorously stir the crème fraîche with a teaspoon and thin it with cream until it falls off the spoon in a thick stream. Hold a spoonful of the cream about 6 inches above the bowl and let it fall in a circular or zigzag pattern onto the soup.

For the Gardener

SPRING HERB SOUP

Make a variation of the sorrel and chive soup with other types of soft-leafed young greens or herbs in place of all or part of the sorrel and chives. Put together a mixture of 4 cups of firmly packed stemmed leaves, choosing from arugula, young mustard greens, mâche, mizuna, spinach, lovage, dill, chervil, mint, lemon balm, very young borage leaves, parsley, or sweet cicely. Be careful not to use a large proportion of greens that have a bitter edge. If sorrel is not included or is a minor part of the mix, stir in a squeeze of fresh lemon juice at the end to brighten the taste. If you like, garnish with a few chive florets or calendula petals.

For the Forager

NETTLE AND CHIVE SOUP

Stinging nettles grow wild in many parts of the United States as well as in Europe. They're the earliest edible green to appear in the spring, usually popping up in late February to mid-March in the Pacific Northwest and in early April in colder parts of the country. In past centuries, when the midwinter diet was lacking green vegetables, the first nettles were gathered and made into soup that was meant to be a spring tonic. As it turns out, nettles are rich in vitamins. They also have a delicious soul-satisfying flavor—the taste of concentrated greenness.

Nettles usually grow waist high in the dappled shade at the edge of woods. They are only good to eat when they are very young and tender, before they flower in the late spring. As they get older, the stems become so tough that Native Americans used them as fishing line. **Warning:** Before you harvest any wild food, you must be 100 percent sure of what you are gathering; if you're not, find a knowledgeable person to guide you. Stinging nettles are so named because they'll give you an irritating rash if you touch them before they're cooked. For gathering them, wear long pants, long sleeves, and rubber gloves. Use a pair of ordinary scissors to cut them and have a large paper bag in which to carry them. If the nettles are just coming up and are less than 6 inches high, snip off the top 2 to 3 inches of the plant. If they are taller, harvest the leaves individually from the top third of the plant, cutting them where the stem meets the leaf and letting them drop into the bag. If you harvest carefully, you won't have to wash, sort, or stem the raw leaves when you bring them in the kitchen. Plunge them directly from the bag into a pot of boiling salted water, using your gloved hand or tongs. Once they are briefly cooked, you can touch them safely with bare hands, and they can be frozen the same way you would freeze blanched spinach leaves.

Using gloves, gather 6 ounces (2 quarts gently packed) young nettle leaves. Use tongs to drop them into a large pot of boiling salted water and boil them for 2 minutes. Drain and plunge them into a large bowl of cold water. Gather the leaves into a ball and squeeze out as much water as you can. They'll look like thawed frozen spinach. Follow the directions for the Spring Sorrel and Chive Soup (page 17), substituting the blanched nettles for the sorrel leaves. You may need to add up to an extra cup of stock at the end if the soup is too thick.

If you add ½ cup lovage leaves along with the chives and nettles, the distinct celery flavor will give even more depth to the piercing green quality of the nettles.

Lettuce and Tarragon Soup

6 servings

In this recipe, an ordinary head of romaine is transformed into something very elegant—a smoothly textured, emerald green soup with a delicate flavor underscored by tarragon. It's remarkably simple and quick to prepare and an impressive starter for a dinner party.

> *2 medium leeks (about 1½ pounds)*
> *4 tablespoons unsalted butter*
> *1 clove garlic, finely chopped*
> *4 cups homemade (page 12) or canned low-sodium chicken stock, or*
>   *Golden Vegetable Stock (page 14)*
> *About 1 teaspoon salt, less if using canned stock*
> *1 medium head romaine lettuce, with the outer, deep green leaves*
> *¼ cup fresh French tarragon leaves*
> *Freshly ground black pepper*
> *Optional garnish: crème fraîche or sour cream, and heavy cream*

1. Soup base. Cut off and discard the tops of the leeks at the point where they turn from light to dark green. Split the remaining portion lengthwise in half, keeping the roots attached so that the layers will not fall apart, and wash thoroughly. Thinly slice them into half circles and discard the roots. Melt the butter in a large (4-quart) saucepan over medium heat. Add the leeks and garlic and cook, stirring often, until softened and just beginning to turn golden, about 10 minutes. Add the stock and salt (omit if using canned stock) and bring to a simmer. Turn the heat to low, cover, and cook at a bubbling simmer for 15 minutes to soften the leeks further. (The soup may be made up to this point up to 2 days ahead and stored covered in the refrigerator.)

2. Lettuce. Meanwhile slice the whole head of romaine crosswise into 1-inch-thick strips (you don't need to separate the leaves first) and discard the base. Wash the lettuce in a deep basin of cold water and drain it in a colander. Stir the lettuce into the soup, increase the heat to medium, and cook uncovered until the lettuce is wilted and softened, about 5 minutes.

3. Finishing the soup. Stir in the tarragon leaves. Put half of the soup in the container of an electric blender (you can use a food processor instead, but the soup will not be as smooth). Hold the lid down with a dry towel and turn the blender on at low speed so that the soup doesn't splash up, then gradually increase the speed to high and blend until very smooth. Pour the puréed soup into a second saucepan and repeat with the remaining soup. When all of the soup is puréed, gently reheat. Taste and season with pepper and additional salt if needed. Serve the soup in warmed bowls.

4. Optional garnish. If you wish to garnish with cream, vigorously stir the crème fraîche with a teaspoon and thin it with cream until it falls off the spoon in a thick stream. Hold a spoonful of the cream about 6 inches above the bowl and let it fall in a circular or zigzag pattern onto the soup.

 HERB SUBSTITUTIONS
- *Use 1 cup chervil, gently packed, or 2 tablespoons lovage leaves in place of the tarragon.*

TOMATO AND FENNEL SOUP

6 servings

In high summer, fresh tomato soups are a delight to prepare and serve, and this easy-to-make version with fennel and tarragon is a favorite. The fennel bulb adds both sweetness and body, mellowing the tangy tomatoes and enriching the soup without resorting to cream. The fresh tarragon amplifies the flavor of the fennel and complements the tomato, allowing the personality of both vegetables to come through clearly.

> *1 large leek (about 1 pound)*
> *1 large fennel bulb, stalks and leaves removed (about 12 ounces trimmed)*
> *2 tablespoons extra-virgin olive oil*
> *2 cups homemade (page 12) or canned low-sodium chicken stock, or*
> *   Golden Vegetable Stock (page 14)*
> *2 pounds vine-ripened tomatoes (about 6 medium), peeled, seeded, and*
> *   coarsely chopped*
> *About ¾ teaspoon salt, less if using canned stock*
> *2 tablespoons coarsely chopped fresh French tarragon leaves*
> *Freshly ground black pepper*

1. Leek and fennel. Cut off and discard the top of the leek at the point where it turns from light to dark green. Split the remaining portion lengthwise in half, keeping the roots attached so that the layers will not fall apart, and wash the leek thoroughly. Thinly slice it into half circles. Cut the fennel bulb in half and slice it ¼ inch thick.

2. Soup base. Heat the olive oil in a medium (3-quart) saucepan over medium heat. Add the leek and cook, stirring often, until it is softened and translucent but not browned, about 8 minutes. Add the fennel, stock, tomatoes, and salt (omit if using canned stock). Bring the soup to a boil, reduce the heat to low, cover, and simmer gently until the fennel is very soft, about 30 minutes. Add the tarragon.

3. Finishing the soup. Transfer the soup to a food processor, filling it no more than half full, and pulse until the soup is partially puréed but still has some texture. Return the soup to the saucepan and reheat if necessary. Taste and season with pepper and additional salt if needed.

VARIATIONS

For a soup with more texture, don't purée it at all but begin with the tomato and fennel cut into even ½-inch dice.

LEEK AND FENNEL SOUP

For a velvety anise-flavored white soup, omit the tomatoes and increase the leeks and fennel bulbs to 2 each. Increase the chicken or vegetable stock to 4 cups. Purée the soup until very smooth in a blender or food processor.

For the Gardener

If you grow the herb fennel, it will produce great quantities of green seed all through tomato season from July until frost. Use 1 tablespoon of these seeds, coarsely chopped, in place of the tarragon. They'll give the soup an even more focused anise flavor. Because the fennel seeds don't lose their flavor with prolonged cooking, as tarragon does, you can add them when you add the tomatoes. As they simmer in the soup, their flavor will have a chance to blend and mellow.

Garnish with some tiny yellow fennel blossoms and a few wispy sprigs of the fennel leaves. For a dramatic presentation, use large feathery fennel fronds to line the plates beneath the soup bowls.

 HERB SUBSTITUTION
  • *Use ¼ cup fresh spearmint leaves in place of the tarragon.*

Umami Carrot Soup with Mint

8 servings

For many years, Jon Rowley—the Northwest's "Seafood Guru" and all-around food expert, enthusiast, and consultant—has been on a mission to introduce the Japanese concept of umami to Americans. *Umami* is difficult to translate. Food is said to have umami when it's at its peak of perfection, at the height of its season, handled with respect, and simply presented—a sublime, ripe peach, an impeccably fresh oyster, a bowl of sugary green peas cooked straight from the garden. Jon has held many workshops at The Herbfarm on this subject, and at one of them he asked me to prepare a luncheon based on the principles of umami. This happened in February, not exactly peak produce season. Kale, pears, leeks, and carrots were all I could find locally grown. I decided to focus on the thick, freshly dug Scarlet Nantes carrots and set about to create a carrot soup that tasted of the essence of the vegetable. I began by cooking the carrots with leeks to caramelize their sugar. Then, instead of adding stock, I added fresh carrot juice, further concentrating the carrot flavor. The soup that resulted had umami. Every spoonful illuminated the essence of the sugary orange roots just pulled from the midwinter soil.

This minted carrot soup evolved from the one I served at the workshop. In this version fresh ginger, toasted coriander, and fresh mint warm and deepen the carrot flavor, though carrot still holds dominion. The mint is added by way of an infusion, both thinning and flavoring the soup as it's puréed.

This soup has very concentrated flavors. Serve it in small bowls or demitasse cups to begin a meal. In the summertime, it's delicious served chilled.

2 medium leeks (about 1½ pounds)
1½ tablespoons dried whole coriander seeds
3 tablespoons unsalted butter
1 pound large sweet carrots (about 4), peeled and cut into ¼-inch slices
½ cup dry white wine
2 teaspoons finely chopped fresh ginger
3 cups fresh carrot juice
1 teaspoon salt
2 cups water
1 large bunch fresh spearmint (about 2 ounces)
2 teaspoons freshly squeezed lemon juice, or more if needed
Garnish: tiny mint leaves or thinly sliced mint leaves

1. Leeks. Cut off and discard the tops of the leeks at the point where they turn from light to dark green. Split them lengthwise in half, keeping the roots attached so that the layers will not fall apart, and wash thoroughly. Thinly slice the leeks into half circles discarding the roots.

2. Toasting the coriander. Put the coriander seeds in a small dry skillet and place it over medium heat. Shake the pan constantly until the seeds begin to darken in color and smell wonderfully fragrant and toasty; be careful not to overcook. Pour them out onto a paper towel to stop the cooking. Using the towel as a funnel, transfer them to a spice mill and grind very fine. If you don't have a spice mill, use a mini processor or blender.

3. Vegetables. Melt the butter in a medium (3-quart) heavy-bottomed saucepan over medium heat. Add the leeks and cook for 5 minutes, stirring occasionally. Add the carrots, wine, and ginger. Cook uncovered until all the liquid has boiled away, about 15 minutes, then continue to cook, stirring often, until the vegetables are slightly browned, about 10 minutes. Don't rush the step, for it allows the natural sugars to slowly caramelize. As the vegetables cook, keep scraping the bottom of the pan with the spoon to gather up any brown bits.

4. Soup. Add the carrot juice, coriander, and salt. Bring to a boil, cover, and gently simmer over low heat until the carrots are very tender, 20 to 30 minutes.

5. Mint tea. Meanwhile bring the water to a boil in a small saucepan. Submerge the mint in the water, remove the pan from the heat, cover, and let steep for about 20 minutes. Strain the tea, squeezing all the liquid out of the leaves.

6. Finishing the soup. Put half of the soup in the container of an electric blender (you can use a food processor instead, but the soup will not be as smooth). Hold the lid down with a dry towel and turn the blender on at low speed so that the soup doesn't splash up, then gradually increase the speed to high. Add half of the mint tea. Blend the soup until it is creamy and very smooth. Pour the puréed soup into a second saucepan and repeat with the remaining soup and tea. When all of the soup is puréed, add the lemon juice and gently reheat. Taste and add additional salt or lemon juice if needed. Ladle the soup into warmed small bowls or demitasse cups. Garnish with tiny mint leaves.

DRIED HERB SUBSTITUTION
- *If you prepare this soup in the winter when fresh mint is harder to come by, you can make the mint tea with 1 tablespoon dried spearmint in place of the fresh.*

CHANTERELLE AND CORN CHOWDER WITH BASIL

6 servings

The first chanterelles begin popping up in Pacific Northwest forests in August, just when corn is ripening in the fields. The nutty mushrooms and sweet kernels make ideal partners, and they frequently show up together on Herbfarm menus—often in a soup. Also at their peak in the herb garden are basil and marjoram; each is a superb complement to both the mushroom and corn flavors.

If you must hunt for wild mushrooms in a market, look for chanterelles that are colored from light chamois to yellow orange. They should be relatively dry and clean, not shriveled, crumbled, or dark brown at the edges. It's always a good idea to give them a sniff before you buy. If the mushrooms are past their prime, they will have an unpleasant odor of decay.

Chanterelles are forest mushrooms, harvested in the wild. If it's been raining where they were gathered—frequently the case in the Pacific Northwest—and they were not given a chance to dry out before being sold, they'll be heavy with rainwater. Wet chanterelles are difficult to sauté because they become mushy, but they can still be used in this soup. You will need to buy (or gather) about fifty percent more wet mushrooms by weight to come up with the same volume as relatively dry ones.

12 ounces fresh chanterelle, shiitake, or oyster mushrooms
5 ears fresh sweet corn, shucked
2 tablespoons extra-virgin olive oil
1 medium onion (about 8 ounces), finely chopped
2 cloves garlic, minced
About ¾ teaspoon salt, less if using canned stock
½ cup dry white wine
2 tablespoons dry sherry
3 cups homemade (page 12) or canned low-sodium chicken stock, or
*   Golden Vegetable Stock (page 14)*
1 cup heavy cream or half-and-half
1 tablespoon finely chopped fresh marjoram or oregano
1 cup coarsely chopped fresh basil
Freshly ground black pepper

1. Mushrooms. Using a brush with soft bristles, thoroughly but gently remove all dirt and pine needles from the chanterelles. If you are using very small chanterelles, tear them into pieces. Cut larger chanterelles with a knife into ½-inch dice. If using shiitakes, remove the stems and thinly slice the caps. If using oyster mushrooms, tear them into ½-inch strips.

2. Corn. Scrape the pulp from the ears of corn. To do this, hold an ear at the top in a large mixing bowl. Draw the tip of a knife down through the rows of corn, cutting down the center of the kernels. With the side of a sturdy tablespoon, firmly scrape the cob to extract the pulp and milk. The skin of the kernels should remain on the cob. If you have an old-fashioned corn scraper, you have just the tool for this task.

3. Soup base. Heat the olive oil in a large (4-quart) saucepan over medium heat. Add the onion and garlic and cook, stirring often, until they soften and begin to turn a light caramel color, about 8 minutes. Add the mushrooms and salt (add only ¼ teaspoon salt if using canned stock) and cook until the moisture the mushrooms release is completely evaporated, about 5 minutes. Pour in the wine and sherry and continue to cook until almost dry. Add the stock and corn. Bring the soup to a boil, reduce the heat, and cook at a bubbling simmer uncovered for 10 to 15 minutes to cook the corn and meld the flavors.

4. Finishing the soup. Stir in the cream, marjoram, and basil and bring the soup to a simmer once again. Taste and season with pepper and more salt if needed.

Pumpkin and Shrimp Bisque

8 servings

Buttery, slightly sweet pumpkin is the perfect mate for the briny flavor of oysters, scallops, or other crustaceans. This soup is made with shrimp, whose shells are turned into an aromatic stock that serves as the soup's liquid. Classic shellfish bisques are thickened with rice, but here pumpkin provides body for the soup. Sage's earthy flavor complements both pumpkin and shrimp and steers the focus of flavor from sweet to savory.

This is a satisfying soup to prepare throughout the fall. If you serve it as a first course for Thanksgiving dinner, you might start a tradition in your family.

1 pound large shrimp (16 to 20)

SHRIMP STOCK
2 tablespoons extra-virgin olive oil
¾ cup dry white wine
3 cups homemade (page 12) or canned low-sodium chicken stock
Pinch saffron threads (about 24)
2 ribs celery, coarsely chopped
1 medium onion (about 8 ounces), coarsely chopped
4 fresh bay laurel leaves, torn, or 2 dried
3 3-inch sprigs fresh sage

2 cups pumpkin purée, fresh (see Note) or canned
½ cup heavy cream
About ¾ teaspoon salt, less if using canned stock
Scant ⅛ teaspoon cayenne pepper
1 tablespoon freshly squeezed lemon juice
Freshly ground black pepper
1 tablespoon extra-virgin olive oil
2 teaspoons finely chopped fresh sage

1. Shrimp stock. Peel and devein the shrimp, reserving the shells. Cover the shrimp and refrigerate. Heat the olive oil in a medium (3-quart) heavy-bottomed saucepan over high heat until it begins to smoke. Add the shrimp shells to the pan and cook, stirring constantly, until they turn deep orange and are just beginning to brown, 3 to 4 minutes. This step—pan-roasting the shells—gives the stock much of its flavor, so take the time to do it carefully. The roasted shells should release a concentrated, toasty, shrimp aroma that will fill your kitchen. Add the wine to the pan, first turning off gas flames to prevent the alcohol from igniting, then boil it over medium heat until all the liquid is evaporated. Add the chicken stock, saffron, celery, onion, bay leaves, and sage. Bring to a boil, then reduce the heat to the lowest setting. Partially cover the pan and simmer gently for 30 minutes. Strain the stock through a fine sieve, pushing down on the solids with the back of a spoon to extract all the liquid. Rinse out the saucepan and pour the stock back into it.

2. Soup. Whisk the pumpkin, cream, salt (omit if using canned stock), and cayenne into the shrimp stock. Bring the soup to a simmer, then cook very gently uncovered over low heat for 10 minutes. Stir in the lemon juice, taste, and season with black pepper and more salt if needed. (The soup can be made up to this point up to 1 day ahead stored covered in the refrigerator. Keep the peeled shrimp in a resealable bag buried in a bowl of ice in the refrigerator.)

3. Finishing the soup. Pour the olive oil into a large sauté pan placed over medium heat. When hot, add the reserved shrimp and the sage and cook, tossing often, until the shrimp is just cooked through, pink, and no longer translucent, but not curled into a circle, 2 to 3 minutes. They should still have a tender snap when you bite into them. Arrange the shrimp in warmed serving bowls or a tureen. Bring the soup back to a simmer and then ladle it over the shrimp. Serve right away.

NOTE

To make fresh pumpkin purée, cut a sugar pumpkin in half and scrape out the seeds. Place it cut side down in a baking dish and pour in about ¼ inch of hot water. Bake it in a 400°F oven until the flesh is tender, 40 to 50 minutes. Turn the pumpkin halves cut side up to cool. Scoop the pumpkin flesh from the skin and purée it in a food processor until smooth. Transfer the purée to a large sieve lined with a double layer of cheesecloth and let it drain for 2–3 hours until it is firm enough to hold its shape on a spoon.

VARIATION

Substitute winter squash purée, such as butternut or acorn, for the pumpkin.

Herbal Chicken Noodle Soup

4 servings

This giant bowl of fresh egg noodles swimming in rich broth with bits of chicken and fresh vegetables makes a substantial meal on its own. Abundant handfuls of fresh herbs are added before the soup is served, scenting the steam that envelops you as you slurp up the chewy noodles. The dish is quick to put together and very healthy. After all, it has double doses of the two oldest forms of medicine—herbs and chicken soup.

> *Salt*
> *6 cups homemade (page 12) or canned low-sodium chicken stock*
> *Freshly ground black pepper*
> *2 cups bite-size pieces asparagus or broccoli, or sugar snap peas*
> *12 ounces fresh thick egg noodles or fettuccine (page 99), or*
>   *9 ounces dried*
> *2 boneless, skinless chicken breast halves (about ¾ pound), very*
>   *thinly sliced*
> *¼ cup torn fresh basil leaves*
> *¼ cup snipped fresh chives or finely chopped green onions*
> *2 tablespoons coarsely chopped fresh French tarragon*
> *2 tablespoons coarsely chopped fresh marjoram*

1. Setting up. Bring a large (6-quart) pot of water to a boil and add 2 teaspoons salt. Bring the chicken stock to a simmer in a large (4-quart) saucepan and add salt and pepper to taste. Put the asparagus, broccoli, or sugar snap peas in a steamer basket or sieve and lower it into the boiling water. Boil the vegetables until they are bright green and still crunchy, 1 to 2 minutes. Lift the basket from the water to drain and run cold water over the vegetables to stop their cooking.

2. Noodles. Stir the noodles into the salted water and cook until tender but still firm. Fresh thick noodles will take 3 to 5 minutes; dried will take 6 to 12 minutes.

3. Finishing the soup. While the noodles are cooking, add the chicken to the chicken stock, turn the heat to low, and poach for 2 to 3 minutes until cooked through. Add the steamed vegetable and the herbs. When the noodles are cooked, drain them and add them to the soup. Ladle the soup into large soup bowls and serve right away with a fork or chopsticks, and a large spoon.

HERB SUBSTITUTIONS

In place of the herbs listed, use:

- ¼ cup coarsely chopped fresh chervil, ¼ cup snipped chives or finely chopped green onions, and 2 tablespoons finely chopped fresh lemon balm
- ¼ cup finely chopped fresh spearmint, ¼ cup coarsely chopped cilantro, and ¼ cup snipped chives or finely chopped green onions
- ¼ cup coarsely chopped fresh dill, ¼ cup thinly shredded sorrel, 2 tablespoons snipped chives or finely chopped green onions, and 1 tablespoon finely chopped fresh lovage

Black Bean Soup with Apple

8 servings

This substantial soup is brimming with the homey flavors of winter. Earthy beans, smoky bacon, and sweet-tart apples are warmed with ginger and allspice and fortified with the workhorse cold-weather herbs—thyme and rosemary.

Black beans require soaking and a longer than average cooking time, so begin this soup early in the day or prepare it several days ahead of time—its flavors will mingle and improve during a night or two in the refrigerator. If you boil dried beans with salt, it can make them cook unevenly and prevent them from becoming tender, so always use unsalted stock and add salt after the beans are partially cooked. This recipe makes a giant pot of soup, but you can freeze half, up to 3 months, for a future supper.

8 cups water
1 pound dried black (turtle) beans (about 2 cups)
6 ounces smoked bacon (6 slices), very finely chopped
1 large onion, finely chopped
5 cloves garlic, finely chopped
4 ribs celery, finely chopped
7 cups homemade (page 12) or canned unsalted chicken stock
½ teaspoon dried red pepper flakes
1½ tablespoons finely chopped fresh ginger
2 teaspoons ground allspice
5 fresh bay laurel leaves, or 3 dried
*3 large tart apples, such as Granny Smith or Newton Pippin, peeled, cored,
   and cut into ¼-inch dice*
2 tablespoons finely chopped fresh thyme
1 tablespoon finely chopped fresh rosemary
1½ teaspoons salt
Freshly ground black pepper to taste
2 teaspoons sherry vinegar or apple cider vinegar
2 tablespoons pure maple syrup or dark brown sugar
*Optional garnishes: chopped chives or green onions and/or shredded sharp
   Cheddar cheese*

1. Beans. Bring the water to a boil in a large (6- to 8-quart) soup pot. Pour in the beans, remove the pan from the heat, and let the beans soak for 1 hour at room temperature or overnight in the refrigerator. Drain the beans in a colander and rinse them thoroughly with cold water.

2. Simmering the soup. Rinse and dry the soup pot and place it over medium heat. Add the bacon and cook, stirring often, until it renders most of its fat but is not quite crisp. Tilt the pot and use a large spoon to remove some of the fat, leaving about ¼ cup behind. Add the onion, garlic, and celery; cook, stirring often, until they are softened, about 5 minutes. Add the beans, chicken stock, red pepper flakes, ginger, allspice, and bay leaves and bring the mixture to a boil. Reduce the heat, cover, and gently simmer until the beans are very soft, 1½ to 2 hours.

3. Finishing the soup. Stir in the diced apples, thyme, rosemary, salt, black pepper, vinegar, and syrup; simmer the soup until the apples are very soft but still hold their shape, about 15 minutes. Remove the bay leaves. Taste and add more salt or vinegar if needed. For a creamier texture, partially mash the beans with a potato masher or handheld immersion blender. Serve the soup in warmed large bowls. If you'd like, garnish it with chives or green onions and/or sharp Cheddar cheese. The soup is delicious with Marjoram Corn Bread (page 242).

VEGETARIAN VARIATION

The soup can be made meatless by substituting ¼ cup olive oil for the bacon and using Golden Vegetable Stock (page 14) in place of the chicken stock.

White Bean and Squash Soup with Parsley Pistou

6 to 8 servings

This soup consists of tender white beans and sweet bits of winter squash in an herbal broth. Pistou is a Provençal sauce, similar to pesto, made in a mortar and pestle with garlic, fresh basil, and olive oil, and often stirred into soups. (Pistou also refers to a Provençal vegetable soup that is served with the sauce of the same name.) For this dish, I've made a parsley pistou. When a brilliant green spoonful of it is swirled into the bowl, its slight saltiness and lively raw garlic punch up the flavor of the soup considerably.

Note: Boiling dried beans with salt can cause them to cook unevenly and prevent them from becoming tender, so always use unsalted stock and add salt after the beans are partially cooked.

8 cups water
12 ounces dried white beans (about 1½ cups), such as Great Northern, navy, borlotti, or cannellini
3 tablespoons extra-virgin olive oil
2 medium onions (about 1¼ pounds), finely chopped
4 ribs celery, finely chopped
6 cloves garlic, finely chopped
7 cups homemade (page 12) or canned low-sodium chicken stock, or Golden Vegetable Stock (page 14)
1¼ teaspoons salt
Freshly ground black pepper to taste
2 tablespoons coarsely chopped fresh winter or summer savory
2 tablespoons coarsely chopped fresh thyme
1 tablespoon chopped fresh sage
4 fresh bay laurel leaves, or 2 dried

PISTOU
1 large bunch parsley, large stems removed (about 3 cups gently packed)
3 cloves garlic, peeled
½ teaspoon salt
½ cup fruity extra-virgin olive oil

4 cups ½-inch cubes peeled delicata squash (about 2 medium) or other hard winter squash, such as turban or kabocha

1. Beans. Bring the water to a boil in a large (6- to 8-quart) soup pot. Pour in the beans, remove the pan from the heat, and let the beans soak for 1 hour at room temperature or overnight in the refrigerator. Drain the beans in a colander and rinse them thoroughly with cold water.

2. Soup base. Rinse and dry the soup pot and place it over medium heat. Add the olive oil and onions and cook, stirring often, until they are softened and begin to turn a light caramel color, about 8 minutes. Add the celery and garlic and cook for several minutes until the garlic no longer smells raw. Add the stock and beans and bring to a boil. Reduce the heat, cover, and gently simmer for 45 minutes. Stir in the salt, pepper, and herbs. Continue to simmer the soup until the beans are very tender but not at all mushy, 15 to 30 minutes. Sometimes a batch of beans will take even longer to become tender, so be patient and allow them the necessary time.

3. Pistou. While the soup is simmering, purée the parsley, garlic, and salt in a food processor, scraping down the sides as necessary. Pour the olive oil through the feed tube in a steady stream and continue to process until it is well incorporated. The pistou should be thick enough to form a soft mound on a teaspoon. Transfer the pistou to a small serving bowl. You can also make the pistou in a mortar and pestle, as they would in Provence. Follow the directions for pesto on page 102.

4. Finishing the soup. Add the squash to the soup and simmer until it is tender but still holds its shape, about 10 minutes. Serve the soup in warmed large bowls. Let each guest swirl in a spoonful of the pistou at the table and pass plenty of crusty bread.

HERB SUBSTITUTION
- *For a late summer or early autumn version of this soup, make traditional basil pistou by substituting 3 ounces stemmed basil leaves (about 3 cups gently packed) for the parsley.*

Herbed Clam Chowder

6 servings

This uncomplicated version of clam chowder takes little more than half an hour to prepare. First, young tender clams are steamed with thyme, bay, and garlic. Once removed from their shells, the meat swims alongside red potatoes and leeks in a light-bodied yet full-flavored broth that's made from the herb-scented clam liquor enriched with cream. At the last minute, fresh marjoram and chervil (or parsley) are stirred in, perfuming the soup further while lending a fresh green contrast.

> *2 cups water*
> *8 to 12 3-inch sprigs fresh English or lemon thyme*
> *2 fresh bay laurel leaves, cracked, or 1 dried*
> *2 cloves garlic, smashed and peeled*
> *3 pounds small live clams, such as Manila or littleneck, purged*
>   *(see page 37)*
> *2 medium leeks (about 1½ pounds)*
> *2 tablespoons unsalted butter*
> *12 ounces small red potatoes, unpeeled, cut into ½-inch cubes*
> *1 cup heavy cream or half-and-half*
> *1 tablespoon finely chopped fresh marjoram or Italian oregano*
> *Salt and freshly ground black pepper*
> *¼ cup coarsely chopped fresh chervil, or 2 tablespoons finely chopped*
>   *fresh parsley*

1. Clams. Pour the water into a large (6-quart) pot and add the thyme, bay leaves, and garlic. Wash the clams in a colander and arrange them on top of the flavorings, then cover the pot and place it over high heat. Steam the clams until all are open, 3 to 5 minutes. Set the colander over a bowl to catch the liquor and empty the clams into it. Let stand until they are cool enough to handle. Remove the meat from the shells, discarding the shells. Strain the clam liquor through a very fine sieve, or a coarser sieve lined with a double layer of cheesecloth.

2. Chowder base. Cut off and discard the tops of the leeks at the point where they turn from light to dark green. Split the remaining portion lengthwise in half, keeping the roots attached, and wash thoroughly. Thinly slice them into half circles, discarding the roots. Melt the butter in a medium (3-quart) saucepan over medium-low heat. Add the leeks and cook, stirring often, until softened but not browned, about 5 minutes. Add the strained clam liquor and the potatoes and bring the mixture to a simmer. Cover, reduce the heat, and gently simmer until the potatoes are very tender, 12 to 15 minutes.

3. Finishing the soup. Stir the cream, marjoram, and reserved clams into the soup and bring it back to a simmer. Taste and season with salt if needed (the clam liquor is quite salty) and pepper. Stir in the chervil and ladle the chowder into warmed shallow serving bowls. Excellent with Dill and Cheddar Three-Grain Biscuits (page 243).

A Note About Clams

Buy live clams from a quality fishmonger. If you want tender meat, Manilas are the best choice on the West Coast, and littlenecks will be a good choice on the East Coast. The shells should be tightly closed, not gaping. Ask the person selling the clams if they were purged. If he doesn't know what you are talking about, seek out another vendor. Purging flushes the clams out with clean water to get rid of any sand they are carrying. Live clams should be purged by the seafood processor before they arrive at the fish counter, but often they are not. Clam shells that feel sandy on the outside are a good indication that they will have sand inside. To purge the clams at home, cover them with a solution of 6 tablespoons salt per 4 cups water and let them soak in the refrigerator for 4 to 8 hours. Drain, rinse, and proceed with the recipe.

SEAFOOD IN SCENTED DASHI

4 servings

This is a simplified home version of an ethereal seafood consommé we often serve at The Herbfarm. Dashi—the all-purpose Japanese fish broth made by steeping dried kelp and bonito flakes in water—serves as an excellent, slightly smoky stand-in for the more complicated clarified seafood stock that I use in the restaurant version. What makes both versions of the soup heavenly is the infusion of a healthy bunch of freshly cut lemon thyme. When the bowls of soup are brought to the table, their steam is heavy with a savory citrus perfume that gently sets off the fresh sweet seafood flavors.

Prepare this dish only if your seafood is of the highest quality. There is nothing in this soup to disguise the flavors that are not brilliantly fresh.

> *1 pound large shrimp (16 to 20), fresh spot shrimp if possible*
> *4 cups cold water*
> *1 3-inch-square piece dried kombu kelp*
> *16 to 24 3-inch sprigs fresh lemon thyme (1 ounce)*
> *½ cup bonito flakes (katsuobushi)*
> *1 tablespoon mirin*
> *2 teaspoons soy sauce*
> *1 pound small live clams, such as Manila or littleneck, scrubbed and*
> *   purged (see page 37)*
> *½ cup water*
> *Salt if needed*
> *8 ounces firm-fleshed white fish, such as halibut, rockfish, or sea bass, cut*
> *   into 1-inch cubes*

1. Dashi. Peel and devein the shrimp. Cover the shrimp meat and refrigerate. Put the shells in a medium (3-quart) saucepan with the 4 cups cold water and the kombu. Bring the mixture to a simmer over medium-low heat, then reduce the heat to very low and poach uncovered at below the simmering point for 5 minutes. Cut off a small handful of the tender tips of the lemon thyme and reserve them for the garnish. Add the rest of the thyme to the pot along with the bonito flakes; continue to cook at this very low heat for another 5 minutes. Don't let the mixture simmer—if necessary set the pan on top of a heat diffuser or in a shallow pan of simmering water. Stir in the mirin and soy sauce and remove the stock from the heat.

2. Finishing the soup. Put the clams in another saucepan of the same size or larger. Pour in the ½ cup water, cover the pan tightly, and steam over high heat until all the clams open. Reduce the heat to low. Pour the dashi through a fine sieve over the clams. Add the shrimp meat and cubes of fish and poach just below the simmering point until the shrimp is pink and no longer translucent, but not curled in a tight circle, and the fish is just cooked through, 2 to 3 minutes. Taste and season with additional salt if needed. Keeping the clams in the shell, ladle the seafood and broth into warmed shallow soup bowls and float a few of the reserved tips of lemon thyme in each bowl.

NOTE
Kombu, bonito flakes, and mirin are available in Asian groceries or in the Asian section of the supermarket.

VARIATIONS
Omit the cubes of fish. When the shrimp is almost done, add ¼ pound crabmeat claws or ¼ pound sea scallops, thinly sliced. Continue to poach just until heated through, about 1 minute.

If pink singing scallops, alive in the shell, are available, reduce the clams to ½ pound and cook ½ pound scallops with the clams in the same pot. The scallops, served in their shells, make an impressive presentation.

Green Gazpacho

6 to 8 servings

There are many versions of gazpacho in Spain. The most familiar to Americans is the tomato-based soup with pieces of raw vegetables, but there are other traditional gazpachos that contain no tomato. I learned a white version from a cook who has taught it while working in Catalonia, Spain. Using the food processor, he would make an emulsion of bread, garlic, olive oil, and sherry vinegar and then stir in chopped green pepper, cucumber, and green onion. The soup was rich and full-flavored, yet still had the refreshing saladlike quality of the familiar tomato version. I've based my soup on his, but along with the vegetables I add handfuls of fresh chopped herbs for another layer of flavor. And they turn it green.

> *4 slices white sandwich bread, crusts removed (about 4 ounces)*
> *2 large cucumbers, peeled and seeded*
> *1 large green bell pepper, cut in half and seeded*
> *2 cloves garlic*
> *¾ teaspoon salt*
> *Several dashes Tabasco sauce*
> *3 tablespoons sherry vinegar or tarragon white wine vinegar*
> *¼ cup fruity extra-virgin olive oil*
> *¼ cup fresh spearmint leaves*
> *¼ cup fresh flat-leaf parsley leaves*
> *¼ cup coarsely chopped cilantro*
> *½ cup ice water*
> *Freshly ground black pepper*
> *Garnish: 3 tablespoons mixed coarsely chopped spearmint, parsley, and*
>   *cilantro*

1. Bread. In a large bowl, pour cold water over the bread to cover and let it soak for 5 minutes. Drain the bread in a colander and lightly press out the excess water.

2. Puréeing the soup. Put the bread in a blender container. Coarsely chop 1 of the cucumbers and half the green pepper and add them to the blender along with the garlic, salt, Tabasco, vinegar, oil, and herbs. Purée on high speed until the mixture is very smooth and uniformly green (you can use a food processor but the texture will not be as smooth). Blend in the ice water. Pour the soup into a medium bowl or plastic container.

3. Finishing the soup. Finely chop the remaining cucumber and green pepper and stir them into the soup. Taste and season with pepper and additional salt if needed. Cover and refrigerate until thoroughly chilled. Serve the soup in chilled small bowls and garnish with the chopped herbs.

HERB SUBSTITUTION

- *Substitute for the cilantro one of the following: ¼ cup fresh dill, 2 tablespoons fresh French tarragon leaves, 2 tablespoons fresh lovage leaves, ¼ cup fresh lemon balm leaves, or ½ cup fresh chervil sprigs.*

Cold Borscht with Dilled Sour Cream

6 servings

When I was very young, my family would drive into Brooklyn on Sundays to visit my grandmothers. The first stop was the tiny one-room studio apartment of my father's mother, Pauline, who was born in Poland and spoke Yiddish to us. The air in her building's hallways was always punctuated with the oniony smells of Sunday dinners cooking in kitchens without exhaust fans. Once in her apartment we would sit on plastic slipcovers and be lavishly fed. In summer the room was oppressively hot, but this cold beet borscht was always on the table. Its refreshing sweet-sour flavor never failed to cool us, yet looking back I think it was the soup's magenta color that enticed me most. Now, it's my favorite summer soup. I don't think my bube (Yiddish for grandmother) ever put fresh dill in hers, but I think she would have approved of this version.

4 cups water
4 medium-large beets (about 1 ¾ pounds), peeled and halved
* or quartered*
1 medium onion, coarsely chopped
1 tablespoon sugar
¾ teaspoon salt
3 tablespoons freshly squeezed lemon juice
½ cup sour cream
2 tablespoons finely chopped fresh dill

1. Beets. Place the water, beets, onion, sugar, and salt in a medium (4-quart) saucepan and bring it to a boil. Reduce the heat, cover, and simmer until the beets are tender, 45 to 60 minutes.

2. Soup. Remove half the beets with a slotted spoon and let cool. Purée the soup with the remaining beets in 2 batches in a blender or food processor until smooth and pour it into a large bowl or plastic container. Add the lemon juice. Grate the cooled beets on the large holes of a hand grater and add them to the soup. Taste and add additional salt or lemon juice if needed. Cover and refrigerate until chilled. The soup will keep for up to 5 days.

3. Garnish. Mix the sour cream with the fresh dill and serve generous dollops of it on the ice-cold soup.

VARIATION

A raw egg is traditionally added to cold borscht. It adds richness and lightens the color. If you are comfortable with the idea of eating raw eggs, blend the freshest one you can find into the soup after it's chilled but before you add the grated beets. If you add egg, don't keep the soup for longer than 2 days in the refrigerator.

CHAPTER 2

Salads

With fresh herbs at hand, it doesn't take much to create an extraordinary salad. Start with a simple bowl of young lettuce leaves. Toss in sprigs of chervil, small leaves of basil and mint, strips of sorrel, spikes of chive, a scattering of brilliant nasturtium blossoms, and a sensitive measure of vinaigrette, and you have an exquisite beginning for a meal. In salad herbs can play two roles: They can season other ingredients, and their leaves can become primary ingredients themselves—a group of tender herbs, lightly dressed, is a salad in its own right.

A stroll through an herb garden provides endless inspiration for all types of salads. Pungent herbs like lemon thyme and marjoram can flavor a simple vinaigrette or creamy dressing, while rosemary and thyme will resonate in a smoky warm dressing for endive and mustard greens. Fennel or dill can infuse a marinade for carrots or beets, and cilantro and mint can add a spark to salads of couscous or lentils, or cool down a salad of spicy grilled peach. Refined herbs like tarragon, chervil, and perilla enliven seafood or chicken salads, and the sweet floral scents of lemon verbena and anise hyssop might perfume a salad of ripe fruits.

Specific examples of adding fresh herbs to salads follow in this chapter. Through these recipes you'll discover which herbs work best with what ingredients, how much of the herbs to use, and how to handle them. But always keep in mind that salad making is not a matter of following strict formulas. Salad recipes are springboards for whatever inspiration grows in the garden.

The Herbfarm Garden Salad

When Ron Zimmerman and Carrie Van Dyck opened The Herbfarm's restaurant in 1986, they both wore many hats. In the first years the chef's toque rested on Ron's head, but Carrie was in charge of the salad course. As the sun was rising on any morning that the restaurant served lunch, Carrie could be found in the garden, individually harvesting each leaf and flower petal. Instead of tossing all the ingredients together with dressing and putting the mix on a plate, the salads were meticulously constructed one leaf at a time, as if each were a carefully considered flower arrangement. No incidental course, the salad was an exciting highlight of the meal—a composition of all the colors, textures, and flavors of the surrounding kitchen garden together on one plate.

By the time I took over as chef in 1990, The Herbfarm had grown so much that Carrie had to delegate her early-morning salad-picking ritual to others, but the same care and attention continues whenever we serve this signature course. Because we have only one seating a day by reservation, we know precisely how many people will be dining with us. If we have thirty-six guests, the salad gatherer will go out in the gardens and pick thirty-six (plus a few extra) of each leaf, sprig, or flower that makes up the salad. At the height of the season the salads can feature up to thirty elements and take the gatherer about three hours to harvest the thousand-plus individually selected pieces. Shallow boxes gradually fill with perfect stacks of colorful young heirloom lettuce, chard, or mustard leaves and mounds of unusual greens like miner's lettuce or purslane. Other boxes contain groups of tender herb sprigs like lovage, lemon balm, or perilla, and an array of dazzling blossoms from borage, calendula, nasturtium, or scarlet runner beans.

Once in the kitchen, the leaves and blossoms are washed, dried, and inspected, then carefully wrapped and set aside until they are needed. When it's time to assemble the salads, thirty-six large white plates are lined up rim to rim on the kitchen counters. All available hands pitch in, cooks and wait staff alike. Each person puts one variety of the largest leaves into a mixing bowl, then tosses them with a precise amount of dressing corresponding to their thickness, toughness, or sharpness of flavor. With bowl in hand, the first person places one leaf on each plate, another shadows with a second leaf of a contrasting color or texture, then another, and so on. These first leaves create a fluffy base from which to build a tall architectural arrangement. Once all the larger leaves are positioned, the delicately dressed smaller leaves and sprigs follow, each one tucked between leaves or balanced on the top. Finally the delicate flower petals are sprinkled or arranged. Sometimes a border of a colorful vinaigrette or juice reduction is drizzled around the salad, and often ingredients like currant tomatoes, slices of Asian pear, clusters of ripe berries, or a wedge of farmstead cheese adorn the plate.

You can easily create the same style of salad at home. It's especially rewarding if you can harvest at least some of the leaves or petals from your own garden, but you can still prepare a salad masterpiece with ingredients purchased from a good market. It's most important that you have a diversity of ingredients. Choose greens that contrast in flavor—hot, sweet, bitter, aromatic, and mild. Select leaves of different shades of green and red and with different shapes and textures—some frilly, some wavy, some flat, some delicate, some chewy, and some with interesting shapes like chives, pea vines, or Belgian endive spears. Pay close attention to how much dressing each leaf requires. Thick and strong-tasting leaves, such as kale or radicchio, need a good coating, but delicate young butter lettuce or tender mâche leaves need only the slightest whisper of vinaigrette. Only dress leaves with similar textures together in the same bowl.

Because the leaves are left whole, these salads should be served with knife and fork. As your guests cut and gather the greens on their forks, they have the choice of which flavors to combine with each bite, and they're sure to have an adventure as they work through the varied tastes and textures.

FOR EACH SALAD

6 3- to 4-inch-long leaves to form the base of the salad, such as young chard, endive, kale, lettuce, mustard, radicchio, or spinach

6 to 12 smaller salad leaves, 1 to 2 inches long, such as amaranth, arugula, beet green, burnet, cress sprigs, dandelion, mâche, miner's lettuce, mizuna, nasturtium, orach, pea tip, purslane sprigs, shungiku, sorrel, tatsoi, or violet leaves

Several leaves or sprigs of soft-leafed herbs, such as anise hyssop, basil, dill, fennel, lemon balm, lovage, mint, perilla, or tarragon

Edible flowers, such as those of arugula, borage, coriander, fennel, nasturtium, pea (not sweet pea), runner bean, sweet cicely, sage, sweet rocket, rosemary, or viola, or petals from calendula, chive, daylily, rose, tuberose begonia, or tulip

About 1 tablespoon Herbfarm Vinaigrette (page 332)

1. **Washing the greens.** Put individual salad plates in the refrigerator to chill. Fill a very large bowl or basin with cool water (if the greens were harvested from gardens where slugs are abundant, like in the Pacific Northwest, add 1 tablespoon of white vinegar to the water to rid the leaves of any small undetected pests). Working with one variety at a time, gently swish the leaves in the water. Lift the leaves from the water, being careful not to stir up the dirt that settles to the bottom, and spin dry or pat between clean towels. If you're not serving the salads immediately, wrap the leaves in damp paper towels, put them in plastic bags, and store them in the refrigerator. Inspect the herb sprigs and flowers for insects and store them in the refrigerator in small bowls or cups, covered tightly with plastic. Don't wash the flowers unless absolutely necessary.

2. **Assembling the base.** Line up the chilled salad plates on your counter. Divide the large leaves between 2 mixing bowls, placing those with coarser textures—like kale, chard, and endive—in one, and those more delicate—like lettuces and spinach—in the other. Ladle in enough vinaigrette to coat the coarse leaves well (about 1 tablespoon for 12 leaves), and the delicate leaves lightly (about ½ tablespoon for 12 leaves). Toss the leaves with your hands, rubbing the dressing onto all the surfaces. It's best to begin the salad with a leaf that doesn't lie flat on the plate, like a Lolla Rossa lettuce leaf or a cupped radicchio leaf. Place one faceup in the center of each plate. Continue to place one leaf of each variety on each plate, alternating colors and textures, and propping and balancing each leaf on its neighbor to form a fluffy, tall mound.

3. **Finishing the salads.** Divide the smaller leaves and herb sprigs in the 2 bowls, again according to their texture and the amount of dressing they require. Put thick leaves like beet green, dandelion, and purslane in one and delicate leaves like mâche, sorrel, and miner's lettuce in the other. Dress the greens in each bowl with the necessary amount of vinaigrette and begin tucking them in between the layers of larger leaves or propping them gently on top. As you build the salad, keep in mind the image of a three-dimensional flower arrangement. When all the leaves and sprigs are placed, it's time to add the flowers. Very lightly dress the larger blossoms, like nasturtiums, or daylily or rose petals, but leave small blossoms like borage or calendula petals undressed, for the vinaigrette will wilt them instantly. Tuck the flowers and petals here and there to give the salad its final flourish. Serve the salads immediately.

Salad Ingredients for The Herbfarm Garden Salad

INGREDIENT	DESCRIPTION
Amaranth	bright red or green or multicolored leaves
Anise hyssop	green, pointed, oval leaves tinged with purple; brilliant purple flowers
Arugula (roquette)	notched leaves, white flowers
Arugula, rustic	finely toothed dark green leaves, yellow flowers, longer lived than regular
Basil	soft green or purple leaves
Beet greens	red-veined leaves
Borage	star-shaped, clear blue flowers; fuzzy gray leaves
Burnet	deeply cut, deep green, compound leaves
Calendula	daisylike orange and yellow flowers
Chervil	lacy, delicate, parsleylike leaves; white flower umbels
Chickweed	tiny light green leaves on trailing thin stems
Chives	reedlike green leaves, purple globelike flowers
Coriander	thin, soft, light green leaves; white flower umbels
Cress, pepper and curly	small green parsleylike leaves
Dandelion	sword-shaped, lanced leaves with thick ribs
Daylily	large lily flowers with thick petals in many colors
Dill	feathery deep green leaves, yellow umbel flowers
Endive, Belgian	tight, long, thin heads, yellow white
Endive, curly (frisée)	frilly leaves in loose heads that are white near the heart
Good King Henry (chenopodium)	green triangular leaves
Kale	coarsely textured leaves with thick ribs in varied shades of green, pink, purple, or white; some flat, some very frilled; yellow flowers
Lemon balm	oval leaves
Lettuce, batavia (crisphead)	crisp leaves with romaine texture in loose round heads
Lettuce, butterhead/Bibb	soft loosely packed heads
Lettuce, looseleaf	frilly loosely packed heads, medium texture, easy to harvest leaf by leaf
Lettuce, romaine (cos)	long vertical heads, very crisp
Lovage	flat, large, wedge-shaped leaves on hollow stems

PARTS TO USE	TASTE	SEASON
leaves under 2 inches long	mild green	summer and fall
small leaves, sprigs with tiny flower buds	very sweet anise	late spring to summer
leaves, flowers	peppery, slightly bitter	all year
leaves, flowers	very peppery, bitter	all year
leaves, sprigs	complex, clove, anise, citrus, spicy	summer
leaves under 2 inches long	sweet green sprouts	all year
flowers, leaves if under 1 inch long	mild cucumber	late spring to early fall
young leaves	mild cucumber	spring to fall
petals	very mild	late spring to fall
leaves, flowers	mild anise	spring and fall
young tender sprigs	grassy	spring
leaves, buds, florets	oniony	spring to fall
leaves, flowers	pungent citrus	spring to fall
leaves, sprouts, flowers	very hot, peppery, can be sweet or bitter	spring to fall
tender young leaves	bitter	spring
petals, buds	sweet, mild, some are perfumed	spring
small sprigs, flowers	caraway, parsley	spring to fall
leaves	sweet, mild, slightly bitter	all year
small leaves	sweet, slightly bitter	all year
leaves	like spinach, grassy	spring
small leaves, flowers	green, some varieties are slightly bitter	fall to spring
leaves	mild lemon	spring to fall
small leaves	sweet, fairly mild	spring to fall
small leaves	sweet, mild	spring and fall
small leaves	sweet, mild	spring to fall
inner leaves	sweet, very slight bitterness	spring to fall
tender young leaves	intense celery	spring and fall

INGREDIENT	DESCRIPTION
Mâche (cornsalad)	very small, very tender, light green heads
Marjoram	green sprigs with knotlike flower buds
Miner's lettuce (claytonia)	round leaf with delicate flower sprigs growing from center
Mint	oval leaves
Mizuna	finely cut, lacy, green leaves with white ribs; yellow flowers
Monarda	light green, pointed oval leaves; composite flowers in red, pink, violet, white
Mustard, Giant Red or Green Wave	wide-ribbed purple or frilly deep green leaves; yellow flowers
Nasturtium	round leaves on vining plants; large bright orange, yellow, or red flowers
New Zealand spinach (tetragonia)	deep green, thick, and fleshy shield-shaped leaves
Orach, red	deep maroon, pointed oval leaves
Parsley	flat or curly deep green leaves on slender stems
Pea, snap	climbing plants with round leaves and tendrils, white blossoms, and edible pods
Perilla	frilly green or purple leaves
Purslane	fleshy round leaves on creeping plants
Radicchio (chicory)	red, green, or white veined leaves in heads, loose or tight, round or elongated
Runner beans	tall vining plants with scarlet or white flowers and flat bean pods
Sage	purple tubular blossoms
Shungiku (edible chrysanthemum)	finely cut leaves, white and yellow daisylike flowers
Sorrel	dark green, long, shield-shaped leaves
Spinach	dark green shield-shaped leaves
Tarragon	narrow dark green leaves on slender stems
Tuberose begonia	brightly colored rose-shaped flowers
Tulip	large brightly colored flowers
Viola	flowers in all shades, sizes from 3-inch pansies to ¾-inch Johnny jump-ups
Violet	heart-shaped leaves; tiny fragrant blue, white, or yellow flowers
Watercress	round deep green leaves of fleshy stems, white flowers

PARTS TO USE	TASTE	SEASON
leaves, sprouts	very mild, soft textured	fall to spring
small tender sprigs	pungent, spicy	summer
leaves, sprigs	very green, grassy sweet	spring
leaves	fruity, cooling	spring to fall
leaves, flowers	very mild green mustard	spring to fall
petals, small leaves	like oregano	early summer
leaves under 4 inches long, flowers	spicy hot, slightly bitter	all year
flowers, leaves, seed pods	peppery sweet	late spring to fall
leaves	green, like spinach	summer
leaves	like spinach	late spring to fall
sprigs	pungent green	all year
tender sprigs of leaf with tendrils, flowers, pods	sweet green	spring
small or torn leaves	like cumin	summer
leaves, sprigs	green, mildly sweet	spring to fall
leaves	bitter	all year
flowers	raw bean flavor	summer
blossoms	pungent, sweet	late spring
leaves, petals	leaves are mild green, petals slightly bitter	summer to fall
small or torn leaves	sour, green	spring and fall
small leaves	green, sweet	all year
tender sprigs	pungent anise	late spring to fall
petals, stems	tart, like sorrel	summer
petals	raw-pea flavor	spring
flowers	sweet, minty violet	all year
small leaves, flowers	leaves are sweet green, flowers mild	spring
leaves, flowers	green, mildly bitter	all year

Green Bean and Nasturtium Salad with Tarragon

6 servings

Paul Bertolli of Oliveto Restaurant in Oakland, California, served this salad for a luncheon he prepared from our kitchen garden at The Herbfarm. I loved the way he handled the nasturtiums, tossing them in as an integral part of the salad rather than placing them on top as a garnish. I've based this recipe on his dish but have added the sweet anise flavor of fresh tarragon to play off the fresh beans and the radishy bite of the flowers.

This dish will taste as good as the green beans you use. Be sure they're freshly harvested and not overmature. You can't go wrong with the tiny French haricots verts, but also try bush, pole, runner, wax, or romano beans as long as they're picked when still young. You can tell your beans are young when you snap one open and it's filled with shimmering translucent matter and the seeds are tiny.

1 medium shallot, very thinly sliced (about ⅓ cup)
2 tablespoons tarragon wine vinegar or sherry vinegar
2 tablespoons fresh French tarragon leaves, very coarsely chopped
Salt
4 quarts water
1 pound tender, young green beans
3 tablespoons extra-virgin olive oil
Freshly ground black pepper
24 nasturtium flowers

1. Marinating the shallot. Toss the shallot, vinegar, tarragon, and ¼ teaspoon salt together in a large mixing bowl. Let sit uncovered for at least 30 minutes to marinate the shallot and blend the flavors.

2. Blanching the beans. Meanwhile bring the water to a boil in a large saucepan and add 1 tablespoon salt. Snap off the stem ends of the beans. If they're small, leave them whole; if they're very large, cut them on a diagonal into 2-inch pieces. Fill a large bowl with ice water and set it to the side. Drop the beans into the boiling water and boil until they are cooked through but still crunchy and brightly colored, 1 to 2 minutes for tiny haricots verts, up to 4 minutes for larger beans. Drain the beans and plunge them into the ice water to stop the cooking. When the beans are thoroughly cooled, drain them again and dry them on a clean dishtowel to prevent water from diluting the dressing. (A steamer basket makes the blanching process simpler. Fill the basket with the beans, plunge it in the boiling water, remove it to plunge it into the ice water, then lift it out again.) You can blanch the beans up to 1 day ahead and store them, refrigerated, in a tightly sealed plastic container or resealable bag.

3. Dressing the salad. Stir the olive oil into the shallot mixture. Add the beans and toss well. Taste and season with black pepper, and additional salt if needed. Check the nasturtiums for insects and gently toss them with the beans. Transfer the salad to a serving platter or individual salad plates, being sure the nasturtiums are evenly distributed.

VARIATION
Sprinkle the salad with Crispy Shallots, below.

HERB SUBSTITUTIONS
- *In place of tarragon, use an equal amount of coarsely chopped fresh dill or summer savory, or ¼ cup torn fresh basil leaves.*

CRISPY SHALLOTS

Makes about ½ cup, enough to garnish 6 servings

> *2 large shallots, peeled*
> *About ½ cup all-purpose flour*
> *About 1 quart vegetable oil*
> *Salt*

Slice the shallots crosswise about 1/16 inch thick, preferably with a mandoline or Japanese Benriner slicer. Separate the rings. Heat the oil in a 3- to 4-quart saucepan until it reaches 325°F. Toss the shallot rings with the flour in a mixing bowl, then tip them into a strainer and shake off the excess flour. Add all the shallots to the oil 1 handful at a time, while stirring with a skimmer to keep the oil from foaming up. Keeping the heat high, turn the shallots constantly with a skimmer until they are a pale golden brown. The oil temperature will drop when all the shallots are first added. When it rises to about 300°F, the shallots should be done. Remove them with the skimmer to paper towels to drain. Sprinkle lightly with salt. If not using immediately, store in a tightly covered bowl for up to 4 hours.

Roasted Asparagus Salad with Fried Sage

6 servings

Roasting asparagus not only concentrates the flavor and sugars but also reduces its water content so that it accepts a dressing more easily than boiled or steamed asparagus would. In this dish the roasted spears are decked with sage, lemon, and curls of Parmigiano-Reggiano cheese, then topped with the delicate crunch of fried sage leaves. You can roast the asparagus ahead of time but don't dress the spears until ready to serve, since the lemon juice drains their color.

> *2 pounds fresh asparagus*
> *1 tablespoon finely chopped fresh sage*
> *1½ tablespoons olive oil*
> *Salt*
> *1 cup vegetable or olive oil, for frying*
> *30 fresh medium sage leaves, patted dry*
> *1 wedge Parmigiano-Reggiano cheese*
>
> DRESSING
> *Thinly sliced zest of 1 large lemon (removed with a zester)*
> *3 tablespoons freshly squeezed lemon juice*
> *1 tablespoon chopped fresh sage*
> *¼ teaspoon salt*
> *Freshly ground black pepper to taste*
> *¼ cup extra-virgin olive oil*

1. **Asparagus.** Preheat the oven to 450°F. Trim the bottoms of the asparagus spears at the point where they turn pale and tough. If the spears are medium to thick, peel the lower two-thirds of the trimmed spears with a sharp vegetable peeler. Thin spears do not need to be peeled. Place them in a bowl and toss with the chopped sage, olive oil, and a light sprinkle of salt. Spread the asparagus in a single layer on a baking sheet and roast until the spears are slightly limp when you hold them from the bottom, 4 to 8 minutes depending on their thickness. They will continue to cook once you remove them from the oven. Let cool.

2. **Fried sage.** Heat the vegetable oil in a 1½- to 2-quart saucepan to 330°F. Drop in half of the sage leaves and turn them in the oil with a wire skimmer or slotted spoon.

They'll sizzle loudly at first, but if they're dry, they won't splatter. Fry for only 10 to 15 seconds, then remove them to paper towels to drain. Do not let the leaves brown. Fry the remaining sage leaves and sprinkle them all lightly with salt. They should crisp when they cool. The sage can be fried up to 1 day ahead of time; it will stay crisp if stored in an airtight container at room temperature.

3. Cheese. Hold the wedge of Parmigiano in your hand and use a sharp vegetable peeler with light pressure to shave thin curls of the cheese into a bowl. You'll want to shave off 2 ounces, about 1 cup.

4. Dressing. Combine all the dressing ingredients except the olive oil in a small mixing bowl, then whisk in the oil.

5. Assembling the salad. When ready to serve, toss the asparagus with the dressing in a large bowl. Arrange the dressed asparagus in a fan shape on a serving platter or individual plates. Sprinkle with the Parmigiano shavings and then with the fried sage leaves. If you have a sage plant that's flowering, sprinkle the salad with some of its blossoms.

VARIATION
WARM ROASTED ASPARAGUS WITH SAGE BUTTER
Roast the asparagus spears as directed. While they are roasting, melt 4 tablespoons unsalted butter in a small (8-inch) skillet over medium-low heat. Add the 30 sage leaves and cook, stirring often, until the butter begins to brown slightly and the sage gives off a nutty, toasty aroma, 3 to 4 minutes. Stir in the finely sliced zest of 1 lemon, 3 tablespoons lemon juice, and ¼ teaspoon salt. Transfer the asparagus to a warm platter and spoon the sage leaves and lemon butter on top. Sprinkle with the Parmigiano shavings and sage blossoms if available.

Carrot and Jalapeño Salad

6 servings

Cilantro, mint, and basil each have a cooling quality that suits them to dishes with chile peppers. All three of these refreshing herbs balance the heat of this sweet and fiery carrot salad. Fresh fennel seeds from your own garden will give the salad another lively layer of flavor, but you can substitute dried seeds for a subtler effect. In either case the seeds are coarsely chopped with a chef's knife rather than used whole or ground.

The flavor of the salad improves greatly if you let it marinate overnight, but expect the herbs to wilt and lose their fresh appearance. Serve this salad with grilled meats or pack it with sandwiches for lunches or picnics—it travels well and keeps up to 3 days in the refrigerator.

> *3 quarts water*
> *1½ teaspoons salt*
> *1½ pounds sweet young carrots, peeled*
> *2 to 5 jalapeño peppers (to taste), seeded and finely chopped*
> *Grated zest and juice of 1 large lime*
> *2 tablespoons extra-virgin olive oil*
> *2 teaspoons honey*
> *1 teaspoon coarsely chopped fresh or dried fennel seeds*
> *2 tablespoons coarsely chopped cilantro*
> *2 tablespoons coarsely chopped fresh spearmint*
> *¼ cup coarsely chopped fresh basil*

1. Carrots. Combine the water and 1 teaspoon of the salt in a large saucepan and bring it to a boil. Slice the carrots ¾ inch thick using a rolling cut: Make the first cut at a 45° angle, then roll the carrot 180° and make another cut at the same angle. The result will be uniform wedge-shaped pieces. Cook the carrots in the boiling water until the tip of a paring knife can pierce them with moderate resistance, 2 to 3 minutes. Drain the carrots in a colander and run cold water over them until they are completely cooled.

2. Dressing the salad. In a mixing bowl, stir together the jalapeños, lime zest, olive oil, honey, fennel seeds, and the remaining ½ teaspoon salt. Add the herbs and blanched carrots and toss to combine. Cover and let the salad marinate for 1 hour at room temperature or overnight in the refrigerator.

MINTED ORANGE AND RED ONION SALAD

4 servings

Salads of sweet orange, sharp onion, and bitter greens are common in Italy and are slowly becoming familiar on American tables. In this version, the refreshing fruitiness of spearmint complements each element well. It's a beautiful and vibrantly flavored salad that serves as an exciting beginning to a meal in any season.

½ medium red onion, peeled
2 tablespoons sherry vinegar
¼ cup coarsely chopped fresh spearmint
¼ teaspoon salt
2 large navel oranges
1 large bunch watercress, thick stems removed
2 tablespoons fruity extra-virgin olive oil
Freshly ground black pepper

1. Onion. Very thinly slice the onion using a mandoline, Japanese slicer, or sharp thin-bladed knife. In a large mixing bowl, toss it with the vinegar, mint, and salt.

2. Oranges. With a large chef's knife or serrated knife, cut off the tops and bottoms of the oranges. Place them cut side down on a cutting board and cut off the peel and white pith with a knife in thick vertical strips, following the curve of the fruit. The oranges should have no part of the peel, orange or white, left on it. Cut the oranges lengthwise into quarters, then slice the quarters crosswise ¼ inch thick. Toss the orange with the onion.

3. Finishing the salad. Wash the watercress by swishing it in a deep basin of cold water. Lift it out of the water and dry it in a salad spinner or on a clean towel. Add the cress and olive oil to the orange mixture and toss. Taste and season with black pepper, and additional salt if needed. Serve at once.

VARIATION
Substitute 1 fennel bulb, shaved or thinly sliced, for the watercress.

Roasted Beet, Dill, and Frisée Salad

6 servings

This eye-catching salad of lacy pale green endive leaves speckled with crimson beets is an exciting alternative to green salad for an autumn meal. Try to find the French curly endive known as frisée. It produces spectacular heads of finely frilled leaves that are light green on the very outside but gradually fade to snowy white in the center. The common type of curly endive, or escarole, is much coarser and tougher but still works as a second choice.

> *8 small beets, about 1½ inches in diameter, or 4 medium beets*
> *1 tablespoon finely chopped lemon zest*
> *2 tablespoons freshly squeezed lemon juice*
> *1 tablespoon pure maple syrup or dark brown sugar*
> *¼ cup chopped fresh dill*
> *1 medium shallot, very thinly sliced (about ¼ cup)*
> *½ teaspoon salt*
> *Freshly ground black pepper to taste*
> *1 medium head frisée, or ½ large head curly endive (escarole)*
> *5 tablespoons extra-virgin olive oil*

1. Roasting the beets. Preheat the oven to 425°F. Trim the stems on the beets to ½ inch and wash the beets. Put them in a shallow baking dish large enough to hold them in a single layer. Pour ½ inch water into the dish and cover the dish with a lid or aluminum foil. Bake the beets until a paring knife easily pierces the center of a beet, 30 to 60 minutes depending on their size. The water will form a syrupy liquid and bubble up. You may need to add a little more water near the end; don't let the dish dry up completely. Remove the pan from the oven, remove the lid, and let the beets cool. Cut the top and tail off each beet and rub them under running water to slip off the skins (wear rubber gloves to avoid staining your hands). Alternatively you can hold each beet in a paper towel and use it to rub the skin off. Cut each small beet into 8 wedges. If the beets are larger, cut them horizontally in half, then cut each half into 8 wedges.

2. Marinating. Stir together the lemon zest, lemon juice, maple syrup, dill, shallot, salt, and pepper. Coat the beets with this dressing and let sit at room temperature for at least 1 hour or cover and refrigerate overnight.

3. Finishing the salad. Wash and dry the frisée and remove any very thick stems. Tear it into bite-size pieces. Pour the olive oil over the beet mixture, then combine with the frisée. Taste and add more salt and pepper if needed.

VARIATIONS

For the curly endive, substitute 3 heads Belgian endive, sliced diagonally into ½-inch-thick strips and separated, or 1 large fennel bulb, thinly sliced.

Right before serving, add 2 cups diced apples, pears, or Asian pears.

Sprinkle the salad with ¾ cup broken lightly toasted walnuts.

HERB SUBSTITUTIONS

- *In place of the dill, use ¼ cup coarsely chopped fresh chervil, 1 tablespoon coarsely chopped fresh tarragon, 2 tablespoons coarsely chopped fresh spearmint, or 2 teaspoons finely chopped fresh fennel seeds.*

goat or

*add Tarragon + red pears + blue cheese
(no dill) sprinkle w/ walnuts*

Fresh Tomato and Herb Salad

6 to 8 servings

The garden behind my house in Seattle is very small, and I have to be ruthlessly choosy about what I can grow. Herbs have nothing to worry about, they're automatically on the guest list; but I can't afford sunny space for vegetables—except tomatoes, of course. Like many Americans, I feel compelled to grow my own every summer without fail, even though Seattle's cool summers typically give us a tomato season that lasts just a few weeks. When the sweet, tangy fruit finally ripens, herbs are growing at full throttle, and I prepare this gorgeous salad combining all their lively flavors.

> *2 pounds perfectly ripe tomatoes, preferably several varieties of contrasting shape and color*
> *1 cup coarsely torn fresh basil leaves*
> *¼ cup fresh French tarragon leaves*
> *½ cup fresh parsley leaves*
> *½ cup small fresh spearmint leaves*
> *2 cups torn arugula or watercress*
> *1 tablespoon red wine vinegar*
> *1 tablespoon balsamic vinegar*
> *¼ cup extra-virgin olive oil*
> *¾ teaspoon kosher salt*
> *Freshly ground black pepper to taste*

Cut the tomatoes into wedges; if they are cherry or currant tomatoes, cut them in half or leave them whole. Combine them in a large mixing bowl with the herbs and arugula. Drizzle the vinegars and olive oil over the top, sprinkle with the salt and a generous grinding of pepper, and toss until everything is evenly coated with dressing. Arrange the salad on a platter or individual serving plates and serve right away.

HERB SUBSTITUTIONS
- *Omit the tarragon and add ¼ cup fresh marjoram leaves, coarsely chopped fresh dill, or coarsely chopped fresh lovage.*
- *In place of the mint leaves, add fresh lemon balm leaves.*

SWEET ONION AND YOGURT SALAD

6 servings

In Indian cuisine, yogurt salads are made with vegetables like cucumber, okra, or onion. Called raitas, they differ from the Western idea of a salad—they are eaten with a spoon, mopped up with bread, or used as a condiment. These refreshing salads inspired me to come up with this herb-garden version. I make it in June when Walla Walla onions are in season and serve it alongside spicy grilled foods as a cool counterpoint.

If you grow nasturtium flowers or can buy them fresh, they'll make this salad dazzle with both their flavor and color, but be sure to add them at the last minute. Without the blossoms, the salad will keep for 2 days covered in the refrigerator.

> *1 large sweet onion, such as Walla Walla or Vidalia, or 1 large red onion,*
>   *peeled and thinly sliced*
> *1 teaspoon minced fresh ginger*
> *2 tablespoons seasoned rice vinegar (used for sushi rice and available in*
>   *Japanese sections of supermarkets)*
> *1 cup plain yogurt*
> *¼ cup fresh basil leaves torn in ½-inch pieces*
> *2 tablespoons coarsely chopped cilantro*
> *1 tablespoon coarsely chopped fresh spearmint*
> *¼ teaspoon salt*
> *Freshly ground black pepper to taste*
> *24 nasturtium flowers, if available*

1. Onion. Combine the onion, ginger, and vinegar in a mixing bowl. Let sit uncovered for at least 1 hour to soften and mellow the onion.

2. Finishing the salad. Pour off most of the liquid from the onion. Stir in the yogurt, basil, cilantro, and mint. Season with the salt and black pepper. Cover and refrigerate until chilled. If you are using nasturtium flowers, check them for insects, remove their stems, and gently fold them in just before serving the salad.

BALSAMIC POTATO SALAD

6 servings

On lazy, hot summer days when the herb garden is taking care of itself and there's little to do but breathe in the fragrances and watch the bees, dinner is an easygoing affair. This sprightly potato salad, full of salty black olives, bold oregano, and cooling mint, is put together quickly. You can serve it warm, as soon as it's tossed, or let its flavors marry all afternoon or overnight in the refrigerator (take it out an hour before you serve and let it lose its chill). Served warm or cool, it's a fitting accompaniment to a simple grilled dinner.

> *½ medium red onion, thinly sliced*
> *1 red bell pepper, seeded and cut into matchsticks*
> *1 clove garlic, minced*
> *¼ cup balsamic vinegar*
> *2½ teaspoons salt*
> *2 pounds small red potatoes or fingerling potatoes*
> *¼ cup extra-virgin olive oil*
> *½ cup coarsely chopped pitted Kalamata, Gaeta, or other briny black*
> *   olives*
> *½ cup coarsely chopped fresh mint*
> *¼ cup coarsely chopped fresh flat-leaf parsley*
> *2 tablespoons coarsely chopped fresh Greek oregano*
> *Freshly ground black pepper to taste*

1. Starting the salad. Combine the onion, red pepper, garlic, vinegar, and ½ teaspoon of the salt in a large bowl and let sit uncovered at room temperature for at least 1 hour to soften and mellow the onion.

2. Potatoes. Meanwhile quarter the red potatoes or slice the fingerlings ½ inch thick and put them in a 4-quart saucepan. Fill the pan with cold water, add the remaining 2 teaspoons salt, and bring to a boil over high heat. Reduce the heat and cook at a slow boil until the potatoes are tender but still hold their shape, 15 to 20 minutes. Since the potatoes firm up a bit when they cool, it's better to slightly overcook than to undercook. Drain in a colander and let cool until the steam stops rising.

3. Dressing the salad. Stir the olive oil, olives, and chopped herbs into the onion mixture. Add the warm potatoes and toss gently. Taste and season with black pepper and additional salt if needed. Serve warm or at room temperature.

HERB SUBSTITUTIONS

In place of the mint and oregano, add one of the following combinations with the ¼ cup parsley:

- *½ cup torn basil leaves and 2 tablespoons coarsely chopped marjoram*
- *1 tablespoon finely chopped rosemary and 2 tablespoons coarsely chopped English thyme*
- *½ cup coarsely chopped dill and 2 tablespoons coarsely chopped lemon thyme*

Roasted Belgian Endive Salad

4 servings

This unusual warm winter salad works well to spark an appetite before a rich main course. The pale, slightly bitter endive are cut in slivers, roasted in a very hot oven with a sweet rosemary dressing, arranged like a chrysanthemum blossom on a platter, and layered with refreshing orange segments.

Belgian endives are sprouts of particular chicory plants that are grown in dark sheds. They should have a mild pleasant bitterness. Purchase heads that are completely pale white or cream colored. Those with green margins on the leaves have been sitting in the light too long and may taste very bitter.

DRESSING
3 tablespoons fruity extra-virgin olive oil
2 tablespoons balsamic vinegar
1 tablespoon sherry vinegar or red wine vinegar
1 tablespoon coarsely chopped fresh rosemary
½ large shallot, coarsely chopped (about 2 tablespoons)
1 clove garlic, coarsely chopped
Finely sliced zest of ½ orange (removed with a zester)
1 tablespoon dark brown sugar
½ teaspoon salt
Freshly ground black pepper

1 pound Belgian endives (3 to 4 medium)
2 large oranges, segmented (see Note)

1. Dressing. Blend all the ingredients for the dressing in a blender or food processor until they are emulsified, meaning the dressing is creamy and does not separate. Set aside.

2. Roasting the endives. Preheat the oven to 500°F. Cut each endive lengthwise in half, then each half into 3 or 4 wedges. In a medium mixing bowl, toss the wedges with the dressing to coat them thoroughly. Spread the endives out in a single layer on a large baking sheet. Roast until their edges begin to brown, 5 to 7 minutes. Let the wedges cool slightly on the pan.

3. Assemble the salad. Using tongs, arrange a row of the warm roasted endive around the edge of the round platter with the pointed tips facing out. Scatter some of the orange segments on top, then continue to arrange the remaining wedges in concentric rows as if they were petals of a flower, scattering the orange segments as you go. Serve the salad slightly warm.

NOTE

To segment an orange, with a large chef's knife or serrated knife, cut off the top and bottom of the orange. Stand it on a cutting board and cut off the peel and white pith with the knife in thick vertical strips, following the curve of the fruit. The orange should have no peel, orange or white, left on it. Hold the peeled orange in your hand and with a sharp paring knife, cut inside the membrane on either side of each segment, letting the flesh drop into a small bowl.

Green Goddess Grilled Chicken Salad

4 servings

I featured this salad on my luncheon menu when I was chef at Seattle's Alexis Hotel in the 1980s. I was interested in serving classic American dishes in an up-to-date form. In my research I came across James Beard's recipe for the original green goddess dressing. I was surprised to find that it originated at the Palace Hotel in San Francisco at the turn of the century and was named after a stage play. The tangy, creamy, and intensely herbal dressing has become a favorite of mine, especially for main-course salads like this one.

2 cups Green Goddess Dressing (page 334)
4 boneless, skinless chicken breasts (about 1½ pounds)
1 tablespoon extra-virgin olive oil
2 cloves garlic, minced
1 tablespoon Dijon mustard
Salt and freshly ground black pepper to taste
6 cups mixed young salad greens, see suggestions for The Herbfarm Garden
*   Salad (page 45), or use commercial mesclun mix, sometimes called field*
*   salad or spring mix*
1 ripe avocado, quartered, peeled, and sliced
2 medium vine-ripened tomatoes, cut into 8 wedges each
Optional garnish: tarragon sprigs, snipped chives, or edible flowers such as
*   mustard, arugula, scarlet runner bean, or nasturtium*

1. Dressing. Prepare the dressing as much as 2 days ahead and store tightly covered in the refrigerator.

2. The chicken. Start a charcoal fire in an outdoor grill or preheat a gas grill to medium-high. In a mixing bowl toss the chicken breasts with the oil, garlic, mustard, salt, and pepper. Adjust the grill rack 4 inches from the fire. When the charcoal is ashed over and medium hot or the gas grill is preheated, lay the chicken on the grill and cook uncovered until the underside is well marked, about 4 minutes. Turn and cook the other side until the chicken is firm to the touch and no pink remains when you peek at the center with the tip of a knife, 4 to 6 minutes. The chicken breasts can also be broiled in the same manner. Let the chicken cool slightly while preparing the greens.

3. Finishing the salad. Wash the salad greens by swishing them in a deep basin of cold water. Lift them from the water and spin dry or pat dry in a clean towel. In a large mixing bowl, toss the salad greens with ½ cup of the dressing until they are well coated. Divide the greens among 4 dinner plates. With a thin-bladed slicing knife, slice the chicken breasts ¼ inch thick on a diagonal. Arrange the slices of chicken on top of the greens in a fan shape and arrange the avocado and tomatoes beside it. Spoon additional dressing in a band across the chicken. Garnish if desired with tarragon, chives, or edible flowers. Serve the salads right away. Pass the remaining dressing at the table.

SEAFOOD VARIATION

Substitute 12 ounces cooked peeled shrimp or 12 ounces fresh crabmeat for the cooked chicken.

HERBED COUSCOUS SALAD

6 servings

This salad gets its inspiration from tabbouleh, the Middle Eastern cracked wheat (bulgur) salad. Couscous is also made from wheat but has a much lighter texture and takes only minutes to prepare. Like tabbouleh, this salad has plenty of parsley and mint, but I've also added cilantro, tangy dried apricots, and red bell pepper. It has a mild but exotic flavor and travels well for picnics or potlucks.

1½ cups water
1 cup quick-cooking couscous

DRESSING
1 tablespoon freshly squeezed lemon juice
1 tablespoon minced fresh ginger
1 teaspoon finely chopped lemon zest (removed with a zester)
¾ teaspoon salt
¾ teaspoon ground cumin
⅛ teaspoon cayenne pepper
3 tablespoons olive oil

6 tablespoons finely chopped fresh spearmint
6 tablespoons finely chopped fresh flat-leaf parsley
¼ cup coarsely chopped fresh cilantro
¼ cup finely chopped green onions
½ cup finely diced red bell pepper
½ cup thinly sliced dried apricots

1. Couscous. Bring the water to a boil in a 2-quart saucepan. Stir in the couscous, cover, and let sit off the heat for 10 minutes. Transfer the couscous to a large mixing bowl and spread it out up the sides of the bowl so that it cools quickly. When cool enough to handle, break up any clumps with your fingertips and check that all the grains are separate.

2. Finishing the salad. Stir together the dressing ingredients in a separate bowl, then pour the mixture over the couscous. Fold in the herbs, green onions, red pepper, and apricots. Let sit at room temperature for at least 1 hour to allow the flavors to meld before serving. You can refrigerate the salad covered for up to 3 days.

GRILLED PEACH SALAD

6 servings

This is a salad of contrasts—sweet, smoky, spicy, bitter, and herbed; warm and cool. It's an exciting beginning for a summer dinner from the backyard grill.

MARINADE

1 to 2 large jalapeño peppers, seeded and finely diced
2 tablespoons coarsely chopped fresh basil
1 tablespoon minced fresh ginger
1 tablespoon freshly squeezed lime juice
⅛ teaspoon salt
1½ tablespoons olive oil

3 large ripe peaches
2 ounces arugula, large stems removed
2 ounces watercress, large stems removed
2 tablespoons fresh basil leaves torn into ½-inch pieces
1½ tablespoons extra-virgin olive oil
1 tablespoon champagne vinegar or rice vinegar
Salt and freshly ground black pepper to taste

1. Peaches. Stir the marinade ingredients together in a mixing bowl. Carefully cut the peaches into quarters, discarding the pits, and toss them gently with the marinade.

2. Greens. Start a medium-hot charcoal fire in an outdoor grill or preheat a gas grill to medium-high. Wash the arugula and watercress and spin dry or pat dry in a clean dishtowel. Toss the greens with the basil, olive oil, vinegar, salt, and pepper. Arrange the greens on a serving platter or individual salad plates.

3. Grilling. Adjust the grill rack 3 to 4 inches from the fire. When the charcoal is ashed over or the gas grill is very hot, place the peaches skin side down on the rack. Don't be concerned if there is a flare-up and the skins blacken. Grill until marked on the skin side, about 2 minutes, then turn and grill briefly on the cut side. Remove the peaches from the grill and let them cool slightly. They should be very warm and slightly blackened in spots but not cooked through or mushy. Rub off any badly charred skin. Arrange the warm fruit on the greens and serve right away.

LEMON VERBENA FRUIT SALAD

8 servings

     The heavenly citrus scent of lemon verbena intensifies the fruit flavors in this refreshing salad. It is perfect for brunch or as a light dessert.

> ¼ *cup sugar*
> ½ *cup (gently packed) fresh lemon verbena leaves, thick center vein*
>   *removed*
> 2 *tablespoons freshly squeezed lime juice*
> 8 *cups mixed sliced ripe fruit and berries, such as melon, peaches,*
>   *nectarines, apricots, plums, pitted sweet cherries, grapes, raspberries,*
>   *strawberries, and blueberries*

Process the sugar and lemon verbena leaves in a food processor to a very smooth green paste, scraping down the sides as necessary. Add the lime juice and process briefly. Shortly before serving, toss this dressing with the fruit in a large mixing bowl.

CHAPTER 3

Little Bites, First Courses, and Egg Dishes

The Herbfarm's nine-course dinners always begin with a plate of small bites to accompany our signature Champagne cocktails. A typical plate might present a sliver of herbed onion tart, some thinly sliced fennel-cured salmon, a plump mussel baked in mint pesto, and a few pieces of herb tempura. This chapter begins with some of these nibbles to serve your own guests before they sit down for dinner. Because they are meant to tease the appetite, the herbal flavors in them can be especially pronounced and daring.

This chapter also has many dishes that can serve as a small course for a dinner party or a main course for lunch or supper. They include silky garlic flan, sweet corn puddings with smoked trout, and delicate squash blossoms filled with warm goat cheese.

Finally, I've included a small collection of egg recipes. When combined with fresh herbs, egg dishes can be most memorable. Eggs have a soft rich flavor that welcomes and embraces mild-tasting herbs like chervil, tarragon, dill, and chives. They make a satisfying meal any time of day.

Herb Tempura

Makes 36 pieces, 6 to 12 servings

Sample the entire herb garden on a platter with these flavorful little fritters. Serve them as an elegant nibble with Champagne or Champagne cocktails (page 318) before dinner.

BATTER
2 cups all-purpose flour (9 ounces)
2 teaspoons baking powder
2 tablespoons cornstarch
2½ to 2¾ cups ice water
4 cups canola, peanut, or olive oil, for deep-frying

36 pieces of a variety of herbs and edible flowers such as:
  Small leaves of mint, sage, perilla, lemon balm, or lovage
  Tender sprigs of French tarragon, flat-leaf parsley, fennel, or dill
  Blossoms of nasturtium, fennel, sweet cicely, or daylily buds
Sea salt or kosher salt

1. Batter. Whisk the dry ingredients together in a mixing bowl. Stir in 2½ cups ice water; don't overmix and don't worry about lumps. The batter should be the consistency of heavy cream. If it's too thick, add more water 1 tablespoon at a time.

2. Frying. Preheat the oven to 175°F. Heat the oil in a 3-quart saucepan until it reaches 350°F on a deep-fry thermometer or heat an electric deep-fat fryer filled with oil. Hold 1 herb or flower by the stem and dip it into the batter. Lift it out and hold it for a moment over the bowl to let the excess drip off, then drop it in the oil. Fry only as many fritters at a time as comfortably fit in the pan without touching, and adjust the heat to keep the oil temperature at 350°F during the entire process. Fry the fritters until lightly browned on the bottom, 30 to 60 seconds, then flip them with a wire skimmer and brown the other side. Drain on paper towels. Keep the fritters warm in the oven as you fry the remaining. When all the herbs are fried, sprinkle them with salt. Transfer them to a serving platter lined with a torn square of handmade paper, rice paper, or fresh grape leaves. Serve right away.

TOMATO AND BASIL CROSTINI

Makes 24 pieces

Here's an example of a familiar dish that can become remarkable when prepared with care and good ingredients. First of all, choose the right bread. An Italian-style bread with a chewy texture (from a small artisan bakery if possible) will provide a better base than a fluffy, light baguette. Then, find juicy vine-ripened tomatoes. Even a pale out-of-season plum tomato will be tasty after it's slow-roasted for 2½ hours with thyme and olive oil, but start with flavorful fruit and the result will be spectacular. For the cheese, seek out delicate fresh mozzarella, sold as snowy white balls that float in water, or even better, use silky mozzarella di bufala, made from water buffalo's milk and imported from Italy. Toast the bread slices carefully, then add the topping just before serving. These crostini will make you sigh.

1 best-quality artisan-style baguette (about 14 ounces and 14 inches long)
*   or a wider loaf*
Extra-virgin olive oil
24 halves Slow-Roasted Tomatoes (page 340), at room temperature
2 tablespoons coarsely chopped fresh marjoram or oregano
8 ounces fresh mozzarella cheese, cut into 24 slices about ¼ inch thick
24 small whole basil leaves

1. Toasting the bread. Preheat the broiler. Cut the bread into ½-inch-thick slices with a serrated knife and spread them out on a baking sheet. If you are using a wider loaf, cut each slice in half. The slices should be no larger than 3 x 2 inches. Brush both sides lightly with olive oil and toast them 4 inches from the heat source until golden brown. Turn the slices and toast the other side. Or toast the bread slices on a grill, away from direct heat, and watch them carefully.

2. Assembling. Reduce the oven temperature to 300°F. Top each toast with a tomato half, a sprinkle of marjoram, and a slice of mozzarella. Warm the crostini in the oven just until the cheese softens, about 3 minutes. Transfer the crostini to a serving platter and arrange a basil leaf on each one. Serve immediately.

BITE-SIZE CHEDDAR AND THYME GOUGÈRES

Makes about 72 puffs

Cheese puffs, really—these are miniature Cheddar versions of a savory French cream puff traditionally enriched with Gruyère cheese. Whatever you call them, fresh from the oven they make the ideal cocktail snack. Once you form the dough into mounds on the baking sheets, you can refrigerate or freeze them and bake the puffs just before your guests are ready to devour them.

¾ cup water
½ teaspoon salt
6 tablespoons unsalted butter, cut into ½-inch cubes
¾ cup all-purpose flour (spoon and level; 3¼ ounces)
4 large eggs
1½ tablespoons finely chopped fresh English thyme
1 cup grated sharp Cheddar or Gruyère cheese (2 ounces)

1. Dough. Preheat the oven to 400°F. Put the water, salt, and butter in a medium (2- to 3-quart) saucepan and bring it to a boil over medium heat. Add the flour all at once and beat vigorously with a sturdy wire whisk, still over heat. It will form a very firm mass of dough that should pull away from the sides of the pan. Remove the pan from the heat. Crack an egg into a small cup. Pour the egg into the saucepan and immediately beat it into the dough using the whisk or a handheld electric mixer. Repeat with the remaining 3 eggs, incorporating each one thoroughly before adding another. The mixture will be satiny and sticky and have a consistency between soft dough and thick batter. Stir in the thyme and ½ cup of the cheese.

2. Forming and baking. Line 2 baking sheets with parchment paper. Using 2 flatware teaspoons, drop balls of dough (each measuring 1 teaspoon in volume) in rows on the paper, allowing 1 inch of space between them for spreading. Or use a pastry bag with a large plain tip and pipe the dough out in ½-inch mounds. Place a pinch of the remaining cheese on top of each gougère. (At this point you can cover the pans tightly with plastic wrap and refrigerate them for up to 24 hours.) Bake the gougères until puffed and golden brown, 20 to 25 minutes. Serve while still warm.

NOTE

Once the dough is formed, you can put the baking sheets in the freezer until the little mounds are solid, then transfer them to resealable freezer bags. When you want to bake a batch, transfer them to a paper-lined baking sheet and bake at 400°F for 25 to 30 minutes.

HERB SUBSTITUTIONS

- *In place of the thyme, use an equal amount of finely chopped fresh summer savory, 2 tablespoons finely chopped fresh marjoram or oregano, or 3 tablespoons finely chopped fresh dill or chives.*

Onion and Sage Tarts

Makes 32 hors-d'oeuvre-size slices

These splendidly rich tarts are my version of French onion galettes. Buttery, flaky pastry crusts are filled with deeply caramelized onions that are generously laced with sage.

The steps to prepare these tarts may seem familiar, but if you take extra care with them, you'll be amazed by the results. Handle the pastry with precision so that it bakes tender, flaky, and shatteringly crisp; spend the time to slowly and thoroughly caramelize the onions until they melt into a golden marmalade; and give the tarts their final baking as close to serving time as possible.

You'll notice the onions are caramelized in a deep saucepan instead of a wide skillet. It makes them easier to stir without flying out of the pan and gives them a chance to soften and stew in their own liquid before it boils away. Once the liquid evaporates, the onions will concentrate and brown, and the balsamic vinegar works to balance the sweetness of the onions and deepen their color. For the best flavor, the whole process should take at least half an hour. Be sure to use regular yellow storage onions, not Walla Walla, Vidalia, or other sweet summer onions—they have too much water and do not caramelize well.

Serve the tarts as an hors d'oeuvre at any elegant occasion, or as an accompaniment to a seasonal salad for a light lunch or supper.

> *2 pounds yellow onions (3 large or 4 medium), sliced*
> *2 ounces bacon (2 slices), finely diced*
> *1 teaspoon sugar*
> *½ teaspoon salt*
> *2 to 3 teaspoons balsamic vinegar*
> *2 tablespoons finely chopped fresh sage*
> *Freshly ground black pepper*
> *¼ cup heavy cream*
> *1 large egg*
> *4 7-inch Free-Form Tart Shells (page 344), prebaked*

1. **Caramelizing the onions.** Peel the onions and cut them in half from root to tip. Cut out the dense core at the root end and slice the onions ¼ inch thick, again from root end to tip. Cook the bacon, stirring often, in a large (4-quart) saucepan over medium heat until almost crisp. Add the onions, sugar, and salt, and cook, stirring often, until they cook down by two-thirds, about 10 minutes. Add 2 teaspoons vinegar, reduce the heat to medium-low, and continue to cook until the onions are an even golden brown and softened to a marmalade consistency, 15 to 30 minutes depending on the onions. Stir often and scrape up any brown bits clinging to the bottom of the pan. The onions need almost constant stirring near the end to prevent them from sticking and burning. They'll let you know they need attention by giving off a sizzling sound. Stir in the sage, allow them to cool slightly, then taste and season with black pepper and additional salt if needed. If the onions seem overly sweet, stir in another teaspoon of vinegar. (The onions can be caramelized up to 2 days ahead and stored covered in the refrigerator.)

2. **Filling and baking.** Preheat the oven to 350°F. Stir the cream and egg into the caramelized onions until thoroughly combined. Divide the filling among the tart shells and spread it evenly with the back of a spoon. Bake in the upper third of the oven until the filling is set, about 15 minutes. The filling should still be soft but not runny. Let cool slightly, then transfer the tarts to a cutting board using a large spatula. Cut each into 8 wedges with the downward pressure of a sharp chef's knife. Serve warm or at room temperature.

VARIATIONS

For larger tarts, prebake 2 10-inch Free-Form Tart Shells (page 344). Divide the onion mixture between them and bake the tarts until the filling is set in the center, 20 to 25 minutes. Using a large spatula, transfer them to a cutting board and cut each into 12 wedges.

The tarts can be made without bacon. Use 3 tablespoons of extra-virgin olive oil to caramelize the onions.

HERB SUBSTITUTIONS
- *In place of sage, use an equal amount of finely chopped rosemary, marjoram, savory, English thyme, or lemon thyme.*

Grilled Figs with Thyme Honey and Gorgonzola Toasts

8 to 12 servings

Next to the fragrances and flavors of herbs, a warm ripe fig plucked from the tree is one of the greatest pleasures my garden offers. This year my heart sank when just as the heavy, soft fruits were weighing down the branches of my Desert King, voracious starlings discovered the tree and devoured them all. Shreds of fig skin hung from the limbs like candy bar wrappers on November 1. (Next year I'll cover the tree with bird netting.)

Fig trees grow quickly and bear young, and the lush plants add drama to the garden with their strapping leaves and drooping limbs. Many varieties of figs, like Brown Turkey, Celeste, and Hardy Chicago, are hardy to 10°F if grown in a sheltered spot along a south wall, though young, unprotected trees are susceptible to damage if the thermometer drops below 25°F. In colder climates, even if the tree is damaged by the cold, it will usually sprout from the roots in the spring. My brother Jon, who lives in Maryland (Zone 6), pots his up every fall and brings it into the garage to spend the winter, watering it every month or so to keep the roots from drying out.

Fortunately, fresh figs are readily available in markets in summer and autumn, and even if they are shy of perfection, they become ambrosial when they're grilled and drizzled with honey infused with thyme. I like to present them on a platter alongside croutons slathered with creamy Gorgonzola. Serve them as an appetizer before dinner or a fruit-and-cheese course to end the meal.

> ¼ cup mild or medium-strength honey, such as clover or blackberry
> 6 3-inch sprigs fresh English thyme
> 12 large ripe figs
> 2 teaspoons extra-virgin olive oil, plus more for brushing
> 2 teaspoons fresh thyme leaves
> 1 best-quality artisan-style baguette
> 6 ounces Gorgonzola cheese, at room temperature

1. Thyme honey. Bring the honey to a simmer in a small saucepan and add the thyme sprigs. Let sit off the heat for 15 minutes or more while grilling the figs and bread.

2. Grilling the figs. Start a charcoal fire in an outdoor grill or preheat a gas grill. Cut the figs in half and toss them in a small bowl with 2 teaspoons olive oil and the thyme leaves. Adjust the grill rack 4 inches from the fire. When the charcoal is ashed over and glowing or the gas grill is medium-hot, grill the figs quickly until they are heated through but not collapsed, 1 to 2 minutes on each side. Transfer them to a platter.

3. Toasts. Cut 24 ½-inch-thick slices from the bread and brush both sides lightly with olive oil. Toast the bread on both sides on the grill away from direct heat. Spread the cheese on the toasts and top them with the figs.

4. Serving. Remove the thyme sprigs from the honey with a fork and discard them, then drizzle the warm thyme honey over the figs and toasts. Serve at once.

Herbed Home-Cured Salmon

Makes 1 pound, 8 to 12 appetizer servings

This is a variation of gravlax, Scandinavia's dill-cured salmon. Traditionally a whole fish is cured at once, but at home I like to use this method for just a small piece of fillet. Removing the skin lets you cut off the strong-tasting gray fat that lies next to it and allows the salt and herb cure to work from both sides of the fillet at once, cutting down on the curing time.

Although the caraway-citrus flavor of dill is perfectly suited to salmon, there are several other herbs that make inspired variations. One of my favorites is fennel flowers, the yellow umbels (umbrella-shaped flower heads) that open above the tall stalks and then turn into seed heads. They have a sweet anise flavor, much more intense than the leaves but not as potent as the mature fresh seeds. A full-grown fennel plant (the herb fennel, not bulbing fennel) will produce baskets full of these flowers for about 6 weeks in the summer. Gather the umbels, then use a pair of scissors to snip off the yellow blooms at the tips.

The best salmon for this preparation is fresh sockeye because it yields thin fillets with a medium fat content and incomparable color. Use the front half or two-thirds of a fillet so that the piece is of an even thickness. If sockeye is not available, use a fillet from a small Atlantic or king salmon, about ½ to ¾ inch thick. It must be absolutely fresh.

Once the salmon is cured, slice it as thin as possible and serve it as you would cold-smoked salmon, though it's more flavorful and salty. Drape it on toasts with crème fraîche and capers, serve it as a first course with a rémoulade sauce and a small salad of seasonal greens, or use it to fill small flaky tart shells, as I describe at the end of the recipe.

> *1 pound salmon fillet, such as sockeye, Atlantic, or king, ½ to ¾ inch thick*
> *1½ tablespoons kosher salt or coarse sea salt*
> *1 tablespoon sugar*
> *½ cup fresh fennel blossoms, small dill sprigs, or cilantro, or ¼ cup fresh*
>   *French tarragon leaves*
> *Freshly ground black pepper*
> *1 tablespoon Pernod or other pastis, dry gin, or tequila if using cilantro*
> *Garnish: fennel leaves and additional blossoms*

1. **Cleaning the fish.** Skin the salmon and feel for the pin bones, the line of small soft bones that run along the front two-thirds of the fish perpendicular to the skin. Pull the bones out with a pair of fish tweezers or needle-nose pliers. Using a sharp, thin knife, cut off the thin layer of gray fat that lies next to the skin.

2. **Curing the fish.** Stir the salt and sugar together in a cup or small bowl. Place a piece of plastic wrap, 18 inches long, on your work surface. Spread half the herbs in the middle of the plastic in an area the size of the fish fillet. Rub half the salt mixture over the top of the fish, liberally grind pepper on top, then turn it over onto the herbs. Rub the remaining salt mixture on the other side, apply more pepper, then cover with the remaining herbs. Sprinkle all over with the liquor. Wrap the plastic wrap tightly around the fish and set it on a large flat plate. Cover with another flat plate, put the whole thing in the refrigerator, and weight it with 4 to 5 pounds (3 large cans tomatoes or a plastic container with 2 quarts liquid). Let the salmon cure for 36 hours, turning the fish over halfway through the curing time.

3. **Serving.** Unwrap the fish, scrape off the herbs, and rinse it briefly under cold water to remove the excess salt. Dry it thoroughly with paper towels. The fish can be stored for up to 2 days, wrapped in a fresh piece of plastic wrap, and refrigerated. When ready to serve, slice the fish as thin as possible using a very sharp, thin-bladed knife held at a 45-degree angle to the board. Sprinkle a few fennel leaves and blossoms on top.

VARIATION
HOME-CURED SALMON AND CHIVE TARTS
Bake 4 7-inch Free-Form Tart Shells (page 344). Just before serving, stir ¼ cup finely chopped chives into ½ cup crème fraîche. Spread the cream on the tart shells. Top with thin slices of the home-cured salmon and carefully cut each tart into 8 pieces with a large serrated knife, using a gentle sawing motion. Top each slice with a tiny leaf or sprig of the herb used to cure the salmon.

Baked Mussels Stuffed with Mint Pesto

6 appetizer servings or 12 hors-d'oeuvre servings

This is a terrific hors d'oeuvre or tapas dish that you can make ahead and bake at the last minute. The mussels are first steamed, then the meat is stuffed back in their shells on a bed of flavorful firm pesto made with spearmint and parsley, but without cheese. Serve them with cocktail forks and make sure your guests scoop up the pesto as they lift each mussel from the shell.

> *2 pounds fresh live mussels, large if possible, washed and beards removed*
> *½ cup dry white wine*
>
> PESTO
> *¼ cup pine nuts*
> *2 cloves garlic, peeled*
> *¾ teaspoon salt*
> *1½ cups (gently packed) fresh spearmint leaves*
> *1 cup (gently packed) fresh flat-leaf parsley leaves*
> *Freshly ground black pepper to taste*
> *¼ cup extra-virgin olive oil*

1. **Steaming the mussels.** Put the mussels in a large (6-quart) pot and pour the wine over them. Cover the pot tightly, place it over high heat, and cook just until all the mussels open. Drain the mussels into a colander set over a bowl to catch the liquor. Allow the mussels to cool until you can easily handle them and reserve the liquor for another use (it freezes well and is good in chowders, bisques, or seafood stews).

2. **Pesto.** Process the pine nuts, garlic, and salt in a food processor until the nuts are finely ground. Add the mint, parsley, and pepper. Pulse the machine until all the leaves are coarsely ground, scraping down the sides if necessary. With the machine running, pour in the olive oil in a steady stream and process until the mixture is a paste with some texture of the leaves remaining. You can also make the pesto with a mortar and pestle (page 102).

3. **Stuffing the mussels.** Detach and discard the top shell of each mussel. Loosen the meat in the bottom shell and check each one to make sure there is no trace of beard left inside the mussel. Lay the mussels in their half-shells on a baking sheet.

Lift a mussel and place ½ to ¾ teaspoon pesto in its shell depending on its size, then lightly press the mussel back in place. Stuff the remaining shells. The mussels can be stuffed earlier in the day, covered with plastic wrap, and refrigerated until ready to bake.

4. **Baking.** Preheat the oven to 375°F. Bake the mussels just until the pesto begins to bubble and the mussels are hot to the touch, 6 to 8 minutes. Serve on plates or platters lined with mint leaves or sprigs.

Stuffed Squash Blossoms on Herbed Tomato Salad

4 servings

At The Herbfarm we grow as much as a quarter acre of zucchini, not for the squash, but for the blossoms. In order to keep the plants producing flowers we need to continuously remove all the fruit, because the plants would rather put their energy into growing seed-producing zucchinis than sending out more blossoms. If you've ever grown them, you know that zucchini plants are zealously procreative, so it takes our gardeners several hours, three times a week, to hunt for and gather all the maturing squash. The reward for their work, however, is a daily supply of one of the loveliest ingredients imaginable—huge sunshine-yellow squash blossoms.

Most often zucchini flowers are dipped in batter and fried to make fritters. They're delicious that way but quite heavy, and it always seems a shame to cook something with such a vibrantly cheerful color to the same shade as a French fry. In this simple preparation the blossoms are briefly blanched so that their color remains vivid, then warmed with herbed goat cheese and placed over a ripe tomato salad.

A squash plant produces both female and male flowers. The females grow from the end of a tiny fruit and the males grow from a long stem. Either sex can be used for this recipe. The petals taste the same, but if you use the females, keep the baby zucchini attached as added interest and flavor.

Squash blossoms only live for one day, on or off the plant. Early in the morning or sometimes in the evening, their petals begin to stretch open in a tulip shape, then when the sun hits them they spread to a large starfish shape, 4 to 5 inches in diameter. That afternoon they'll close, which means they are starting to die, and the petals will become withered and twisted. Sometimes zucchini blossoms are available in markets beginning in early June and throughout the summer, but they are very perishable and fragile and rarely are they in good shape. Only buy those that were harvested that morning and cook them the same day. The petals should be large and bright orange-yellow and not wilted or twisted over each other at the tips.

FILLING

4 ounces fresh soft goat cheese or mild chèvre
1 tablespoon coarsely chopped fresh basil
1 tablespoon finely chopped fresh marjoram

BLOSSOMS

Salt

8 large fresh zucchini blossoms, female with fruit attached, male with stem attached

1 tablespoon extra-virgin olive oil, plus more for brushing

Freshly ground black pepper

2 cups vine-ripened cherry or other small tomatoes, halved or quartered, or 2 large vine-ripened tomatoes, cut into bite-size pieces

1 tablespoon coarsely chopped fresh marjoram

12 fresh basil leaves, torn into ½-inch pieces

1. **Filling.** Stir the filling ingredients together in a small bowl. Form the mixture into 8 balls, using about 1 tablespoon for each. Cover and set aside.

2. **Blanching the flowers.** Bring a large (6-quart) pot of water to a boil with 1 tablespoon salt. Shake each blossom and check inside for insects. Carefully snap off and discard the pistil inside the female flowers and leave the fruit attached. The male flowers just need their stems trimmed to about 1 inch. Set up a large bowl of cold water next to the stove. Plunge 4 blossoms at a time into the boiling water and boil for 10 seconds. Remove them with a slotted spoon or wire skimmer and plunge them into the cold water.

3. **Stuffing.** Line a baking sheet with parchment paper or lightly oil it. Keep the blossoms submerged in water where the petals are easier to separate. Cup your hand and scoop up one of the flowers, while you use your other hand to drape the petals over the top of your thumb and index finger. Lift the flower from the bowl of water and tilt your hand to drain it. Put a ball of the filling into the center, gently drape the petals back into a closed position, and lay it on the baking sheet. Repeat with the remaining blossoms. Brush the blossoms lightly with olive oil and season them very lightly with salt and pepper. At this point they can be covered with plastic wrap and refrigerated for up to 8 hours. Let them warm to room temperature before proceeding.

4. **Tomato salad.** Toss the tomatoes with 1 tablespoon olive oil, the marjoram, and basil. Season with salt and pepper to taste. Arrange the tomatoes on 4 salad plates.

5. **Finishing.** Preheat the oven to 350°F. Heat the blossoms in the oven until they begin to sizzle at the base and the cheese is warmed through, 5 to 7 minutes. Using a small spatula, carefully place 2 blossoms on each plate of tomatoes, crossing them in an X. Serve the blossoms with knife and fork.

Smoked Trout and Corn Puddings

4 servings

Sweet, smoky, and vibrantly flavored with marjoram, these little custards can start a meal or make a satisfying luncheon or supper dish on their own. Prepare them when plump ears of local sweet corn come into the market. In this recipe the corn is scraped off the cob instead of cut off. By first piercing the skin of each kernel then scraping down the cob with a sturdy spoon, you extract the flesh and juice but leave the skin of the kernels behind.

Serve these puddings surrounded by a small salad of summer greens or arugula or with Runner Beans with Summer Savory and Bacon (page 130).

About 1½ tablespoons unsalted butter, softened
⅓ cup fine dry bread crumbs
4 ears mature sweet corn, shucked
2 large eggs
2 tablespoons all-purpose flour
¼ cup heavy cream
¼ cup whole milk
1½ tablespoons finely chopped fresh marjoram
¼ teaspoon salt
Small pinch cayenne pepper
Freshly ground black pepper to taste
1 large red pepper, roasted, peeled, seeded, and diced (about ½ cup; page 331)
4 ounces smoked trout, skinned and flaked (about ⅔ cup)

1. Preparing the molds. Generously coat the interiors of 4 6-ounce ramekins with the softened butter, using a pastry brush or your fingers. Half fill one of the ramekins with bread crumbs and tilt and rotate it until all surfaces are coated, then tip the crumbs out into the next ramekin. Repeat the process until they all have a thorough coating of crumbs. Set the prepared molds in a large shallow baking pan.

2. Scraping the corn. Preheat the oven to 350°F. To scrape an ear of corn, hold it by the top in a large mixing bowl. Draw the tip of a knife down through the rows, cutting through the center of each kernel. With the side of a sturdy tablespoon, firmly scrape down along the cob to extract the pulp and milk. The skin of the kernels should remain on the cob. Keep scraping the ears until you have 1 cup of scraped corn pulp and milk.

3. Custards. In a large mixing bowl, whisk 1 egg with the flour until smooth. Add the remaining egg, the cream, and milk and whisk again until smooth. Stir in the scraped corn, then stir in the marjoram, salt, cayenne, black pepper, roasted red pepper, and trout. Ladle the corn mixture into the prepared molds and put them in their pan on the center rack of the oven. Fill the pan with ½ inch hot tap water from a pitcher or teakettle. Bake the puddings until puffed and beginning to brown, 30 to 35 minutes.

4. Serving. Let the puddings cool for 5 to 10 minutes. Run a knife around the side of each pudding. Unmold the puddings by carefully shaking them out into your hand, then flipping them right side up onto warmed salad plates. (You can bake the custards up to 24 hours ahead of time and store them covered, in their ramekins, in the refrigerator, but do not store the unbaked batter. Reheat the puddings in another water bath in a 350°F oven for about 20 minutes.)

VARIATION
Instead of smoked trout, use an equal amount of crumbled hot-smoked salmon, chopped cold-smoked salmon, or smoked mussels.

HERB SUBSTITUTIONS
- *In place of the marjoram, use an equal amount of finely chopped fresh lemon thyme or sage, or 3 tablespoons finely chopped fresh dill or chives.*

HERBED GARLIC FLANS WITH ARUGULA

6 servings

These custards have a mild, soothing flavor, and their warm silkiness is amplified by the contrasting sharpness of lightly dressed arugula. This is an example of a savory dish that uses the technique of herbal infusion. Instead of chopping and adding the herbs to the custard, the herb sprigs are steeped in the hot milk and cream and then strained out. You end up with just enough of the herbs' flavors but none of their leafy texture. Don't be alarmed by the amount of garlic; it becomes quite mild after the lengthy cooking.

> *8 large cloves garlic, peeled*
> *1 cup homemade (page 12) or canned low-sodium chicken stock, Golden Vegetable Stock (page 14), or water*
> *1 tablespoon unsalted butter, plus more for buttering the ramekins*
> *1½ cups whole milk, or low-fat (2%) milk for slightly less rich custards*
> *½ cup heavy cream*
> *1 2-inch sprig fresh rosemary*
> *3 large fresh sage leaves*
> *3 3-inch sprigs fresh thyme*
> *2 fresh bay laurel leaves, cracked, or 1 dried*
> *2 large eggs*
> *2 large egg yolks*
> *½ teaspoon salt*
> *¼ teaspoon ground white pepper*

SALAD

> *1 large bunch arugula, washed, dried, stemmed, and torn into bite-size pieces (about 4 ounces)*
> *¼ head radicchio, cut into thin strips (about ½ cup)*
> *1½ teaspoons fruity extra-virgin olive oil*
> *1½ teaspoons walnut oil*
> *1 tablespoon sherry vinegar*
> *Kosher salt and freshly ground black pepper*

1. Flavoring the custard base. Cut each garlic clove into 4 or 5 slices and put them in a medium (2-quart) saucepan with the stock and 1 tablespoon butter. Cook at a gentle simmer until almost all the liquid is evaporated and the garlic is coated with a glaze, about 20 minutes. Mash the garlic with the back of a fork against the side of the pan. Add the milk and cream, increase the heat, and bring it to a full boil. Immediately add the herbs, cover, and remove the pan from the heat. Let the mixture steep for at least 30 minutes.

2. Custards. Preheat the oven to 325°F. Butter 6 4-ounce ramekins and set them in a shallow baking pan. Pour the garlic mixture through a fine sieve into a medium mixing bowl, pressing down on the solids to extract all the liquid. Whisk in the eggs, salt, and white pepper. Ladle the mixture into the ramekins. Put the baking pan with the ramekins into the oven and fill it with ½ inch of hot tap water from a pitcher or teakettle. Bake the flans until fully set but still jiggly, 25 to 30 minutes. Remove them from the oven and let them sit in the water bath while you prepare the salad.

3. Salad. Toss the arugula and radicchio with the oils, vinegar, and salt and pepper to taste. Arrange the salad on 6 large salad plates. When the flans have cooled down but are still warm, run a thin knife around the edge and carefully unmold them by tipping them upside down onto the middle of the salads. If they don't release right away, use your finger coax the custard away from the side of the mold as you tilt it. Serve right away.

VARIATION
Sprinkle Crispy Shallots, page 53, over the flans for a crunchy and delicious complement.

Oysters on the Half-Shell with Lemon Verbena Ice

4 to 6 servings

To a purist anything that adorns a raw oyster is anathema, but for the less devout this is a refreshing alternative to mignonette sauce. Tiny scoops of tart, lemony, peppered ice are scooped onto the quivering oysters just before your guests slurp them down, giving them an extra chill and a little kick of vibrant, but not overbearing, flavor.

> *½ cup (gently packed) fresh lemon verbena leaves, center veins removed*
> *½ cup seasoned rice vinegar*
> *2 teaspoons finely chopped shallot*
> *2 dashes Tabasco sauce*
> *10 grinds black pepper*
> *24 small live oysters, 1½ to 2 inches long, Kumamotos if possible or small*
>   *Pacific oysters such as Westports or Quilcenes*
> *Crushed ice*
> *Garnish: lemon verbena sprigs*

1. Ice. Put the lemon verbena leaves, vinegar, shallot, Tabasco, and pepper in a blender (not a food processor) and blend on high speed until the liquid is bright green and no bits of leaf are visible, about 1 minute. Pour the mixture into a small container and freeze it until it's solidly frozen, at least 3 hours.

2. Serving. When ready to serve, shuck the oysters (or have your fishmonger do it no more than 2 hours in advance). Using a sturdy table fork, scrape the lemon verbena ice to create a flaky texture similar to a snowcone. Fill a large (9-inch) serving bowl with plain crushed ice and submerge a small (3-inch) bowl in the center. Fill the small bowl with the lemon verbena ice, place several demitasse or caviar spoons in it for serving, and arrange the shucked oysters on the crushed ice around it. Garnish with the lemon verbena sprigs, weaving them around the shells. Serve immediately. The lemon ice will melt quickly. Your guests can pick up an oyster, spoon some ice on top, and slurp it down.

 HERB SUBSTITUTIONS
- *Substitute an equal amount of French tarragon, Mexican tarragon, or cilantro for the lemon verbena. Or use ¼ cup red perilla (shiso) for a stunning and wonderfully peppery pink ice.*

SOUFFLÉS

At the age of twelve I made my first cheese soufflé after Julia Child gave me a lesson on our little black-and-white TV. She made it seem easy. It was, and I've been making them ever since. A soufflé, sweet or savory, towering from a demitasse cup or erupting from a hollow eggshell, appears on nearly every Herbfarm nine-course menu. Rushed to the table, they add drama to the meal.

A soufflé looks like it must be difficult to make but it is not. The following recipe is simply a flour-thickened white sauce with flavoring ingredients stirred in, and then beaten egg whites folded in. Even the timing is easy to control. The base (white sauce with flavoring) can be prepared up to 2 days ahead of time and stored in the refrigerator. After you fold in the egg whites, the soufflés can still wait on the kitchen counter for up to an hour before they bake with little effect on their rise. The only time the soufflés will not wait is when they are risen and ready to serve.

The first important step for success is preparing the molds properly. The soufflé doesn't just rise up at the top, its sides slide straight up (this is why soufflé dishes should always have straight sides). If there is an unbuttered spot on the side of the dish, the batter will stick to it and inhibit the rise. Also be sure that no batter is touching the unbuttered rim of the dish. You can use your thumb to wipe off any slips. When I use individual molds, I like to fill them to ¼ inch from the top with batter and I don't use a collar. These soufflés are stable enough that they'll rise a good 2 inches above the rims without spilling over and make a grand entrance when rushed to the table.

Second, be sure you beat the egg whites sufficiently. They should be as firm and high as they will get without becoming dry or grainy. When I use my Kitchen Aid stand mixer, I wait until the vortex in the middle of the egg whites that's formed by the whisk rotating around rises and disappears. If using a handheld mixer in a mixing bowl, I beat the whites until I can tip the bowl on its side and they don't slide down. When you fold the whites in, use a large stiff rubber spatula and work quickly and decisively—you don't have to baby them.

The following soufflé makes an excellent brunch dish or an elegant light meal with a salad and a loaf of bread. The recipe calls for 6-ounce straight-sided ramekins, but you can bake the soufflé in a 1½-quart soufflé dish as well. The large soufflé will have a looser interior, even though it needs to bake longer. As another alternative, you can bake the soufflé for a shorter time in 9 4-ounce espresso cups (unless the cups are made of very delicate china, they should do fine in the oven because they are insulated with a water bath). They'll make a show-stopping first course for a special-occasion dinner.

Individual Crab and Lemon Thyme Soufflés with Chervil Sauce

6 servings

These soufflés, perfumed with the gentle scent of lemon thyme, are airy delights. The soft delicacy of the eggs and the crab complement each other perfectly. A drizzle of lemony chervil sauce lifts their flavor even higher.

About 1½ tablespoons unsalted butter, softened
⅓ cup fine dry bread crumbs
3 tablespoons unsalted butter
3 tablespoons all-purpose flour
1 cup whole milk
4 large egg yolks
¼ teaspoon salt, plus more to taste
1 tablespoon finely chopped fresh lemon thyme
6 ounces fresh crabmeat, picked over for shell and cartilage
Freshly ground black pepper
6 large egg whites, at room temperature
Blended Herb and Butter Sauce (page 324), made with ½ cup fresh
  chervil

1. Preparing the molds. Generously coat the interiors of 6 6-ounce straight-sided ramekins with the softened butter, using a pastry brush or your fingers. Half fill one of the ramekins with bread crumbs and tilt and rotate it until all surfaces are coated, then tip the crumbs out into the next and repeat the process until all the ramekins have a thorough coating of crumbs. Set the prepared molds in a large shallow baking pan.

2. Soufflé base. Melt the butter in a medium (2-quart) saucepan over medium heat. Add the flour and whisk until the roux (flour and butter mixture) bubbles and turns lighter in color, less than 1 minute. Pour in the milk all at once and whisk over the heat until the mixture thickens and boils. Off the heat, whisk in the egg yolks and salt, then return it to the heat and continue to whisk vigorously until the mixture comes to a boil again. Whisk in the lemon thyme. This is the soufflé base. Transfer it to a large mixing bowl, place a piece of plastic wrap directly on the surface of the base, and set it aside until you are ready to fold in the whites, up to 1 hour. (The soufflé base can also be refrigerated covered for up to 2 days. Let it warm to room temperature before proceeding.)

---

3. Egg whites. Preheat the oven to 375°F. If you made the base ahead of time, whisk it to make sure there are no lumps, then, using a large rubber spatula, stir in the crabmeat. Taste and season with black pepper, and more salt depending on the saltiness of the crab. Beat the egg whites until they form stiff peaks but are not dry. Fold one-third of the egg whites into the base to lighten it, then fold in the rest gently but quickly. Distribute the batter among the prepared dishes, filling them to within ¼ inch of the top. Wipe up any spills on the sides of the dishes, and using your thumb, wipe off any mixture that is touching the rims. (At this point the soufflés can be held for up to 1 hour at room temperature.)

4. Baking. Put the baking pan holding the soufflés in the oven and fill the pan with about ½ inch of hot tap water from a pitcher or teakettle. Bake until they are lightly browned and have risen about 1½ to 2 inches above the rims, 20 to 25 minutes. While they are baking, prepare the chervil sauce. When the soufflés are done, use tongs or hot pads to immediately transfer the hot dishes to individual serving plates and rush them to the table accompanied by a pitcher of the sauce. Each guest pokes a hole in their soufflé and pours the sauce in.

VARIATIONS

For a large soufflé, pour the batter into a straight-sided 1½-quart soufflé dish generously coated with butter and fine dry bread crumbs. Bake the soufflé in a shallow water bath at 375°F for 30 to 35 minutes if you like a loose interior, 35 to 40 minutes if you like the eggs firmer. Makes 4 to 6 servings.

To bake the soufflés in espresso cups, generously butter the interiors of 9 4-ounce espresso cups, coat them with fine dry bread crumbs, and set them in a shallow baking dish. Fill them to within ⅛ inch of the top with the soufflé batter and bake them in a shallow water bath at 375°F until they are risen at least 2 inches above the rims and are lightly browned, 20 to 25 minutes. Use tongs or hot pads to transfer the cups to their saucers and serve immediately, accompanied by pitchers of chervil sauce. Makes 9 first-course servings.

FOUR-HERB OMELET

1 serving

This is an omelet of just eggs and herbs, and that's all it needs. I hesitate to suggest the option of filling it with cheese or vegetables, because its elegance lies in its simplicity—anything more will detract from the delicate flavors of the fresh herbs.

> *2 large eggs*
> *2 teaspoons finely chopped fresh basil*
> *1 teaspoon finely chopped fresh marjoram*
> *1 teaspoon finely chopped fresh chives*
> *1 teaspoon finely chopped fresh parsley*
> *¼ teaspoon salt*
> *2 teaspoons unsalted butter*
> *Freshly ground black pepper*

In a small mixing bowl, whisk together the eggs, herbs, and salt. Heat a medium (8-inch) nonstick skillet or omelet pan over medium heat. Add the butter—it should sizzle as it hits the pan. When the sizzling subsides but before the butter browns, pour in the egg mixture. As soon as the eggs begin to set around the sides, reduce the heat and quickly shake the pan and stir the eggs with a small rubber spatula or the back of a table fork. When most of the egg is softly set but there is still some that is runny, less than half a minute, spread the egg out to cover the bottom of the pan. Allow the omelet to firm up until it is no longer runny but still soft and custardlike on the top. Hold the pan over a warmed dinner plate, tilt the pan, and using the rubber spatula or fork, flip the omelet over itself several times as you roll it onto the plate. Serve immediately and grind fresh pepper over the top at the table.

 HERB SUBSTITUTIONS
Substitute for the herbs:
- *Fines herbes—1 teaspoon each finely chopped fresh French tarragon, chervil, chives, and parsley*
- *½ teaspoon finely chopped fresh lemon thyme, 2 teaspoons finely chopped parsley, and 1 teaspoon finely chopped fennel leaves*
- *2 teaspoons finely chopped fresh dill and 2 teaspoons finely chopped chives*

Softly Scrambled Eggs with Chervil and Chives

2 servings

These eggs are fluffy and creamy, almost like custard, and laced with the gentle flavors of chervil and chives. They're cooked in the French style—slowly in a double boiler instead of over direct heat—and the result is very far from the scrambled eggs that Americans are accustomed to, though just as easy to make. For richness, I like to add cream cheese instead of butter because it contributes a little extra body to the eggs and ensures they stay soft.

4 large eggs
⅛ teaspoon salt
2 tablespoons finely chopped fresh chervil
1 tablespoon finely chopped chives
2 tablespoons cream cheese, preferably without stabilizer
Freshly ground white pepper

1. Double boiler. Create a double boiler by selecting a medium (10- to 12-inch) stainless-steel mixing bowl that will rest on top of a large (6-quart) pot filled with about 2 inches of water. The top of the bowl can extend beyond the rim of the pot, but the bottom of the bowl must not touch the water. Put the pot (without the bowl) over medium heat and bring the water to a boil.

2. Eggs. Whisk together the eggs and salt until very smooth. With a rubber spatula, stir in the chervil, chives, and cream cheese. Place the bowl on top of the boiling water and stir steadily and continuously with the spatula, scraping the bottom and sides of the bowl as the eggs begin to set. While the eggs cook, the cream cheese will melt and incorporate itself. Cook until the eggs are thick enough to hold their shape on a spoon but are still soft, custardlike, and slightly underdone, 1½ to 2 minutes. Immediately remove the bowl from the larger pan. Stir the eggs for a few more seconds as they continue to cook from the heat of the bowl. Spoon the eggs onto warmed plates or into a warmed serving dish and serve immediately. If there is a thin layer of egg that sticks to the sides of the bowl, just leave it behind. Offer freshly ground white pepper and additional salt at the table.

SMOKED SALMON BENEDICT WITH SORREL SAUCE

4 servings

This combination of sorrel, smoked salmon, and eggs makes one of the best brunch dishes I've ever eaten. When sorrel leaves are shredded and cooked in butter, they wilt dramatically and quickly turn into a purée, almost as if they melted. Add some cream, and you have a lemony sauce that complements the smoked salmon more keenly than a rich hollandaise. Just remember it takes a lot of sorrel leaves to make a little bit of sauce, so make this dish when you have plenty to harvest or can buy big bunches at the market, usually in the spring or early fall.

Crumpets are worth searching out. They're often sold packaged next to English muffins. They have more body than English muffins and remain softer when toasted, so they make the dish easier to eat with knife and fork. Don't split the crumpets—use a whole one under each egg.

SAUCE
2 tablespoons unsalted butter
1 small shallot, finely chopped (about 3 tablespoons)
8 ounces sorrel, stems removed, leaves coarsely chopped
*   (3 to 4 cups gently packed)*
¼ cup heavy cream
¼ teaspoon salt
Freshly ground pepper

1 tablespoon white wine vinegar
8 crumpets, whole, or 4 English muffins, split
8 large or extra-large eggs
8 wide slices cold-smoked salmon or Nova lox, about 4 x 2 inches, at room
*   temperature*
Garnish: snipped chives or chive blossoms

1. Sauce. Melt the butter in a medium (10-inch) skillet over medium heat. Add the shallot and cook until it is softened but not browned, less than 1 minute. Add half the sorrel, stir until it is wilted, then add the rest of the sorrel and continue to cook until it is melted into a purée, 2 to 3 minutes. Stir in the cream and salt. Taste and season generously with pepper, and additional salt if needed.

2. Poaching the eggs. Meanwhile fill a wide (12-inch), deep pan with water, add the vinegar, and bring it to a simmer. Toast the crumpets or muffins and keep them warm in a very low oven. Crack 1 egg into a saucer and gently slide it into the simmering water. Repeat with the remaining eggs. Adjust the heat so that the water stays just below a simmer. You should see bubbles at the bottom of the pan, but they should not rise rapidly to the top. Cook until the whites are firm but the yolks are still soft, about 4 minutes. (The eggs can be poached ahead of time, transferred to cold water, and refrigerated in the water for up to 1 day. When ready to serve, reheat in a pan of simmering water for 1 minute.)

3. Assembling. Arrange 2 of the toasted crumpets or 2 English muffin halves on each of 4 warmed plates. Lift the eggs from the water with a slotted spoon and hold them over a paper towel to soak up any excess moisture. Place an egg on each crumpet or muffin. Arrange a slice of smoked salmon on each egg. Reheat the sorrel sauce and spoon it over the salmon, dividing it evenly among the 8 pieces. Sprinkle with chives and serve right away.

For the Gardener
Several times each season, depending on how often you cut them back, your chives will send up lovely globes of pink florets held on sturdy stems. These little flowers have a flavor very similar to the chive leaf but are even stronger tasting. Tear the individual florets from the flower heads with your fingers and sprinkle them with restraint onto eggs, salads, grilled fish, or any dish that benefits from the onion flavor of chive leaves. Never garnish with the whole blossom, for it's much too overpowering to eat, and always discard the stem that carries the blossom—it will be much tougher than the leaves it resembles.

CHAPTER 4

Pasta and Risotto

It's hard to think of a pasta dish that would not welcome a fresh herb, whether it be a light sprinkling of parsley or a bold handful of thyme. Herbs can be pounded into a silky pesto, simmered in a deeply flavored ragout, tossed with abandon over fresh egg noodles with warmed ripe tomatoes, or folded into a filling for delicate handmade ravioli. Of all the chapters in this book, I was sorry to complete this one because I never tire of eating pasta. The miracle of these dishes is that many can be prepared in a flash, often in the time it takes to bring a large pot of water to a boil and cook the pasta.

I always find that I have the most success with pasta if I keep the sauce simple and make sure it complements the pasta instead of drowning it. Fight the temptation to add everything in the refrigerator. Even more important, make sure the ingredients you do put in are of top quality. You're bound to have great results if you cook with excellent olive oil, real Parmigiano-Reggiano, local vegetables in season, carefully made pasta, whether fresh or dried, and, of course, plenty of gorgeously fragrant just-picked herbs.

Fresh Egg Pasta

Makes 1 pound

I learned to make this style of pasta from my friends Jordi Viladas and Carla Leonardi, who make superb fresh pasta by hand every day in their Seattle restaurant, Café Lago. The two of them have taught many classes at The Herbfarm in which they demonstrate how to prepare the very refined pasta dishes they're known for. The dough they use is made with whole eggs and regular bread flour, not semolina, and then rolled extremely thin. They showed me a very useful trick to keep the pasta dough from sticking to itself after it's rolled out. A dusting of regular flour is quickly absorbed into the dough, but a dusting of rice flour remains dry on the surface and keeps the sheets separate. Rice flour is available in most natural food stores and some supermarkets.

> *2 cups unbleached bread flour (spoon and level; 9 ounces)*
> *2 large eggs*
> *¼ teaspoon salt*
> *2 teaspoons olive oil*
> *About 2 tablespoons water*
> *Rice flour, for dusting*

1. Dough. Pulse the flour, eggs, salt, and olive oil together in a food processor until the mixture looks like cornmeal. Add 2 tablespoons water and process briefly. Take a small piece of the dough in your hand and squeeze it. If it stays together in a firm dough that feels like an earlobe, you've added enough water. If the dough barely comes together and seems crumbly, add another teaspoon of water. Continue to process the dough until it spins itself into a ball that bounces around the workbowl, about 1 minute. If it doesn't come together, add more water 1 teaspoon at a time. When the dough forms a smooth firm ball, remove it from the machine and wrap it in plastic wrap. Let the dough rest for at least 15 minutes at room temperature. It will feel softer after it has had time to relax.

2. Rolling the dough. Set up a roller-type pasta machine on a large work surface. Divide the dough in half. Keep one piece wrapped in plastic while you roll the other. Shape the dough into a rectangle roughly 5 x 4 inches, dust it lightly with bread flour, and pass it through the machine on the #1 setting. Fold it in thirds like a business letter, rotate the dough so that the open side feeds into the machine first, and roll it through again. Now fold the dough in half instead of thirds and repeat the rolling and folding process about 3 more times in order to knead the dough and form it into a smooth rectangle that is the width of the rollers. Adjust the rollers to #2, lightly dust the dough with bread flour, but don't fold it, and pass it through the machine again. Continue to roll the dough thinner, setting the dial one notch higher each time, and dusting with flour as needed. When you have rolled it through the number #4 setting, cut the dough crosswise in half so that it is easier to handle, and cover one piece with plastic wrap. Continue to roll the second piece of dough until it is the desired thickness; on my Atlas machine it's #5 for thick noodles and #6 for delicate noodles and ravioli, but different brands of pasta machines will vary. Before the dough goes through the machine the last time, dust it generously with rice flour.

3. Cutting. Cut the dough into the desired shape, then continue to roll and cut the remaining dough.

For ravioli, leave the sheets of dough whole.

For pappardelle, use a fluted pastry wheel to cut the sheets into long ribbons about 1½ inches wide.

For fettuccine, either pass the sheet through the fettuccine cutter on the pasta machine, or fold the sheets lengthwise in half and in half again until you have a 2-inch-wide strip, cut ¼-inch-wide strips, then unfold the ribbons. Dust the noodles again with rice flour. If you are not cooking the noodles right away, let them dry for about 30 minutes, then store them in a tightly sealed plastic bag.

VARIATION
FRESH BASIL PASTA
This pasta is a brighter green than spinach pasta, with an understated but distinct basil flavor. Increase the flour to 2¼ cups. Process it with 2 ounces stemmed sweet basil leaves (about 2 cups, gently packed) until very finely ground. Proceed with the Fresh Egg Pasta recipe but omit the water because the basil leaves contain the necessary moisture to make a malleable dough.

PASTA WITH PESTO

Pesto, the voluptuous and fragrant herb paste made by pounding fresh basil with pine nuts, garlic, fruity olive oil, and Parmigiano-Reggiano or pecorino cheese, is as venerable to an herb lover as chili is to a Texan. Though many worthy variations and improvisations exist, nothing comes close to the perfect balance of flavors in the classic basil version, and though pesto can be used in many ways, none is better than tossing the sauce into a bowl of pasta.

It's no coincidence that pesto became familiar to Americans at the same time the food processor became a common kitchen appliance. With the processor you can make a perfectly good batch of pesto in minutes with very little effort, or you can turn a mountain of basil into a year's supply of sauce in about an hour. But pesto gets its name from the Italian verb *pestare,* to pound, because traditionally it's made in a mortar and pestle. The consistency of hand-pounded pesto is distinct. Unlike the smooth and uniform machine-made version, it has an irregular, chewier texture with visible shreds of leaf, yet at the same time it's silky and emulsified. The color is different as well—more of a creamy shade of olive than bright green. I was always a bit skeptical of claims that hand-pounded pesto tasted better until I made the two versions side by side with the same ingredients. The difference is subtle, but I'm now convinced that hand-pounded pesto somehow develops a rounder and fuller flavor. It's certainly worth getting hold of a mortar and pestle to discover the difference yourself.

Perhaps the best reason to make pesto by hand is for the pleasure of the process. You'll see the separate ingredients slowly transform into the unctuous sauce, smell the powerful clove, mint, and licorice fragrances of the basil as it combines with the garlic and cheese, and listen to the soft pounding and grinding of the pestle instead of the unyielding whir of an electric motor. It certainly takes more effort, but it really doesn't take that much time, and it's worth the muscle—the calories you burn can justify a second helping of pasta.

Though there's nothing to compare with freshly made pesto, it does have excellent keeping qualities. To store your pesto, pack it in a glass jar being sure there are no air pockets, and either pour a ½-inch layer of olive oil on top or press a piece of plastic wrap directly on the surface. Cover the jar tightly and refrigerate it for up to 2 weeks. For longer storage, you can freeze the pesto for up to 6 months. I like to pack small amounts into resealable freezer bags for a ready-made sauce to use throughout the year. Because oil is extremely effective at capturing and holding fresh herb flavors, the high olive-oil content of pesto makes it one of the best vehicles to preserve the flavors of the summer garden for the winter months.

CLASSIC BASIL PESTO

Makes 1 cup, enough to sauce 1 pound dried pasta

> 2 cloves garlic, peeled
> 3 tablespoons raw pine nuts
> ¼ teaspoon salt
> 3 ounces stemmed sweet basil leaves (about 3 cups gently packed)
> ½ cup extra-virgin olive oil
> ½ cup freshly grated Parmigiano-Reggiano

Mortar and Pestle Method

1. Put the garlic, pine nuts, and salt in a large mortar. Use the pestle with a gentle downward pounding action to crush the ingredients and start to form a paste.

2. Coarsely chop the basil leaves on a cutting board with a sharp knife. Add the leaves to the mortar one handful at a time as you begin to rotate the pestle in a circular grinding movement, working mostly at the bottom of the bowl. From time to time use the mortar to pound the mixture with downward strokes. After several minutes it will start to form a paste.

3. When all the leaves are added, begin to pour in the olive oil a little at a time, while continuing to use the mortar with the rotary grinding motion. When all the oil is added, the color with be lighter and the oil will be suspended in the thick spoonable sauce, but you will still be able to see shreds of the basil leaves. Stir in the cheese.

Food Processor Method

Process the garlic, pine nuts, and salt until finely ground, about 15 seconds. Add the basil leaves and process in spurts just until no whole leaves remain. With the machine running, pour the oil through the feed tube in a steady stream. Stop and scrape down the sides, then process for several more seconds. The mixture should be ground to a pastelike consistency but a little bit of the leaves' texture should remain. If necessary, quickly pulse the mixture again. Add the cheese and pulse until just incorporated.

VARIATIONS

Classic pesto is a stepping-off place for a wide range of herb sauces. Using the same method of pounding or puréeing other types of herbs, nuts, cheese, and oil, it's easy to make delicious herb pastes with flavors from around the globe. But at some point the flavor can veer so far from the Genovese herb sauce that the word *pesto* loses its meaning. I've provided 2 recipes for broader interpretations of pesto on pages 328 and 329. Here are some of the more traditional variations:

Use 1 cup loosely packed fresh flat-leaf parsley or spearmint in place of 1 cup of the basil.

Use walnuts instead of pine nuts.

Add only ¼ cup olive oil, then stir in ¼ cup softened butter with the cheese.

In place of raw garlic, use 2 tablespoons Roasted Garlic Paste (page 341).

In place of Parmigiano-Reggiano, use any other hard grating cheese such as pecorino Romano or dry Jack.

Stir in 1 cup fresh whole-milk ricotta with the Parmigiano-Reggiano.

PASTA WITH PESTO

4 servings

>6 quarts water
>1½ tablespoons salt
>1 pound dried pasta, or 1¼ pounds Fresh Egg Pasta (page 99),
>   such as linguine or fettuccine
>1 cup Classic Basil Pesto (page 102)

Fill a large (8-quart) pot with the water, add the salt, and bring it to a boil over high heat. Add the pasta, stir, and cook until tender but still firm, 1 to 3 minutes for fresh pasta depending on the thickness, or 7 to 10 minutes for dried. Ladle out about ½ cup of the cooking water and set it aside. Drain the pasta and empty it into a large mixing bowl. Scoop the pesto on top of the noodles, add ¼ cup of the cooking water, and toss with tongs or 2 wooden spoons. Add more of the pasta water if necessary to thin the sauce so that it coats the ribbons of pasta evenly. Serve on warmed plates or in shallow bowls.

FETTUCCINE WITH SAGE BUTTER AND PEAS

4 servings

When sage is slowly browned in butter, it crisps, mellows, and gives off a nutty and mouthwatering flavor. Sage butter makes a wonderful sauce on its own, but in this pasta dish I've tossed it with sweet garden peas and accented it with a bit of salty prosciutto. This dish is most successful when prepared with delicate fresh egg noodles, homemade if possible, but it's still worth preparing with quality dried pasta.

> *6 quarts water*
> *1½ tablespoons salt*
> *1½ cups fresh shelled garden peas, or 8 ounces frozen peas*
> *6 tablespoons unsalted butter*
> *½ cup small fresh sage leaves, or large sage leaves cut into ¼-inch-wide strips*
> *3 ounces prosciutto, cut into thin strips (about ¾ cup)*
> *1 pound fresh fettuccine (page 99), or 12 ounces dried*
> *½ cup freshly grated Parmigiano-Reggiano*
> *Freshly ground black pepper*
> *Garnish: sage blossoms, if available*

1. **Peas.** Fill a large (8-quart) pot with the water, add the salt, and bring it to a boil over high heat. Put the peas in a steamer basket and drop it in the water. Boil until the peas are bright green and crisp-tender, about 1 minute. Remove the basket to drain the peas and set them aside. If using frozen peas, cook just until warmed. Leave the water boiling for the pasta.

2. **Sage butter.** Melt the butter in a large (12-inch) skillet over medium-low heat. Add the sage leaves and cook, stirring often until the butter begins to brown slightly and the sage gives off a nutty, toasty aroma, 3 to 4 minutes. Add the prosciutto and cook for about 1 minute until it loses its rosy color. Add the peas and cook briefly to reheat.

3. **Finishing the pasta.** While you are preparing the sauce, add the pasta to the boiling water. Cook until tender but still firm, 1 to 3 minutes for fresh pasta depending on the thickness, or 7 to 10 minutes for dried. Drain the noodles and add them to the skillet. Sprinkle with the cheese and a generous grinding of black pepper and toss with tongs or 2 wooden spoons. Serve right away in warmed bowls or plates and sprinkle with sage blossoms if available.

FUSILLI CARBONARA WITH FINES HERBES

4 servings

Bette Stuart is the grande dame of Fall City, Washington. People are always asking her if she will be their grandmother. She's been involved with The Herbfarm since its very beginning—teaching and assisting with cooking classes, and most important keeping us well fed with baked treats from her kitchen. One of the many other things she does is raise chickens behind her Victorian farmhouse. The eggs Bette's chickens lay are amazing. The shells are beautiful shades of ochre, chestnut, and pale blue, the whites are firm and clear, the yolks are the deepest marigold yellow. The flavor of one poached or over easy makes you pause and appreciate the pleasure of something so simple.

When Bette gave me a dozen of these eggs to take home one day, I was inspired to make a variation of pasta carbonara, the divine pasta dish sauced with pancetta, eggs, and Parmigiano-Reggiano. In place of the pancetta, I thought of another great match—eggs and fines herbes, the French herb mixture of fresh tarragon, chives, parsley, and chervil. The result is a pasta that feels as satisfying and indulgent as the classic version but is fresher tasting and not as heavy.

This is another very quick-to-prepare pasta dish. The egg yolks cook and thicken the sauce as they are tossed with the hot pasta in the bowl.

6 quarts water
1½ tablespoons plus ¼ teaspoon salt
4 large egg yolks
⅓ cup heavy cream
¼ cup finely chopped fresh chervil if available
¼ cup finely chopped fresh chives
¼ cup finely chopped fresh parsley
2 tablespoons finely chopped fresh French tarragon
Freshly ground black pepper
12 ounces dried fusilli, spaghetti, or gemelli
½ cup freshly grated Parmigiano-Reggiano

1. Setting up. Fill a large (8-quart) pot with the water, add 1½ tablespoons of the salt, and bring it to a boil over high heat. Whisk together the egg yolks and cream in a large stainless-steel mixing bowl. Stir in the herbs, the remaining ¼ teaspoon salt, and a generous grinding of pepper.

2. Pasta. When the water is at a boil, stir in the fusilli and cook at a steady boil until tender but still firm, 8 to 12 minutes. While the pasta is cooking, warm the egg yolk mixture by briefly holding the bowl over the pot of boiling water and whisking rapidly. Heat the mixture just to lukewarm; don't let the eggs cook. When the pasta is done, drain and add it to the egg mixture. Sprinkle with the cheese and toss well. The egg yolks will cook from the heat of the pasta and form a thick sauce. Serve right away in warmed pasta bowls.

FETTUCCINE WITH FRESH TOMATO AND HERBS

4 servings

   Here's my essential summer pasta. Make it when tomatoes are drip-ping with flavor and herbs are overflowing from their beds. Since the sauce is nothing more than a warmed tomato salad, it's a quick and casual dish and the herbs should be treated accordingly. Give them a brief chopping or a few tears and let them mingle with the chunks of tomato and ribbons of pasta.

> *6 quarts water*
> *1½ tablespoons plus 1 teaspoon salt*
> *6 medium vine-ripened tomatoes (about 2½ pounds)*
> *3 tablespoons fruity extra-virgin olive oil*
> *3 cloves garlic, minced*
> *⅓ cup coarsely chopped fresh flat-leaf parsley*
> *⅓ cup torn fresh basil leaves*
> *2 tablespoons coarsely chopped fresh oregano or*
> *marjoram*
> *2 tablespoons coarsely chopped fresh spearmint*
> *Freshly ground black pepper*
> *1 pound fresh fettuccine (page 99), or 12 ounces dried*
> *Freshly grated Parmigiano-Reggiano*

1. Tomatoes. Fill a large (8-quart) pot with the water, add 1½ tablespoons of the salt, and bring it to a boil over high heat. Fill a large bowl with cold water. Drop the tomatoes into the boiling water and cook them for 15 seconds. Scoop them out with a slotted spoon and put them in the cold water. Slip off the skins, using a paring knife if necessary. Cut them in half through the middle and poke out the seeds with your finger (this is easier to do with the tomato immersed in the bowl of cold water). Coarsely dice the tomatoes.

2. Sauce. Heat the olive oil in a large (12-inch) skillet over medium-low heat. Add the garlic and cook gently until it loses its raw fragrance but is not browned, about 1 minute. Add the tomatoes and toss them in the oil until just warm; don't allow them to simmer. Remove the pan from the heat. Stir in the herbs and the remaining ½ teaspoon salt. Taste and season with pepper, and additional salt if needed.

3. Finishing the pasta. Bring the large pot of water back to a rolling boil, add the fettuccine, and cook until tender but still firm, 3 to 4 minutes for fresh, or 7 to 10 minutes for dried. Drain and add the pasta to the tomato mixture in the skillet. Toss with tongs or 2 wooden spoons until the pasta is evenly coated. Serve it in warmed plates or shallow bowls. Pass the cheese at the table.

 HERB SUBSTITUTIONS

- *Any one of the herbs can be omitted if not available.*
- *Substitute 1 tablespoon coarsely chopped summer savory or 1 tablespoon coarsely chopped fresh thyme for the oregano or the mint.*

Spaghetti with Roasted Cherry Tomatoes and Thyme

4 servings

This is another simple fresh-tomato pasta, this time using cherry tomatoes tossed with thyme and flashed in a hot oven until their juices release and concentrate. The better the tomatoes taste raw, the better the sauce will taste. Try to get hold of varieties like Red or Yellow Currant or Sungold, which have small fruit and an intense sweet and tangy flavor.

> *6 quarts water*
> *1½ tablespoons plus ¼ teaspoon salt*
> *1 pint small ripe cherry or currant tomatoes*
> *2 tablespoons extra-virgin olive oil*
> *2 tablespoons very coarsely chopped fresh English thyme*
> *Freshly ground black pepper*
> *12 ounces dried spaghetti*
> *¼ cup coarsely chopped fresh flat-leaf parsley*
> *Freshly grated Parmigiano-Reggiano*

1. Tomatoes. Preheat the oven to 450°F. Fill a large (8-quart) pot with the water, add 1½ tablespoons of the salt, and bring it to a boil over high heat. Using a very sharp thin knife, cut each tomato in half and put them on a baking sheet. Drizzle with the olive oil, then sprinkle with the thyme, the remaining ¼ teaspoon salt, and several grinds of black pepper. Using your fingers, gently toss the tomatoes to coat them evenly.

2. Spaghetti. When the water is at a rolling boil, stir in the spaghetti. Put the tomatoes in the oven and roast until they are sizzling, slightly shriveled, and have released some juice into the pan, about 6 minutes. Rinse a large mixing bowl with hot tap water to warm it, then empty the roasted tomatoes into it. Taste and season with additional salt and pepper if needed. Cook the spaghetti until tender but still firm, 7 to 9 minutes. Drain and add the pasta to the mixing bowl. Sprinkle with the parsley and toss gently with tongs or 2 wooden spoons. Serve in warmed shallow bowls or plates and pass the cheese at the table.

Penne Arrabbiata with Herbs

4 servings

The Italians call this dish pasta all'arrabbiata, or angry pasta, because of the fiery heat from hot chile flakes. To give character to the gutsy sauce, I've added rosemary and Greek oregano because they are both sturdy and aggressive enough to assert their flavors over the heat of the red pepper. A handful of parsley tossed in at the end adds color and balances the dish. If it's not tomato season, good-quality canned tomatoes will give better results than mediocre fresh ones.

6 quarts water
1 ½ tablespoons plus ½ teaspoon salt
¼ cup extra-virgin olive oil
3 cloves garlic, finely chopped
2 pounds very ripe fresh tomatoes, peeled, seeded, and coarsely chopped
(about 3 cups) or 1 28-ounce can whole plum tomatoes, coarsely
chopped, with their juice
½ to 1 teaspoon dried red pepper flakes
1 tablespoon finely chopped fresh rosemary
½ cup coarsely chopped fresh flat-leaf parsley
3 tablespoons coarsely chopped fresh Greek oregano
12 ounces dried penne or spaghetti
¼ cup freshly grated Parmigiano-Reggiano

1. Sauce. Fill a large (8-quart) pot with the water, add 1½ tablespoons of the salt, and bring it to a boil over high heat. Heat the oil in a large (12-inch) skillet over medium-low heat. Add the garlic and cook, stirring constantly, until it loses its raw fragrance but is not browned, 1 to 2 minutes. Add the tomatoes, red pepper, rosemary, and remaining ½ teaspoon salt. Bring the sauce to a boil and cook uncovered at a steady gentle boil until most of the liquid evaporates and the sauce is quite thick, about 15 minutes. Stir occasionally, mashing any large pieces of tomato. Stir in the parsley and oregano.

2. Penne. When the water is at a rolling boil, add the penne and boil until tender but still firm, 8 to 12 minutes. Drain the pasta, add it to the skillet of sauce, sprinkle with the cheese, and toss to coat it evenly. Serve in warmed shallow bowls.

HERB SUBSTITUTION
- *Substitute an equal amount of coarsely chopped fresh basil for the parsley.*

Fettuccine with Red Onion, Blue Cheese, and Thyme

4 servings

If you love creamy sauces and blue cheese, as I do, this is as good as it gets. Sweet red onions, cooked until they are tender but still have some crunch, and a liberal amount of pungent fresh thyme provide just the right counterpoints.

> *6 quarts water*
> *1½ tablespoons salt*
> *1 large red onion*
> *2 tablespoons extra-virgin olive oil*
> *3 tablespoons coarsely chopped fresh English thyme*
> *⅓ cup dry white wine*
> *¾ cup heavy cream*
> *1 pound fresh fettuccine (page 99), or 12 ounces dried*
> *¾ cup crumbled blue cheese (3 ounces), such as Danish blue, Gorgonzola,*
> *   Bleu d'Auvergne, or Roquefort*
> *Freshly ground black pepper*

1. Onion. Fill a large (8-quart) pot with the water, add the salt, and bring it to a boil over high heat. Peel the onion and cut it in half from root to tip. Cut out the dense core at the root end and slice the onion ¼ inch thick, again from root end to tip. Heat the oil in a large (12-inch) skillet over medium heat. Add the onion and cook, stirring very often, until they begin to soften but still hold their shape and have some snap when you bite into a piece, about 4 minutes. Add 2 tablespoons of the thyme and the wine and let the mixture boil for a minute or two to evaporate the alcohol. Stir in the cream and remove the pan from heat.

2. Pasta. Stir the pasta into the boiling water and cook until tender but still firm, 3 to 4 minutes for fresh pasta, or 7 to 10 minutes for dried. Bring the sauce to a simmer. Drain the pasta and add it to the skillet. Sprinkle with the cheese and toss, using tongs or 2 wooden spoons, until about half the cheese melts into the sauce but small pieces remain. Taste and add black pepper, and additional salt depending on the saltiness of the cheese. Transfer the pasta to warmed shallow bowls or plates and sprinkle with the remaining 1 tablespoon thyme. Serve right away.

LINGUINE WITH HERBED CLAM SAUCE

4 servings

"Linguine with clam sauce is mankind's crowning achievement."
—Fran Lebowitz, *Social Studies*

I have to agree. When heated in wine, fresh clams release a perfectly seasoned sauce, readily soaked up by silky strands of pasta. A dose of chopped garlic cooked in good olive oil will capably finish the dish, but naturally I think it only becomes a true chef-d'oeuvre with the addition of a few fresh herbs. In my version, rosemary sprigs subtly flavor the liquor as the clams steam, then a liberal handful of marjoram and parsley finishes the pasta as it's tossed.

This dish is a good example of one where dried pasta is preferred to fresh. Here the noodles are cooked until they are slightly underdone, then tossed with the shelled clams and their liquor over heat until they absorb some of the excess liquid and finish cooking. Fresh noodles are much too delicate and would quickly become overdone if treated this way.

3 pounds small live clams, such as Manila or littleneck, purged (page 37)
2 4-inch sprigs fresh rosemary
1 cup dry white wine, such as Sauvignon Blanc or Pinot Gris
6 quarts water
1½ tablespoons salt
6 tablespoons extra-virgin olive oil
5 cloves garlic, finely chopped
1 pound dried linguine
½ cup coarsely chopped fresh parsley
¼ cup finely chopped fresh marjoram or Italian oregano
Freshly ground black pepper

Clams. Wash the clams in a colander, then put them in a large (6-quart) pot with the rosemary and wine. Cover tightly and bring to a boil over high heat. Reduce the heat to medium-low and steam the clams until they all open. Empty the clams into a fine-mesh strainer set over a bowl to catch the liquor. (If you with to serve some of the clams in their shells as garnish, put 24 in a small bowl, cover with aluminum foil, and set in a warm place like the back of the stove.) When the clams are cool enough to handle, remove the meat from the shells, discarding the shells, rosemary sprigs, and any clams that did not open.

2. Sauce. Fill a large (8-quart) pot with the water, add the salt, and bring it to a boil over high heat. Heat the olive oil in a large (12-inch) skillet or the same pot you steamed the clams in over medium-low heat. Add the garlic and cook, stirring, until it loses its raw fragrance but is not browned, about 1 minute. Pour the clam liquor into the pot through a very fine strainer, being careful to hold the last tablespoon or two back if you can see grit or other sediment. (If your strainer is not very fine, line it with a coffee filter.) Increase the heat and boil the liquid until it is reduced to half its original volume.

3. Finishing the pasta. Meanwhile stir the linguine into the boiling water. Cook until the noodles are slightly underdone, 5 to 8 minutes, so they can finish cooking in the sauce without becoming mushy. When you break a strand you should see a small white line in the center of the noodle that is still raw. Drain the pasta and add it to the clam sauce with the reserved clam meat and the parsley and marjoram. Toss the pasta over medium heat until it absorbs over half of the liquid, about 3 minutes. Taste and season with pepper and additional salt if needed. Serve the pasta right away in warmed shallow bowls, dividing any remaining clam liquor among them. Garnish with the clams in their shells if they've been set aside.

INDULGENT VARIATION
Add 1 cup heavy cream along with the clam liquor to the garlic. Cook the sauce until reduced by half.

 HERB SUBSTITUTIONS
- *Substitute 1 tablespoon finely chopped fresh lovage for the marjoram.*
- *Omit the rosemary and marjoram and add 2 tablespoons finely chopped fresh tarragon, ¼ cup coarsely chopped fresh chervil, or ½ cup coarsely chopped fresh basil with the parsley.*

TARRAGON AND CHIVE RAVIOLI

6 first-course servings

For devoted cooks, making ravioli by hand is a lot of fun. But why spend the considerable time it takes to produce them unless the result is remarkable? I promise you these ravioli are worth every minute. They are nothing less than delicate and ethereal. Disks of whisper-thin dough enclose a creamy ricotta filling highlighted with tarragon and chive and are napped with a subtle herbed butter.

The ravioli will taste best if you use quality fresh ricotta from a cheese shop or good Italian grocer. Compare it side by side with low-fat ricotta packed in plastic tubs from the supermarket. One is sweet, creamy, and hard to resist eating with a spoon; the other is grainy and bland. Be aware, though, that fresh ricotta is very perishable and will usually keep for less than a week in the refrigerator.

FILLING
1 cup fresh whole-milk ricotta
1 large egg
3 tablespoons finely chopped fresh tarragon
¼ cup finely chopped fresh chives
¼ cup finely chopped fresh flat-leaf parsley
¼ cup freshly grated Parmigiano-Reggiano

½ recipe Fresh Egg Pasta (page 99)
Rice flour, for dusting
Egg wash made with 1 egg yolk and 1 tablespoon water
6 quarts water
1½ tablespoons salt
6 tablespoons unsalted butter
¼ cup small fresh flat-leaf parsley leaves
2 tablespoons fresh tarragon leaves
2 tablespoons chives snipped into 1-inch pieces
Freshly ground black pepper
Garnish: sage, chive, or thyme blossoms if available

1. Filling. Stir all the filling ingredients together in a small mixing bowl. Cover and refrigerate if you're not assembling the ravioli right away.

2. Dough. Roll out one sheet of the pasta dough (one-quarter of the recipe) as thin as a wonton wrapper, keeping the remaining dough covered. When you lay it on a printed page, you should be able to see the text through it; however, it needs to be just thick enough to contain the moist filling without disintegrating when it's cooked, so you can't allow it to stretch after you roll it. On most machines you'll stop at the second-to-the-highest setting. Cut the sheet lengthwise in half again and lay the pieces on a work surface dusted with rice flour. You will have 2 strips of dough about 18 x 6 inches each.

3. Stuffing the ravioli. Brush the bottom half of one sheet of dough with egg wash. Drop 5 or 6 heaping teaspoons of the filling along the bottom half of the dough, spacing them 3 inches apart. Beginning at one end, carefully fold the top half of the dough over the bottom and use your finger to press the dough around the filling while you squeeze out as much air as you can (don't worry if you don't get all the air out—once the dough sticks together you can't undo it). Cut the ravioli into 3-inch squares. The best tool to use is a crimper-cutter, which presses and seals the dough together as it slices, but a straight or fluted pastry wheel will work as well. First cut a thin strip from the top and bottom of the long line of ravioli, then cut in between the mounds. Stuff and cut the second strip of dough, then roll, stuff, and cut the remaining dough. Divide the finished ravioli evenly between 2 baking sheets that have been sprinkled with more rice flour. You should end up with a total of about 32 to 36 ravioli. This recipe makes ample dough; you can roll out the leftovers and make a small batch of fettuccine. The ravioli can sit uncovered at room temperature for about 2 hours until you're ready to boil them. If you want to make them ahead of time, put the trays of ravioli into the freezer uncovered. When they harden, you can transfer them to resealable freezer bags and store them for up to 3 months.

4. Cooking the ravioli. Fill a large (8-quart) pot with the water, add the salt, and bring it to a boil over high heat. Melt the butter in a small saucepan and spread a few teaspoons of it onto a warmed large platter. Reduce the heat under the pot of water to a simmer and drop in half the ravioli one at a time. Cook the ravioli below the simmering point until the pasta is cooked through but still firm and the filling is hot, 1½ to 2 minutes. (If the ravioli were frozen, drop them directly from the freezer into the hot water and allow an extra minute of cooking time.) Use a slotted spatula to carefully lift out the ravioli and transfer them to the buttered platter. Keep them warm while you cook the remaining ravioli.

5. Finishing the ravioli. Stir the parsley, tarragon, and chives into the melted butter. Divide the ravioli among warmed serving plates and spoon on the herbed butter. Grind a little black pepper over each serving and sprinkle with a few herb blossoms if available

Risotto

Elegant, comforting, and made in one pot, risotto deserves its popularity. With gradual additions of hot stock, medium-grain rice turns into a creamy and receptive base for a great variety of flavorings and enrichments. Like many pasta dishes, a risotto can be made very quickly—in less than three-quarters of an hour—but in that period of time it asks for your undivided care and attention.

Just as there are many varieties of potatoes or beans, there are many varieties of rice. To make a proper risotto, you need a variety with a medium grain that will absorb a large amount of liquid and slowly release its starch as it cooks. Since Italians have been making risotto for hundreds of years, they've bred varieties that are perfectly suited. Three that are imported to the United States are Carnaroli, Arborio, and Vialone Nano. Carnaroli is my first choice. It produces the creamiest risotto, and the cooked grains have a firm and very pleasing texture that resist turning mushy. The second variety, Arborio, is the most commonly available Italian rice. It produces a risotto that has both creaminess and firm-textured grains as long as you're careful not to overcook it. The last, Vialone Nano, has very fat grains that plump many times their original size but don't seem to release as much starch. It is often used for risotto dishes that have a looser consistency.

Nearly all risotto dishes start with cooking onion, shallot, or leek in butter or olive oil. The rice goes in the pot next and is stirred over heat to gently toast the grains. Then, unlike other rice dishes, you add the liquid a little at a time, and the pot is stirred and left uncovered as the rice boils. There will always be differing opinions concerning how much the risotto has to be stirred. Some cooks say to stir it constantly; others say you only need to stir when you add stock. I take the middle ground. I always stay close to the pot and stir every couple of minutes, but while the risotto is cooking, I'll prepare the herbs, grate the cheese, or do other tasks on a workspace adjacent to the stove. The most important thing is not to get distracted. Never leave the rice so long that it begins to stick.

Perhaps the most difficult step in making risotto is assessing the exact moment when it's done. If you've eaten a well-prepared risotto, you know that the grains should be cooked through but not mushy, firm but not chalky. The grains should be suspended in a velvety coat, and when a large spoonful is dropped on a plate, it should spread slowly but not run. If you don't serve it immediately, the rice will continue to absorb liquid and you may need to add a little extra stock to loosen the risotto to the proper consistency.

Robust herbs like thyme and sage can go in the pot when you first start cooking the risotto, so that the rice absorbs the flavor as it soaks up the liquid. But I most often stir in liberal amounts of fresh herbs after the rice cooks along with cheese and other enrichments. Leave the herbs coarsely chopped so that you see them in the finished dish—they'll enhance the size and texture of the rice grains.

GREEN RISOTTO

4 servings

Like Pasta with Pesto (page 104), this is a dish where the herbs are the main event. This rendition includes a well-balanced mixture of tangy sorrel, fragrant basil, peppery arugula, verdant parsley, and sharp chives, but gather your own inspirations from the herb garden and try other combinations of soft-leafed herbs. Some other suggestions follow the recipe.

5½ to 6 cups homemade (page 12) or canned low-sodium chicken stock, or
*   Golden Vegetable Stock (page 14)*
5 tablespoons unsalted butter
1 medium onion, finely chopped
1½ cups Italian medium-grain rice, such as Carnaroli, Arborio, or
*   Vialone Nano*
½ cup dry white wine
1 teaspoon salt, less if using canned stock
1½ cups coarsely chopped fresh basil
1 cup coarsely chopped stemmed sorrel
1 cup coarsely chopped stemmed arugula
½ cup coarsely chopped fresh parsley
½ cup finely chopped or snipped chives or green onions
¾ cup freshly grated Parmigiano-Reggiano
Freshly ground black pepper

1. Starting the risotto. Bring the chicken stock to a simmer in a medium (2-quart) saucepan and set it over very low heat. Melt 2 tablespoons of the butter in a large (4-quart) saucepan over medium heat. Add the onion and cook, stirring often, until it is softened but not browned, about 5 minutes. Add the rice, reduce the heat to medium-low, and stir for 1 minute.

2. Adding the liquid. Add the wine and salt (omit the salt at this point if using canned stock). Stir the rice continuously with a large wooden spoon until all the liquid is absorbed. Ladle in 1 cup of the hot stock. At this point you will need to stir the rice very often, but you don't have to stir it continuously. It's all right to set the spoon down for a few minutes at a time, but stay close by and don't get distracted. You never want the rice to get so dry that it sticks to the bottom of the pan. Keep the heat at medium-low so that the rice is at a steady but very gentle bubble when you stop stirring. When the rice absorbs the first cup of stock, add another. Continue stirring and adding stock in this way, always waiting until the rice absorbs the liquid before adding more. The risotto will take 25 to 30 minutes to cook from the first addition of stock, depending on the type of rice you use. When done, the mixture will be creamy and the rice will be puffed and somewhat tender but still have a little bit of a bite in the interior when you chew it. It should not be mushy.

3. Finishing the risotto. When the rice is done, stir in the remaining 3 tablespoons butter over low heat until it melts, then stir in the herbs and cheese. If necessary, add a little more stock to keep the risotto moist and creamy—it should form a spreading mound if spooned onto a plate. Taste and season with black pepper, and additional salt if necessary. Spoon the risotto into warmed shallow bowls and serve at once.

HERB SUBSTITUTIONS
In place of the herbs above, use:
- *½ cup coarsely chopped fresh dill, 2 tablespoons finely chopped fresh lovage, 1 cup stemmed mustard greens cut into fine strips, 1 cup coarsely chopped stemmed spinach*
- *1½ cups coarsely chopped fresh basil, ¼ cup coarsely chopped fresh marjoram, ½ cup coarsely chopped fresh mint, ½ cup coarsely chopped fresh parsley*
- *⅓ cup coarsely chopped fresh French tarragon, ½ cup coarsely chopped fresh lemon balm, ½ cup finely chopped chives, 2 cups coarsely chopped stemmed spinach*

Shrimp and Tarragon Risotto

4 servings

This splendid risotto, pairing fresh sweet shrimp with the clear anise flavor of tarragon, gains its depth of flavor by using the shrimp shells to flavor the stock.

1 ½ pounds fresh large shrimp in the shell

STOCK
1 tablespoon olive oil
1 cup dry white wine, such as Sauvignon Blanc or Pinot Gris
4 cups homemade (page 12) or canned low-sodium chicken stock
3 cups water
½ medium onion, coarsely sliced
1 rib celery, coarsely chopped
About 10 fresh parsley stems
About 8 3-inch sprigs fresh thyme
2 fresh bay laurel leaves, or 1 dried

4 tablespoons unsalted butter
1 medium shallot, finely chopped (about 6 tablespoons)
1 ½ cups Italian medium-grain rice, such as Arborio, Carnaroli, or Vialone Nano
1 teaspoon salt, less if using canned stock
⅓ cup coarsely chopped fresh French tarragon
¼ cup coarsely chopped fresh parsley
Freshly ground black pepper

1. Shrimp stock. Peel and devein the shrimp, reserving the shells. Cover the cleaned shrimp and refrigerate. Heat the olive oil in a medium (3-quart) heavy-bottomed saucepan over high heat until it smokes steadily. Add the shells to the pan and cook, stirring constantly, until they turn a deep orange and are just beginning to brown, 3 to 4 minutes. Pan-roasting the shells gives the stock much of its flavor, so take the time to do it carefully. The roasted shells should release a concentrated, toasty, shrimp aroma that will fill your kitchen. Add the wine to the pan, first turning off the gas flame to prevent the alcohol from igniting, then return it to medium heat and boil until all the liquid is evaporated. Add the chicken stock, water, onion, celery, parsley stems, thyme, and bay leaves and bring it to a boil. Reduce the heat to the lowest setting and simmer gently uncovered for 30 minutes. Strain the stock through a fine-mesh sieve into another medium saucepan and place it over low heat. You should have 5 to 6 cups stock. Discard the solids.

2. Starting the risotto. Melt the butter in a large saucepan over medium-low heat. Add the shallot and cook, stirring often, until softened but not browned, less than 1 minute. Add the rice and stir over heat for 1 minute.

3. Adding the liquid. Ladle in 1 cup of the hot stock and add the salt (omit at this point if you used canned chicken stock to make the shrimp stock). Stir the rice continuously with a large wooden spoon until all the liquid is absorbed. After the first addition of stock, you will need to stir the rice very often, but you don't have to stir it continuously. It's all right to set the spoon down for a few minutes at a time, but stay close by and don't get distracted. You never want the rice to get so dry that it sticks to the bottom of the pan. Keep the heat at medium-low so that the rice is at a steady but very gentle bubble when you stop stirring. When the rice absorbs the first cup of stock, add another. Continue stirring and adding stock in this way, always waiting until the rice absorbs the liquid before adding more. The risotto will take 25 to 30 minutes to cook from the first addition of stock. When done, the mixture will be creamy and the rice will be puffed and somewhat tender but still have a little bit of a bite in the interior when you chew it. It should not be mushy.

4. Finishing the risotto. When the rice is done, add the shrimp and continue to stir the risotto until the shrimp are no longer translucent and just cooked through, but not curled into a tight circle, 3 to 5 minutes. They should still have a tender snap when you bite into them. If necessary, add a little more stock as the shrimp are cooking to keep the risotto moist and creamy—it should form a spreading mound if spooned onto a plate. Stir in the tarragon and parsley. Season with black pepper, and additional salt if necessary. Spoon the risotto into warmed bowls and serve right away.

Asparagus and Mushroom Risotto with Lemon Thyme

4 servings

It can be hard to tell when it's spring in the Pacific Northwest because it will most likely be fifty degrees and the rain will not have stopped since the previous September, but when we see local asparagus at the market we know that the sun might soon shine down on us. I, for one, never seem to tire of eating asparagus when it's in season. I prefer to roast the spears, even when I add them to a risotto or pasta, because roasting intensifies their sweet flavor and keeps their texture firm.

In this dish that combines the simple flavors of asparagus, rice, and mushrooms, lemon thyme adds a welcome vibrancy. Try to use freshly picked lemon thyme and chop it as close to using it as you can—its remarkable flavor vanishes into the air quickly.

> 1 pound medium or thick asparagus
> 2 teaspoons olive oil
> Salt
> 12 ounces fresh button, shiitake, and/or oyster mushrooms
> 5½ to 6 cups homemade (page 12) or canned low-sodium chicken stock, or
>   Golden Vegetable Stock (page 14)
> 3 tablespoons unsalted butter
> ½ medium onion, finely chopped (about 1 cup)
> 1½ cups Italian medium-grain rice, such as Carnaroli, Arborio, or
>   Vialone Nano
> ½ cup dry white wine
> 3 tablespoons coarsely chopped fresh lemon thyme
> ½ cup freshly grated Parmigiano-Reggiano
> Freshly ground black pepper

1. Asparagus. Preheat the oven to 450°F. Cut off and discard the bottom quarter of the asparagus spears. If they are thick, peel the lower half of the trimmed spears with a sharp vegetable peeler. Place the spears on a baking sheet, drizzle them with the olive oil, and sprinkle lightly with salt. Toss the spears to coat them evenly and then spread them out in a single layer. Roast the asparagus until the spears just begin to sag when you hold them by the bottom, 4 to 8 minutes depending on the thickness. They should be slightly underdone, for they will continue to cook once you remove them from the oven. Cool slightly, cut them into 1½-inch pieces, and set aside (to save time, you can roast the asparagus while you cook the risotto).

2. Mushrooms and stock. If using button mushrooms, cut them into quarters. If using shiitakes, remove the stems and save them for the stockpot, then slice the caps. If using oyster mushrooms, tear them apart into separate "shells." Bring the chicken stock to a simmer in a small (2-quart) saucepan and hold it over very low heat.

3. Starting the risotto. Melt the butter in a large (4-quart) saucepan set over medium heat. Add the onion and cook, stirring often, until softened but not browned, about 5 minutes. Add the mushrooms, season lightly with salt, and continue to cook until they release their moisture and the liquid boils away, about 8 minutes. Add the rice, reduce the heat to medium-low, and stir for 1 minute.

4. Adding the liquid. Add the wine and ¾ teaspoon salt (omit the salt at this point if using canned stock). Stir the rice continuously with a large wooden spoon until all the liquid is absorbed. Ladle in 1 cup of the hot stock. At this point you will need to stir the rice very often, but you don't have to stir it continuously. It's all right to set the spoon down for a few minutes at a time, but stay close by and don't get distracted. You never want the rice to get so dry that it sticks to the bottom of the pan. Keep the heat at medium-low so that the rice is at a steady but very gentle bubble when you stop stirring. When the rice absorbs the first cup of stock, add another. Continue stirring and adding stock in this way, always waiting until the rice absorbs the liquid before adding more. The risotto will take 25 to 30 minutes to cook from the first addition of stock. When done, the mixture will be creamy and the rice will be puffed and somewhat tender but still have a little bit of a bite in the interior when you chew it. It should not be mushy.

5. Finishing the risotto. When the rice is done, add the asparagus, lemon thyme, and cheese. Stir over heat for another minute or two to warm the asparagus. If necessary, add a little more stock to keep the risotto moist and creamy—it should form a spreading mound if spooned onto a plate. Season with black pepper, and additional salt if necessary. Spoon the risotto into warmed bowls and serve.

CHAPTER 5

Vegetables

Cooking with vegetables is all about cooking with the seasons. It's a clever gift of nature that foods that ripen at the same time inherently taste good together, and it follows that herbs and vegetables that share the same soil make good partners when they share the same saucepan. In spring, the flavors of young peas and carrots are gently heightened by the flavors of chervil and chives. In summer, sun-blessed eggplant, peppers, and tomatoes are perfect with pungent basil and oregano, and marjoram and summer savory work magic with corn and beans. For a cozy winter's dinner, squash, parsnips, and potatoes are even more inviting when paired with the deep flavors of hardy evergreen herbs, like sage, thyme, and rosemary.

If your vegetables are fresh from the garden, a light hand with herbs is sufficient. A few sprigs of mint tossed into the blanching water for peas, a sprinkle of thyme on roasting parsnips, or a shower of casually chopped chives and lemon balm on garnet-colored beets all serve to highlight the vegetables' own flavors. On the other hand, fresh herbs can turn an ordinary vegetable dish into something very exciting. Mint and sorrel add fragrance and piquancy to freshly sautéed spinach, Greek oregano and thyme spice up a soothing chard gratin, and a basil-walnut filling adds rich flavor to baked artichokes. The recipes in this chapter will teach you a few of the ways to pair these kitchen-garden neighbors. The vegetables and herbs in your garden or market can inspire others.

Snap Peas with Mint and Chervil

4 servings

Snap peas did not exist until quite recently—the first variety, Sugar Snap, was introduced in 1979. With shelling peas, you need pounds to make a bowl of 4 servings, and to be at their best they have to be cooked soon after they're picked. Snap peas, on the other hand, produce fat little 1½-inch pods that are completely edible, shells and all, and they keep their sweet flavor for days after harvesting. They have much more flavor and crunch than the more familiar flat-podded snow peas. If you grow snap peas in your garden, they yield a lot of pea per square foot. Sugar Snap climbs to 6 feet, but now there are other varieties that grow only 2 to 3 feet tall, like Sugar Daddy or Super Sugar Mel. Snap peas are also available in markets, though not as widely as they should be. In this simple preparation the peas are first boiled with fresh mint sprigs (a typically English way to prepare them), which is like cooking them in mild mint tea, and they pick up just a shadow of the mint flavor. Then the peas are tossed with butter and showered with tender chervil just before they make it to the table.

> *4 quarts water*
> *1 tablespoon salt*
> *1 pound fresh snap peas*
> *2 tablespoons unsalted butter, at room temperature*
> *6 4-inch sprigs fresh spearmint, tied together with kitchen twine*
> *½ cup coarsely snipped fresh chervil*

Bring the water with the salt to a boil in a large pot. Snap the stems off the peas, pulling down to remove any strings. Put the butter in a serving bowl and set it in a warm spot like a warm oven. When the water is at a rolling boil, drop in the peas and the mint bundle. Boil until the peas are crisp-tender, 1½ to 3 minutes. Drain the peas in a colander and let them sit for a minute to evaporate excess moisture. Discard the mint. Toss the peas with the butter in the serving bowl and sprinkle with the chervil. Serve right away.

Young Carrots with Tarragon

4 servings

Not long ago, baby vegetables were a staple of fine restaurants. Now I think most chefs realize that tiny immature vegetables are not necessarily superior, just different. Young carrots lack the sweetness and developed flavors of the grownups, but they shouldn't be banished from the table. They're delicate and tender, and when cooked whole with a bit of their little green tops attached and glistening with butter, they're very elegant. I like to cook them when they're finger width; any smaller they aren't worth the bother. Here I've glazed them in chicken stock and tossed in fresh tarragon, making a beautiful accompaniment to a simple spring dinner of roasted chicken or poached fish.

> *2 bunches young carrots, finger width and any length (1 pound trimmed)*
> *1 cup homemade (page 12) or canned low-sodium chicken stock or water*
> *½ teaspoon sugar*
> *½ teaspoon salt, less if using canned stock*
> *1 tablespoon unsalted butter*
> *2 tablespoons coarsely chopped fresh French tarragon*

Cut off the tops of the carrots, leaving ½ inch of green stem. Peel them with a sharp vegetable peeler and wash them carefully to remove any dirt where the stems meet the roots. Put them in a sauté pan large enough to hold them in a single layer (10 to 12 inches) and add the stock, sugar, salt, and butter. Bring to a boil over medium heat, cover, and let the carrots boil gently until they can be easily pierced with the tip of a paring knife but are still firm, 5 to 6 minutes. Remove the lid and continue to boil until all the liquid evaporates and the carrots are coated with a glaze. Add the tarragon to the pan, toss, and transfer to a warmed serving dish.

NOTE

If you can't find young carrots, substitute 1 pound trimmed larger carrots, cut diagonally into ¼-inch-thick slices.

HERB SUBSTITUTIONS

- *In place of tarragon, use an equal amount of coarsely chopped mint, dill, or chives, 1 tablespoon coarsely chopped marjoram or lemon thyme, or ¼ cup coarsely chopped chervil.*

SPINACH WITH SORREL, MINT, AND ANCHOVY

4 servings

This is spinach with punchy flavor. Anchovies lend saltiness and depth, sorrel lends tang, and mint lends aroma. It's an exciting dish to serve alongside roasted leg of lamb or to place underneath grilled tuna steaks.

> *1 large bunch fresh spinach (about 1 pound)*
> *2 tablespoons extra-virgin olive oil*
> *4 anchovy fillets*
> *1 medium shallot, finely chopped (about ⅓ cup)*
> *1 cup thinly slivered sorrel leaves (gently packed)*
> *¼ cup coarsely chopped fresh spearmint*
> *¼ teaspoon salt*
> *Freshly ground black pepper*

1. Spinach. Remove the stems from the spinach and wash the leaves thoroughly by swishing them in a deep basin of cold water. Lift the leaves from the water and let them drain in a colander. Repeat the washing process if the spinach was very gritty.

2. Sautéing. Heat the oil in a large (12-inch) skillet over medium-low heat. Add the anchovies and shallot and cook, stirring and mashing the anchovy fillets with the back of the spoon, until the shallot is softened but not browned and the anchovy is dissolved. Add as much spinach as will fit in the pan, increase the heat to medium-high, and toss it in the pan with tongs until it is wilted. Add the remaining spinach along with the sorrel, mint, and salt. Continue to toss until all the spinach is wilted and most of the liquid that collects in the pan has boiled away, about 3 minutes. Taste and season with black pepper, and additional salt if needed. Serve right away.

ARTICHOKES STUFFED WITH BASIL AND WALNUTS

4 servings

Because you must eat these artichokes with your hands, they're a bit messy, but they're so delicious you won't mind. A pestolike mixture is fortified with fresh bread crumbs and packed between the leaves of an artichoke, then baked. At the table, you remove the leaves one by one, maneuvering some of the herby stuffing onto each one, and scrape them between your teeth. When all the leaves are skeletons you have the best part—the heart—left to savor, and just enough stuffing to enjoy it with.

Be sure to use fresh soft bread crumbs—dried bread crumbs from a cardboard carton will make the stuffing too heavy. You can easily make fresh crumbs from stale, but not dry, bread that has some body, like rustic Italian or dense white sandwich bread. Trim the crust, tear the bread in pieces, and whirl it in a food processor.

> *½ cup walnuts, lightly toasted*
> *2 cloves garlic, peeled*
> *1 cup (gently packed) fresh basil leaves (1 ounce)*
> *1 cup (gently packed) fresh flat-leaf parsley leaves*
> *4 anchovy fillets*
> *¾ teaspoon salt*
> *½ cup extra-virgin olive oil*
> *1½ cups fresh bread crumbs*
> *¼ cup freshly grated Parmigiano-Reggiano*
> *4 large artichokes*
> *Lemon wedges*

1. Stuffing. Preheat the oven to 400°F. Purée the walnuts, garlic, basil, parsley, anchovies, and salt in a food processor until they form a rough paste. With the machine running, add the olive oil in a steady stream. Add the bread crumbs and cheese and pulse until incorporated.

2. Preparing the artichokes. Cut the stems off the artichokes so that they will sit upright. Remove about 3 rows of the outer leaves by bending them backward until they snap, then peeling down. Cut off the top quarter of the artichokes with a sharp chef's knife. With a pair of scissors, cut the spiny tips off any leaves that still have their

---

points. Using your thumbs, coax the leaves apart to expose the center of the artichoke. Firmly grip the very fine pale leaves in the middle and twist and tug them out. With a small sturdy spoon, scrape out the chokes—the fuzzy material in the very center of the vegetable that covers the hearts.

3. Stuffing the artichokes. Divide the filling into 4 even portions and stuff each portion between the leaves of an artichoke and into the center cavity. Don't be concerned about being neat—just separate the leaves with one hand as you use the other to work the stuffing in. Some of the stuffing should remain on the surface of the artichoke to become brown and crunchy in the oven.

4. Baking. Place the stuffed artichokes in a casserole or Dutch oven just large enough to hold them comfortably and deep enough that it can be covered tightly once the artichokes are in place. Pour 1 inch of hot water into the bottom of the casserole and cover with the lid. Bake for 40 to 50 minutes, checking near the end to make sure the water has not dried up completely and replenishing it if necessary. Test for doneness by removing an outer leaf. It should come off easily and the tiny bit of flesh at the bottom of the leaf should be tender enough to scrape off with your teeth. When the artichokes are tender, remove the lid and bake until the stuffing is browned, about 10 minutes longer. Let the artichokes rest for 5 to 10 minutes, then serve them on plates with the lemon wedges, forks for eating the hearts, a bowl for discarding the scraped leaves, and plenty of napkins.

Runner Beans with Summer Savory and Bacon

4 servings

Runner beans should be in every kitchen garden. Beautiful, delicious, easy to grow, they have it all. Because they climb vertically, they demand very little real estate, and they can even be grown in large containers if you give them something to climb on. After the last frost, bury the large bean seeds near a tall fence or beneath a tepee made of bamboo poles, and stand back. Twining stems will shoot up 8 to 10 feet and send out brilliant sprays of scarlet, white, pink, or bicolored blossoms depending on the variety. Scarlet runner beans are the most common, and they're my favorite for the saturated color of the blossom and the sweetness of the beans. Many people grow these towering vines merely as ornamentals, but they're missing out on half the pleasure. First of all, the blossoms are edible and delicious. They taste like an ultrasweet tender green bean and are spectacular sprinkled on a salad or tossed on top of buttered corn kernels. When the flowers set seed (they are reluctant to do so in very hot weather), they send out elegant clusters of fast-growing long, flat beans, ½ inch wide and up to 12 inches long. Pick these pods while they're still young and the seeds are still tiny. Briefly steamed or boiled, they're surprisingly tender, despite their imposing size. After the seeds inside begin to plump and the bean pods become rounded, they can still be cooked as fresh shell beans if removed from the pods. If left to mature completely, then shelled and dried, you'll have delicious dried beans to store for the winter.

Prepare young runner beans as you would tender green beans or Romano beans. They're particularly delicious with a little bacon and fresh summer savory. Savory is appropriately tagged the "bean herb" because its pungent flavor works so well with all kinds of them, fresh and dried. This recipe illustrates that point well.

4 quarts water
1 tablespoon salt
1 pound fresh runner beans with flat pods and small seeds
2 slices bacon or pancetta (2 ounces), finely diced
2 cloves garlic, finely chopped
2 tablespoons coarsely chopped fresh summer savory
Freshly ground black pepper

1. Beans and bacon. Bring the water with the salt to a boil in a large pot. Trim the stems of the beans and cut them diagonally into 2-inch lengths. Heat a large (12-inch) skillet over medium-low heat. Add the bacon and cook, stirring, until it renders most of its fat and is nearly crisp. Pour off all but 1½ tablespoons of the fat. Add the garlic to the skillet and stir over medium-low heat until it loses its raw fragrance but is not browned, less than 1 minute. Remove the skillet from the heat.

2. Finishing. Drop the beans into the rapidly boiling water and boil them until they are tender but still have a little snap when you bite into one, 2 to 4 minutes. Drain the beans in a colander. (If you are not ready to serve the beans, run cold water over the beans to cool them quickly.) Place the skillet with bacon and garlic back over medium-high heat. Add the beans and savory and toss for a minute or two to heat the beans and blend the flavors. Taste and season with pepper, and additional salt if needed.

HERB SUBSTITUTIONS
- *In place of summer savory, use an equal amount of coarsely chopped marjoram or oregano or 1 tablespoon winter savory.*

BRAISED FENNEL BULB

5 to 6 servings

This dish uses both kinds of fennel—the vegetable fennel, called Florence fennel, finocchio, or sometimes sweet anise, which produces the enlarged white bulbs just above ground level, and the herb fennel, which produces heads of pungent seeds on top of tall stalks with feathery leaves. Wild fennel and bronze fennel are types of the herb fennel.

Fennel bulb's anise flavor is pronounced when it's raw but weakens considerably when it's cooked for a long period of time. In this preparation, the fresh green seeds of the herb reinforce the anise flavor. Slices of the bulb are cooked in a skillet with chicken stock, butter, and fennel seeds until the liquid boils down to a glaze and the fennel slices brown. Fresh fennel seeds form in midsummer after the yellow color of the flower clusters fades. If you don't grow the herb fennel in your garden, you can give the dish a similar flavor by adding pastis (anise-flavored liquor) such as Pernod or Ricard.

When you purchase fennel bulbs, look for ones that are round, smooth, and very white. Avoid any that have brown spots or deep ribs that indicate stringiness. Also stay clear of any bulbs that are flat, elongated, and stretching their layers upward. This means they're getting ready to bolt (send up flower stalks), and the bulbs will be tough and have very large cores.

> *2 large fennel bulbs (about 1½ pounds without tops)*
> *2 tablespoons unsalted butter*
> *1 cup homemade (page 12) or canned low-sodium chicken stock, Golden Vegetable Stock (page 14), or water*
> *2 teaspoons fresh green fennel seeds, or 2 tablespoons pastis, such as Pernod or Ricard*
> *¾ teaspoon salt, less if using canned stock*

1. Slicing the fennel bulb. Cut the stalks off the bulbs. Cut the bulbs lengthwise from stem to root into ½-inch slices. Try to get a bit of the core in each slice so that they will hold together as they cook. You should end up with 10 to 12 flat slices.

2. Browning. Melt the butter in a very large (12- to 14-inch) skillet, preferably non-stick, over medium-high heat. When sizzling, add the fennel slices to the pan in a single layer and cook until the undersides begin to brown, about 2 minutes. Turn the slices over and brown the second side.

3. Braising. Add 1 inch hot water to the pan, then add the stock, fennel seeds or pastis, and salt. Cook the fennel at a steady boil until the liquid is reduced to a glaze, 15 to 20 minutes. It will announce when it gets to this point by making a sizzling sound, and you will need to watch the pan very closely to avoid scorching. As soon as the liquid evaporates completely and the fennel begins to brown further, turn the heat to low, flip the slices, and cook them briefly until the other side starts to brown, then remove them from the pan. (The fennel can be braised ahead of time and stored covered in the refrigerator for up to 2 days. Reheat it on a baking sheet in a 400°F oven until heated through, 10 to 12 minutes.) The braised fennel is particularly good as an accompaniment to fish, shellfish, pork, or lamb dishes.

Swiss Chard Gratin

4 servings

This vegetable gratin is boldly flavored with oregano and thyme and is memorable as an accompaniment to a simple roast or served as a main course. There are several steps to the preparation, but they're all easy, and the dish can be prepared up to a day ahead of time, ready for its final baking.

Swiss chard is a generous plant. It's easy to grow, and if you harvest only the outer leaves of the chard and don't let them bloom, the plants will give you a continuous supply of greens well into the fall. Red chard, like the variety Rhubarb, is my favorite. It's so striking that I often plant it here and there in my flower border. The stems appear to be lacquered with countless coats of brilliant ruby, and when the sun hits them from behind, the broad red-veined leaves shine like intricate stained glass. White Swiss chard is just as tasty, though not as showy. There is also a new seed strain called Bright Lights chard—a rainbow-colored variety with red, orange, yellow, and white stems.

About 2 teaspoons butter, softened
2 to 3 tablespoons fresh bread crumbs
1 pound Swiss chard, any color, with stems
1 tablespoon extra-virgin olive oil
1 medium shallot, or ½ small onion, finely chopped
2 cloves garlic, finely chopped
½ teaspoon salt
Freshly ground black pepper

SAUCE
2 tablespoons unsalted butter
2 tablespoons all-purpose flour
1½ cups whole or low-fat (2%) milk
¼ teaspoon salt
2 fresh bay laurel leaves, cracked, or 1 dried bay leaf and
  ⅛ teaspoon nutmeg
2 tablespoons finely chopped fresh Greek oregano
2 teaspoons finely chopped fresh English thyme
½ cup grated Gruyère cheese (2 ounces)

¼ cup fresh bread crumbs
½ cup grated Gruyère cheese (2 ounces)

1. Prepare the dish. Coat the interior of a 1½-quart gratin dish with the softened butter. Spoon in the bread crumbs and tilt the dish until they adhere to the buttered surface. Preheat the oven to 400°F.

2. Chard. If the chard stems are an inch or more in thickness, split the leaves through the rib from the tip of the leaf to the bottom of the stem. Slice the chard stems and the leaves with ribs attached into 1½-inch pieces. Wash the chard in a deep basin of cold water and drain it in a colander but don't dry it. Heat the olive oil in a 6-quart Dutch oven or soup pot over medium heat. Add the shallot and garlic and cook, stirring constantly, until softened but not browned, about 1 minute. Add the damp Swiss chard to the pot, sprinkle with the salt, and cover tightly. Let the chard steam until it is wilted to half its original volume, 2 to 3 minutes. Remove the lid and continue to cook the chard, turning it occasionally with tongs, until all the water in the pan evaporates, 3 to 5 minutes. Season with black pepper to taste and set it aside while you prepare the sauce.

3. Sauce. Melt the butter in a small (1- to 2-quart) saucepan over medium heat. Whisk in the flour and continue to whisk until the mixture bubbles up and turns lighter in color, about 1 minute. Pour in the cold milk all at once and whisk vigorously. Add the salt and bay leaves and continue to whisk the sauce until it comes to a boil and thickens. Reduce the heat to low and simmer the sauce for about 2 minutes. Stir in the oregano, thyme, and cheese. Remove and discard the bay leaves.

4. Assembling and baking. Stir the sauce into the Swiss chard in the large pot. Taste and add additional salt or pepper if necessary. Spoon the mixture into the gratin dish. For the topping, sprinkle the bread crumbs and then the cheese evenly over the top. At this point you can cover the dish with plastic wrap and refrigerate it for up to 1 day. Bake the gratin until it bubbles over the entire surface and the top is browned, 25 to 35 minutes, depending on if it was warm or chilled. If you wish, you can turn on the broiler for the last minute or two of baking to further brown the top. Serve hot.

ZUCCHINI STRANDS WITH MINT

4 servings

Sometimes if you cut a vegetable in a different fashion it will make it seem entirely new. It's certainly the case in this dish where zucchini are sliced into spaghetti strands, then salted before cooking. The salt draws out all the excess moisture and ensures a firm texture, and the strands are so thin that they cook extremely fast.

To achieve the spaghetti shape you'll need some sort of a mandoline or vegetable slicer. I use an inexpensive Japanese-made Benriner slicer, which is simply a plastic rectangular board holding a razor-sharp angled blade. If you don't have one of these slicing tools in your kitchen, you can shred the zucchini in a food processor using a shredder disk or grate it on the largest holes of a hand grater.

> 2 small to medium zucchini squash (1 pound)
> ½ teaspoon salt
> 1 tablespoon unsalted butter or olive oil
> 1 clove garlic, finely chopped
> 2 tablespoons finely shredded fresh spearmint
> Freshly ground black pepper

1. Cutting and salting the zucchini. Cut the stems and bottom tips off the zucchinis and slice them on a mandoline or other vegetable slicer into long spaghetti-like strips, about ⅛ inch wide and ⅛ inch thick. Toss them with the salt in a medium mixing bowl, then transfer them to a fine sieve or colander and set it over the mixing bowl. Let the zucchini sit for 15 minutes at room temperature, then gently squeeze it in your hands to extract some of the water. It will give off at least ½ cup.

2. Sautéing. Melt the butter in a large (12-inch) skillet over medium-low heat. Add the garlic to the pan and stir until it loses its raw fragrance but is not browned, less than 1 minute. Add the zucchini and mint and toss with tongs just until heated through, about 1 minute. Taste and season with pepper.

HERB SUBSTITUTIONS
- *In place of the mint, use an equal amount of shredded basil, lemon balm, or perilla.*

Roasted Beets with Chives and Lemon Balm

6 servings

Green snips of chives and bits of lemon balm are dazzling tossed among deep garnet slices of beets, while the onion and citrus flavors of the respective herbs are a pleasant accent to the beetroot's sweet earthiness.

6 medium beets (about 2 pounds trimmed)
2 tablespoons unsalted butter
¼ teaspoon salt
Freshly ground black pepper to taste
2 tablespoons coarsely snipped fresh chives
2 tablespoons coarsely chopped fresh lemon balm
About 1 tablespoon freshly squeezed lemon juice

1. Roasting the beets. Preheat the oven to 425°F. Trim the beet stems to ½ inch and wash the beets. Put them in a shallow baking dish large enough to hold them in a single layer, pour in ½ inch water, and cover the dish with a lid or aluminum foil. Bake until a paring knife easily pierces the center of a beet, 30 to 60 minutes, depending on their size. The water will form a syrupy liquid and bubble up. You may need to add a little more water near the end—don't let it dry up completely. Remove the pan from the oven, uncover, and let the beets cool. Cut the top and tail off each beet and rub them under running water to slip off the skins (wear rubber gloves to avoid staining your hands). Alternatively you can hold the beets in paper towels and use the towels to rub the skins off. Cut each beet into 8 wedges. If the beets are larger, cut them horizontally in half, then cut each half into 8 wedges.

2. Finishing. Melt the butter in a medium (10-inch) skillet over medium heat. Add the beets, sprinkle with the salt and pepper, and toss until the beets are heated through, about 2 minutes. Toss in the chives and lemon balm and remove the pan from the heat. Taste and season with the lemon juice and additional salt and pepper if needed.

HERB SUBSTITUTIONS
- *In place of lemon balm, use an equal amount of coarsely chopped fresh chervil or parsley, or 1 tablespoon coarsely chopped fresh dill, lemon thyme, or tarragon.*

GRILLED MARJORAM-SCENTED CORN

6 servings

When you grill corn in its husk, it presents a handy opportunity to flavor the ears with fresh herbs. Tuck whole herb sprigs and pats of butter next to the kernels and the husk will hold them in place. As it cooks on the grill, the corn becomes perfumed with the fragrance of the herbs, while the charred husk injects a mild hit of smokiness. Marjoram is my favorite herb to pair with fresh corn, but lemon thyme is a runner-up.

> *6 ears fresh sweet corn in their husks*
> *3 tablespoons unsalted butter, softened*
> *24 3-inch sprigs marjoram*
> *Sea salt*
> *Optional: lime wedges*

1. Preparing the corn. Build a medium fire in a charcoal grill with the coals concentrated at the center or off to one side, or preheat a gas grill to medium. Peel back the husk of each ear of corn, trying to make as few tears in it as possible and keeping it attached to the ear at the bottom. Remove and discard the silk. Smear ½ tablespoon of the butter over each ear and then press the marjoram sprigs into the butter. Pull the husk back into place to completely cover the kernels. Tear off a piece of the husk about 1 inch wide and tie it around the end of the ear in a knot to keep the husk firmly closed.

2. Grilling. When the coals are ashed over and glowing or the gas grill is preheated, arrange the corn on the rack, away from the concentration of coals, and cover the grill. Cook for 10 to 20 minutes over the indirect heat, turning the ears from time to time. The cooking time depends on many factors—the heat of the grill, the tenderness of the corn itself, and your own preference. Test the corn by piercing a kernel with the tip of a paring knife—it should go in easily but still have some "pop" to it. As it grills, the husks will brown and blacken and they might split apart in places and expose the kernels, but the corn will be fine. If the husks catch on fire when you lift the lid to turn them, replace the lid right away.

3. Serving. The grilled ears look beautiful when you present them on a platter in their husks, but it can be a struggle to remove the husks at the table. You'll do your guests a favor if you bring the platter into the kitchen to unwrap the corn and remove the marjoram sprigs that flavored it. You can then line a platter with some of the browned husks and stack the hot ears on top, using the cooked marjoram to garnish. Allow your guests to sprinkle the corn with salt to their own taste, and pass lime wedges if you wish.

 HERB SUBSTITUTION

- *In place of marjoram, use an equal quantity of lemon thyme sprigs.*

GRILLED EGGPLANT WITH ROSEMARY

4 servin

This simple recipe has converted many eggplant haters. Soy sauce, olive oil, and garlic make an all-purpose grilling marinade that is particularly delicious on eggplant, especially when fresh rosemary is added to the mix.

Raw eggplant can act as a sponge, so don't let the slices soak in the marinade or they will become saturated. Just give them a quick dip before they go on the grill. Serve the grilled eggplant as a side dish to accompany other grilled foods, and use the leftovers to fill a sandwich along with goat cheese, roasted red peppers, and basil.

> *¼ cup extra-virgin olive oil*
> *¼ cup soy sauce*
> *¼ cup fresh rosemary leaves*
> *2 cloves garlic, peeled*
> *1 medium eggplant, or 4 small Japanese eggplants*

1. Setting up. Build a medium-hot fire in a charcoal grill or preheat a gas grill to medium-high. Put the oil, soy sauce, rosemary, and garlic in a food processor or a blender and purée until the rosemary is finely chopped. Pour the marinade into a shallow dish. Cut the large eggplant into 8 wedges or the small eggplants in half.

2. Grilling. When the coals are ashed over and glowing or the gas grill is preheated, pick up 1 piece of eggplant at a time, dip all sides into the marinade, and place it on the grill about 4 inches above the coals. Grill the eggplant on all sides until deep brown in color and the slices are soft and limp, 6 to 8 minutes. If any marinade is left, brush it on the slices after you turn them. If the eggplant blackens a little, don't worry—the soy sauce can make it seem charred but it should not taste burnt. Let the eggplant cool slightly before serving.

Roasted Ratatouille

4 to 6 servings

The traditional version of ratatouille, a summer vegetable stew from the south of France, is cooked on the stovetop, but this dish is cooked entirely in the oven. The vegetables are brushed with a mixture of herbs and olive oil and then are roasted together on the same baking sheet. They come out of the oven tender, but not mushy, and imbued with the fragrance of the roasted herbs. You scoop the eggplant from its skin and chop it with all the rest of the roasted vegetables, mix everything together with some fresh basil, stuff it back in the eggplant shells, and bake it again. The second time in the oven, all the flavors have a chance to meld.

1 medium eggplant (about 1 ¼ pounds)
1 medium zucchini (about 4 ounces)
1 large red bell pepper
1 pound ripe plum tomatoes (about 6)
1 head garlic
¼ cup plus 1 tablespoon extra-virgin olive oil
2 tablespoons finely chopped fresh rosemary
2 tablespoons finely chopped fresh sage
1 tablespoon finely chopped fresh thyme
About ¾ teaspoon salt
Freshly ground black pepper to taste
2 teaspoons red wine vinegar or sherry vinegar
¼ cup coarsely chopped fresh basil
2 tablespoons fresh bread crumbs

1. Roasting the vegetables. Preheat the oven to 425°F. Line a large baking sheet with parchment paper. Cut the eggplant in half, leaving the cap on. With the tip of a chef's knife, score the flesh in a diamond pattern, making cuts 1 inch apart and almost to the bottom without piercing the skin. Cut the zucchini lengthwise into 4 slices. Pierce the pepper in several places with the tip of a knife. Cut the tomatoes crosswise in half and poke out the seeds with your finger. Cut off the top quarter of the head of garlic. Stir ¼ cup oil, the rosemary, sage, and thyme together in a small bowl. Spread out all the vegetables on the baking sheet and brush them with the herb mixture, coating all sides of the zucchini and pepper. Sprinkle the vegetables with the salt and black pepper and roast until the eggplant is tender, the zucchini begins to brown slightly, the pepper skin is blackened, the tomatoes are shriveled, and the garlic is soft, about 40 minutes. All the vegetables should cook in approximately the same amount of time. Let the vegetables cool until you can handle them.

2. Assembling. Preheat the oven to 375°F. With a large spoon, scoop out the flesh of the eggplant without breaking the skin. Peel and seed the red pepper under running water. Chop the eggplant pulp, red pepper, zucchini, and tomatoes coarsely and combine them in a large mixing bowl. Squeeze the garlic out of its skin into a small bowl and mash it with the back of a fork, then stir it into the chopped roasted vegetables along with the vinegar and basil. Taste and season with additional salt and pepper if needed. Put the eggplant shells in a shallow baking dish in which they fit comfortably and spoon in the ratatouille, dividing it between the halves. At this point the dish can be covered and refrigerated for up to 2 days. Drain any liquid that accumulates in the baking dish. Sprinkle the top with the fresh bread crumbs and drizzle with the remaining 1 tablespoon olive oil. Bake the ratatouille until it's heated through and starts to bubble around the edges, 25 to 35 minutes. Serve hot or warm.

DELICATA SQUASH WITH ROSEMARY, SAGE, AND CIDER GLAZE

6 servings

This is my favorite way to cook winter squash. You peel and slice it, then cook it in a skillet with cider and winter herbs. When most of the liquid boils away, the cider forms a tart-sweet glaze around the now-tender squash.

Delicata is a wonderfully firm-textured squash that's not too sweet and almost like a potato. Other varieties like acorn, turban, or kabocha will make good substitutes, but they may not hold their shape quite as well through the braising.

2 medium delicata squash (about 2 pounds) or other firm winter squash
3 tablespoons unsalted butter
¼ cup very coarsely chopped fresh sage
1 tablespoon coarsely chopped fresh rosemary
1½ cups fresh unfiltered apple cider or juice
1 cup water
2 teaspoons sherry vinegar
1 teaspoon salt
Freshly ground black pepper

1. Squash. If using delicata squash, peel it with a vegetable peeler, cut it lengthwise in half, and scrape out the seeds with a spoon. Cut each piece lengthwise in half again, then crosswise into ½-inch-thick slices. Other types of squash should be peeled with a chef's knife, seeded, cut into 1-inch wedges, then sliced ½ inch thick.

2. Herb butter. Melt the butter in a large (12-inch) skillet over low heat. Add the sage and rosemary and cook, stirring, until the butter just begins to turn golden brown, 3 to 5 minutes. Do not brown the herbs. Cooking the herbs in butter mellows their flavor and improves their texture.

3. Cooking the squash. Add the squash to the skillet, then the apple cider, water, vinegar, and salt. Cook, stirring occasionally, over medium heat at an even boil until the cider has boiled down to a glaze and the squash is tender, 20 to 30 minutes. Taste and season with pepper, and additional salt if needed.

Spicy Red Cabbage with Apple and Cilantro

6 servings

Here's a vibrant take on braised sweet-and-sour red cabbage with apples. It's spiced with red pepper flakes, showered with cilantro and green onion, and comes to the table a brilliant magenta color. Just like the traditional long-simmered version, it makes a terrific accompaniment to rich meats like pork or duck, but because of its lighter and livelier nature, it also makes a fitting side dish for grilled or broiled fish.

½ medium head red cabbage (about 1 pound)
2 tablespoons vegetable oil
½ teaspoon dried red pepper flakes
1 large or 2 small apples, peeled, cored, and cut into ¼-inch dice
¼ cup freshly squeezed lime juice
1 ½ tablespoons sugar
¾ teaspoon salt
3 green onions, thinly sliced
1 cup coarsely chopped fresh cilantro

1. Cabbage. Cut the ½ head of cabbage in half again and cut out the cores. Slice the cabbage very thin, less than ⅛ inch thick, preferably using a mandoline, cabbage shredder, or the shredding disk of a food processor.

2. Cooking. Heat the oil with the red pepper flakes in a large (12-inch) skillet or wide saucepan over medium heat. Add the apple and cook, stirring, for about 1 minute. Add the red cabbage and toss it with tongs to coat it with the hot oil. Add the lime juice, sugar, and salt, cover the pan, and reduce the heat to low. Cook until the cabbage is tender, 5 to 10 minutes. Add the green onions and cilantro and toss together with the tongs. Taste and season with additional salt or sugar if needed.

ROASTED PARSNIPS WITH THYME

4 servings

I love the nutty, sweet, and spicy flavor of parsnips. Their unpopularity is a mystery to me—it seems many people don't realize how delicious they can be. This dish brings out their best qualities. It's very simple to prepare and can share the oven with Bay Laurel Roasted Chicken (page 196) or Maple-and-Herb-Brined Pork Roast (page 224).

2 pounds parsnips (5 to 6 medium)
3 tablespoons unsalted butter
1½ tablespoons (packed) dark brown sugar
1 tablespoon balsamic vinegar
½ teaspoon salt
¼ teaspoon freshly ground black pepper
3 tablespoons coarsely chopped fresh thyme

Preheat the oven to 425°F. Peel the parsnips and cut them into 2-inch lengths. Quarter the thickest pieces, halve the medium ones, and leave the thinnest ones whole. You want all the pieces to be about the same size. Put the butter in a shallow baking dish large enough to hold the parsnips in a single layer and put the dish in the oven until the butter melts. Stir in the brown sugar and vinegar. Add the parsnips, salt, and pepper and stir to coat all the pieces evenly. Bake for 20 minutes. Remove the pan from the oven and stir in the thyme. Continue to bake until the parsnips are browned and tender when pierced with a fork, about 10 minutes longer.

HERB-ROASTED POTATOES

6 servings

Who wouldn't love these crispy little potatoes roasted with plenty of fresh herbs and garlic? They will fill your kitchen with mouthwatering aromas and can accompany nearly any roasted or braised meat or poultry dish. You'll find them easy enough to prepare for everyday meals, but they are also ideal for a dinner party because they can be parboiled, seasoned, and set out on a baking sheet early in the day, then roasted when needed.

> *2 quarts cold water*
> *2½ teaspoons salt*
> *2 pounds small potatoes, such as Yellow Finn, Yukon Gold, fingerling, or*
> *   new red or white potatoes*
> *3 tablespoons coarsely chopped fresh herbs, such as rosemary, thyme,*
> *   summer or winter savory, sage, and/or oregano*
> *4 cloves garlic, finely chopped*
> *3 tablespoons extra-virgin olive oil*
> *Freshly ground black pepper to taste*

1. Parboiling the potatoes. Wash the potatoes and cut them in halves or quarters so that the pieces are no larger than 1 inch across. If using fingerlings, slice them crosswise ¾ inch thick. Put the potatoes in a large (4-quart) saucepan and add the water and 2 teaspoons of the salt. Bring the potatoes to a boil over high heat and continue to boil them until they are easily pierced with the tip of a paring knife but are still firm, about 10 minutes. Drain the potatoes in a colander.

2. Roasting. Preheat the oven to 425°F. Transfer the potatoes to a large mixing bowl and toss them with the herbs, garlic, olive oil, the remaining ½ teaspoon salt, and the pepper. Spread them out on a baking sheet or shallow roasting pan. (At this point the potatoes can be covered with plastic wrap and held for up to 2 hours at room temperature or up to 1 day in the refrigerator.) Roast the potatoes until golden brown, 15 to 20 minutes, turning them once halfway through the baking time so that they brown evenly.

POTATOES WITH LAVENDER AND ROSEMARY

6 servings

Many people are skeptical when I suggest how good lavender can be in savory foods, but this dish can change their minds. When lavender is cooked with simple boiled potatoes, its sweet and floral flavor turns earthy and mysterious, especially when its savoriness is amplified with fresh rosemary.

As in most dishes with lavender, you can use either sweet-scented English lavender, like Hidcote or Munstead, or the larger and more pungent flower spikes of lavendin hybrids like Grosso or Provence. The flowers can be used at any stage, but the flavor is best when the spikes are in bud but showing full color, just before the individual blossoms are about to open. If fresh lavender flowers are not available, dried buds, often available at natural food stores, are a good substitute. Make sure they are food grade and not treated with oils for use in potpourri.

2 pounds small potatoes, such as Yellow Finn, Yukon Gold, fingerling, or new red or white potatoes
6 fresh lavender sprigs, or 1 teaspoon dried lavender buds
3 tablespoons unsalted butter
4 teaspoons finely chopped fresh lavender buds, or 2 teaspoons dried
2 teaspoons finely chopped fresh rosemary
½ teaspoon salt

1. **Parboiling the potatoes.** Wash the potatoes and cut them in halves or quarters. If using fingerlings, slice them crosswise ¾ inch thick. Put them in a saucepan with the lavender sprigs and cover with cold water. Bring to a boil over high heat and continue to boil until the potatoes are tender when pierced with a fork but still hold their shape, 12 to 15 minutes. Drain. Some of the lavender buds will cling to the potatoes.

2. **Final cooking.** Melt the butter in a large skillet over medium heat. Add the potatoes, chopped lavender and rosemary, and salt; cook, tossing occasionally, until the potatoes are very hot and the flavors have a chance to meld, 5 to 8 minutes.

 HERB SUBSTITUTION
- *Omit the rosemary and add 2 tablespoons coarsely chopped fresh spearmint to the potatoes just before they are through cooking in the skillet.*

POTATOES IN HERBED CREAM

4 servings

Just homey scalloped potatoes, really, but with generous quantities of whole herb sprigs steeped in the cream. The technique of infusion works perfectly here. In addition to being fast, it allows just the right amount of flavor to be released into the cream, which in turn is absorbed by the potatoes, making them taste as if they were grown deep in an herb bed.

> *1 cup whole milk*
> *½ cup heavy cream*
> *4 cloves garlic*
> *3 4-inch sprigs fresh marjoram or Italian oregano*
> *2 4-inch sprigs fresh rosemary*
> *3 4-inch sprigs fresh thyme*
> *1 2-inch sprig fresh sage*
> *6 fresh bay laurel leaves, torn, or 2 dried plus ¼ teaspoon ground nutmeg*
> *¾ teaspoon salt*
> *Freshly ground black pepper to taste*
> *2 tablespoons unsalted butter, softened*
> *2 large russet (Idaho) potatoes (about 1½ pounds)*

1. Cream. Place the milk and cream in a small saucepan over medium heat. Smash the garlic cloves with the side of a chef's knife and remove the peels. When the milk and cream are boiling, add the garlic, herb sprigs, bay leaves, salt, and pepper. Bring the mixture back to a boil, then immediately remove it from the heat, cover, and let steep for 30 minutes or longer while you prepare the potatoes.

2. Gratin. Preheat the oven to 425°F. Butter a shallow 1½-quart baking dish with 1 tablespoon of the butter. Peel the potatoes, slice them ⅛ inch thick, and arrange them in the dish. Bring the herbed cream back to a simmer. Hold a large fine sieve over the baking dish and pour the cream through it and over the potatoes, coating all the slices. The liquid will not completely cover the potatoes at this point. Dot with the remaining 1 tablespoon butter. Bake until the top is nicely browned and the potatoes are tender, 30 to 35 minutes. Halfway through the cooking, use the back of a large spoon to lightly press down any potatoes that are not yet submerged into the cream.

VARIATIONS

You can omit the cream and use additional milk in its place, but the top won't brown quite as well. To forgo the dairy altogether, use a rich chicken stock, infusing it in exactly the same way as the milk.

HERB SUBSTITUTIONS

- *You can omit any of the herbs listed above, for instance, adding only the thyme and bay leaves, or marjoram and rosemary.*
- *For a lavender-scented potato gratin, add 6 fresh English lavender sprigs and 3 3-inch sprigs fresh rosemary or thyme in place of the herbs listed above.*

GREEN MASHED POTATOES

6 servings

A tablespoon of chopped herbs, like thyme or marjoram, is a welcome addition to ordinary mashed potatoes, but these very herby potatoes are taken one step further. They're made with a pestolike mixture of parsley and chives, which turns them a brilliant green and gives them a green onion flavor. They're gorgeous served with salmon.

> *2 pounds russet (Idaho) potatoes (about 3 large)*
> *6 3-inch sprigs fresh English thyme, tied together with cotton string*
> *½ cup coarsely snipped fresh chives*
> *1 cup (lightly packed) fresh parsley leaves*
> *¼ cup extra-virgin olive oil*
> *¾ teaspoon salt*
> *½ cup whole milk*
> *¼ cup heavy cream*
> *Freshly ground black pepper*

1. Boiling the potatoes. Peel the potatoes and cut them into quarters. Put them in a large (4-quart) saucepan, fill the pan with cold water to cover the potatoes by 1½ inches, and add the thyme bundle. Bring the potatoes to a boil over medium-high heat and continue to boil them until they are easily pierced with a fork, about 20 minutes.

2. Pesto. While the potatoes are cooking, purée the chives, parsley, olive oil, and salt in a food processor until they form a fairly smooth paste.

3. Mashing. When the potatoes are done, drain them in a colander and discard the thyme. Return the saucepan to the stove, add the milk and cream, and bring it to a simmer over medium heat. Remove the pan from the heat and press the potatoes through a ricer, letting them fall into the hot cream. Whip the potatoes with a sturdy wire whisk or portable electric mixer. At this point you can keep the potatoes warm by holding them in a covered metal bowl set over a pan of simmering water for up to 1 hour. Just before serving, add the pesto and continue to whip until it is thoroughly incorporated. Taste and season with pepper, and additional salt if needed.

MASHED POTATOES WITH TOASTED CORIANDER

6 servings

When Ron Zimmerman, The Herbfarm's co-owner and an ardent potato lover, makes mashed potatoes, he adds toasted ground coriander and roasted garlic. Coriander seeds take on a nutty deep flavor when toasted—completely different from the taste of the raw dry seeds—and lend a savory and delicious earthiness.

> *3 tablespoons dried coriander seeds*
> *2 pounds russet (Idaho), Yellow Finn, or Yukon Gold potatoes*
> *¼ cup whole milk*
> *¼ cup heavy cream*
> *4 tablespoons unsalted butter*
> *1½ tablespoons Roasted Garlic Paste (page 341)*
> *¾ teaspoon salt*
> *Freshly ground black pepper*

1. Toasting the coriander. Put the coriander seeds in a small dry skillet and place it over medium heat. Toast, shaking the pan constantly, until the seeds begin to darken in color and smell wonderfully fragrant and toasty; be careful not to overcook. Pour them out onto a paper towel to stop the cooking. Using the towel as a funnel, transfer them to a spice mill and grind very fine. If you don't have a spice grinder, use a mini food processor or blender.

2. Boiling the potatoes. Peel the potatoes and cut them into quarters. Put them in a large (4-quart) saucepan and fill the pan with cold water to cover the potatoes by 1½ inches. Bring the potatoes to a boil over medium-high heat and continue to boil them until they are easily pierced with a fork, about 20 minutes.

3. Mashing. When the potatoes are done, drain them in a colander. Return the saucepan to the stove, add the milk and cream, and bring it to a simmer over medium heat. Remove the pan from the heat and press the potatoes through a ricer, letting them fall into the hot cream. Whip the potatoes with a sturdy wire whisk or portable electric mixer. Add the coriander, butter, roasted garlic paste, and salt and continue to whip until the butter is melted and thoroughly incorporated. Taste and season with pepper, and additional salt if needed. Serve right away, or keep the potatoes warm by holding them in a covered metal bowl set over a pan of simmering water for up to 1 hour.

MINTED FRENCH LENTILS

6 servings

French lentils are smaller, rounder, and darker than the common green or gray-green varieties, and they also cook quite differently—instead of turning to mush, they retain their shape and texture. You can buy lentils imported from France called lentilles du Puy, but the same variety is grown in the Pacific Northwest in the area known as the Palouse, which straddles the border between Washington and Idaho. They're usually sold as "French-style lentils" and are very similar to the imported ones, but they seem to cook faster.

Although lentils don't require presoaking, I like to do so and then boil them until they are just tender. Handled this way, you can cook them to exactly the right stage of doneness and they stay perfectly separate. If done ahead of time, all they need is final cooking with the flavorings shortly before you serve them.

> *3 quarts water*
> *1 cup French-style lentils*
> *2½ teaspoons salt*
> *3 slices bacon, finely diced (3 ounces)*
> *1 teaspoon finely chopped garlic*
> *1 tablespoon finely chopped fresh ginger*
> *½ cup finely diced carrots*
> *1 cup unfiltered apple cider or juice*
> *3 tablespoons sherry vinegar or apple cider vinegar*
> *½ cup chopped fresh spearmint*
> *Freshly ground black pepper to taste*
> *Garnish: ¼ cup fresh mint leaves cut into fine strips (chiffonade)*

1. Soaking the lentils. Bring the water (unsalted) to a boil in a large (4-quart) saucepan. Add the lentils, turn off the heat, and let them soak for at least 1 hour or overnight in the refrigerator.

2. Parboiling the lentils. Drain the lentils and rinse them under cold running water. Refill the saucepan with 3 quarts of fresh water, add 2 teaspoons of the salt, and bring it to a boil. Add the lentils and boil until just tender but still firm and not mushy. French lentils vary greatly and may take anywhere from 2 to 10 minutes to cook.

Watch them carefully, for they overcook quickly. Drain and rinse under running water. (The lentils can be cooked ahead of time up to this point. Refrigerate them until you are ready to proceed.)

3. Finishing. Heat the same saucepan over medium heat. Add the bacon and cook, stirring often, until almost crisp. Pour off all but 2 tablespoons fat in the pan. Add the garlic, ginger, and carrots and cook, stirring constantly, until the garlic loses its raw fragrance, about 2 minutes. Add the lentils, cider, and remaining ½ teaspoon salt. Cook uncovered, stirring occasionally, until the liquid is absorbed, about 10 minutes. Add the vinegar and chopped mint. Taste and season with pepper and additional salt if needed. Transfer the lentils to a serving dish and garnish with the fine strips of mint leaves.

VEGETARIAN VARIATION
Substitute 2 tablespoons olive oil for the bacon and increase the salt by ¼ teaspoon.

Baked Herb Polenta

6 servings

Cheesy polenta laced with fresh herbs is a reliable crowd-pleaser. Traditional polenta must be stirred constantly for about 45 minutes, but this baked version is a snap to make because it requires only 5 minutes of stirring on top of the stove, just until it begins to thicken. The rest of the cooking takes place in the oven while you're doing other things. When just out of the oven, this polenta will make soft mounds when spooned on the plate. If left to sit, it will become much firmer.

1 tablespoon unsalted butter, softened
4½ cups water
¾ teaspoon salt
1 cup medium-coarse ground cornmeal
2 tablespoons finely chopped fresh marjoram
1 tablespoon finely chopped fresh thyme
1½ cups grated Gruyère cheese (about 3 ounces)

1. Polenta. Preheat the oven to 350°F. Coat a shallow 1½-quart baking dish with the butter. Bring the water with the salt to a boil in a medium (3-quart) saucepan. Slowly sprinkle in the cornmeal as you whisk constantly. Continue to whisk over medium heat until the mixture is as thick as Cream of Wheat, about 5 minutes. Remove the pan from the heat and stir in the marjoram, thyme, and half the cheese.

2. Baking. Spread the polenta evenly in the prepared dish and sprinkle the remaining cheese on top. Bake until the polenta is bubbling all over and the edges begin to brown, about 1 hour.

HERB SUBSTITUTION
- *Substitute 1 tablespoon finely chopped sage for either the thyme or the marjoram.*

White Beans with Herbed Onion-Garlic Confit

4 servings

These richly flavored beans make a wonderful side dish for lamb or chicken, or they can be served as a main course with garlicky wilted greens. While the beans are boiling, you cook onions, garlic, and herbs in olive oil and chicken stock until they turn into a soft marmalade, and then stir the two together. You have the option of leaving the beans whole or mashing them once the dish is done. If you purée them in a food processor or blender, you'll have a fabulous spread or dip.

> *4 quarts water*
> *8 ounces dried white beans, such as great Northern, navy, flageolet, or*
>   *cannellini (about 1 ¼ cups)*
> *Bouquet garni of 2 bay laurel leaves, fresh or dried, and 1 small bunch*
>   *English thyme tied in a bundle*
> *3 tablespoons extra-virgin olive oil*
> *1 large onion, finely chopped*
> *6 cloves garlic, finely chopped*
> *2 cups homemade (page 12) or canned low-sodium chicken stock, or*
>   *Golden Vegetable Stock (page 14)*
> *1 tablespoon coarsely chopped fresh rosemary*
> *1 tablespoon coarsely chopped fresh winter savory, or 1 ½ tablespoons*
>   *coarsely chopped fresh summer savory*
> *1 teaspoon salt, less if using canned stock*
> *Freshly ground black pepper*

1. Soaking the beans. Bring 2 quarts water to a boil in a large (4-quart) saucepan. Add the dried beans, turn off the heat, and let them soak uncovered for 1 hour.

2. Boiling the beans. Drain the soaked beans in a colander, rinse them under cold running water, and return them to the saucepan. Add 2 quarts cold water and the bouquet garni. Gently boil the beans uncovered until they are very soft but still hold their shape, 35 to 60 minutes depending on the type of bean.

3. Onion and garlic. While the beans are cooking, heat the olive oil in a small (1½- to 2-quart) saucepan over medium heat. Add the onion and garlic and cook, stirring often, until softened but not browned, about 8 minutes. Pour in the stock and add the rosemary and savory. Boil until the level of the liquid is below the level of the onion and garlic, about 30 minutes. The onion and garlic should be very soft, but not caramelized, and have a consistency like marmalade.

4. Finishing. When the beans are cooked, drain them in a colander and discard the bouquet garni. Return the beans to the large saucepan. Stir in the onion confit and the salt (omit the salt at this point if using canned stock). Cook, stirring often, over medium heat for 5 minutes to blend the flavors. Taste and season with black pepper, and additional salt if needed.

NOTE
For convenience, 3 cups drained canned beans can be substituted for the cooked dried beans.

VARIATION
WHITE BEAN PURÉE
Using an old-fashioned potato masher or a handheld immersion blender, purée the beans until no beans are left whole but the mixture still has some texture. If the consistency is thin, put them back over medium heat and stir them until they firm up. For a smoother texture, good for a spread or dip, purée the beans in a food processor or blender.

CHAPTER 6

Fish and Shellfish

Herbs and seafood come together in exquisite ways: The sweet spice of marjoram is just the right complement to the sugared brininess of fat fresh shrimp roasted in their shells. Verdant dill supports the delicate flavor of halibut wrapped in lettuce leaves and steamed over fresh mint. A whole salmon grilled over fennel stalks picks up an anise smokiness that intensifies its rich ocean freshness. Full-flavored swordfish resonates with aromatics when skewered with fresh bay on rosemary branches.

From simple pan-fried trout to home-smoked salmon, all steps of cooking seafood require care. Success relies on diligent shopping for the freshest ingredients, exact timing in the pan, oven, or grill, and a balanced hand with seasoning. Pairing herbs with seafood also takes some finesse, but it's simple if you think about matching the boldness and subtleties of the ingredients. Mild-flavored lean white seafood does better with soft-leafed herbs like tarragon, chervil, cilantro, and basil. Darker and richer fish and shellfish with fuller flavors, like swordfish, tuna, and mussels, can stand up to herbs like thyme, rosemary, and sage. All seafood has an affinity for herbs with anise and lemon flavors and for parsley. Begin with small amounts of an herb that you know will harmonize with the flavor of the seafood and add more as you go.

The recipes in this chapter cover varied techniques for cooking fish and shellfish, from baking to poaching, steaming, sautéing, grilling, and smoking. Use them to become familiar with how best to pair the herbal flavors and the specific ways to incorporate them, then explore how you can introduce what's fresh in your local seafood market to what you have in your own herb garden.

Fish Fillets en Papillote, Many Ways

4 servings

The French call the method of steaming food in a parchment paper envelope *en papillote,* or in a paper bag. I first learned about it in chef's school many years ago. This technique has become familiar to many cooks since then, and with good reason, for it's one of the quickest, easiest, and most healthful methods of cooking fish. You can do all the preparation ahead of time, then pop the packets in the oven at the last minute. Best of all, it presents a splendid opportunity to use fresh herbs. You assemble the fish fillets, herbs, and other flavorings on heart-shaped pieces of parchment paper, then fold the paper around the food to create sealed envelopes. In the oven the envelopes turn into individual steamers in which the herbs infuse their flavor into the steam, which in turn flavors the fish. A heavenly bouquet is released when the packets are cut open.

The one disadvantage to cooking in paper is that you cannot test how well cooked the fish is until the packets are ripped open; so if you're longing for fish cooked to the exact breath of doneness, you might want to prepare it another way. The timing I suggest will work quite accurately, however, and the steamy environment inside the packets will keep the fish moist even if it cooks a hair longer than it should.

These packets are easiest to make if you can find the 24 x 16-inch sheets of baking parchment that restaurants and bakeries use to line their large sheet pans. They are called "pan liners" and are packed in boxes of 1,000, which can be bought at restaurant or bakery supply stores. If you invest in a whole box, you can share some with friends and neighbors, and you'll still have enough to use in your own kitchen for years. Besides being ideal for these packets, they can be used to line baking sheets every time you bake breads, pastries, or desserts.

Here is a basic recipe for fish en papillote, with many options for flavoring.

ALL VERSIONS
1½ to 2 pounds skinless delicate or medium-firm fish fillet, such as halibut, salmon, snapper, or sea bass
Salt and freshly ground black pepper
2 tablespoons unsalted butter

Choose one of the following flavoring combinations:

GRAPEFRUIT AND TARRAGON
1 shallot, thinly sliced
Zest of ¼ grapefruit, cut into thin strips
Segments from 1 large grapefruit (page 65)
¼ cup very coarsely chopped fresh French tarragon leaves

SLOW-ROASTED TOMATO AND BASIL
12 to 16 halves of Slow-Roasted Tomatoes (page 340)
20 large fresh basil leaves
4 teaspoons balsamic vinegar

LEMON THYME AND GINGER
8 thin slices whole lemon
¼ cup coarsely chopped green onions
2 tablespoons fresh ginger cut into small matchsticks
16 3-inch sprigs fresh lemon thyme
2 tablespoons dry white wine

FENNEL BULB AND BLOSSOM
1 small fennel bulb (8 ounces), very thinly sliced
¼ cup snipped fennel blossoms, yellow part only (page 395)
4 thin slices whole lemon
½ small shallot, very thinly sliced
¼ cup dry white wine

SPRING VEGETABLE AND HERB
16 asparagus tips
1 small carrot, peeled and cut into matchsticks
4 medium fresh shiitake mushrooms, stemmed and sliced, or
    4 medium button mushrooms, cut into quarters
½ medium shallot, very thinly sliced
¼ cup coarsely snipped fresh chives or chopped green onions
2 tablespoons coarsely chopped fresh dill
Optional: 2 teaspoons finely chopped fresh lovage
¼ cup dry white wine

1. **Fish.** Preheat the oven to 425°F. Trim any dark gray flesh on the skin side of the fish and check for and remove any remaining bones. Cut the fillet into 4 equal pieces.

2. **Cutting the paper.** Fold 4 sheets parchment paper (24 x 16 inches) in half, so they are now 12 inches wide. (If you are using 12-inch-wide parchment from a roll, begin with sheets 12 x 20 inches.) As if you were making a grade-school valentine, cut out a half-heart shape as large as the paper. Unfold the hearts and lay them out side by side on a large counter.

3. **Filling and sealing the packets.** Season all sides of the fish fillets with salt and pepper. Place a piece of fish in the center on the right side of each heart. Cover the fish with the remaining ingredients except any wine, dividing them evenly among the packets. Season again with salt and pepper and dot each with ½ tablespoon butter. If you are using wine, pour it over the fish just before you seal the packet. Fold the left half of the parchment paper over to cover the fish. Starting at the top left corner, fold over a piece of the edge about 1 inch deep and 2 inches wide and crease firmly. Make the second fold to the right of it, overlapping the last by half. Continue to fold the edge over, each time overlapping half of the last crease and following the shape of the paper, until you get to the bottom and are left with a pointy tail. Twist this piece around several times like a hard candy wrapper and tuck it under. You should have a totally sealed packet with a straight side and a rounded side, like a butterfly wing. Seal the remaining packets in the same way and put them on 2 large baking sheets. (The packets can be prepared up to this point 4 hours ahead and stored in the refrigerator.)

4. **Baking.** Bake the packets until they are puffed and the edges of the paper begin to brown, 10 to 12 minutes. If you are baking the packets on 2 racks in the same oven, switch their positions halfway through so that they bake evenly. You can transfer the packets to dinner plates and open them at the table, but I prefer to remove the paper in the kitchen so that my guests are not faced with a big soggy piece of paper in front of them. Slide the packages onto plates and cut them open with scissors. Use a spatula to push the contents onto the plates while pulling the paper out. Remove and discard any whole herb sprigs. Serve right away with rice, couscous, or crusty bread.

GREEN-ROASTED FISH FILLETS

4 servings

This is a wonderfully flavorful and very easy way to prepare fish. The fillets are marinated and roasted in a thick coat of fresh herb purée made from cilantro, parsley, and mint. It keeps them especially moist in the oven and imparts a vivid freshness without overpowering delicately flavored white fish.

HERB PASTE
½ cup (gently packed) fresh cilantro leaves
½ cup (gently packed) fresh flat-leaf parsley leaves
½ (gently packed) fresh spearmint leaves
1 tablespoon freshly ground dried coriander seeds, untoasted, or
    1 teaspoon fresh green coriander seeds, finely chopped
2 green onions, white and green parts, coarsely chopped
2 cloves garlic, peeled
1 teaspoon salt
½ teaspoon freshly ground black pepper
Thinly sliced zest of ½ lime (removed with a zester)
¼ cup freshly squeezed lime juice
6 tablespoons extra-virgin olive oil

1 ½ to 2 pounds skinless medium-firm white-fleshed fish fillet, such as
    halibut, sea bass, cod, or rockfish

1. Herb paste. Process all the ingredients for the paste in a food processor to a fairly smooth purée. Transfer it to a glass or stainless-steel mixing bowl.

2. Marinating the fish. Remove any bones that may remain in the fillet, cut off any gray fat that was next to the skin, and cut the fish into 4 equal pieces. Toss them with the herb paste until all surfaces are evenly coated. Cover the bowl loosely with plastic wrap and let the fish set at room temperature for 15 to 30 minutes.

3. Baking. Preheat the oven to 425°F. Arrange the pieces of fish in a shallow baking dish large enough to hold them in a single layer without touching. Spoon any of the herb paste left in the bowl over the fish so that they are covered with an even coating. Bake until, when you peek inside a piece, the last bit of translucence is fading from the interior of the flesh, 10 minutes per inch of fish thickness. Serve right away.

Halibut Baked with Leeks, Apple, and Lovage

4 servings

Tender and mellow leek, sweet-tart apple, and the piercing green flavor of lovage create a breathtaking harmony of flavors that especially suits the delicate sweetness of halibut. Here they cook into a sort of ragout in which the fresh fish fillets bake. The whole dish is brought to the table, and each piece of fish is served with a generous portion of the apple and leek ragout.

> *3 medium leeks (about 2¼ pounds untrimmed)*
> *3 tablespoons unsalted butter*
> *¾ cup dry white wine*
> *1½ cups unfiltered apple cider or apple juice*
> *¾ teaspoon salt*
> *1 large tart apple, such as Granny Smith, Jonagold, or Braeburn*
> *2 tablespoons coarsely chopped fresh lovage*
> *2 tablespoons sherry vinegar*
> *Freshly ground black pepper*
> *1½ to 2 pounds skinless halibut fillet or other medium-firm flaky fish*
> *fillet, such as salmon, sea bass, or snapper*
> *1 tablespoon unsalted butter, softened*

1. The ragout. Cut off and discard the tops of the leeks at the point they turn from light to dark green. Split the bottom portion lengthwise in half, keeping the roots attached so that the layers will not fall apart. Rinse thoroughly. Cut the leeks into 3-inch lengths, discard the roots, then slice each section into ⅛-inch-thick matchstick. Melt 3 tablespoons butter in a large (4-quart) saucepan over medium heat. Add the leeks and cook, stirring often, until they are softened and beginning to brown, about 10 minutes. Add the wine and cook until most of the liquid evaporates. Add the apple cider and salt and gently boil uncovered until the leeks cook down further and the liquid evaporates down to below the level of the leeks in the pan, about 10 minutes. Peel, core, and cut the apple into ¼-inch cubes and stir it into the leek mixture along with the lovage. Stir in the vinegar, taste, and season with pepper, and additional salt if necessary. (The ragout can be made ahead up to this point. Let it sit on the back of the stove for up to 2 hours or cover and refrigerate for up to 2 days.)

2. Fish. Preheat the oven to 425°F. Trim any dark gray flesh from the skin side of the halibut fillets and check for and remove any stray bones. Cut the fillet into 4 equal pieces and sprinkle both sides with salt and pepper. Reheat the leek ragout on the stove until it simmers, then pour it into an ungreased 12 x 9-inch shallow baking dish. Arrange the fish fillets on top of the hot ragout and press them down so that their sides are submerged in the mixture but their tops are not covered by it. Cut a piece of parchment paper slightly larger than the baking dish and smear it with the softened butter. Press it, butter side down, directly on the fish. Bake the fish with the parchment cover until it is milky, firm, and just barely translucent at the inside center, 10 to 15 minutes. It's best to underbake the fish slightly because it will continue to cook once the dish is removed from the oven. Bring the dish to the table. Use a spatula to serve the fish fillets and then spoon some of the ragout and the sauce over each piece.

HERB SUBSTITUTIONS

- *Fresh lovage really defines the flavor of this dish and nothing else can approximate it, but if you don't grow lovage yourself, you can use an equal amount of coarsely chopped fresh lemon thyme or dill, or ¼ cup coarsely chopped fresh parsley.*

Rainbow Trout with Browned Herb Butter

2 servings

Here's a beautifully simple way to cook fresh trout, perfect for a quick dinner for two. The fish are stuffed with sprigs of fresh herbs, then dredged in flour, browned in a skillet, and baked in the oven. Additional herbs are coarsely chopped, crisped in butter, and then spooned over the fish, and lemon is squeezed on at the table. The herbs highlight the fresh flavor of the fish without taking over.

You can leave the trout whole when you serve them, but they'll probably be enjoyed more if you remove the bones in the kitchen and present the fillets.

> *2 12- to 16-ounce fresh rainbow trout, cleaned, with heads and tails left on*
> *Salt and freshly ground black pepper to taste*
> *2 3-inch sprigs fresh sage*
> *6 3-inch sprigs fresh English thyme*
> *About 1 cup all-purpose flour, for dredging*
> *3 tablespoons extra-virgin olive oil*
> *3 tablespoons unsalted butter*
> *2 teaspoons fresh whole English thyme leaves*
> *1 tablespoon finely shredded fresh sage leaves*
> *2 tablespoons coarsely chopped fresh flat-leaf parsley*
> *Lemon wedges*

1. Setting up. Preheat the oven to 400°F. Rinse the trout and pat dry with paper towels. Salt and pepper both sides of the trout and the cavities. Stuff the cavities with the sage and thyme sprigs. Spread the flour on an oval platter and set it beside the stove.

2. Cooking the trout. Heat the olive oil in a large (12-inch) ovenproof skillet over medium-high heat until it begins to smoke. Pick up 1 trout at a time and coat both sides with flour. Pat the fish to shake off any excess flour, then carefully lower it into the oil, allowing the head and tail to rest on the sides of the pan if necessary. As soon as the fish are in the skillet, move them around with a spatula to be sure they are not sticking. Fry the trout until the underside turns golden brown, 2 to 3 minutes, then turn them. Immediately put the skillet in the oven and bake until the fish is cooked through, 8 to 12 minutes. If you're not sure the fish is done, remove the skillet from the oven and lift a fillet from the frame below the gills using a knife or narrow spatula. It should separate easily and the flesh should be opaque. Let the fish rest in the skillet while you prepare the herb butter.

3. Herb butter. Melt the butter in your smallest skillet or saucepan over medium-low heat. Stir in the thyme and sage leaves and cook, stirring often, until you see golden brown specks in the butter, 3 to 4 minutes. Immediately remove the pan from the heat and stir in the parsley to stop the cooking. Set the sauce aside while you fillet the fish.

4. Filleting the trout. Make a shallow cut with a thin narrow spatula along the back of one of the fish. Loosen the top fillet by working the spatula underneath it, being sure to keep it above the fish frame and follow the contour of the bones upward over the herb-stuffed cavity. Using a fork and the spatula, lift the fillet off the bones and turn it skin side down onto a warmed serving plate. Grab hold of the tail with tongs or your fingers and lift it. The entire fish frame should lift off the bottom fillet in one piece with the head attached. Remove any fins that remain on the bottom fillet and use the spatula to set it alongside the top fillet, slightly overlapping. Repeat with the other fish. Spoon the herbs in browned butter over the fillets. Serve right away, passing lemon wedges at the table. The trout is good served with Potatoes with Lavender and Rosemary (page 147) or its variation with lavender and mint.

 HERB SUBSTITUTION
- *Substitute 1 tablespoon coarsely chopped spearmint for the parsley.*

Herb and Peppercorn–Crusted Tuna Steaks with Perilla Salad

4 to 6 servings

Tuna is well suited to cooking with an herb crust because you can achieve a deep brown exterior while the interior stays rare. Here it gets a peppery crust that's just vibrant enough to lend excitement without overtaking the flavor of the fish. The fish is accompanied by a salad of cucumber, radish, avocado, and a generous handful of perilla, whose cuminlike flavor is at the same time earthy and refreshing. If you don't grow it, perilla can sometimes be found in Asian markets under the Japanese name shiso.

High-quality fresh tuna is delicious when cooked rare—when you slice it the center will be warm but still translucent and pink or red. To keep the interior rare and still have a well-browned crust, it's vital that the tuna steak be cut 1½ inches thick no matter what the diameter of the fish is. If it's too thin, it will overcook in the time it takes to brown the crust.

2 pounds skinless tuna steaks, such as yellowfin, bluefin (ahi), or albacore,
*   sliced 1½ inches thick (2, 3, or 4 steaks depending on the diameter of*
*   the fish)*
Salt and freshly ground black pepper to taste
4 teaspoons whole black peppercorns
1 tablespoon dried coriander seeds (untoasted)
1 tablespoon fresh thyme leaves
¾ cup finely chopped fresh parsley

SALAD

2 cucumbers, peeled, seeded, and cut into ¼-inch dice
10 radishes, cut into thin wedges
1 ripe avocado, peeled and cut into ¼-inch dice
½ cup finely shredded fresh perilla (shiso) leaves, red or green
2 tablespoons finely chopped fresh chives or green onions
Zest of ½ lemon, cut into fine strips
¼ cup freshly squeezed lemon juice
½ teaspoon salt
Freshly ground black pepper to taste

3 tablespoons extra-virgin olive oil
Garnish: 2 tablespoons finely shredded fresh perilla (shiso) leaves,
red or green

1. Crusting the fish. If the tuna has a section of dark blood-stained flesh, trim it off and discard it. Salt and pepper all sides of the fish. Grind the peppercorns, coriander, and thyme in a spice mill or blender to a medium-coarse consistency. Toss the spices with the parsley in a shallow dish. Coat the tuna with the herb mixture by firmly pressing the fish into it on all sides. Transfer the crusted fish steaks to a platter. (At this point the fish can be covered with plastic wrap and refrigerated for up to 2 hours.)

2. Salad. Right before you are ready to cook the tuna, toss all the ingredients for the salad together in a mixing bowl.

3. Searing the tuna. Heat the olive oil in a large (12-inch) skillet over high heat until it is very hot and smoke is rising steadily. Carefully lower the crusted fish into the pan using tongs. Cook the fish until it is an even medium-brown on the bottom, about 3 minutes. Turn the steaks and cook until the other side is browned, about 2 minutes. The fish should still be rare. Transfer the fish to a cutting board and let it rest for 2 to 3 minutes before slicing.

4. Finishing. Put a mound of the perilla salad on each dinner plate or on one end of a large platter. Using a sharp thin knife in a sawing motion, slice the tuna steaks about ¼ inch thick. A band about ¾ inch thick in the middle of each slice should still be translucent. Arrange the slices over or beside the salad. Garnish the plates with the shredded perilla. Serve right away.

 HERB SUBSTITUTION
- *If you cannot find perilla, substitute an equal amount of finely shredded fresh spearmint leaves.*

BRAISED MONKFISH WITH FENNEL BULB AND LEMON THYME

4 servings

Braising—the method of searing and them simmering in a covered pan with a little bit of liquid—is not often used for fish, but it's a terrific way to prepare thick, firm-fleshed fish like monkfish. Here the whole fillets are braised with fennel bulb, saffron, and lemon thyme and then sliced before serving. The lemon thyme is handled like a bouquet garni—it's tied up with string and simmered in the cooking liquid. In the brief time it takes to braise the fish, its heady lemon fragrance infuses the whole dish.

> *2 pounds monkfish fillet*
> *Salt and freshly ground black pepper to taste*
> *1 large fennel bulb (about 12 ounces trimmed)*
> *16 3-inch sprigs fresh lemon thyme*
> *2 bay laurel leaves, fresh or dried*
> *2 tablespoons extra-virgin olive oil*
> *1 medium shallot, thinly sliced*
> *2 cloves garlic, minced*
> *¾ cup dry white wine*
> *18 saffron threads*
> *Thinly sliced zest of ½ lemon (removed with a zester)*
> *1 tablespoon freshly squeezed lemon juice*

1. Setting up. Trim the monkfish by removing any tough gray membrane on its surface. This is easiest to do with the tip of a sharp thin knife in the same way you would remove the silver skin from a piece of meat. Insert the tip of the knife under the membrane and cut loose a small piece. Grab this piece to serve as a handle and pull it taut. Hold the knife under the membrane with the blade angled up, so that you won't cut into the flesh, and guide it along gently in a sawing motion, freeing thin strips of the membrane. Take the time to do a thorough job of trimming, for this membrane toughens when cooked and is quite unpalatable. Leave the fillets in large pieces (you'll probably have 2 or 3) and season them with salt and pepper. Remove any stalks from the fennel bulb and cut the bulb into quarters. Cut out the core and slice the bulb ¼ inch thick. Divide the lemon thyme into 2 bunches and tie each with a bay leaf using kitchen twine.

2. Searing the fish. Heat the olive oil in a large (12-inch) heavy-bottomed skillet over high heat until it begins to smoke. Carefully lower the pieces of fish into the oil and sear on all sides until they turn light golden brown, 2 to 3 minutes total. Transfer the fish to a platter and set it aside.

3. Braising. Reduce the heat under the skillet to medium and add the fennel, shallot, garlic, and ½ teaspoon salt. Cook uncovered, stirring often, until the fennel begins to soften, 4 to 5 minutes. Add the wine, saffron, and lemon zest. Place the fish fillets on top of the fennel mixture and tuck the herb bundles between them. Reduce the heat to low and cover the pan tightly. Let the fish braise until it feels quite firm, 6 to 10 minutes, depending on its thickness. Once you slice the fish you'll be able to judge its exact degree of doneness, and you can put it back in the braising liquid and cook it longer if you need to.

4. Finishing. Transfer the fish to a cutting board. Let it rest for a few minutes, then cut it on a diagonal into ½-inch-thick slices. Arrange the slices on a warmed serving platter or individual plates. Boil the fennel braising liquid over high heat for several minutes to concentrate the flavors. Remove the lemon thyme bundles. Taste and add the lemon juice and additional salt and pepper if needed, then spoon the sauce around the fish. Serve immediately.

HERB SUBSTITUTION
- *In place of the lemon thyme bundles, make 2 herb bundles, each with 4 3-inch sprigs fresh English thyme, 1 3-inch sprig fresh sage, and 1 bay laurel leaf.*

POACHED SALMON FILLETS WITH TARRAGON SAUCE

4 servings

When salmon is poached very gently and not overcooked, it has a wonderfully tender texture. Most often court bouillon—a simple vegetable stock with white wine or vinegar—is used as the poaching liquid. My poaching liquid is closer to a tisane, or herb tea, and infuses the fish with a very subtle herbal flavor as it cooks. I make the tisane by steeping several kinds of herbs in water, then I add the wine and salt. Once the fish has been poached in this liquid, it becomes fish stock. Don't throw it out. Cool it down and freeze it to use later in a fish chowder, stew, or sauce, or to use again the next time you poach fish.

Anise-flavored herbs are a perfect match to the rich flavor of salmon. That's why I like to serve a sauce loaded with fresh tarragon with the poached fish. It's a brilliant green and looks gorgeous next to the salmon.

POACHING LIQUID

3 cups water

3 sprigs fresh parsley

2 4-inch sprigs fresh French tarragon

2 4-inch sprigs fresh lovage, or 1 rib celery, coarsely chopped

1 bay laurel leaf, fresh or dried

¾ cup of dry white wine, such as Sauvignon Blanc or Pinot Gris

½ teaspoon salt

2 pounds skinless salmon fillet, wild king if possible (1 inch thick)

SAUCE

4 tablespoons unsalted butter, at room temperature

1 small shallot, finely chopped (about 3 tablespoons)

¼ cup dry white wine

⅓ cup fresh French tarragon leaves

2 tablespoons coarsely chopped fresh parsley

2 teaspoons freshly squeezed lemon juice

¼ teaspoon salt

Freshly ground white pepper

Garnish: 1 tablespoon mixed very coarsely chopped fresh French tarragon
and parsley leaves

1. **Poaching liquid.** Bring the water to a boil in a wide 3-quart saucepan or deep 10-inch skillet. Add the parsley, tarragon, lovage, and bay leaf. Remove the pan from the heat, cover, and let it steep for about 10 minutes. Add the white wine and salt.

2. **Salmon.** While the herbs are steeping, prepare the salmon. Using a pair of fish tweezers or needle-nose pliers, remove the pin bones, the line of thin bones that run in a row through the front two-thirds of the fish. Cut away any gray fat that was next to the skin. Cut the fish into 4 equal pieces.

3. **Beginning the sauce.** Melt 1 tablespoon of the butter in a small (1-quart) saucepan over medium-low heat. Add the shallot and cook until softened but not browned, less than 1 minute. Add the wine and gently boil uncovered until all of the liquid is evaporated and the shallot makes sizzling noises. Remove from the heat and set aside.

4. **Poaching the salmon.** Return the poaching liquid to a simmer. Slide in the fish fillets and turn the heat to very low. The poaching liquid should just cover them. If it doesn't, add more water. Cook the fish very gently, below the simmering point, uncovered, until just barely translucent at the center, 8 to 10 minutes. Lift the pieces of fish from the liquid with a slotted spatula and carefully transfer them to warmed serving plates. Blot up any poaching liquid that collects on the plates with a paper towel.

5. **Finishing the sauce.** While the fish is poaching, warm the container of an electric blender by filling it with hot tap water and then emptying it. (If you don't have a blender, you can use a food processor or immersion blender, but the sauce will not be as smooth.) Put the tarragon and parsley in the blender and set it aside. Ladle ¼ cup of the fish poaching liquid into the saucepan with the shallot mixture and bring it to a simmer over medium heat. Rapidly whisk in the remaining 3 tablespoons butter, 1 tablespoon at a time, allowing each addition to melt before adding the next. Add the lemon juice and salt and continue to whisk the sauce over heat until it comes to a boil. Immediately pour the sauce over the herbs in the blender and blend on high speed until it is smooth and bright green, at least 30 seconds. Taste and season with white pepper, and additional salt if needed. Pour the sauce around the salmon fillets. Casually garnish each plate with a light sprinkle of the coarsely chopped herb leaves.

 HERB SUBSTITUTIONS
- *In place of the tarragon in the sauce, use ½ cup (gently packed) fresh chervil leaves or ½ cup (gently packed) shredded sorrel leaves, stems and veins removed.*

Striped Bass Steamed with Lemon Verbena and Cilantro

2 main-course or 4 first-course servings

In this recipe, a whole fish is cooked in an Asian style. The fish is slashed, and an herb paste is stuffed into the slashes, almost to the bone. The fish is then set on a plate and placed in a steamer, and in the steaming process an aromatic broth collects on the plate. My paste consists of lemon verbena, cilantro, and green onion. Lemon verbena is not an Asian herb, but it's used here in place of lemon grass. It offers a similar citrus intensity, and its supple leaves are easier to grind into a paste than tough lemon grass.

Asian cooks traditionally prepare this type of dish in a very large bamboo steamer set over a wok, but the bamboo steamers seen in most American kitchens are not large enough to accommodate a 2-pound fish with its head and tail. I improvise a steamer with a covered turkey roaster and set 2 or 3 ovenproof ramekins or custard cups in the bottom of the pan to serve as a rack.

HERB PASTE

⅓ cup (gently packed) fresh lemon verbena leaves, tough central veins removed

¾ cup (gently packed) fresh cilantro leaves

2 green onions, white and green parts, coarsely chopped

½ teaspoon salt

¼ small jalapeño pepper, seeded

1 2-pound striped bass, cleaned and scaled with head and tail left on, or other whole mild-tasting fish, such as sea bass, red snapper, or Pacific rockfish

Steamed rice

1. Herb paste. Pulse all the ingredients for the herb paste in a food processor until they are finely chopped but not completely smooth.

2. Setting up the steamer. Choose a large covered turkey roaster, or another large deep roasting pan or kettle, and a heatproof oval platter that is big enough to accommodate the fish but fits comfortably inside the pan. Place 2 or 3 heatproof ramekins or custard cups of equal height on the bottom of the pan for the platter to sit on. Fill the pan and the cups with 1 inch water.

3. Stuffing the fish. Rinse the fish inside and out and pat dry with paper towels. Cut 3 diagonal slits almost down to the bone on one side of the fish, then cut 3 slits slanted at right angles to the first ones, like a tic-tac-toe grid. Cut slits in the other side of the fish in the same way. Put the fish on the heatproof platter. Using your fingers, work the herb paste into the slashes on both sides, allowing the excess to spread out over the skin of the fish.

4. Cooking the fish. Place the steamer setup over high heat, straddling 2 burners if the pan is big enough and bring the water to a boil. Set the platter on top of the ramekins and cover the pan tightly with a lid or a large piece of heavy-duty aluminum foil tucked tightly over the rim. Steam for 15 to 20 minutes. It's easy to see if the fish is cooked through by uncovering the pan and peeking inside the slashes of the fish. The flesh should lift from the bone easily and there should be no sign of translucence. Put scoops of rice in warmed shallow serving bowls. To serve the fish, use a small slotted spatula or a spoon and a fork to separate and lift the fish flesh from the frame. When the top fillet is served, lift the tail and the entire fish frame should lift up with it, exposing the bottom fillet. Serve the fish on top of the rice and spoon the broth from the platter over it.

 HERB SUBSTITUTIONS
- *If fresh lemon verbena is not available, substitute an equal amount of fresh spearmint or lemon balm.*

Fish Fillets Steamed in Lettuce Leaves with Lemon-Dill Sauce

4 servings

In this recipe, fish fillets are nestled in between leaves of tender lettuce with fresh dill, then steamed over an aromatic fresh mint tea. Napped with a buttery sauce of lemon and more dill, this elegant dish is not about bold flavors—it's about subtlety, the taste of the fish, and the flavors of spring.

1½ to 2 pounds skinless delicate or medium-firm fish fillet, such as
*   halibut, salmon, rockfish, or sea bass*
Salt and freshly ground white pepper
1 large head Bibb lettuce
¼ cup very coarsely chopped fresh dill
6 4-inch sprigs fresh spearmint

SAUCE
4 tablespoons unsalted butter
1 small shallot, finely chopped (about 3 tablespoons)
½ teaspoon grated lemon zest
2 tablespoons freshly squeezed lemon juice
¼ cup coarsely chopped fresh dill
¼ teaspoon salt
Freshly ground white pepper

Garnish: Dill flowers or small dill sprigs

1. **Wrapping the fish.** Check the fish for any stray bones and cut off any dark flesh that was next to the skin. Cut the fillet into 4 equal pieces (square shapes will be easier to wrap than long rectangular pieces). Season both sides of the fish lightly with salt and pepper. Separate the large outer leaves from the head of lettuce, without tearing them. Place a leaf cupped side up and center a piece of fish in the middle of the leaf (use two leaves side by side if necessary). Sprinkle the fish with 1 tablespoon of the dill. Top with another one or two lettuce leaves, this time cupped side down, so that the fillet is completely enclosed in lettuce. Wrap the remaining fillets in lettuce, sprinkling each one with dill, and arrange them, without crowding, in a steamer rack or basket.

2. Steaming the fish. Bring several inches of water to a boil in the bottom of a steamer. Drop in the mint sprigs, put the steamer rack or basket in place, cover, and steam the fish 8 minutes for each inch of thickness (for instance, if the fish is ¾ inch thick, steam it 6 minutes). Turn off the heat, uncover the steamer, and let the fish rest for 1 to 2 minutes. To check for doneness, carefully lift the top leaf from one of the packets and peek inside the fillet. If it is still translucent in the center, cover and steam for 1 to 2 minutes more.

3. The sauce. While the fish is steaming, make the sauce. Melt 1 tablespoon of the butter in a small (1-quart) saucepan or 6-inch skillet over medium-low heat. Add the shallot and cook, stirring, until it is softened but not browned, about 1 minute. Add the lemon zest and juice and bring the mixture to a simmer. Vigorously whisk in the remaining butter, 1 tablespoon at a time, allowing each addition to melt before adding the next. The sauce should be slightly thickened and the butter emulsified. Stir in the dill and season with the salt and pepper to taste. If you are not ready to serve the sauce, set the saucepan in a larger pan filled with an inch of simmering water.

4. Finishing. Carefully transfer the fish packets to warm serving plates. Pour the sauce over and around the fish and garnish with the dill flowers. Serve with Young Carrots with Tarragon (page 126) or Snap Peas with Mint and Chervil (page 125).

VARIATION

Instead of the dill sauce, serve the steamed wrapped fish with the carrot sauce on page 188.

HERB SUBSTITUTIONS
- *In place of the dill, use an equal amount of coarsely chopped basil, cilantro, or chervil, or one-third as much tarragon.*

GRILLED FISH WITH HERB SALAD

4 servings

   A salad of tiny fresh herb leaves tossed with chive oil and marinated shallots makes a lovely full-flavored stand-in for a sauce or chutney. This effortless dish requires little more than a bowl and a grill.

> *2 medium shallots, peeled*
> *2 tablespoons sherry vinegar, or champagne vinegar*
> *Thinly sliced zest of 1 lemon (removed with a zester)*
> *1½ to 2 pounds medium-firm fish fillet, such as halibut, snapper, salmon, or sea bass, with or without skin*
> *5 tablespoons Chive Oil (page 337), or ¼ cup fruity extra-virgin olive oil mixed with 2 tablespoons very finely chopped fresh chives*
> *Kosher salt*
> *Freshly ground black pepper*
>
> HERB SALAD
> *¼ cup fresh small spearmint leaves*
> *¼ cup fresh French tarragon leaves*
> *¼ cup fresh flat-leaf parsley leaves*
> *½ cup watercress leaves*
> *¼ cup torn sorrel leaves, or additional watercress*
> *Optional: 8 to 12 nasturtium flowers*

1. Shallots. Cut the shallots in half from root to tip and remove the dense core at the base with a small V-shaped cut. Very thinly slice the shallots, again from root to tip, using a sharp thin knife or a mandoline. Toss the shallots with the vinegar and lemon zest and let sit at room temperature for at least 30 minutes to soften and mellow.

2. Fish. Build a hot fire in a charcoal grill or preheat a gas grill on high. Make sure your grill rack is very clean and lightly oiled. Check for and remove any bones in the fish and cut it into 4 equal pieces. Place the fish in a shallow bowl with 2 tablespoons of the chive oil, ½ teaspoon salt, and a few grinds of pepper. Turn the fish to coat each piece evenly.

3. Finishing the salad. Stir 2 tablespoons of the remaining chive oil into the shallots. Add the herb leaves, nasturtiums if using (inspect first for insects), a large pinch of salt, and a few grinds of pepper; toss gently.

4. Grilling the fish. When the coals are ashed over and glowing or the gas grill is very hot, grill the fish 4 inches from the coals until the bottom is well marked, 3 to 5 minutes. Turn the fish and grill it on the other side until the fish is barely translucent at the inside center, 3 to 4 minutes longer. Transfer the fish to warmed dinner plates. Loosely arrange the herb salad in a band across the fish and drizzle the remaining chive oil on the plates.

Herb-Skewered Swordfish

4 servings

Swordfish has a unique and robust flavor that blends deliciously with astringent tough-leafed herbs. Here chunks of the fish are skewered on rosemary branches in between bay leaves, which flavors them from inside out. If fresh bay laurel is not available, do not use dried or California bay leaves. Fresh sage leaves are an excellent substitute.

> *2 pounds swordfish, sliced 1 inch thick*
> *3 tablespoons extra-virgin olive oil*
> *3 cloves garlic, minced*
> *1 lemon*
> *8 fresh stiff rosemary branches, 8 to 9 inches long, or bamboo skewers*
> *24 fresh bay laurel leaves or large sage leaves*
> *Salt and freshly ground black pepper to taste*

1. Setting up. Start a medium fire in a charcoal grill with the clean grill rack positioned 4 inches from the coals, or preheat a gas grill to medium-high. Remove the skin from the swordfish and cut it into 32 equal pieces, about 1 inch square. Toss them in a mixing bowl with the olive oil and garlic. Cut 3 ¾-inch-thick slices from the lemon, then cut each slice into 8 wedges, yielding 24 pieces. Strip the needles off the rosemary branches, leaving some at the top for appearance, and cut the bottoms at a 45° angle so that you have a sharp point. If using bamboo skewers, soak them in hot water for 30 minutes to prevent them from burning.

2. Skewering the fish. Thread the fish, bay leaves, and lemon on the skewers in this order: lemon, fish, bay, fish, bay, lemon, fish, bay, fish, lemon. (The skewers can be assembled up to 8 hours ahead of time. Cover and refrigerate.)

3. Grilling. Season all sides of the skewers with salt and pepper. When the coals are ashed over and glowing, or the gas grill is preheated, arrange the skewers on the rack facing out so that the needles at the tops are not directly over the coals or gas jets. Grill for 2 to 3 minutes on each side until the fish is thoroughly cooked but still moist. Break open a piece of the fish to check it. Unlike tuna, swordfish should never be served rare. If the skewers begin to burn, move them away from the direct heat. Serve the skewers right away with Roasted Tomato and Herb Salsa (page 219) and Minted Orange and Red Onion Salad (page 57).

Whole Fish Grilled on Fennel Stalks

4 to 6 servings

From midsummer to midautumn, fennel towers over the herb garden with its bamboolike stalks that shoot 6 feet in the air. Around the Mediterranean, these stems are put to use as a bed on which to grill fish, and it's easy to do the same on your own backyard grill. Fish grilled on the bone is full of flavor to begin with, and the smoldering fennel infuses the meat with a mouthwatering smokiness that tastes subtly of anise. Cooking a whole fish directly on the grill is notoriously tricky because it often sticks or cooks unevenly, but the fennel stalks make it much easier by acting as a buffer between the fish and the coals. The fish won't stick to them, yet there's enough transfer of heat to achieve a nice crispy skin. The more leaves and seed heads that remain on the fennel stalks, the more smoke they create, and the stronger the smoke and fennel flavor will be on the fish. You can adjust it to your own taste by removing them.

1 to 2 6-foot fennel stalks with seed heads, or 3 to 4 3-foot stalks
1 4- to 6-pound or 2 2- to 3-pound whole fish, such as striped bass, sea
*   bass, rockfish, red snapper, coho or sockeye salmon, or steelhead,*
*   cleaned and scaled with head and tail left on*
1 tablespoon extra-virgin olive oil
Salt and freshly ground black pepper
Optional: lemon wedges and clarified butter

1. **Fennel bed.** Remove the rack from a kettle grill and start a medium charcoal fire in it. Use scissors to cut the fennel stalks into lengths slightly smaller than the width of the grill rack and place them side by side in a single layer on the rack to create a bed. Reserve 3 or 4 of the whole seed heads and distribute the rest over the stalks. Rinse the fish inside and out under cold water and pat dry with paper towels. Rub it with the olive oil and season all sides and the cavity generously with salt and pepper. Stuff the reserved seed heads in the cavity. Place the fish on top of the fennel stalks (the rack is still off the grill).

2. **Grilling the fish.** When all the charcoal is ashed over and the coals are glowing, carefully set the rack holding the fennel bed and the fish on the grill. Immediately cover the grill. Cook the fish covered for a total of 20 to 30 minutes for 2- to 3-pound

fish, or 35 to 50 minutes for a 4- to 6-pound fish, turning the fish over halfway through the cooking. The fish is done when the flesh under the head is easily lifted from the frame with a knife, and the fish is no longer translucent next to the bone. An instant-read thermometer inserted under the head and downward toward the tail should register 140°F. Carefully transfer the fish to a warmed platter and fillet it at the table. Serve with lemon wedges and clarified butter if desired.

NOTE
Since the racks on gas grills are usually made of several separate pieces, you can't first set up the fennel bed off the grill. Preheat the grill to medium with the racks in place, then quickly lay out the bed of fennel and place the fish on top. Cover the grill and proceed as directed for the charcoal grill.

HERB-SMOKED SALMON

It's an unwritten rule that every Northwest chef must have a signature salmon dish, and this is mine. I like this preparation so much that I sometimes have to force myself to cook salmon any other way. There are two types of smoked salmon. The first, cold-smoked salmon, is smoked in an environment that doesn't get hot enough to actually cook the fish. It's usually thinly sliced and served at room temperature. Lox is a type of cold-smoked salmon. The second type is hot-smoked salmon, which cooks as it is smoked, and that's the kind we're talking about here. To make it, individual portions of the fish are placed on a rack set over a stovetop smoking pan (I use a roasting pan), and dried herb twigs are used for the smoker's fuel. The pan is tented with aluminum foil and placed over high heat for only 4 to 5 minutes, then the heat is turned off and the fish continues to cook in the smoky chamber from the heat of the pan. Its finished texture is somewhere between a piece of salmon that's been grilled and one that's been slow roasted—tender and melting, but perfectly cooked. Herb twigs give off a much subtler smoke than hardwood chips, vaguely hinting at the flavor of the herb that the twigs come from. The mild smokiness gives the fish a deep savoriness without overwhelming its own flavor. Countless Northwesterners, who are jaded from a steady diet of salmon, have told me it's the best they've ever had.

Smoker

This stovetop smoking method requires only a roasting pan, wire rack, and aluminum foil. Any sort of metal pan of a medium weight with sides at least 2 inches deep will work, even a rectangular cake pan. Speckled enamel-coated roasters (granite ware) are common and work especially well. Since the smoking pan will blacken and might even warp, you will have to devote one solely to this purpose. If you don't have an old roasting pan lying around in your basement or dark corner of a cupboard, you can always find them at thrift stores or garage sales for a few dollars. I used the same roasting pan for all the smoking I did at the restaurant for 6 years. It started out as a flat shallow pan, but after about 500 uses it resembled a piece of wreckage from an auto accident. It became so badly warped it practically turned itself inside out, and the rack holding the food to be smoked had to precariously teeter on top of it. But it turned out perfectly smoked foods every time, and I was very reluctant to replace it. I finally did purchase another one that will never bend, a mighty commercial roasting pan, girded with metal straps for reinforcement, but I kept the old one for good luck.

When you have your smoking pan, find a sturdy wire rack that is just large enough to sit on top of the rim instead of falling in. A sturdy cake-cooling rack will work well. The smoking process should not damage the rack—it will just need a good scrubbing when you're done with it.

Fuel

Certain herbs are more successful in the smoker than others. One of the best choices is basil wood. When burned, dried basil stems give off an aromatic smoke with almost no hint of resin. It might seem odd that a soft herb like basil could produce a stem that's woody enough to smoke with, but the branches of the mature plants become quite tough and thick at the end of the season. Fennel stalks are another excellent choice. Also free of any tarry qualities, the smoke from fennel imparts a seductive but very understated anise flavor. Or try lemon verbena stems. They produce a pleasant smelling smoke that will give the fish a very subtle citrus flavor. Lemon thyme, tarragon, and thick mint stems work well also. Thyme, lavender, and sage stems have some resin, though they can still be used, but the herb to stay away from is rosemary. Lamb or beef might be able to stand up to it, but rosemary imparts a pitchy, resinous taste that overpowers fish.

Herb stems can be dried at any time of the year. If you want to harvest a large quantity, it's best to gather them at the end of the season when most of the foliage has died and the stems are hardened. For basil, fennel, and lemon verbena—my favorites for smoking—cut the plants down near ground level (but don't cut your lemon verbena back this far if you want it to live till next season) and shake off any loose leaves. Tie the plant material in small bundles and hang it upside down in an airy dark place like an attic, garage, or shed. In a week or two it will be dry enough for smoking. When you're ready to use the branches, shake or strip off as many leaves as you can and then clip the branches with a pair of hand pruners into 1-inch pieces. A few leaves mixed in with stems won't hurt, but if there are many, they burn very fast and give off an overpowering smoke.

If you don't have an herb garden and have to buy fresh herbs at the market, you can still collect material for the smoker. Every time you use fresh herbs with tough stems, like thyme, sage, oregano, basil, tarragon, or savory (but not rosemary), instead of throwing the stems out, toss them into a shallow box to dry out. Pretty soon you'll have more than enough to prepare this recipe many times.

If you want to prepare this recipe right away and have no stems, you can sometimes buy dried bunches of herbs on their stems in herb shops or specialty food stores. Strip the leaves off and store them in a jar, then smoke the fish with the stems. Or you can simply substitute the wood chips that are widely available for home smokers, such as apple wood or alder.

Brining and Drying

Before the salmon is ready for the smoker, it needs to be soaked in brine and then dried. I use a relatively mild brine (a salt solution) sweetened with sugar and infused with fennel seeds and fresh herbs. It accomplishes several things. First, it flavors the fish not only with saltiness and sweetness but also quite distinctly with the herbs that you add to it. Second, it firms the fish and makes it especially moist and succulent because the fish actually absorbs some of the liquid brine. And finally, the small amount of sugar that remains on the surface enables a better skin to form on the fish in the next step, the drying. Don't let the fish soak in the brine for too long or it will become overly salty—2 hours is just right.

The drying step might seem to be a lot of trouble, but it makes an enormous difference in the final result. The fish needs to develop what is called a pellicle, or thin dry skin. It enables it to pick up a better smoke flavor, while it seals the fat and moisture within the fillet. As odd as it may sound, the best way to achieve this skin is to prop the rack of fish in front of an ordinary household electric fan set on high speed. After about 1 hour the pieces of fish will feel dry to the touch, with no stickiness, very much like the skin between your thumb and index finger (to an almost unsettling degree). Alternatively you can allow the fish to sit on the rack overnight in the refrigerator, uncovered. If you allow this pellicle to develop properly, the fish will have a beautiful sheen when it comes out of the smoker. If you don't dry it properly, it will seep bits of white protein (albumen) as seen on a baked salmon fillet.

This is an excellent dish to prepare for a large dinner party. Depending on the size of your roasting pan and rack, you could probably accommodate at least 12 portions of fish. You can smoke the salmon early in the day or even the day before, cover it on the rack, and store it in the refrigerator. Bring it to room temperature before giving it its final baking. Unlike ordinary cooked fish, it reheats beautifully.

HERB-SMOKED SALMON

6 servings

BRINE

4 cups water
3 tablespoons salt
¼ cup sugar
4 2-inch sprigs fresh thyme
1 tablespoon dried whole fennel seeds
1 bay laurel leaf, fresh or dried

*2 to 2½ pounds very fresh skinless salmon fillet, such as king, sockeye, or
Atlantic*
*2 ounces dried herb twigs or stems, such as basil, lemon verbena, thyme,
and/or fennel, cut into 1-inch pieces (about 4 cups)*

1. Brine. Bring the water, salt, sugar, thyme, fennel seeds, and bay to a boil in a medium (2-quart) saucepan. Remove the pan from the heat and let cool. Pour the brine into a medium mixing bowl or 1-gallon plastic storage container and refrigerate until thoroughly chilled.

2. Cutting the salmon. Feel along the fish for the pin bones, the line of small soft bones that runs along the front two-thirds of the fish and remove them with a pair of fish tweezers or needle-nose pliers. Using a sharp thin knife, cut off the thin layer of gray fat that lies next to the skin. Cut the fish into 6 equal pieces. If your salmon fillet is very wide (over 6 inches) cut it lengthwise in half first, down the center of the fillet, then cut each half into thirds. Place the fish in the cold brine and refrigerate it for 2 hours, no more than that or it will become salty.

3. Drying the fish. Drain the brine from the fish. Cover the fish fillets with fresh cold water and swish them gently to remove excess salt. Drain again. Lightly brush your smoking rack with oil. Dry the fillets by patting them between a double thickness of paper towels. Place the pieces of fish on the rack with the side that had skin facing down, spacing them so that they don't touch. Put the rack on a baking sheet and prop up one side with an object 3 to 4 inches high, like a box or a plastic storage container, so that the rack rests at a 30° angle. Point an electric fan (make sure all the blades are clean) at the fish about 12 inches away and turn it on high. Leave the fan on until the fish forms a skin and feels dry to the touch, 45 to 60 minutes depending on the strength of the fan and the humidity of the room. Alternatively you can let the fish sit on its rack uncovered in your refrigerator for about 8 hours or overnight, but it will not achieve as dry a skin and, therefore, not smoke as beautifully.

4. Smoking. Place the dry herb stems in the bottom of the roasting pan, concentrating them near the middle. If the roasting pan is large enough to straddle 2 burners of your stove, concentrate the stems in 2 piles above where the burners will be. Place the rack of fish on top of the pan. The dried stems should not touch the rack. Tear off a piece of wide heavy-duty aluminum foil that is about 12 inches longer than the pan. If your pan is very wide, attach 2 pieces together by folding a seam. Brush the foil lightly with oil or spray it with vegetable oil cooking spray. Turn the foil oiled side down and, keeping it several inches above the fish, place it over the smoking setup to form a tent. Tightly tuck all the edges of the foil under the rim of the pan. Using the tip of a paring knife, make a small slit in the top of the foil. If using a gas stove, place the pan over a large burner or over 2 burners and turn them on high. If you have an electric stove, preheat the burner(s) on high until they are red-hot before placing the pan on top. Set a timer for 4 minutes. When the time is up, you should start to see a steady stream of smoke escaping from the slit at the top; if you don't, leave it on the heat another minute or two. Turn off the heat and let the pan sit for 30 minutes, without opening the foil tent or even peeking, to allow the fish to continue smoking.

5. Opening the smoker. Remove the aluminum foil and transfer the smoking rack of fish to a baking sheet. Examine the fish. Because there are many variables, like the thickness of the fish, the heat of your stove, and the type of roasting pan, the fish can be anywhere from rare and still soft to nearly fully cooked and firm. It will come out fine in the end in either case because you can adjust the timing of the final baking. At this point you have 3 options: You can bake the fish right away, or let the pan sit at room temperature for up to 1 hour, or wrap the pan with plastic wrap and refrigerate it for up to 1 day. Let it warm at room temperature for 1 hour before the final baking.

6. Final baking. Preheat the oven to 400°F. Place the fish (still on the smoking rack on top of the baking sheet) in the oven. Bake the fish anywhere from 3 minutes if it just came from the smoker and is fully cooked, to 12 minutes if it is cool and rare. To tell if the fish is baked enough, lift a piece and gently bend it backward until it cracks open enough that you can peek inside. It should have just a faint bit of translucence in the center and be very moist but cooked through. If it has the texture of lox, it needs more time in the oven. Serve the fish hot as a main course with one of the following sauces or accompaniments.

ACCOMPANIMENTS
- *Serve with Carrot-Marjoram Sauce or the beet variation (page 188).*
- *Serve with Lemon-Dill Sauce (page 174).*

- *Serve with any Blended Herb and Butter Sauce (page 324).*
- *Serve over a bed of Minted French Lentils (page 152).*
- *Serve with herb salad and chive oil as directed for Grilled Fish with Herb Salad (page 176).*
- *Serve with the perilla salad that accompanies the Herb and Peppercorn-Crusted Tuna (page 166).*

VARIATION

Use sturgeon or black cod (sablefish) fillet in place of the salmon.

ROASTED SHRIMP WITH MARJORAM

3 to 4 main-course or 8 tapas servings

If you get hold of big beautiful shrimp, especially fresh spot shrimp from the cold waters of the Pacific, one of the tastiest ways to prepare them is also one of the simplest. Here, large shrimp are tossed with garlic, oil, lemon, and marjoram and quickly roasted in their shells, which is like cooking meat or fish on the bone—it adds an enormous amount of flavor. You can make a meal of these shrimp with crusty bread and a salad or serve them as a tapas dish with cocktails. To eat them, you must dig in with your fingers and peel them as you go.

> *1½ pounds large shrimp in the shell (18 to 30), fresh spot shrimp if possible*
> *3 tablespoons extra-virgin olive oil*
> *1 tablespoon coarsely chopped fresh marjoram*
> *½ teaspoon finely chopped lemon zest*
> *2 teaspoons freshly squeezed lemon juice*
> *2 cloves garlic, finely chopped*
> *¼ teaspoon salt*
> *Freshly ground black pepper to taste*

1. Cleaning the shrimp. Preheat the oven to 425°F. Using scissors and beginning at the head end, split the shrimp along their backs, through the shells, and two-thirds of the way into the flesh (as if deveining a shrimp but cutting through the shell and a little deeper into the flesh). The shrimp should still remain in one piece. Remove the black vein, using the tip of a paring knife.

2. Roasting. Put the shrimp in a mixing bowl, add the remaining ingredients, and toss to coat them evenly. Lay the shrimp split side up in a single layer on a baking sheet. (At this point, the shrimp can be covered and refrigerated for up to 4 hours.) Roast until the shells turn pink and the flesh is no longer translucent, 3 to 5 minutes. Don't overcook. Serve the shrimp hot or warm in their shells.

 HERB SUBSTITUTIONS
  • *In place of marjoram, use 2 teaspoons coarsely chopped English or lemon thyme or rosemary.*

Seared Sea Scallops with Carrot-Marjoram Sauce

4 servings

This is my most requested recipe. People are always amazed that a sauce so colorful and tasty can come from such an ordinary vegetable. It has a stunning orange color and rich sweet-sour flavor that complements a wide range of seafood, but I especially like this sauce against the delicate sweetness of sea scallops. You make it by reducing fresh carrot juice with white wine, shallots, and lemon juice, then whisking in butter. After this basic sauce is made, a small bunch of marjoram sprigs, stems and all, steeps in the hot sauce. This method of infusing the herb is a very quick and easy way to give the finished sauce a subtle but forward herb flavor without changing its color or texture.

The seared sea scallops themselves are no trouble to prepare once you get the knack of working quickly over high heat. Use a heavy skillet and wait until it's very hot before the scallops go in the pan. Brown the scallops well on both sides, then let them rest briefly on a warmed platter. At that point they should be perfectly cooked, meaning heated through but still tender and moist.

Although fresh sea scallops are a first choice, previously frozen sea scallops can also be excellent if they have not been treated with phosphates, which acts as a preservative and causes them to absorb water. When you try to sear treated scallops, some of the water oozes and they stew in their juices instead of browning in the dry pan. Furthermore, treated scallops lack the fresh, sweet, and briny sea flavor of dry-packed scallops. If the sea scallops you see in the store are uniformly pure white, they are most likely treated. Untreated scallops are also called dry-pack scallops, and they range in color from off-white to light orange pink.

You can buy fresh carrot juice in a market or juice bar, or you can make it at home if you have a vegetable juicer.

SAUCE

2 cups fresh carrot juice
½ cup dry white wine or dry vermouth
3 tablespoons freshly squeezed lemon juice
1 medium shallot, finely chopped (about ⅓ cup)
¼ teaspoon salt
4 tablespoons unsalted butter, at room temperature, cut into 8 pieces
8 3-inch sprigs fresh marjoram, tied together with kitchen twine

1 ½ pounds large sea scallops (about 12 to 16), untreated (dry-pack)
Salt and freshly ground black pepper to taste
2 tablespoons vegetable or olive oil

1. **Carrot reduction.** Combine the carrot juice, ¼ cup of the white wine, the lemon juice, shallot, and salt in a medium (3-quart) saucepan. Bring to a boil over high heat. Reduce the heat just enough to maintain a steady boil and cook the mixture until only about ½ cup liquid remains and the sauce is slightly thickened, about the same consistency as pulpy orange juice. Allow 20 to 30 minutes for this process. (This reduction can be made several hours ahead and left to sit beside the stove, or up to 2 days ahead if covered and stored in the refrigerator.)

2. **Adding butter and infusing.** Reduce the heat so that the sauce very gently simmers and whisk in the butter 1 piece at a time, waiting until each piece is melted and incorporated before adding another. The sauce should be thickened enough to lightly coat the back of a spoon. Return the sauce to a simmer, whisking constantly. Drop in and submerge the bundle of marjoram and remove the pan from heat. Let the herbs infuse the sauce while you're cooking the scallops.

3. **Searing the scallops.** Preheat the oven to 175°F. Turn off the oven and put in a platter to warm. If the scallops have a small, loosely attached, rectangular piece of white muscle on their sides, pull it off and discard it. Pat the scallops dry with paper towels and season all sides lightly with salt and pepper. Heat the oil in a large (12-inch) heavy-bottomed sauté pan over high heat until it is very hot and smoking. Using tongs, carefully place the scallops flat side down in the pan. Let the scallops cook undisturbed until they are a deep golden brown, 2 to 3 minutes. Turn and cook until the other side is browned, 1 to 2 minutes. Transfer the scallops to the warmed platter and put them in the oven (turned off) to stay warm while you finish the sauce. Reduce the heat to medium and pour in the remaining ¼ cup wine. Scrape up the browned bits, then add the liquid to the carrot mixture.

4. **Finishing.** Remove the marjoram bundle from the carrot sauce, squeeze it dry, and discard. Reheat the sauce over medium heat, whisking constantly. Taste and season with pepper and additional salt if needed. For an utterly smooth texture, pass the sauce through a very fine strainer. If you have any problem with the sauce separating or the butter coming to the surface in droplets, blend it with an immersion blender or transfer the sauce to the warmed container of a blender and whiz it for a few seconds. Divide the scallops among warmed dinner plates and pour the carrot sauce around them. If you wish, you can put the scallops on a bed of sautéed fresh

spinach or other greens or on a small mound of herb salad (page 176), then pour the sauce around them.

(page 176)

VARIATION
SEARED SEA SCALLOPS WITH BEET SAUCE
Substitute an equal amount of beet juice for the carrot juice. The sauce will be a glistening deep garnet color and have a fabulous sweet-tart flavor. Fresh beet juice is harder to find than carrot, so you will probably need to juice the beets yourself. Because beet juice becomes syrupy as it reduces, boil the reduction to just ¾ cup instead of ½ cup. If the sauce seems too sweet, add a little more lemon juice.

 HERB SUBSTITUTIONS
- *For the marjoram, substitute an equal amount of fresh French tarragon or fresh lemon thyme sprigs or 2 3-inch sprigs fresh lovage.*

STEAMED MUSSELS WITH ROSEMARY AND ROASTED GARLIC SABAYON

4 light-supper or first-course servings

A sabayon is a wine custard, usually served as dessert, made by whisking egg yolks, wine, and sugar in a bowl over heat until it turns airy, thick, and voluminous. The Italians make it with Marsala or vin santo and call it zabaglione. The same method, without the sugar of course, is used here to make a sauce for mussels. Sprigs of fresh rosemary are steamed with mussels and wine, and the liquor that collects in the pot carries their fragrance and flavor. Whisk egg yolks and roasted garlic into this nectar, whip it in the top of a double boiler, and you end up with a heavenly savory sabayon that enrobes the mussels and begs to be mopped up with crusty bread. This dish takes about 10 minutes to prepare.

> *5 large egg yolks*
> *1½ tablespoons Roasted Garlic Paste (page 341)*
> *2 pounds fresh live mussels, washed and beards removed*
> *½ cup dry white wine*
> *4 3-inch sprigs fresh rosemary*
> *3 tablespoons freshly squeezed lemon juice*
> *½ teaspoon salt*
> *Freshly ground black pepper*

1. Setting up. Create a double boiler by resting a medium-size stainless-steel mixing bowl (10 to 12 inches across at the top) on top of a large (6-quart) pot filled with about 2 inches water. The top of the bowl can extend beyond the rim of the pot, but the bottom of the bowl must not touch the water. Put the pot (without the bowl) over medium heat and bring the water to a boil. Whisk the egg yolks and roasted garlic together in the bowl and set it aside.

2. Steaming the mussels. Put the mussels in another large (6- to 8-quart) pot, add the wine and rosemary, and cover tightly. Place it over high heat and cook just until the mussels are steamed open, about 5 minutes. Remove the pan from the heat.

3. Straining the liquor. Set a fine strainer over a medium bowl. Pour the mussel liquor from the pot of mussels through the strainer into the bowl, holding the mussels back with the lid of the pan. Cover the pan of mussels with the lid and set it aside on the back of the stove.

4. Sabayon. Whisk the strained mussel liquor into the egg yolk mixture along with the lemon juice and salt. Set the bowl on top of the pot of boiling water. Whisk vigorously until the mixture is frothy and thickened and there is no trace of liquid at the bottom of the bowl, about 3 minutes. You don't have to worry about overcooking as long as do you not stop whisking. (You can use a handheld electric mixer if you wish.) When cooked enough, the sauce should register 160° to 180°F on an instant-read thermometer and heavily coat a spoon. Remove the bowl from the boiling water. Taste the sabayon and season it generously with pepper, and additional salt if needed.

5. Serving. Arrange the mussels, facing up in concentric circles, in 4 warmed serving bowls. Spoon the sabayon on top, dividing it evenly among the bowls. Serve immediately with crusty French bread.

VARIATION
Substitute 3 pounds small live Manila or littleneck clams for the mussels.

HERB SUBSTITUTIONS
- *In place of rosemary, use an equal amount of fresh marjoram or lemon thyme sprigs.*

The Herbfarm Garden Salad (page 45)
and Herbed Focaccia (page 234)

1

*Roasted Asparagus Salad
with Fried Sage (page 54)*

2

*Baked Mussels Stuffed with
Mint Pesto (page 82)*

Individual Crab and Lemon Thyme Soufflé with Chervil Sauce (page 92)

Fusilli Carbonara with
Fines Herbes (page 106)

5

*Grilled Halibut with
Herb Salad (page 176)*

6

Bay Laurel Roasted Chicken (page 196)

7

Lemon Verbena Ice Cream (page 258),
Candied Lemon Verbena Leaves (page 313),
and Lavender Shortbread (page 288)

THIRTY-MINUTE SEAFOOD STEW WITH LOADS OF HERBS

6 servings

There are countless versions of seafood stew from around the world, all based on the catch from local waters. This version from Seattle uses what's best in this area—fresh clams, mussels, spot shrimp, and halibut—but it's easy to re-create anywhere you have access to good seafood. This stew is colorful, brimming with green herbs, and quick to prepare once the ingredients are ready.

> 2 medium leeks (about 1½ pounds)
> ¼ cup extra-virgin olive oil
> 2 bell peppers, red, yellow, orange, or combination, seeded and sliced
>   into ⅜-inch-thick strips
> 6 cloves garlic, finely chopped
> 2 teaspoons coarsely chopped fresh fennel seeds (page 395) or coarsely
>   chopped fresh English thyme
> ½ teaspoon dried red pepper flakes
> 2 pounds vine-ripened tomatoes, peeled, seeded, and chopped (about
>   3 cups)
> 1 cup dry white wine
> 1 teaspoon salt
> 2 pounds small live clams, purged (page 37)
> 1 pound live mussels, washed and beards removed
> 1 pound large shrimp (16 to 20), fresh spot shrimp if possible, peeled and
>   deveined
> 1 pound white-fleshed fish fillet, such as halibut or halibut cheeks, red
>   snapper, or true cod, cut into ¾-inch pieces
> Optional: 1 cup small orange or yellow cherry tomatoes, halved
> 2 tablespoons coarsely chopped fresh marjoram
> 1 cup (gently packed) coarsely chopped fresh flat-leaf parsley
> 2 cups (gently packed) torn fresh basil leaves
> Freshly ground black pepper

1. Vegetable base. Cut off and discard the tops of the leeks at the point they turn from light to dark green. Split the bottom portion lengthwise in half, keeping the roots attached so that the layers will not fall apart. Rinse the leeks thoroughly. Cut the leeks into 3-inch lengths, discarding the roots, then slice each section into ⅛-inch-thick matchsticks. Heat the oil in a large (8-quart) Dutch oven over medium heat. Add the leeks, bell peppers, garlic, fennel seeds, and red pepper flakes; cook, stirring often, until the vegetables are softened but not browned, 5 to 7 minutes. Stir in the chopped tomatoes, wine, and salt. Increase the heat to medium-high and gently boil the mixture for 5 minutes.

2. Adding the seafood. Add the clams and mussels to the pot, cover tightly, and cook until the shellfish open. Discard any clams or mussels that stay tightly shut. Gently stir in the shrimp and fish chunks and cover again. Reduce the heat to medium-low and cook until the fish is no longer translucent and the shrimp is opaque and firm but not curled into a tight circle. Stir in the cherry tomatoes if using, the marjoram, parsley, and basil. Taste and season with black pepper, and additional salt if needed. Serve right away in warmed shallow bowls, accompanied with crusty French bread.

CHAPTER 7

Poultry and Meat

Even if I were not an herb zealot, I would be hard-pressed to prepare a grilled leg of lamb, a roasted pork loin, or a kettle of braised chicken without using a sprig of rosemary, some leaves of sage, or a sprinkle of thyme. Meats and poultry receive herbal flavors graciously. Grilled or roasted at high heat, they welcome bold quantities of assertive herbs. In a long-simmered braise, they slowly absorb the herbs all the while, creating a deeply flavored sauce. And when quickly sautéed, meats pair elegantly with lively herbs like tarragon, mint, and cilantro. You can coat the outside of meat with herb rubs and crusts, soak meat in herb-infused brines or marinades, stuff it with herb leaves, braise it with bouquets garnis, shower it with chopped leaves, or serve it with an herbal sauce or condiment like a chutney or relish. The recipes in this chapter illustrate all these techniques in dishes that range from 10-minute chicken breasts to long-simmered lamb shanks.

BAY LAUREL ROASTED CHICKEN

4 servings

For an informal dinner, there's no more satisfying dish than a perfectly roasted chicken, and this version, saturated with the aroma of fresh bay laurel, is incomparable. The bay leaves along with slivers of garlic are stuffed under the skin of the chicken, and as their sweet complex flavors permeate the flesh, they create a little air space that allows the skin to become especially crispy. Because the leaves have a sharp and tough texture, they are used to flavor the meat but are then removed.

Dried bay leaves are fine for stocks, stews, and braises, but not for this dish. They taste overly strong and lack the sweet and floral characteristics that give this chicken sensational flavor. If fresh bay is unavailable, an equal amount of English or lemon thyme, marjoram, or sage leaves can take its place, with different but still exciting results.

One caveat—the chicken is roasted at a very high heat and will create a considerable amount of smoke. If you don't have a good exhaust fan above your range, be sure your kitchen is well ventilated while the bird is roasting.

> *1 3½- to 4-pound chicken, preferably free-range*
> *12 fresh bay laurel leaves (not California bay or dried bay leaves)*
> *2 cloves garlic*
> *1½ tablespoons extra-virgin olive oil*
> *Salt and freshly ground black pepper*
> *½ cup dry white wine*

1. **Chicken.** Preheat the oven to 450°F. Remove the giblets and any excess fat from the chicken cavity. Wash it inside and out under cold water and pat dry with paper towels. Bend the wing tips back and tuck them behind their first joints. Using your fingertips, carefully loosen the chicken skin from the flesh. Begin at the bottom of the breast and, without tearing the skin, work your hand under the skin all the way up the breast and down into the thigh on each side. Crack the bay leaves to release their flavor by holding both ends of the leaf and twisting (don't break them in half). Cut the garlic cloves into about 5 slices each. Place 2 bay leaves in the cavity of the bird. Insert the remaining leaves under the skin of the chicken, positioning them as evenly as possible—2 under the skin of each thigh and 3 under the skin of each side of the breast. Distribute the garlic slices evenly under the skin as well. Tie the legs together with a short piece of kitchen twine.

2. Roasting. Place the chicken breast side up in a shallow roasting pan, about 11 x 8 inches. Rub the bird with the olive oil on all sides and season it very generously with salt and pepper. Roast until an instant-read thermometer inserted in the thickest part of the thigh registers 165° to 170°F, 50 to 60 minutes. The chicken should be beautifully browned, and the juices that run out of the bird when it is tilted should have no sign of pink. If you are still not certain the bird is done, cut between the thigh and body and peek inside near the hip joint to be sure there is no sign of pink flesh. Remove the chicken from the oven and let rest for 10 minutes in a warm place.

3. Jus and serving. Tilt the roasting pan, and using a flatware tablespoon, skim off as much fat as you can. Place the roasting pan over medium-low heat and add the wine. As it simmers, scrape up and dissolve the sticky bits at the bottom of the pan. Add ¼ cup hot water if more liquid is needed. Pour the jus into a sauceboat to pass at the table. Cut the twine holding the legs together and carve the bird. Remove and discard the bay leaves from under the skin before you serve the chicken or instruct your guests to do so at the table.

VARIATION
Cut 1½ pounds potatoes, such as Yukon Gold or Yellow Finn, into 1½-inch chunks. Place the chicken in a 12 x 9-inch baking dish, surround it with the potatoes, then season the potatoes with salt and pepper. Roast as directed. Remove the chicken from the pan to rest for 10 minutes. Stir the potatoes, scraping up any browned bits sticking to the pan, and return them to the oven for 10 minutes to crisp and brown further. Since the potatoes absorb the cooking juices, no jus can be made.

HERB SUBSTITUTIONS
- *Don't substitute dried bay leaves for fresh in this dish. If you can't get hold of fresh bay leaves, substitute 12 2-inch sprigs thyme, lemon thyme, or marjoram, or 16 to 20 sage leaves.*

ROSEMARY GRILLED CHICKEN

4 servings

This quickly prepared grilled chicken is one of my summertime staples. The piquant marinade, full of fresh rosemary, garlic, lemon, and mustard is a welcome alternative to sweet red barbecue sauces. It's good hot off the grill, at room temperature, or even straight from the refrigerator the next day.

If you have access to large woody rosemary branches from a big shrub and you use a kettle-style charcoal grill, you can infuse the chicken with even more rosemary flavor. Put the branches directly on the coals right before you put the chicken on the grill, and they will fill the covered kettle with thick savory smoke that will do the job effectively.

2 tablespoons stone-ground, whole-grain, or Dijon mustard
¼ cup coarsely chopped fresh rosemary
¼ cup freshly squeezed lemon juice
1 tablespoon dark brown sugar
3 tablespoons extra-virgin olive oil
4 cloves garlic, finely chopped
½ teaspoon salt
½ teaspoon freshly ground black pepper
1 3½- to 4-pound chicken, preferably free-range, cut into 8 serving pieces
  without the back
Optional: about 5 8-inch branches thick woody rosemary

1. Marinade. In a large mixing bowl, stir together the mustard, chopped rosemary, lemon juice, brown sugar, olive oil, garlic, salt, and pepper. Toss the chicken pieces in this marinade until thoroughly coated. Refrigerate covered for 1 to 2 hours.

2. Grilling the chicken. Start a medium-hot fire in a charcoal grill or preheat a gas grill to medium. If you are using a charcoal kettle grill, when the coals are ashed over and glowing, toss the rosemary branches (if using) directly on the coals, put the grill rack in position, and quickly arrange the chicken on the rack. Cover. If using a gas grill, arrange the chicken on the grill when it is preheated and cover. Tend the chicken carefully, lifting the lid and checking it every 3 to 5 minutes. Move the chicken away from hot spots as they become apparent and don't let it blacken. Cook the chicken covered for 10 to 15 minutes on each side. The breast pieces will be done first—

remove them from the grill when they feel firm to the touch and when no pink is visible when you cut into the thickest part with a paring knife. Continue to cook the legs and wings until they are all cooked through. The flesh at the base of the drumsticks will shrink to expose the bone, and when you poke the thigh with a fork, the juices that run out will be clear. Serve the chicken hot, warm, or at room temperature with Balsamic Potato Salad (page 62) and Grilled Marjoram-Scented Corn (page 138).

VARIATIONS

To reduce the fat, remove the skin from the chicken before marinating. The meat will pick up even more of the herb flavor.

You can broil the chicken instead of grilling it. Preheat the broiler on medium-high with the oven rack set 6 to 8 inches from the heat source. Arrange the chicken in a broiler pan and cook for 10 to 15 minutes per side as directed for the grilled chicken.

 HERB SUBSTITUTIONS

- *In place of chopped rosemary, use an equal amount of coarsely chopped fresh sage, marjoram, oregano, or summer savory, or 2 tablespoons coarsely chopped fresh English or lemon thyme.*

Braised Chicken with Leeks and Porcini

4 servings

This is a sumptuous dish of tender chicken pieces braised on the bone and cloaked in a sauce richly flavored with leeks, porcini, and fresh herbs. The herbs are added in two stages. First, whole sprigs simmer with the braising liquid to flavor the bird while it's cooking, then chopped herbs are stirred into the sauce at the last minute to add a bright finish.

Porcini mushrooms are the Italian variety of *Boletus edulis* (the French call them cèpes) and they are widely available dried. Not all dried porcini come from Italy—many are harvested in China, Eastern Europe, and South America. They are graded according to the quality of the mushroom, not the place of origin (less mature mushrooms with few wormholes are higher grade). To reconstitute them, you soak them in hot water, and that water then becomes a flavorful ingredient itself. Just ½ ounce dried mushrooms adds an enormous depth of flavor to this dish, proving the benefits of having porcini in your pantry.

> *½ ounce dried porcini mushrooms (about ¼ cup)*
> *1 cup very hot tap water*
> *2 medium leeks (about 1½ pounds)*
> *1 4-inch sprig fresh rosemary*
> *1 4-inch sprig fresh sage*
> *6 3-inch sprigs fresh English thyme*
> *2 fresh bay laurel leaves, or 1 dried*
> *1 3½- to 4-pound chicken, preferably free-range, cut into 8 serving pieces and the back*
> *Salt and freshly ground black pepper*
> *2 tablespoons extra-virgin olive oil*
> *6 large cloves garlic, coarsely chopped*
> *½ cup dry white wine*
> *1 tablespoon coarsely chopped fresh English thyme*
> *1 tablespoon finely chopped fresh sage*
> *¼ cup finely chopped fresh parsley*
> *½ cup crème fraîche or heavy cream*

1. Mushrooms. Place the dried mushrooms in a deep bowl and cover them with the hot water. Let them soak for 30 minutes. Gently lift the mushrooms out of the water, being careful not to stir up any of the grit that will have settled to the bottom of the bowl. Holding them over the bowl, lightly squeeze out the excess water. Pour the mushroom water through a very fine strainer, holding back any sediment left in the bottom of the bowl. To ensure there is no grit remaining in the mushrooms, swish them in a second bowl of hot water, lifting them out and squeezing them in the same way, but discard this water. Put the mushrooms on a cutting board and finely chop them.

2. Leeks and bouquet garni. Cut off and discard the tops of the leeks at the point where they turn from light to dark green. Split the remaining portion lengthwise in half, keeping the roots attached so that the layers will not fall apart. Rinse the leeks thoroughly, then thinly slice them in half circles, discarding the roots. Tie the herb sprigs and bay leaves together with a piece of kitchen twine.

3. Browning the chicken. Wash the chicken under cold water and pat dry with paper towels. Generously sprinkle the chicken pieces with salt and pepper. Heat the oil in a large (6-quart) Dutch oven or deep 12- to 14-inch skillet over high heat. Using tongs, add the chicken pieces skin side down in a single layer. You may need to brown the chicken in two batches. Cook over high heat, using a splatter screen or partially covering the pan, until the underside is golden brown, 6 to 8 minutes. Turn the pieces over and brown them lightly on the other side, 3 to 4 minutes. Transfer the chicken to a platter, leaving the oil in the pan.

4. Braising. Reduce the heat to medium and add the leeks and garlic to the pan. Cook uncovered, stirring often, until the vegetables are softened and start to turn a light caramel color, about 8 minutes. Add the wine, let it boil for a minute or two, then add the strained mushroom water, the chopped porcini, ½ teaspoon salt, and the bouquet garni. Return the chicken to the pan, skin side up. Cover the pan tightly, reduce the heat to very low, and braise the chicken at the gentlest simmer until it is tender when poked with a fork but not yet falling off the bone, 50 to 60 minutes.

5. Finishing the sauce. Remove and discard the back. Transfer the remaining chicken pieces to a warmed clean platter, cover them loosely with aluminum foil, and keep them warm in a very low oven or on the back of the stove. The stewed leeks and mushrooms, submerged in a fragrant stock, will be left in the pan. Remove and discard the bouquet garni and stir the chopped thyme and sage into the pan. Increase the heat to high and boil until the sauce thickens slightly and the liquid evaporates to below the level of the leeks, 5 to 8 minutes. Stir in the parsley, crème fraîche, and any juices that have collected on the chicken platter. Return to a boil. Taste and season with black pepper, and additional salt if needed. Pour the sauce over the chicken. Serve with buttered egg noodles, Herb-Roasted Potatoes (page 146), or Green Mashed Potatoes (page 150).

Almond-and-Herb-Breaded Chicken

4 servings

Skinless chicken soaked in buttermilk to tenderize it and baked with a savory coating of almonds, rosemary, thyme, and parsley makes an easy weeknight dinner or picnic food that everyone will love. Because of the firm crust, this is chicken you eat with your fingers.

1 ½ cups whole or low-fat buttermilk
2 tablespoons Dijon mustard
2 cloves garlic, minced
½ teaspoon salt
1 3½- to 4-pound chicken, preferably free-range, cut into 8 pieces without the back and skinned (leave the skin on the wings)

CRUST
¾ cup almonds, whole or sliced, blanched or unblanched
½ cup fine dry bread crumbs
2 tablespoons coarsely chopped fresh rosemary
2 tablespoons fresh English thyme leaves
1 cup (gently packed) fresh parsley sprigs
⅛ teaspoon cayenne pepper
¼ teaspoon freshly ground black pepper
¾ teaspoon salt

About 1 cup all-purpose flour

1. Marinating the chicken. Whisk together the buttermilk, mustard, garlic, and ½ teaspoon salt in a mixing bowl large enough to accommodate the chicken. Toss the chicken pieces in the buttermilk mixture until they are evenly coated. Refrigerate covered for 1 hour.

2. Crust. Preheat the oven to 400°F. Lightly oil a large baking rack and set it on top of a baking sheet. Whirl all of the ingredients for the crust in a food processor until the nuts are finely ground and the herbs are finely chopped. Empty the coating mixture into a wide shallow bowl and put the flour in a second shallow bowl. Lift the chicken pieces from the buttermilk mixture and place them on a platter. Working with 1 piece at a time, coat the chicken piece in the flour and shake off any excess. Put it in the bowl of buttermilk and turn to coat all sides. Lift and let it drain for a moment, then drop it into the almond mixture and turn it to coat all sides. Gently put the piece onto the prepared baking rack. Coat the remaining pieces of chicken. (At this point the chicken can be refrigerated uncovered on its baking rack for up to 4 hours.)

3. Baking. Bake the chicken for 45 to 55 minutes. When done, the crust will be browned, the flesh at the base of the drumsticks will have shrunk to expose the bone, and when you poke the thigh with a fork, the juices that run out will be clear. Remove the chicken from the oven and let it cool on the rack for 10 minutes. Carefully loosen the pieces with a large spatula and transfer them to a large serving platter. Serve warm or at room temperature.

Herb-Crusted Chicken Le Cordon Bleu

4 servings

In 1998, Le Cordon Bleu cooking schools and the National Broiler Council sponsored a chef's contest for the best new version of Chicken Cordon Bleu—the classic dish of breaded chicken breasts stuffed with ham and cheese. This recipe took first prize and I won a trip to Paris. In my version, a flavorful fresh herb crust replaces the heavy breading, and for the stuffing, I specify Gruyère and Black Forest ham. Real Black Forest ham is made in Germany and it's very smoky with a consistency like dry prosciutto. Don't confuse it with the domestic deli ham of the same name. If you can't find it, substitute Westphalian ham, which is very similar, or prosciutto, which doesn't have the smokiness but will nevertheless give delicious results.

4 large boneless, skinless chicken breast halves (about 1 ½ pounds)
Salt and freshly ground black pepper
4 thin 4 x 2-inch slices Black Forest or Westphalian ham or prosciutto
4 4 x 2-inch slices Gruyère cheese
½ cup finely chopped fresh parsley
¼ cup finely chopped fresh rosemary
¼ cup finely chopped fresh sage
2 tablespoons olive oil

1. Pounding the chicken breasts. Put each chicken breast half between 2 pieces of plastic wrap and pound with a meat pounder or the side of an empty wine bottle, using just enough force to gently spread the meat without tearing it, until each piece is less than ¼ inch thick and about 5 inches wide and 7 inches long.

2. Stuffing. Lay out the chicken pieces with the short ends facing you and season lightly with salt and pepper. Lay a slice of ham and a slice of cheese horizontally along the bottom half of each breast. Fold a ½-inch strip of each side inward and then fold the top over to enclose the filling completely.

3. Herb crust. Mix the parsley, rosemary, and sage together in a wide shallow bowl. Coat the chicken breast packages in the herb mixture, pressing to adhere as many herbs as you can. Set the coated packages on a plate until ready to cook. (At this point they can be covered with plastic wrap and refrigerated for up to 24 hours.)

4. **Cooking the chicken.** Heat the oil in a large skillet or sauté pan over medium-high heat until hot. Season the breasts with salt and pepper. Using tongs, carefully lower the chicken into the pan, reduce the heat to medium, and cook uncovered until the underside is deep brown, 5 to 6 minutes. Turn the chicken over and cook the other side until it is well browned and the chicken is cooked through, another 5 to 6 minutes. To test for doneness, cut a breast in half on a cutting board with a sharp knife (they will be sliced before serving anyway) and check that there is no sign of pink and the cheese is melted. Transfer the chicken to a warmed platter and let rest in a warm place, on the back of the stove, for 3 to 5 minutes. On a cutting board, cut each breast diagonally into 3 to 5 slices to reveal the filling and arrange the slices in a fan shape on warmed dinner plates.

DILLED CHICKEN PICCATA

2 servings

      In 1983, I cooked at Ernie's in San Francisco, a restaurant that was famous for being a location in Alfred Hitchcock's movie *Vertigo*. Staid customers would often order veal piccata, though it hadn't been on the menu since the talented young Frenchman Jacky Robert had become chef. We grumbled but gave customers what they wanted, and I learned to prepare a classic piccata sauce by deglazing the sauté pan with white wine, and adding lemon juice, parsley, and sometimes capers. This simple and delicious sauce is perfect for sautéed chicken breast scallops as well, and it's receptive to many herbs, particularly dill. It makes a lovely, and nearly instant, dinner for two.

> *2 boneless, skinless chicken breast halves (about 12 ounces)*
> *Salt and freshly ground black pepper*
> *1½ tablespoons extra-virgin olive oil*
> *½ cup dry white wine*
> *Thinly sliced zest of ½ lemon (removed with a zester)*
> *1 tablespoon freshly squeezed lemon juice*
> *1 tablespoon unsalted butter*
> *2 tablespoons coarsely chopped fresh dill*
> *2 tablespoons coarsely chopped fresh parsley*

1. Pounding the chicken breasts. Put each chicken breast half between 2 pieces of plastic wrap and pound them with a meat pounder or the side of an empty wine bottle, using just enough force to gently spread the meat without tearing it, until each piece is ¼ inch thick and about 5 inches wide and 6 inches long. Season both sides of the chicken with salt and black pepper.

2. Sautéing the chicken. Heat the olive oil in a large (10- to 12-inch) skillet over medium-high heat until the oil begins to smoke. Using tongs, lower the chicken breasts into the oil. Cook until lightly browned on the underside, 2 to 3 minutes, then turn and brown the other side for the same amount of time. At this point the chicken should be firm and fully cooked. If you are not certain, cut into the thickest part with a paring knife to be sure there is no longer any sign of pink or translucence. Remove the skillet from the heat and transfer the chicken to warmed dinner plates.

3. Sauce. Pour off any oil in the skillet, then pour in the wine and stir to dislodge the browned bits in the pan. Cook over medium heat until the wine boils down to half its volume. Add the lemon zest, lemon juice, and butter; swirl the pan until the butter is melted and incorporated. Stir in the dill and parsley. Taste and add additional salt and pepper if needed. Spoon the sauce over the chicken and serve right away.

VARIATION
Add 2 tablespoons drained capers to the sauce along with the wine.

HERB SUBSTITUTIONS
- *Replace the dill with one of the following: 3 tablespoons coarsely chopped fresh basil, 2 tablespoons finely snipped fresh chives, 1 tablespoon coarsely chopped fresh marjoram or Italian oregano, 2 tablespoons coarsely chopped fresh spearmint or French tarragon, or 2 teaspoons coarsely chopped fresh English or lemon thyme.*

Chicken Breasts in Tarragon Cream

4 servings

If you're an herb lover, this dish, which takes 10 minutes to prepare from start to finish, will become a standard in your repertoire.

4 boneless, skinless chicken breast halves (about 1½ pounds)
Salt and freshly ground black pepper
2 teaspoons extra-virgin olive oil
1 small shallot, finely chopped (about 3 tablespoons)
¼ cup dry vermouth or dry white wine
¾ cup heavy cream
2 to 3 tablespoons coarsely chopped fresh French tarragon
1 teaspoon freshly squeezed lemon juice

1. Browning the chicken. Season both sides of the chicken breasts with salt and pepper. Heat the oil in a large (10- to 12-inch) skillet over medium-high heat. Using tongs, carefully lower the chicken breasts into the pan and cook them for about 1 minute on each side just until they begin to brown slightly. Transfer the still-raw chicken to a plate.

2. Poaching in cream. Reduce the heat under the skillet to low. Add the shallot and cook, stirring constantly, until softened but not browned, less than 1 minute. Add the vermouth and cook for 30 seconds, then add the cream and half the tarragon. Return the chicken breasts to the pan and adjust the heat so that the cream gently simmers. Cover and cook until the chicken is firm and just cooked through, 4 to 6 minutes. To check for doneness, cut into the thickest part of a breast with a paring knife—there should be no sign of pink or translucence.

3. Finishing. Transfer the chicken breasts to a warmed serving platter or individual dinner plates. The sauce should be thick enough to lightly coat a spoon. If it is too thin, continue to simmer it for about 1 minute and it will thicken. Stir in the remaining tarragon and the lemon juice, then taste and season with additional salt and pepper if needed. Pour the sauce over the chicken and serve right away with buttered egg noodles.

THYME GRILLED QUAIL

4 servings

Quail are the smallest of farm-raised game birds, and you can often find them at specialty butchers or Asian markets. They weigh 4 to 8 ounces and 2 are needed for a main-course serving. In restaurants they are usually served semiboneless (ribs and back removed but bones remaining in the legs and wings), making them easier to eat with knife and fork. But for me, the true pleasure of eating quail can only be experienced when it is both cooked and served on the bone for the meat comes out far more succulent and flavorful. I also like picking and eating the treasured bits off the bone with my hands. This two-ingredient marinade of olive oil and thyme brings out the best in the birds, giving them extra moistness and just the right touch of aromatic flavor. Though a bit messy to eat, they are worthy of a special occasion.

8 whole quail (5 to 6 ounces each)
1 large bunch fresh thyme, about 1½ inches in diameter and
 4 inches long
¾ cup fruity extra-virgin olive oil
Salt and freshly ground black pepper

1. Marinating. Remove and discard the backbones of each quail by cutting along both sides with kitchen shears. Rinse the birds under cold water, removing any viscera left inside, and dry them on paper towels. Bend the wing tips back and tuck them behind their first joints. With the tip of a sharp knife, pierce two ¼-inch slits between the thighs and the base of the breast. Insert the tips of the legs into these slits, swiveling the thighs so the knee joints face inward. Put 2 or 3 quail in a single layer in a deep glass or ceramic baking dish. Top them with about one-quarter of the thyme sprigs and drizzle with 3 tablespoons of the olive oil. Layer the remaining quail with the remaining thyme and oil in the same manner. Cover tightly and let marinate in the refrigerator for 8 to 24 hours.

2. Grilling. Build a medium-hot fire in a charcoal grill or preheat a gas grill to medium-high. Lift the quail from the marinade and place them on a baking sheet lined with paper towels to drain. A thin coat of oil and some of the loose thyme leaves should remain on the birds. Season both sides of the birds generously with salt and pepper. When the coals are ashed over and glowing or the gas grill is preheated, arrange the quail breast side down on the grill and cook until the skin browns and crisps slightly, 6 to 8 minutes. Be careful not to char the birds; move them away from hot spots, and if the grill flares up, cover it immediately to extinguish the flame. Turn the quail over and grill until cooked through, 6 to 8 minutes longer. To test for doneness transfer a quail to a plate and lift the thigh to peek underneath it. The flesh at the hip joint should be tender and slightly pink but not have a raw, translucent appearance. (If you prefer your quail rare, and some people do, cook it only about 5 minutes per side.) Remove the quail to a platter and let them rest for about 5 minutes before serving. Serve with crusty bread and a salad of sharply dressed arugula, watercress, or other greens.

Herb-Rubbed Duck with Tart Cherry and Sage Sauce

4 very generous servings or 6 to 8 servings when accompanied with other courses

When the weather turns chilly, a dinner of perfectly cooked duck, with crispy skin, rosy succulent meat, and a balanced fruity sauce, is something to dream about. This duck dish delivers all these things. It calls for whole ducks, which can be found fresh or frozen in most supermarkets for a price per pound not much more than chicken.

The breast and leg meat are removed from the carcass and marinated. The carcass is made into stock, strained, and boiled down into a rich sauce. When it's time to cook the duck, the legs are baked in the oven until fully cooked, tender, and crispy, and the breasts are sautéed on top of the stove until the skin crisps but the meat is still rosy. If you are not confident cutting up the duck yourself, buy a fresh duck from a butcher, who will cut it for you. Don't let the many steps scare you off. The result is well worth it, and you can do much of the work the day ahead.

The day before, or the morning of serving day: **Cut up the duck and marinate it; make the duck stock (3 hours); and strain the stock and boil it down to make the sauce (1 hour).**

20 minutes before serving: **Begin cooking the duck breasts.**

45 minutes before serving: **Begin cooking the duck legs; reheat the sauce.**

5 minutes before serving: **Allow the duck to rest, then slice and serve.**

HERB RUB

6 fresh bay laurel leaves, or 2 dried

¼ cup fresh rosemary leaves

2 tablespoons fresh English thyme leaves

4 teaspoons juniper berries

Thinly sliced zest of ½ orange (removed with a zester)

2 teaspoons salt

2 teaspoons freshly ground black pepper

2 whole 5-pound ducks, Peking or Muscovy

STOCK

2 tablespoons vegetable oil

1 small onion, coarsely chopped

1 small carrot, coarsely chopped
1 rib celery, coarsely chopped
6 3-inch sprigs fresh English thyme
2 bay laurel leaves, fresh or dried

SAUCE

2 cups full-bodied red wine, such as Cabernet Sauvignon or Merlot
1 medium shallot, finely chopped (about ⅓ cup)
1 cup dried tart cherries (see Note, page 213)
2 tablespoons finely chopped fresh sage
1 teaspoon finely chopped fresh English thyme
2 teaspoons balsamic vinegar
Salt and freshly ground black pepper

1. Herb rub. If using fresh bay leaves, pull out the center veins. Combine all the ingredients for the herb rub in a spice mill or blender and grind to a coarse paste.

2. Marinating the duck. Cut up the ducks by removing the 2 legs and the 2 boneless breasts (with skin) from each bird. Reserve the necks and carcasses. Score the skin on the breasts by drawing a very sharp knife across the skin in a diagonal crisscross pattern, 4 or 5 lines in each direction. Be careful to cut only into the skin and not into the flesh. This helps render the fat quickly when the breasts are cooked. Rub the duck breasts and legs with the herb paste as evenly as you can, rubbing some inside the scored cuts. Put them in a medium bowl, cover, and let marinate in the refrigerator for at least 3 hours or as long as 24 hours.

3. Stock. Cut the wings off the duck carcasses, remove as much skin and fat as comes off easily, and cut the carcasses in half (you can bend them until they snap, then cut between bones, or use a cleaver). You should now have 4 wings, 4 pieces of carcass, and 2 necks. Heat the oil in a large (6- to 8-quart) heavy-bottomed pot over high heat. Add these 10 pieces to the pot and brown them for 10 to 12 minutes, turning once or twice. This step is important for building flavor in the stock but not all of the surfaces need to be evenly brown. Pour off the fat that has accumulated in the pan, then pour in enough cold water to barely cover the bones. Bring the stock to a boil, turn the heat to very low, and skim off any fat or foam that rises to the surface. Add the onion, carrot, celery, thyme, and bay leaves and gently simmer uncovered for 2 to 3 hours.

4. Sauce. Strain the stock, discard the bones, and return the stock to the pot. Add the wine, shallot, and cherries. Boil the sauce until it is thickened and reduced to about 2 cups, 45 to 60 minutes. (The sauce can be made a day ahead and refrigerated for up to 2 days.)

5. Roasting the legs. Preheat the oven to 425°F. About 45 minutes before serving, heat a large (10- to 12-inch) ovenproof skillet (cast iron works well) over medium-high heat. Pour in a film of vegetable oil and heat. Add the duck legs skin side down and cook until the skin side browns, 4 to 5 minutes. Without turning the legs over, put the pan in the oven and roast for 10 minutes. Turn the duck legs and continue to roast until the skin is very brown and crisp and the meat is tender when pierced with a fork, about 20 minutes longer. Remove them from the oven and let rest on a plate in a warm spot.

6. Sautéing the breasts. When the legs have been in the oven for 20 minutes, begin to cook the breasts. Pour a thin film of oil into another large (12-inch) skillet and heat it over medium heat until hot. Add the duck breasts skin side down, reduce the heat to medium-low, and let cook slowly and undisturbed. After 5 minutes, about ½ inch of fat will have rendered into the pan, which will help render the remaining fat from under the skin. Continue to cook the breasts until the skin is very brown and crisp, another 5 to 10 minutes. If the rendered fat rises above the level of the skin and the duck meat begins to be submerged, pour some of it off into a small bowl. This will prevent the breast meat from overcooking before the skin is crisp. When the skin is crisp but not blackened, turn the breasts over and cook just 1 minute for rare or 2 to 5 minutes for medium-rare to medium. The meat should feel firm but still springy and an instant-read thermometer inserted horizontally into the breast should register 120° to 125°F for rare, 130° to 135°F for medium-rare to medium. The temperature will continue to rise about 10° as they rest. Transfer them to the plate with the legs and let them sit on the back of the stove for 4 to 5 minutes before carving.

7. Finishing. Bring the sauce to a simmer and stir in the chopped sage, thyme, and balsamic vinegar. Taste and season with salt and pepper as needed. Arrange the duck legs on a warmed platter or individual plates. Using a sharp thin knife, slice the breasts on a diagonal ⅜ inch thick and arrange the slices in a fan shape leaning against the legs. Pour the sauce over and around the duck. Serve promptly with Roasted Parsnips with Thyme (page 144), Minted French Lentils (page 152), or Herb-Roasted Potatoes (page 146).

NOTE

Resembling giant raisins, sweet and sour varieties of dried cherries from Yakima Valley in Washington are exciting and relatively new ingredients. Dried sweet cherries have a prunelike flavor, but the tart (sour or pie) cherries, which are usually processed with sugar, have a brilliant tangy flavor. When simmered with wine and duck stock, they make a balanced, savory, and full-flavored sauce that plays beautifully off the crispy citrus-herb-rubbed duck in this recipe.

Sautéed Duck Breasts with Mint, Coriander, and Olives

4 servings

If fresh skin-on duck breasts, which the French call *magrets*, are available from your butcher, this stovetop recipe will turn them into a spectacular dish, quick enough for a weeknight (marinate them the night before) or elegant enough for a special dinner.

SPICE RUB

2 tablespoons whole dried coriander seeds
2 teaspoons whole black peppercorns
2 teaspoons salt
Thinly sliced zest of 2 lemons (removed with a zester)
1 cup (gently packed) fresh spearmint leaves

4 duck breast halves with skin, Peking or Muscovy (about 8 ounces each)
1 tablespoon vegetable oil
1 large shallot, or 2 small shallots, finely chopped (about ½ cup)
½ cup dry vermouth or dry white wine
¾ cup homemade (page 12) or canned low-sodium chicken stock
½ cup coarsely chopped pitted brined black olives, such as Kalamata
  or Gaeta
½ cup very coarsely chopped fresh spearmint
Freshly ground black pepper

1. **Spice rub.** Grind the coriander, peppercorns, salt, and lemon zest in a spice mill or blender until very fine. Add the mint leaves and grind until it forms a smooth paste.

2. **Marinating the duck.** Score the skin on the breasts by drawing a very sharp knife across the skin in a diagonal crisscross pattern, 4 or 5 lines in each direction. Be careful to cut only into the skin and not into the flesh. This helps render the fat quickly when the breasts are cooked. Rub both sides of the breasts with the spice paste as evenly as you can, rubbing some inside the scored cuts. Stack them on a plate and cover tightly with plastic wrap. Let marinate in the refrigerator for at least 1 hour or as long as 24 hours.

3. Sautéing the breasts. Pour the oil into a large (12-inch) skillet and heat over medium heat until hot. Add the duck breasts skin side down, reduce the heat to medium-low, and let them cook slowly and undisturbed. After 5 minutes, about ½ inch of fat will have rendered into the pan, which will help render the remaining fat from under the skin. Continue to cook the breasts until the skin is very brown and crisp, another 5 to 10 minutes. If the rendered fat rises above the level of the skin and the duck meat begins to be submerged, pour some of it off into a small bowl. This will prevent the breast meat from overcooking before the skin is crisp. When the skin is crisp but not blackened, turn the breasts over and cook just 1 minute for rare or 2 to 5 minutes for medium-rare to medium. The meat should feel firm but still springy and an instant-read thermometer inserted horizontally into the breast should register 120° to 125°F for rare, 130° to 135°F for medium-rare to medium. The temperature will continue to rise about 10° as they rest. Transfer them to a warmed plate and let them sit on the back of the stove for 4 to 5 minutes while you make the sauce.

4. Sauce. Pour off all but 1 tablespoon of the duck fat from the skillet. Add the shallot and cook, stirring constantly, over medium-low heat until softened but not browned, less than 1 minute. Pour in the vermouth and increase the heat to medium. Scrape up any browned bits with a wooden spoon and cook until most of the liquid has boiled away. Add the stock and any juice that has collected on the plate holding the duck breasts; continue to boil the sauce until it is reduced to about half its volume and is slightly thickened. Stir in the olives and mint. Taste and season with pepper. Because the olives are salty, additional salt will probably not be needed.

5. Slicing and serving. Using a sharp thin knife, slice the duck breasts on a diagonal about ⅜ inch thick. Keeping the shape of the duck breasts together, use a spatula to transfer them to warmed serving plates and then spread the slices apart slightly into a fan shape. Spoon the sauce over. Serve with Minted French Lentils (page 152), Baked Herb Polenta (page 154), or Herb-Roasted Potatoes (page 146).

BEEF TENDERLOIN STEAKS WITH RED ONION AND TARRAGON RELISH

4 servings

I'll always remember the first fancy French restaurant my parents took me to. It was my twelfth birthday and my father and I shared a Châteaubriand (the large tip of a beef tenderloin) with béarnaise sauce. Béarnaise is a butter and egg yolk sauce, like hollandaise, flavored with wine and tarragon. I thought it the most marvelous thing I had ever tasted. Inspired by the memory of this splendid combination of tarragon and tender beef, I came up with this dish of seared or grilled tenderloin steaks, draped with a relish of red onions that are slowly cooked with red wine, sherry vinegar, and plenty of fresh tarragon. The relish lightens the classic considerably, but if you're up for it or it's your birthday, you can indulge and serve the steaks with the classic béarnaise sauce (page 326) instead.

RELISH

2 tablespoons olive oil
1 large red onion (about 10 ounces), peeled and thinly sliced
1 tablespoon sugar
½ teaspoon salt
½ cup full-bodied red wine, such as Cabernet Sauvignon or Merlot
1½ tablespoons sherry vinegar or use tarragon-flavored red wine vinegar
½ cup very coarsely chopped fresh French tarragon
Freshly ground black pepper

4 beef tenderloin steaks (filet mignon), about 8 ounces each and 1 to
* 1¼ inches thick*
Salt and freshly ground black pepper
2 tablespoons extra-virgin olive oil

1. Relish. Heat the olive oil in a medium (3-quart) saucepan over medium heat. Add the onion, sugar, and salt and cook, stirring often, over medium heat until the onion is softened but not browned, about 5 minutes. Add the red wine and gently simmer, stirring often, until all the wine evaporates and the onion is very tender, 5 to 10 minutes. Stir in the vinegar and tarragon. Taste and season with pepper and additional salt if needed. (The relish can be made ahead of time and refrigerated covered for up to 1 week.)

2. Searing the steaks. Season both sides of the steaks generously with salt and pepper. Heat the olive oil in a large (12-inch) skillet over high heat until the pan is very hot and the oil is smoking. Using tongs, carefully lower the steaks into the pan. Cook until the underside is a deep brown, 3 to 5 minutes, then turn and continue to cook until the steaks are done to your liking. An instant-read thermometer inserted horizontally into the center of a steak should register 120°F for rare, 130°F for medium-rare, or 140° to 145°F for medium. Transfer the steaks to a warmed plate, cover them very loosely with aluminum foil, and let them rest for 5 minutes in a warm place, such as the back of the stove.

3. Serving. If the onion relish has cooled, warm it in the pan over medium-low heat. Put the steaks on warmed serving plates and drape the relish over the top. Serve with Herb-Roasted Potatoes (page 146), or Green Mashed Potatoes (page 150).

GRILLED FLANK STEAK IN OREGANO MARINADE

4 servings

Flank steak begs for a marinade. Bold seasonings enliven its flavor, and the thin, firm meat can stand the tenderizing acids of vinegar or wine without becoming mushy. I like to use this soy and balsamic marinade that's loaded with brash and fiery Greek oregano. Flank steak cooks very quickly, so that in order to keep the center medium-rare but still achieve a slightly charred crust, you must cook it on a very hot grill. A charcoal grill is preferred here because most gas grills cannot get hot enough.

> *1 large bunch fresh Greek oregano sprigs, about 1½ inches in diameter and 4 inches long*
> *12 3-inch sprigs fresh English thyme*
> *¼ cup soy sauce*
> *¼ cup balsamic vinegar*
> *¼ cup extra-virgin olive oil*
> *6 cloves garlic, finely chopped*
> *1 small jalapeño pepper, seeded and coarsely chopped*
> *1 tablespoon sugar*
> *1 teaspoon ground cumin*
> *1 teaspoon salt*
> *1 2-pound flank steak*

1. Marinating. Roughly strip the large stems from the oregano and thyme sprigs. It's okay if small stems remain. Put them in a shallow baking dish just large enough to hold the steak. Stir in the rest of the ingredients except for the steak. Put the steak in the marinade and turn it to coat all surfaces. Cover the dish and let the steak marinate in the refrigerator for 8 to 24 hours. (If you prefer, you can fold the steak in half and marinate it in a 1-gallon resealable freezer bag.)

2. Grilling. Build a very hot charcoal fire in a charcoal grill. Position the grill rack 3 inches from the coals. Remove the steak from the marinade and wipe off the excess marinade, allowing some of the herb leaves to remain. When the charcoal is ashed over and blazing hot, grill the steak for 3 to 4 minutes on each side for medium-rare. An instant-read thermometer inserted horizontally into the center of the steak should read 125° to 135°F. Remove the steak from the grill and let it rest for 5 minutes on a board or platter. Very thinly slice it with a knife held at a 45° angle to the board, so that the pieces end up twice as wide as the steak is thick. The steak is fabulous with Roasted Tomato and Herb Salsa, below.

ROASTED TOMATO AND HERB SALSA

Makes 2 cups

This lively chunky sauce is just the thing to serve on marinated flank steak, broiled swordfish steaks, or a platter of mixed grilled vegetables. It also makes a superb topping for bruschetta.

> *1 pound ripe plum tomatoes (about 6 large)*
> *1 tablespoon olive oil*
> *¼ teaspoon salt*
> *1 teaspoon sugar*
> *2 tablespoons minced red onion*
> *1 to 2 teaspoons seeded and finely chopped jalapeño pepper*
> *¼ cup finely shredded fresh spearmint leaves*
> *2 tablespoons coarsely chopped fresh marjoram*
> *2 tablespoons coarsely chopped fresh parsley*
> *2 tablespoons red wine vinegar*

1. **Tomatoes.** Preheat the oven to 450°F. Cut the tomatoes lengthwise in half and toss them with the olive oil, salt, and sugar in a medium mixing bowl. Arrange them cut side up on a baking sheet and roast until the skin is shriveled and the tomato halves are softened and beginning to collapse, 10 to 15 minutes, depending on ripeness. Remove them from the oven and let cool.

2. **Salsa.** Coarsely dice the tomatoes. Return them to the mixing bowl and stir in the remaining ingredients. Let the salsa sit at least 1 hour at room temperature to blend the flavors. Taste and season with additional salt if needed.

VARIATION
Instead of roasting the tomatoes, grill them over a medium-hot fire until they are slightly blackened and soft, about 2 minutes each side.

HERB-BRAISED SHORT RIBS OF BEEF

6 to 8 servings

Winter savory, sage, and thyme are sturdy thick-leafed herbs that can stay in the garden all winter and make this hearty dish reverberate with rich flavor. You can complete it up to 3 days ahead of time and its flavor will improve while it rests in the refrigerator, making it a comforting family dish to serve for several meals or a convenient dish for a dinner party. Purchase short ribs that are block shaped, 3 to 4 inches long and about 2 inches thick—sometimes called English style—not the Asian-style short ribs that are very flat, thin, and long.

> *5 pounds beef short ribs*
> *Salt and freshly ground black pepper*
> *2 tablespoons vegetable oil*
> *2 slices bacon (2 ounces) cut into ¼-inch dice*
> *2 medium onions (about 1 pound) thinly sliced*
> *12 cloves garlic, each cut into 3 slices*
> *2 cups full-bodied red wine, such as Cabernet Sauvignon, Merlot, or Zinfandel*
> *1 28-ounce can whole plum tomatoes*
> *12 3-inch sprigs fresh winter savory*
> *12 3-inch sprigs fresh English thyme*
> *2 4-inch sprigs fresh sage*
> *4 fresh bay laurel leaves, or 2 dried*
> *¼ cup coarsely chopped fresh winter savory*
> *¼ cup coarsely chopped fresh sage*
> *½ cup coarsely chopped fresh parsley*

1. Browning the ribs. Season the short ribs generously with salt and pepper on all sides. Heat the oil in a large (6- to 8-quart) Dutch oven over high heat until it begins to smoke. Using tongs, lower half the ribs into the pan in a single layer. Brown all sides very well, 8 to 12 minutes, then remove the browned ribs to a platter and brown the remaining ribs.

2. Braising mixture. Pour off most of the fat in the pan, reduce the heat to medium, and add the bacon. Cook, stirring often, until it renders most of its fat and is almost crisp. Add the onions and garlic and cook until softened, scraping up the browned bits on the bottom of the pan, about 4 minutes. Stir in the wine, tomatoes, ¾ teaspoon salt, and a generous grinding of pepper. Return the ribs to the pot and bring the liquid to a simmer.

3. Bouquet garni. Divide the savory and thyme sprigs into 2 piles and add a sage sprig and half the bay leaves to each. Tie each bundle with a piece of kitchen twine and tuck them between the ribs in the braising pan. Cover the pot and reduce the heat to very low. Gently simmer the ribs until they are tender enough to pierce with a fork and the meat easily pulls off the bone, 2½ to 3 hours.

4. Finishing the sauce. Transfer the ribs to a warmed large platter. Remove and discard the herb bundles. If you see any fat on the surface of the braising liquid, skim it off. Stir in the chopped savory and sage and increase the heat under the pan to medium-high. Boil the sauce until it is thickened enough to coat a spoon, 10 to 15 minutes. Stir in the parsley. Taste and season with additional salt and pepper if needed. Spoon the sauce over the ribs and serve with Herb-Roasted Potatoes (page 146), Baked Herb Polenta (page 154), or crusty bread.

Pork Tenderloin Crusted with Mediterranean Herbs

6 servings

Pork tenderloin is easy to cook and reasonably priced. Rolled in a mixture of robust Mediterranean herbs and seared in olive oil, it takes on an intensely aromatic, almost smoky flavor. When served with tangy red pepper and hazelnut sauce, it is a gastronomic triumph.

You must use enough finely chopped herbs to form a generous crust on the pork, but if you use only robust herbs, the flavor will be overly strong. For this reason, parsley makes up the majority of the mixture in this recipe. Parsley is bulk—the herbal green version of bread crumbs; it contributes flavor to the dish, but you can use quantities without it taking over.

If you have leftovers, spread the sauce on a split baguette, stuff it with the sliced cold meat and some arugula, and you'll have an unforgettable sandwich.

> *Red Pepper and Hazelnut Sauce (page 331)*
> *2 pork tenderloins (about 1 pound each)*
> *Salt and freshly ground black pepper*
> *½ cup finely chopped fresh parsley*
> *¼ cup finely chopped fresh rosemary*
> *2 tablespoons finely chopped fresh sage, savory, marjoram, or oregano*
> *3 tablespoons extra-virgin olive oil*

1. Sauce. Prepare the red pepper sauce up to 1 week ahead; store covered in the refrigerator. Let it warm to room temperature before serving or warm the sauce gently by stirring it in a stainless-steel bowl set over simmering water. Don't overheat the sauce or the oil will separate.

2. Herb crust. Trim the pork tenderloins of any fat. On one side of the meat you will see a thin tough membrane called the silver skin. Remove as much as you can with the tip of a sharp thin knife. Sprinkle the pork liberally on all sides with salt and pepper. Combine the herbs in a large shallow dish. Pressing firmly, roll the tenderloins in the herbs, coating all sides of the meat with a thick layer. If there are any herbs left that do not stick, sprinkle them over the top. Wrap each herbed tenderloin tightly in plastic wrap and refrigerate for 2 to 24 hours to give the herbs a chance to flavor the meat.

3. Cooking the pork. Preheat the oven to 400°F. Heat the olive oil in a large (12-inch) ovenproof skillet over high heat until the pan is very hot and the oil smokes steadily. Unwrap the herbed tenderloins. Using tongs, carefully lower the pork into the pan. Sear the pork, still over high heat, until the herbs on the underside turn a deep brown color, about 3 minutes. Be patient—don't turn the meat until the crust has lost all green color. Rotate the meat a quarter turn and continue to brown the meat on each side. When 3 sides are browned, turn the last side into the oil and place the skillet in the oven (the last side will brown in the oven). Roast the pork until an instant-read thermometer inserted horizontally into the center of a tenderloin registers 145° to 150°F, about 8 minutes. Remove the pork from the oven, transfer it to a plate, cover very loosely with aluminum foil, and let it rest in a warm place, such as the back of the stove, for 5 to 10 minutes.

4. Serving. Using a sharp thin knife, slice the meat on a diagonal against the grain ¼ to ½ inch thick. Arrange the slices on warmed serving plates or a serving platter. Spoon some of the red pepper sauce over the top of the meat in a zigzag pattern and pass the remaining sauce in a serving dish at the table. Serve with Herb-Roasted Potatoes (page 146) or Baked Herb Polenta (page 154).

MAPLE-AND-HERB-BRINED PORK ROAST

6 servings

Pork that is sold today is so lean that cooks need to devise ways to help keep it moist in the oven. Brining is one solution. When the meat is soaked overnight in a brine (salt solution), it absorbs some of the liquid, which not only flavors it but also keeps it from drying out. The brine in this recipe combines the rich flavor of maple with fresh rosemary, sage, and thyme and has just enough salt to yield good results without making the meat seem overly salty.

A boneless pork loin roast can look very different depending on where you buy it. Sometimes you'll find a long piece of the loin, just as it's cut from the ribs, but often the roast will consist of 2 pieces tied together so that it's twice as thick around. I prefer the thin untied roast because it cooks faster and more evenly, and there's more surface to become browned and flavorful. If your roast is 2 pieces tied together, you'll have to untie them for the brining, then you have the choice of retying them or roasting them separately.

BRINE
¾ cup pure maple syrup (grade A or B)
1 cup water
4 teaspoons salt
4 4-inch sprigs fresh rosemary
2 4-inch sprigs fresh sage
6 3-inch sprigs fresh English thyme
4 fresh bay laurel leaves, or 2 dried
2 teaspoons yellow mustard seeds, or 1 teaspoon dried yellow mustard
Ice cubes

1 3-pound boneless pork loin roast
Freshly ground black pepper
Optional: 3 to 5 8-inch branches rosemary, sage, or bay
¾ cup white wine, such as Riesling or Chardonnay

1. Making the brine. Bring the maple syrup, the water, and the salt to a boil in a small saucepan. Stir in the herbs and mustard, cover, and let steep off the heat for 10 minutes. Pour the brine into a large measuring cup and add enough ice cubes to measure 2 cups.

2. Brining the pork. If your roast consists of 2 pieces of loin tied together, cut the string and separate the pieces. Put the pork in a container in which it will fit snugly but comfortably and pour in the cold brine. The liquid should just cover the meat; if it doesn't, add more water. Cover and refrigerate for 16 to 24 hours.

3. Roasting. Preheat the oven to 450°F. Remove the pork from the brine and discard the brine. Rinse the pork under cold water and pat it dry with paper towels. If the pork is in 2 pieces, you can tie them back together as they were or keep them separated. Season the outside of the pork generously with pepper. Put the whole herb branches in the bottom of a small roasting pan or shallow baking dish and set the pork on top. If large herb branches are not available, set the meat directly in the pan. Pour the wine into the pan. Roast the pork for 20 minutes. Reduce the heat to 325°F and continue to roast until an instant-read thermometer inserted in the center of the roast registers 145° to 150°F. Be sure to take readings in more than one place in the roast and use the lowest. If the roast is untied, it will take 30 to 60 minutes after the oven temperature is lowered. If the roast is 2 pieces tied together, it will take 1 to 1½ hours.

4. Serving. Transfer the roast to a platter and let it rest for at least 10 minutes. Pour the jus that formed in the bottom of the pan into a sauceboat and skim off any fat that rises to the surface. Taste for seasoning and serve the jus separately. Slice the roast and serve with Potatoes in Herbed Cream (page 148) or Mashed Potatoes with Toasted Coriander (page 151).

PORK CHOPS WITH SAGE, ONION, AND PROSCIUTTO

4 servings

These pan-seared and braised chops, quick and easy enough for a busy weeknight, are proof that the traditional combination of pork, sage, and onion is unbeatable. Though it might seem that ½ cup sage would be overly strong for 4 chops, the flavor mellows when it is slowly cooked with the onions and blends deliciously with the pork and prosciutto flavors.

> *4 bone-in thick-cut loin or rib pork chops (about 1¼ inches thick and 10 to 12 ounces each)*
> *Salt and freshly ground black pepper*
> *2 tablespoons extra-virgin olive oil*
> *1 large onion (about 10 ounces), sliced ¼ inch thick*
> *½ cup very coarsely chopped fresh sage or very small whole sage leaves*
> *4 ounces thinly sliced prosciutto, cut into ¼-inch-wide strips*
> *1½ cups homemade (page 12) or canned low-sodium chicken stock*
> *2 teaspoons Dijon mustard*

1. Searing the pork. Generously season both sides of the chops with salt and pepper. Heat the oil in a large (12-inch) skillet over medium-high heat until it begins to smoke. Using tongs, lower the pork chops into the pan and brown well on both sides, about 3 minutes per side. Transfer the chops to a large plate and set them aside.

2. Onion mixture. Reduce the heat under the skillet to medium-low and add the onion and sage. Cook uncovered, stirring often, until the onion is softened and light brown in color, about 4 minutes. Stir in the prosciutto and cook until it loses its rosy color, about 1 minute. Add the stock and mustard.

3. Braising. Return the pork chops to the pan, reduce the heat to low, and cover the pan. Very gently simmer the chops until an instant-read thermometer inserted horizontally into the center of a chop registers 145° to 150°F, 10 to 12 minutes. Transfer the chops to warmed serving plates or a platter. Increase the heat under the skillet to high and boil the sauce until it is slightly thickened. Taste and season with additional salt and pepper if needed. Spoon the sauce over the pork and serve right away. Accompany with Baked Herb Polenta (page 154) or Mashed Potatoes with Toasted Coriander (page 151).

HERB-CRUSTED RACK OF LAMB

4 to 5 servings

Superb lamb is raised in Ellensburg, Washington, just on the other side of the Cascade Mountains from The Herbfarm. It often appears on our menu in this signature dish, and countless guests have commented that it's the best they have ever had. This preparation differs from most other versions of herbed rack of lamb in that the fresh herbs are pressed directly onto the uncooked meat, and then the racks are seared in hot olive oil until the herbs form a deep brown crust and take on an intensely aromatic and toasty flavor.

This recipe calls for frenched lamb racks, which means the thin pieces of fatty meat between the ribs are removed and the bones scraped clean. They are often sold this way in supermarkets. If you buy the racks from a butcher, ask him or her to remove the fat and silver skin from the rib-eye as well.

2 trimmed and frenched racks of lamb (about 1¼ pounds each trimmed;
* 2½ pounds each untrimmed)*
6 tablespoons finely chopped fresh parsley
¼ cup finely chopped fresh rosemary
2 tablespoons finely chopped fresh thyme, sage, or savory
Salt and freshly ground black pepper
3 tablespoons extra-virgin olive oil

SAUCE
½ cup full-bodied red wine, such as Cabernet Sauvignon or Merlot
1 cup homemade (page 12) or canned low-sodium chicken stock
2 teaspoons Roasted Garlic Paste (page 341)
2 teaspoons Dijon mustard
4 teaspoons balsamic vinegar

1. Trimming and coating the lamb. Peel away any remaining fat that covers the rib-eye (the large piece of meat) and remove the thin tough membrane called the silver skin, using a sharp thin knife (if your butcher did not do this for you already). The top of the rib-eye should now be completely bare but still firmly attached to the bones. Mix the herbs together on a shallow platter. Firmly press the racks into the herbs, coating all sides of the exposed meat with a thick layer. If there are any herbs left that do not stick, sprinkle them over the rib-eyes. Wrap each herbed rack tightly in plastic wrap and refrigerate for 2 to 24 hours. The herbs will act as a dry marinade and flavor the meat.

2. Cooking the lamb. Preheat the oven to 450°F. Unwrap the lamb racks and season both sides generously with salt and pepper. Heat the olive oil in a large (12-inch) ovenproof skillet over high heat until the pan is very hot and the oil smokes steadily. Carefully lower the lamb racks with the top of the rib-eye facing down into the pan. Keeping the heat high, sear the lamb until the herbs on the underside turn a deep brown color, about 3 minutes. Turn the racks over and put the pan in the oven (the underside will brown while they roast). Roast the racks until an instant-read thermometer inserted into the center of the eye registers 120° to 125°F for medium-rare or 130° to 135°F for medium, 10 to 15 minutes. The temperature will continue to rise about 5° once they are out of the oven. Remove the skillet from the oven and put it on the stovetop. Transfer the racks to a platter and cover them very loosely with aluminum foil. Let them rest while you prepare the sauce.

3. Sauce. Pour off any oil that remains in the skillet but leave behind any browned herbs (keep a hot pad or dry towel over the skillet handle to remind you it is extremely hot). Put the skillet over medium heat, add the wine, and stir and scrape up the browned bits on the bottom of the pan. Whisk in the stock, roasted garlic, and mustard and cook at a steady boil until the sauce is reduced to about one-third of its original volume and lightly thickened, 4 to 5 minutes. Stir in the balsamic vinegar. Taste and season with salt and pepper if needed.

4. Carving and serving. Cut the racks between the ribs on a cutting board, allowing your knife to find the spot where it can easily slip between the bones. Arrange the chops on warmed serving plates, allowing 3 or 4 per person. Pour the sauce over top and serve right away. The lamb is good with White Beans with Herbed Onion-Garlic Confit (page 155), Herb-Roasted Potatoes (page 146), or Minted French Lentils (page 152).

HERB SUBSTITUTIONS

- *In place of the 2 tablespoons thyme, sage, or savory, add 2 teaspoons finely chopped fresh lavender buds or 1 teaspoon finely chopped dried lavender buds and increase the chopped parsley to ½ cup.*

Roast Boneless Leg of Lamb with Rosemary and Lavender

6 servings

To me, roasting leg of lamb without rosemary and garlic is like baking bread without salt. Of course, this lamb preparation uses lots of both, but the understated addition of lavender imparts an intriguing bit of aroma that blends deliciously with the other ardently savory flavors. I like to use a boneless leg of lamb because I can remove more fat and tendon, and the herb paste can be distributed inside and out. It also roasts more evenly and is much easier to carve. This recipe calls for a boned sirloin end (top half of the leg). If your market doesn't offer this cut boned, it's simple to remove the bones yourself with a sharp boning knife or ask your butcher to do it for you. This roast needs a lengthy marinade, so start it the day before you plan to serve it.

HERB PASTE
½ cup fresh rosemary leaves
4 teaspoons fresh lavender buds, or 2 teaspoons dried
1 tablespoon fresh English thyme leaves
6 cloves garlic, peeled
1 tablespoon Dijon mustard
1 teaspoon salt
1 teaspoon freshly ground black pepper
6 tablespoons extra-virgin olive oil

1 boneless sirloin end leg of lamb (top half of the leg; about 3 pounds)
Optional: 6 thick woody branches rosemary, about 8 inches long

SAUCE
¼ cup red wine
1 teaspoon mustard
1 teaspoon balsamic vinegar

1. Herb paste. Process all the herb paste ingredients except the olive oil in a food processor until the herbs are coarsely chopped. With the machine running, slowly pour in the oil. Stop the machine and scrape down the sides, then process to a coarse, thick sauce consistency.

2. Marinating the lamb. If the lamb is tied with string, untie it. Spread the lamb open; it should be shaped somewhat like a fan and about 3 inches thick at the widest part. With a sharp thin knife, remove as much fat and tendon from both sides of the meat as you can. Put the lamb in a glass or ceramic baking dish in which it fits snugly. Smear the top with half the herb paste, then turn the meat over and smear it with the rest of the paste. Cover tightly with plastic wrap and refrigerate for 8 to 24 hours.

3. Roasting. Preheat the oven to 425°F. Without scraping off the marinade, roll the lamb back into its original shape. Using 3 lengths of kitchen twine, snugly tie the roast in 3 places, spaced equally, to create an evenly shaped roast. Lay the thick rosemary branches in a single layer in the bottom of a small roasting pan or shallow baking dish. Set the roast on top of the branches. If rosemary branches are not available, set the roast directly in the pan. Roast the meat in the hot oven for 10 minutes. Reduce the heat to 350°F and continue to roast until an instant-read thermometer inserted into the center registers 130° to 135°F for medium-rare, about 1½ hours. The temperature in the interior will rise about 10° after it is removed from the oven. Be sure to take readings in more than one place in the roast and use the lowest. Transfer the roast to a board or platter, cover it very loosely with aluminum foil, and let it rest for 10 minutes while you prepare the sauce.

4. Sauce. Remove the rosemary branches from the pan. Tilt the roasting pan so that the drippings collect in one corner and use a spoon to skim off as much fat as you can. Pour the red wine into the pan and put it over low heat. Use a whisk to stir up and dissolve any browned bits clinging to the bottom. Stir in the mustard and vinegar. Taste and season with salt if necessary. It will be very strong but only a small amount is used on each serving. Remove the strings from the roast and thinly slice the meat. Arrange the meat on a platter and pour the sauce over. Serve with White Beans with Herbed Onion-Garlic Confit (page 155), Herb-Roasted Potatoes (page 146), or Minted French Lentils (page 152).

Braised Lamb Shanks with Sun-Dried Tomatoes, Orange, and Rosemary

4 servings

If it's your first time preparing braised lamb shanks, you're likely to discover a dish that will become a longtime favorite. When seared and patiently simmered with red wine, herbs, orange zest, and sun-dried tomato, the shanks turn meltingly tender and deeply flavored. Here the herbs become a bouquet garni—little bundles of the sprigs are tied with string to release their flavor throughout the braise and then are pulled out. The dish is ideal for a dinner party because each lamb shank is an individual serving size, and the dish can be prepared up to 3 days ahead of time. As it rests in the refrigerator, the flavor will improve.

> *4 lamb shanks (about 1 pound each)*
> *Salt and freshly ground black pepper*
> *12 4-inch sprigs fresh thyme*
> *8 4-inch sprigs fresh rosemary*
> *3 fresh bay laurel leaves, or 2 dried*
> *3 tablespoons extra-virgin olive oil*
> *2 medium onions (about 1 pound), thinly sliced*
> *1 carrot, peeled and sliced ½ inch thick*
> *8 cloves garlic, coarsely chopped*
> *2 ounces sliced dry-packed sun-dried tomatoes (about 1½ cups)*
> *Thinly sliced zest (removed with a zester) and juice of 2 oranges*
> *2 cups full-bodied red wine, such as Cabernet Sauvignon or Merlot*
> *¼ cup coarsely chopped fresh parsley*

1. Shanks and bouquet garni. Trim the excess fat from the lamb shanks until you expose the red meat on about half the surface of the shank. Season them liberally with salt and pepper. Divide the thyme and rosemary sprigs into 3 bunches. Place a bay leaf on each pile and tie each one into a bundle using a small piece of kitchen twine.

2. Browning the shanks. Heat the oil in a 6-quart Dutch oven or other heavy pot wide enough to hold the shanks in a single layer comfortably over high heat until the oil smokes. Using tongs, carefully lower the shanks into the pan and cook until the undersides are well browned. Turn the shanks and continue to brown all sides. Don't take shortcuts, for much of the flavor of the sauce develops in this step. It will take a total of 8 to 12 minutes. Remove the shanks to a plate.

3. Braising. Reduce the heat to medium-low and add the onions, carrot, and garlic to the pan. Cook, stirring often and scraping up the browned bits on the bottom, until the vegetables are softened and beginning to turn a caramel color, about 8 minutes. Stir in the tomatoes, orange zest and juice, ¾ teaspoon salt, and a dozen grinds of pepper. Return the lamb shanks to the pan and nestle them amongst the vegetables. Pour in the wine and tuck the herb bundles between the shanks. Cover the pan tightly, reduce the heat to the lowest setting, and let the meat slowly braise at a gentle simmer until the shanks are so tender that the meat falls from the bones, 2 to 3 hours. (At this point the dish can be cooled, covered, and refrigerated for up to 3 days. Heat covered in a 375°F oven until heated through, about 40 minutes.)

4. Finishing the sauce and serving. Carefully transfer the shanks to a warmed platter. To serve without the bones, hold the meat in place with a fork while you gently pull out and discard the bones with tongs, leaving the meat as intact as possible. Still using your tongs, pull out and discard the 3 herb bundles from the sauce. Bring the sauce to a simmer and stir in the parsley. Taste and season with additional salt and black pepper if needed. Pour the sauce over the braised meat on the platter. Serve the shanks with Baked Herb Polenta (page 154), Green Mashed Potatoes (page 150), Mashed Potatoes with Toasted Coriander (page 151), or crusty bread.

CHAPTER 8

Breads

Like all areas of cooking, bread making engages all of your senses, but it is a particularly soulful pursuit. The bouncy, silky feel of the soft, elastic dough, the hollow thump of a crusty brown loaf, and the earthy flavor of slowly fermented wheat flour all contribute to the experience, but what's most captivating is the blessed smell of the loaf of bread as it bakes in your own kitchen. Add a measure of fresh rosemary, sage, or thyme and the fragrance is even more heavenly.

This chapter will show you some of the ways you can incorporate fresh herbs into both yeasted and quick breads. In the following recipes fresh thyme melds with buttery onions on plush potato rolls, lavender adds intrigue to walnut bread, and a combination of thyme, rosemary, and sage encrusts a chewy flatbread. Soft-leafed herbs have a place as well. Basil pesto is irresistible when it is rolled like a spiral in a crusty loaf, marjoram is delicious in a moist corn bread, and dill gives character to whole-grain Cheddar biscuits. I've even included a recipe for turning a quality loaf from the bakery into a festive and fragrant herbed garlic bread.

Measuring Flour

The method you use to measure flour affects the accuracy of the recipe. Flour that is measured by scooping it up with the measuring cup will be more compacted than flour that is spooned into the cup. All the recipes in this book call for the spoon-and-level method, meaning you fill the cup by spooning the flour into it, then you use a knife to sweep the top level. The most accurate and easiest way to measure flour is with a scale, so I've also included the dry weight whenever flour is used in a recipe. One cup of all-purpose flour or white bread flour, spooned and leveled, weighs 4½ ounces.

HERBED FOCACCIA

Makes 1 large bread, 8 servings

When you pull this handsome bread from the oven, you can't help but feel a sense of great accomplishment, yet it's quite simple to prepare. This recipe makes an impressive large rustic bread, about 1½ inches thick, topped with loads of fragrant toasty herbs. Serve it with soup or salad—it needs no butter at the table because it's baked with a coating of olive oil. Or slice it horizontally and make a giant sandwich that you can cut into wedges.

> *2 cups lukewarm water (105° to 110°F)*
> *1 package active dry yeast (2½ teaspoons)*
> *2 tablespoons coarsely chopped fresh rosemary*
> *2 tablespoons coarsely chopped fresh sage*
> *1 tablespoon coarsely chopped fresh thyme, winter savory, or oregano*
> *1½ teaspoons salt*
> *4½ cups unbleached bread flour (spoon and level; 20 ounces), plus*
> *   additional flour as needed*
> *3 tablespoons extra-virgin olive oil*

1. Dough and first rise. Pour the water into the bowl of a heavy-duty electric mixer or a large mixing bowl. Sprinkle the yeast over the water and let sit for several minutes to dissolve. Stir the herbs together in a small bowl. Add half the herb mixture to the yeasted water. Cover the remaining herbs and refrigerate. Stir the salt and flour into the yeast mixture to form a soft dough. Knead for 8 minutes with the dough hook or paddle at medium speed, or knead the dough by hand on a lightly floured surface until it is elastic and satiny, 8 to 10 minutes. The dough should be very soft and will stick to the bottom of the electric mixer bowl as it is kneaded, but if it is too sticky to pull away from the sides of the bowl after 5 minutes of kneading, add another ¼ cup flour. If you are kneading by hand, add only as much flour as needed to keep the dough from sticking. Put the dough in a large bowl, cover it with plastic wrap and then a clean towel, and let it rise at room temperature until doubled in bulk, 1½ to 2 hours.

2. Second rise. In another large mixing bowl, stir the olive oil and reserved herbs together and spread the mixture evenly over the bottom of the bowl. Punch down the dough and scoop it into the second bowl on top of the herb mixture. Let the dough rise again until doubled, about 40 minutes.

3. Forming the loaf. Place a baking stone on the center rack of your oven and preheat the oven to 400°F. Place a sheet of parchment paper on a large cookie sheet or the back side of a large baking sheet. This will serve as the peel that you will use to transfer the bread to the baking stone. Without punching down the dough, turn the dough out onto the paper, letting it fall out with the herbs and oil on top. Use your fingertips to poke the dough while at the same time gently pulling it into an oval about 12 inches long. The dough will deflate somewhat, but keep as much rise in it as you can. Use a paper towel to blot any oil that runs down the sides. Let the dough rise again for 10 to 15 minutes to restore its puffiness.

4. Baking. With a pair of scissors, trim the excess parchment paper extending beyond the edges of the dough so that the paper doesn't burn in the oven. Set the edge of your peel on the edge of the oven rack in front of the baking stone. Carefully grab one edge of the parchment and slide it with the loaf onto the stone. Bake the bread until golden brown on top and well browned on the bottom, about 25 minutes. It will puff a little more in the oven. Remove the loaf from the oven with a large spatula and let it cool on a wire rack for at least 10 minutes. Slice it into rectangles with a serrated knife or break it at the table.

 HERB SUBSTITUTIONS
- *Instead of the herb mixture, use a single herb, such as ¼ cup coarsely chopped fresh rosemary, thyme, savory, oregano, or sage.*

PESTO SPIRAL LOAVES

Makes 2 14-inch loaves

Here's a bread for pesto lovers, so flavorful you'll want to make it a meal. Basil pesto is rolled, jelly-roll fashion, into basic white bread dough to form loaves shaped like a bâtard, the wider softer-crusted version of a baguette. The fragrant stuffing is not revealed until the loaves are sliced, but the irresistible aroma gives away their secret before a knife comes near it. If you make and freeze your own pesto when basil is flourishing, you can enjoy baking these loaves in any season.

> *2 cups lukewarm water (105° to 110°F)*
> *1 package active dry yeast (2½ teaspoons)*
> *1 teaspoon sugar*
> *2 teaspoons salt*
> *5 cups unbleached bread flour (spoon and level; 22½ ounces), plus
> additional as needed*
> *⅔ cup Classic Basil Pesto (page 102)*

1. Forming the dough and first rise. Pour the water into the bowl of a heavy-duty electric mixer or a large mixing bowl. Sprinkle the yeast over the water and let sit for several minutes to dissolve. Stir in the sugar, salt, and flour to make a medium-soft dough. Knead for 8 minutes with the dough hook at medium speed, adding up to ½ cup more flour if necessary so that the dough pulls away from the sides of the bowl; or knead the dough on a lightly floured surface until it is elastic and satiny, 8 to 10 minutes, adding the minimum amount of additional flour needed to keep the dough from sticking. Put the dough in a large mixing bowl, cover it with plastic wrap and then a clean towel, and let it rise at room temperature until doubled in bulk, 1½ to 2 hours.

2. Shaping and second rise. Punch down the dough, turn it out onto a lightly floured surface, and cut it in half. With a large rolling pin, roll one of the pieces into an oval, about 15 x 10 inches. The dough will be elastic, and you will need to be persistent until it stays the size you want. Using a rubber spatula, spread half the pesto over the surface of the dough, leaving a ½-inch border all around. Beginning from the short end, roll up the dough tightly. Pinch the seam to seal it well. Gently stretch and shape the loaf until it is an even cylinder about 14 inches long. Place the loaf seam side down on a large parchment-lined baking sheet. Shape the second loaf in the same way and place it alongside the first, allowing space for them to spread. Sprinkle the tops of the loaves with a little more flour, cover them with a clean towel, and let them rise until again doubled in bulk, 1 to 1½ hours.

3. Baking. Preheat the oven to 375°F. Slash 4 shallow slits in the top of each loaf with a sharp serrated knife or straight-edged razor blade. Bake the loaves on the center oven rack until they are well browned and sound hollow when tapped on the bottom, 40 to 45 minutes. Cool them on a rack for at least 30 minutes before slicing.

POTATO, THYME, AND ONION BOULES

Makes 6 small round breads

These small round breads have a distinct and very appealing texture—plush and airy, yet at the same time chewy and substantial. They're topped with lightly cooked thyme-flavored onions that become beautifully brown in the oven. The very soft and sticky dough is best kneaded in a heavy-duty electric mixer, but if you don't own one, you can knead it in a food processor (instructions follow the recipe). The dough shaped into smaller rolls makes great hamburger buns.

> *1 large russet (Idaho) potato (about 12 ounces)*
> *2 cups lukewarm water (105° to 110°F)*
> *1 package active dry yeast (2½ teaspoons)*
> *2 teaspoons sugar*
> *1 tablespoon fresh whole thyme leaves, all stems removed*
> *2 teaspoons salt*
> *5 cups unbleached bread flour (spoon and level; 22½ ounces), plus*
>   *additional as needed*
>
> TOPPING
> *1½ tablespoons unsalted butter*
> *1 large onion, thinly sliced*
> *1 tablespoon fresh whole thyme leaves, all stems removed*
> *½ teaspoon salt*

1. Potato. Preheat the oven to 425°F. Pierce the potato with a fork in several places and bake until it is cooked through and soft, about 50 minutes. (If you prefer, you can cook the potato in a microwave oven until soft, 10 to 12 minutes on high power.) Split the potato open to let steam escape and let stand until cool enough to handle. Scoop out the flesh into a small bowl and mash it with a fork. Discard the skin. Measure 1 cup of the mashed potato.

2. Dough. Pour the water into the bowl of a heavy-duty electric mixer fitted with the paddle. Sprinkle the yeast and sugar over the water and let sit for several minutes to dissolve. Add the potato, thyme, salt, and half the flour and mix on low speed until all the ingredients are incorporated. Add the remaining flour and knead for about 5 minutes on medium speed. At this point the dough should pull away from the sides of the bowl, but it will stick at the bottom. If the dough sticks to the sides of the bowl, add up to ½ cup more flour, a little at a time. Place the dough in a large mixing bowl and cover with plastic wrap and then a clean towel. Let it rise at room temperature until doubled in bulk, about 2 hours.

3. Topping. Melt the butter in a medium saucepan over medium heat. Add the onion and cook, stirring often, until they are softened but not browned, about 6 minutes. Stir in the thyme and salt. Cool.

4. Shaping the breads. Line 2 baking sheets with parchment paper. Turn the dough out onto a heavily floured surface. Divide it into 6 equal pieces and sprinkle them with more flour. Shape each piece into a ball by gently tucking the sides under and rotating the dough ¼ turn with each tuck. Repeat 5 to 6 times until the dough is a perfect round. Place 3 rounds on each baking sheet and pat them gently into circles about 4 inches in diameter. Top them with the onion mixture, dividing it equally and spreading it to the edges. Let the breads rise again until doubled, about 45 minutes.

5. Baking. Preheat the oven to 375°F. Bake the breads until the crust underneath the topping is golden brown and they feel firm when you lightly press on the tops, 35 to 40 minutes. The onion might become slightly blackened at the tips, but they will not taste burnt. If you are baking both trays on separate racks in the same oven, switch their positions halfway through the baking time. Let the breads cool on a rack—they will seem doughy if they are eaten while still hot.

FOR HAMBURGER BUNS

Divide the dough into 12 pieces, instead of 6, and pat them into 3-inch circles. Proceed as directed but reduce the baking time to 30 to 35 minutes.

FOOD PROCESSOR VARIATION

If you have a large-capacity food processor (11 cups or larger), follow the same procedure as for the electric mixer but process with the steel blade for 30 seconds after the first addition of flour and 30 seconds after the second. If you have a smaller food processor, divide the ingredients in half and process the dough in 2 separate batches.

 HERB SUBSTITUTIONS
  • *These breads are equally delicious with 1 tablespoon finely chopped rosemary, 2 tablespoons finely chopped sage, or ¼ cup coarsely chopped fresh dill substituted for the thyme. Whichever herb you use, divide it equally between the dough and topping.*

Lavender, Walnut, and Honey Slipper Breads

Makes 2 loaves

These breads are shaped like ciabatte, the flat, oval Italian breads named for their resemblance to a slipper. They are mildly sweet, with a touch of lavender accentuating the pronounced flavor of honey, and a generous scattering of walnuts to lend an earthy flavor. Thin slices of this bread are superb served for brunch with jams and marmalade or to present on a tray of cheeses after dinner.

This recipe makes a soft dough, which is easiest to knead with a heavy-duty electric mixer or in a food processor.

> 1½ cups lukewarm water (105° to 110°F)
> 1 package active dry yeast (2½ teaspoons)
> 2 tablespoons medium- to strong-flavored honey, such as blackberry or fireweed
> 1 tablespoon coarsely chopped fresh lavender buds, or 1½ teaspoons coarsely chopped dried
> 1¼ teaspoons salt
> 3½ cups unbleached bread flour (spoon and level; 16 ounces), plus additional as needed
> 1 cup coarsely chopped walnuts (4 ounces)

1. Dough. Pour the water into the bowl of a heavy-duty electric mixer fitted with the paddle. Sprinkle the yeast over the water and let sit for several minutes to dissolve. Add the honey, lavender, salt, and flour and mix on low speed until all the ingredients are incorporated. Knead for about 6 minutes on medium speed. At this point the dough will be very soft and stick to the bottom of the bowl as you knead it, but it should pull away from the sides of the bowl. If the dough sticks to the sides of the bowl, add up to ¼ cup more flour, a little at a time. (To knead the dough in a food processor with the steel blade, follow the same procedure as for the electric mixer but process for only 50 to 60 seconds.) Spread the walnuts on a work surface and turn the dough out on top of them. Sprinkle the dough lightly with flour and knead briefly until the walnuts are evenly incorporated, using a dough scraper if it sticks to the board. Place the dough in a large mixing bowl and cover with plastic wrap and then a clean towel. Let rise at room temperature until doubled in bulk, about 1½ hours.

2. Shaping. Turn the dough out onto a lightly floured surface. Dust with flour and pat the dough into a 10-inch square. Fold it in half, pat it out a little, then fold it in quarters and pat it again so that you end up with a 6-inch square of dough. Cut the dough in half with a sharp knife. Dusting it with flour as necessary, lift a piece of dough and stretch it out to a 12 x 4-inch oval. It should look like the sole of a very big shoe. Repeat with the other piece of dough. Transfer the loaves to a parchment-lined baking sheet and dust again with flour. Cover the loaves with a clean towel and let them rise at room temperature until doubled, about 45 minutes.

3. Baking. Preheat the oven to 375°F. Bake the loaves on the center oven rack until they are dark brown and sound hollow when thumped on the bottom, 30 to 35 minutes. Cool completely on a rack before slicing.

Marjoram Corn Bread

Makes 1 8-inch-square bread, 9 servings

Because fresh marjoram is such a good match with sweet corn, I had the inspiration to add it to corn bread, and it turned out a winner. This especially moist bread is delicious with main-course soups or bean dishes.

2 teaspoons unsalted butter, softened, for the pan
1 cup all-purpose flour (spoon and level; 4½ ounces)
1½ teaspoons baking powder
¼ teaspoon baking soda
1 teaspoon salt
¾ cup stone-ground cornmeal
1 tablespoon sugar
1 cup whole or low-fat buttermilk
2 large eggs
2 tablespoons finely chopped fresh marjoram
¼ cup finely chopped green onions
4 tablespoons unsalted butter, melted

Preheat the oven to 400°F. Butter an 8-inch-square baking pan. Sift the flour, baking powder, baking soda, and salt into a medium mixing bowl. Stir in the cornmeal and sugar. In a separate bowl, whisk together the buttermilk and eggs. Pour the liquid into the dry ingredients and stir just until all the ingredients are moistened. Stir in the marjoram, green onions, and melted butter. Pour the mixture into the prepared pan. Bake until the cornbread is lightly browned and pulls away from the sides of the pan, about 25 minutes. Cool slightly in the pan before cutting and serving.

DILL AND CHEDDAR THREE-GRAIN BISCUITS

Makes 8 large biscuits

These shaggy biscuits are crisp and light, but their whole-grain character means they're substantial and decidedly not fluffy. Fresh dill plays beautifully off the sharpness of the cheese and the nuttiness of the grains. You can have them ready for the oven in minutes, and they are a wonderful accompaniment to nearly any kind of soup.

1 cup all-purpose flour (spoon and level; 4½ ounces)
½ cup whole-wheat flour
¼ cup rye flour
¼ cup cornmeal
1 tablespoon baking powder
½ teaspoon salt
4 tablespoons unsalted butter, slightly softened and cut into ½-inch cubes
1 cup grated sharp Cheddar cheese (2 ounces)
¼ cup coarsely chopped fresh dill
1 cup plus 1 tablespoon whole or low-fat (2%) milk

1. Dough. Preheat the oven to 400°F. Stir together the flours, cornmeal, baking powder, and salt in a medium mixing bowl. Cut in the butter with a pastry blender until the largest pieces are smaller than a pea (or pulse the mixture in a food processor). Stir in the cheese and dill. Pour in the milk and stir just enough to moisten all the ingredients. The dough should be soft enough to scoop with a spoon.

2. Shaping and baking. With a large spoon or your hands, form 8 large shaggy mounds of the dough, each a little more than 2 inches in diameter, and space them evenly on a parchment-lined baking sheet. Bake the biscuits until they are speckled brown on top and deeply browned on their bottoms, 20 to 25 minutes. Let the biscuits cool slightly on the pan but serve while still warm.

CORIANDER-ORANGE SCONES

Makes 12 scones

These scones are as quick and easy to make as any biscuit or muffin and are just the thing for a leisurely Sunday morning breakfast or brunch. If you didn't know they were made with coriander, you probably wouldn't guess it was one of the ingredients. The flavor of the seeds blends in mysteriously, making the scones seem extra buttery and slightly toasty. Always buy coriander seeds whole and grind them shortly before you use them in a spice mill or blender.

2 cups all-purpose flour (spoon and level; 9 ounces)
2 teaspoons baking powder
¾ teaspoon salt
1 tablespoon freshly ground dried coriander seeds, not toasted
5 tablespoons sugar, plus 2 teaspoons for the topping
Finely chopped zest of 1 orange
4 ounces (1 stick) unsalted butter, slightly softened and cut into ½-inch cubes
¾ cup dried currants or raisins
¾ cup plus 2 tablespoons whole milk
Egg wash made with 1 large egg and 1 tablespoon milk

1. Dough. Preheat the oven to 425°F. Sift the flour, baking powder, and salt into a medium mixing bowl. Stir in the coriander, 5 tablespoons sugar, and the orange zest. Cut in the butter with a pastry blender until the largest pieces are smaller than a pea (or pulse the mixture in a food processor). Stir in the currants, then add the milk and stir just until it forms a firm dough.

2. Shaping. Turn the dough out onto a lightly floured surface and divide it in half. Dust with a little flour and pat each piece into a circle 6 inches in diameter and ¾ inch thick. Cut each circle into 6 wedges with a large chef's knife. Transfer the scones to a baking sheet lined with parchment paper, spacing them 1 inch apart.

3. Glazing and baking. Brush the scones with the egg wash and sprinkle them with the additional sugar. Bake until they are a deep golden brown, 16 to 18 minutes. Lift one to check that the underside is well browned before you remove them from the oven. Transfer to a cooling rack. The scones are best while still warm. To reheat the scones, put them on a baking sheet in a 250°F oven for 6 to 8 minutes.

Herbed Olive Oil Crackers

Makes 24 crackers

The flavors of rosemary, sage, and fruity olive oil come through vividly in these hearty and chewy crackers. Serve them with dips or cheeses or for a nibble on their own. They're fun to make on the spur of the moment because the dough is very quick to mix and easy to handle, and it requires no resting or rising.

1½ cups all-purpose flour (spoon and level; 6¾ ounces)
½ cup medium rye flour
¾ teaspoon salt
2 teaspoons finely chopped rosemary
5 tablespoons fruity extra-virgin olive oil
¼ cup whole milk
¼ cup cold water, plus more if needed
¼ cup thinly slivered fresh sage leaves
½ teaspoon coarse kosher salt

1. Dough. Preheat the oven to 425°F. Stir the flours, ¾ teaspoon salt, and rosemary together in a medium mixing bowl. Stir in 4 tablespoons of the olive oil, then rub the mixture between your fingers to break up any lumps and work the crumbs into the texture of cornmeal. Stir in the milk and water to form a medium-stiff dough. If it is too dry to easily come together into a dough, add more water 1 tablespoon at a time.

2. Rolling. Line a large cookie sheet or the back of a baking sheet (about 16 x 12 inches) with parchment paper. Roll the dough into a rectangle the same size as the pan. Roll it up on the rolling pin and unroll it on the parchment. With a pastry wheel or pizza cutter, cut the dough into a 6 x 4 grid for 24 crackers. (They don't have to be uniform.) Brush the tops of the crackers with the remaining 1 tablespoon olive oil and sprinkle them with the sage leaves and kosher salt.

3. Baking. Bake the crackers until they are browned around the edges and in spots throughout, 16 to 18 minutes. Slide the crackers onto a wire rack. If the crackers that were baked in the middle of the pan seem softer and less done, return them to the oven for 3 to 5 minutes. Cool the crackers for at least 30 minutes before serving to give them a chance to crisp. Store in an airtight container for up to 1 week.

HERB-BUNDLED GARLIC BREAD

8 to 10 servings

Small bakeries that produce excellent European-style breads are popping up across the nation. The chewy, slowly raised loaves from these artisan bakeries have an earthy character that is very difficult to achieve in a home kitchen. Here's a showy way to incorporate fresh herbs into one of these fine loaves.

This recipe is based on the garlic bread my mother, and probably many other mothers, once made to accompany spaghetti dinners. She'd brush garlic butter between the slices of an airy Italian loaf, wrap the whole loaf in aluminum foil, and bake it. I've done almost the same thing here, but I start out with a terrific artisan loaf and tuck lavish sprigs of fresh herbs between the slices. In the oven, the herbs boldly flavor the bread, and at the table they make a splendid presentation. As the bread is served, the herb sprigs are discarded.

> *4 to 6 tablespoons unsalted butter or extra-virgin olive oil, depending on the size of the bread*
> *3 to 5 cloves garlic, minced*
> *1 fresh loaf European-style crusty, chewy bread (1 to 1 ½ pounds)*
> *18 to 24 3-inch herb sprigs, such as rosemary, sage, thyme, marjoram, oregano, and/or savory*

1. Garlic butter or oil. Preheat the oven to 400°F. Melt the butter or heat the oil in a small skillet over medium-low heat. Add the garlic and cook, stirring often, until it loses its raw fragrance but does not brown, about 2 minutes.

2. Assembling the loaf. With a large serrated knife, cut the loaf into ¾-inch-thick slices without cutting all the way through the bottom crust, so the loaf remains in one piece. Brush the garlic butter or oil on either side of each slice. Tuck the herb sprigs between the slices, allowing them to poke up out of the loaf by about ½ to 1 inch. Put the loaf in the center of a large square of heavy-duty aluminum foil and gather the foil up to loosely wrap it, leaving the top open. Bake the bread until it is heated through, about 12 minutes. Remove the foil and transfer the bread to a board or platter. As you serve the bread, pull out the herb sprigs and set them aside.

CHAPTER 9

Desserts

I've always loved creating desserts, and I've especially relished the opportunity to explore the ways fresh herbs and flowers can flavor them. I have discovered many. Herbs add thrilling dimension and sophistication to a wide range of sweets, from custards and ice creams to cakes and pastries. The sweet scent of lavender gives an exotic highlight to shortbread or meringue; lemon verbena's brilliant citrus flavor is fantastic in ice cream and fool; fresh bay laurel lends a soothing sweet spice flavor to custard; fresh rosemary sprigs infused in maple syrup will warm a pear clafoutis; and even basil can weave complex flavor into ice cream or warm fruit shortcake. And working with the herbs and fruits that come into season together year after year, I discovered how certain combinations strike perfect pitch—rhubarb with angelica, berry with rose geranium, lavender with plum, peach with anise hyssop, and apple with rosemary to name a few. While the idea of herbs in desserts may be exotic to many of us, it's nothing new, for herbs and flowers have been used to flavor confections throughout the centuries in many cultures.

Incorporating the flavors of fresh herbs into desserts is a matter of learning a few simple techniques and basic recipes. Herb sprigs can be steeped in milk or cream to flavor custards and ice creams, or infused in wine, honey, or simple sugar syrup to flavor fruit desserts. The chopped leaves can be added to cake batters or cookie doughs, or the herbs can be ground with sugar in a spice mill or food processor for a smoother textured flavoring. Once you learn these techniques and formulas, you'll gain a sense of how to add herbs to sweet things as confidently as you do savory dishes.

HERB-INFUSED MILK OR CREAM—MASTER RECIPE

Makes 2 cups

Whenever you make a dessert that features milk or cream as a main ingredient, you are given an opportunity to add the flavor of fresh herbs with this infusion technique. Just as you would tea, you bring the milk or cream to a boil, add whole herb leaves or sprigs, and steep the mixture for 30 minutes, covered and off the heat. Then you pass it through a strainer, chill it if necessary, and proceed with the recipe. The flavor of the herb is thus captured in the milk or cream, giving it the aromatic essence of the fresh herb without its green vegetable characteristics. The strained infusion also prevents the rough texture of the herb leaves from spoiling the silky consistency of custards and ice creams.

You can use this method to infuse skim milk, low-fat milk, whole milk, half-and-half, light cream, heavy cream, or any combination of these, but the higher the fat content, the more herbal flavor will be captured. Once the liquid is infused and strained, it can be stored in a covered container in the refrigerator up to the product's expiration date, but the flavor will be best if used within 3 days.

2 cups milk or cream, plus an additional 2 tablespoons if needed
Your choice of herb (see Herbal Infusions for Desserts, page 250)
Additional flavoring if desired (see Herbal Infusions for Desserts)

Pour the milk or cream into a small (1- to 2-quart) saucepan and place it over medium-high heat. Watch the pan carefully. As soon as the milk or cream comes to a full boil, add the herbs and any additional flavoring, push them under the surface of the liquid with a spoon, and immediately remove the pan from the heat. Cover the pan and let the herbs steep for 30 minutes. If they steep longer, it will have little effect on the flavor, but you should uncover the pan so that the milk or cream can cool faster. Strain the liquid though a fine sieve into a large liquid measuring cup, pressing down firmly on the herbs with the back of a spoon to extract all the liquid from the leaves. Add fresh milk or cream if needed to measure 2 cups.

Herb-Infused Simple Syrup—Master Recipe

Makes 1 cup

Use this syrup to sweeten fruit compotes, fruit soups or sorbets, or to soak genoise or sponge cakes. It also makes a delicious drink when mixed with sparkling water (page 321) or when used as sweetener for lemonade or iced tea. Poured into attractive bottles, a selection of several flavors make a wonderful gift.

> *1 cup sugar*
> *¾ cup water*
> *Your choice of herb (see Herbal Infusions for Desserts, page 250)*
> *Additional flavoring if desired (see Herbal Infusions for Desserts)*

Combine the sugar and water in a small (1-quart) saucepan and place it over medium-high heat. As soon as the syrup comes to a full boil and the sugar is completely dissolved, add the herbs and any additional flavoring, push them under the surface with a spoon, and immediately remove the pan from the heat. Cover the pan and let the herbs steep for 30 minutes. Pour the syrup through a fine sieve and press down firmly on the herbs with a back of a spoon to extract any syrup that is held in the leaves. Store in a covered bottle or jar in the refrigerator for up to 3 months.

HERBAL INFUSIONS FOR DESSERTS

Use the quantities of fresh herbs in this table as a guide. You can increase or decrease the amount specified depending on the strength of the particular herbs that you are using, how the infusion will be used, and your personal taste. Measurements for fresh sprigs are for healthy, full stems. If your herb sprigs are sparse or spindly, use more.

FRESH HERB	SUGGESTED AMOUNT FOR 2 CUPS MILK OR CREAM, OR SIMPLE SYRUP MADE WITH 1 CUP SUGAR	GOOD WITH
Angelica	½ cup coarsely chopped leaf and stem	apricot, ginger, rhubarb, orange
Anise hyssop	4 4-inch sprigs, with flower buds if possible	apricot, red berries, currants, nectarine, peach
Basil (sweet, cinnamon, licorice, or lemon)	3 or 4 4-inch sprigs	apricot, berries, cinnamon, citrus, nectarine, peach
Bay laurel	8 to 10 leaves, 2 to 3 inches long	apple, caramel, fig, pear, strawberry, vanilla
Fennel	2 teaspoons coarsely chopped green seeds	apple, fig, nectarine, orange, peach
Lavender	6 to 8 flower clusters, 2 to 3 teaspoons fresh buds, or 1 to 1 ½ teaspoons dried buds	berries, black currents, cherry, fig, ginger, lemon, orange, plum, vanilla
Lemon balm	6 4-inch sprigs	apricot, berries, melon, nectarine, peach
Lemon thyme	6 3-inch sprigs	fig, orange, pear, quince
Lemon verbena	6 4-inch sprigs	apricot, berries, melon, nectarine, peach, rhubarb
Meadowsweet	1 cup flowers, lightly packed	apricot, cherry, fig, vanilla
Mexican tarragon	4 4-inch sprigs	apricot, citrus, nectarine, peach
Mint	6 to 8 4-inch sprigs	berries, chocolate, melon
Rosemary	2 4-inch sprigs	apple, caramel, fig, grape, pear
Sage	2 4-inch sprigs	blueberry, cherry, lemon
Scented geranium	8 to 12 medium leaves, 1 ½ to 2 inches long	apple, apricot, berries, chocolate, lemon
Tarragon	4 to 6 4-inch sprigs	apricot, chocolate, citrus
Thyme, English	4 to 6 3-inch sprigs	cranberry, date, fig, orange, pear

OTHER FLAVORINGS	IF STEEPED WITH HERBS	IF STEEPED ALONE	GOOD WITH
Vanilla bean,* split and scraped**	¼ to ½	½ to 1	angelica, bay, lavender, rose geranium, rosemary
Cinnamon stick, 3 inches	½	1 to 2	basil, bay, rose geranium
Fresh ginger	3 (¼-inch-thick) slices	6 (¼-inch-thick) slices	angelica, basil, bay, lavender, lemon balm, lemon verbena, mint, rose geranium
Thinly sliced orange, lemon, or lime zest (removed with a zester)	From ½	From 1	angelica, basil, bay, lavender, mint, rose geranium, sage, tarragon

* To substitute vanilla extract for vanilla bean, use ½ teaspoon for each ¼ vanilla bean and add it to the liquid after it is infused.

** To split and scrape a vanilla bean, hold the bean on a cutting board and split it lengthwise with the tip of a sharp paring knife. Open the bean up. Hold it against the board and scrape the seeds off by drawing the knife down the length of the bean with the blade pointed in the opposite direction. Wipe the seeds that stick to the knife blade back onto the pod and toss it into the liquid.

HERB-INFUSED CUSTARD SAUCE (CRÈME ANGLAISE)—MASTER RECIPE

Makes 2½ cups

My method for making custard sauce, or crème anglaise, is different from most other methods. In fact it's radical. I discovered this shortcut during the year I worked as a pastry chef in San Francisco, when I had to make several gallons of the sauce every day, and I've found it to be foolproof. In the standard technique, you beat egg yolks with sugar in a bowl, whisk in hot milk, then return the mixture to the stove and carefully cook it just to the point when it thickens but does not curdle—a distinction that takes practice. In my fool-proof version the milk and sugar are heated together and the egg yolks are warmed separately in a mixing bowl. When you whisk the boiling milk mix-ture into the lukewarm egg yolks, there is enough heat retained in the ingredi-ents to bring the sauce to the required temperature in the bowl without the need to return it to the saucepan, and you run no risk of overcooking it.

The key steps for success are:

- The egg yolks, and the mixing bowl that holds them, must be warmed in a water bath to a temperature of 90° to 100°F.
- The milk and sugar must be at a true rolling boil when they are whisked into the yolks.
- When you add the milk mixture to the egg yolks, stir with the whisk at a moderate stroke. Whisking rapidly will cool the custard down before it has a chance to cook.
- Do not reduce the quantities in the master recipe or the milk will not retain enough heat to cook the yolks. You can double or triple the recipe, though, with no change in results.
- Do not use low-fat milk.

Serve the herb-infused custard sauces as an accompaniment to desserts, referring to Herbal Infusions for Desserts (page 250) for suggested pairings. For instance, serve rose geranium custard sauce with a chocolate soufflé, cinnamon basil custard sauce with apricot turnovers, lavender custard sauce with a ginger cake, or rosemary custard sauce over baked apples. Custard sauce is also used to make Rose Geranium Bavarian Cream (page 264).

2 cups herb-infused whole milk (page 248)
½ cup sugar
6 large egg yolks

1. Heating the milk and warming the yolks. Pour the milk and sugar into a small (1- to 2-quart) saucepan and set it over medium heat. Put the egg yolks in a medium stainless-steel mixing bowl and float that bowl in a larger bowl half full of hot tap water. Whisk the yolks until they are lukewarm, about 90° to 100°F (it will take less than 1 minute), then lift the bowl out of the water.

2. Cooking the custard. The instant the milk mixture comes to a rolling boil and rises in the pan, lift it off the heat. With the whisk in one hand and the saucepan in the other, pour the boiling milk into the egg yolks as you whisk constantly but gently. Continue to gently stir the sauce with the whisk for 30 seconds. At this point it should be fully cooked. An instant-read thermometer set in the sauce should register 170° to 180°F. It should coat a teaspoon, but it will become much thicker when it cools. (If for some reason the sauce did not get hot enough to thicken, you can place the bowl on top of a saucepan of boiling water and stir it with a rubber spatula until it reaches 170°F. Do not heat the sauce above 180° F or it will curdle.) Now whisk the sauce rapidly for 30 seconds to cool it and then pour it through a fine sieve. Store it in a covered container in the refrigerator for up to 5 days.

HERB-INFUSED WHIPPED CREAM—MASTER RECIPE

Makes 2 cups

Once you infuse heavy cream with an herbal flavor and then chill it, you can whip it. It's important that the cream be very cold (below 40°F) before you begin to whip it and that you use heavy cream with at least 36 percent milk fat. If the carton says only "whipping cream," it probably has less. Butterfat content is usually not stated on the carton, but you can check the nutrition facts on the side of the carton. There should be at least 5 grams of fat per 1 tablespoon cream, but 6 is better. Also avoid cream that has been ultra-pasteurized, a process where it is heated to 300° F in order to prolong its shelf life. After ultrapasteurized cream has been heated and chilled again in the infusion process, it can be impossible to whip into soft peaks.

Serve the flavored whipped cream as an accompaniment to fruit desserts, referring to Herbal Infusions for Desserts (page 250) for suggested pairings. For instance, serve bowls of fresh berries with dollops of rose geranium whipped cream, a slice of peach cobbler with anise hyssop whipped cream, plum tart with lavender whipped cream, or apple charlotte with rosemary whipped cream.

1 cup herb-infused heavy cream (not ultrapasteurized), very well chilled
2 tablespoons sugar

Pour the cold infused cream into a chilled mixing bowl or the bowl of an electric mixer. Add the sugar and whisk or beat until soft peaks form. Use the cream right away.

Herb-Infused Pastry Cream—Master Recipe

Makes 2½ cups

Pastry cream is a stovetop custard, thickened with flour or cornstarch, that is used as a filling in tarts and other pastries. When you make it with herb-infused milk, you can create a whole range of flavored custards to complement fruit flavors. Rose geranium pastry cream makes an out-of-this-world filling for a raspberry tart (page 280) or strawberry napoleon, pastry cream flavored with basil and cinnamon is luscious in an apricot tart, and angelica or lavender pastry cream is fabulous under poached rhubarb.

> *4 large egg yolks*
> *½ cup sugar*
> *6 tablespoons all-purpose flour (1.7 ounces)*
> *⅛ teaspoon salt*
> *2 cups herb-infused whole milk (page 248) or substitute low-fat (2%) milk*
> *   for a slightly less rich custard*
> *2 tablespoons unsalted butter*

1. Egg yolk mixture. In a medium mixing bowl, beat together the egg yolks and sugar with a sturdy wire whisk until smooth. Add the flour and salt and whisk again until smooth.

2. Adding the milk. Bring the infused milk to a simmer in a 2-quart saucepan. Thin the egg yolk mixture by whisking in ¼ cup of the hot milk until completely incorporated. Whisk in the remaining hot milk and pour the mixture back into the saucepan.

3. Cooking the custard. Whisk the custard over medium-high heat until it is very thick and begins to boil. Remove it from the heat and transfer it back to the mixing bowl. Add the butter and whisk until melted and incorporated. Scrape down the sides of the bowl with the rubber spatula and place a piece of plastic wrap directly on the surface of the pastry cream to prevent a skin from forming. Let cool. The pastry cream will keep covered in the refrigerator for up to 5 days.

Cinnamon Basil Ice Cream—Master Recipe

Makes 1½ quarts

Like herb-infused whipped cream, custard sauce, and pastry cream, you can make ice cream with any "flavor" of herb-infused milk and cream. I've chosen cinnamon basil to use as an example because it's one of my favorites. Cinnamon basil is a specific variety of basil with a cinnamon flavor, not a combination of herb and spice. If you don't have this herb, you can approximate the flavor very closely by combining sweet basil and cinnamon sticks. Even when using cinnamon basil, add a small piece of cinnamon stick to the infusion to accentuate the flavor. This ice cream has a subtle warm spice flavor. It's fantastic served with warmed sweetened blueberries or alongside a slice of apricot pie.

The procedure for making the custard base of an ice cream like this one is identical to making a custard sauce (page 252), but cream is substituted for half of the milk and there are fewer egg yolks. As in the custard sauce, I use my foolproof method of cooking the mixture off the heat in the mixing bowl.

> *2½ cups whole milk, plus an additional 2 tablespoons if needed, or substitute low-fat (2%) milk for a slightly less rich ice cream*
> *1½ cups heavy cream*
> *8 4-inch sprigs cinnamon basil and ½ cinnamon stick, or 6 4-inch sprigs sweet basil and 1½ cinnamon sticks*
> *¼ vanilla bean, split and scraped (page 251), or ½ teaspoon vanilla extract*
> *8 large egg yolks*
> *1 cup plus 2 tablespoons sugar*

1. Infuse the cream. Pour the milk and cream into a 2-quart saucepan and bring it to a boil over medium-high heat. Add the basil, cinnamon stick, and vanilla bean if using, push them under the surface of the liquid with a spoon, and immediately remove the pan from the heat. Cover the pan and steep for 30 minutes. Strain the liquid through a fine sieve into a large liquid measuring cup, pressing down firmly on the herbs to extract all the liquid from the leaves. Add fresh milk if needed to measure 4 cups. Return the infused cream to the saucepan.

---

2. Egg yolks. Put the egg yolks in a medium stainless-steel mixing bowl and float that bowl in a larger bowl half full of hot tap water. Whisk the yolks until they are lukewarm, 90° to 100°F (it will take less than 1 minute), then lift the bowl out of the water.

3. Ice cream base. Add the sugar to the infused cream and bring it back to a boil over medium-high heat. The instant the cream comes to a rolling boil and rises in the pan, lift if off the heat. With the whisk in one hand and the saucepan in the other, pour the boiling cream into the egg yolks as you whisk constantly but gently. Don't whisk rapidly or you will cool the custard before the yolks have a chance to set. Continue to stir the custard with the whisk for 1 minute. At this point it should be fully cooked. An instant-read thermometer set in the custard should register 170° to 180°F. It will coat a teaspoon, but it will become much thicker when it cools. (If for some reason the custard did not get hot enough to thicken, you can place the bowl on top of a saucepan of boiling water and stir it with a rubber spatula until it reaches 170°F. Do not overheat the custard or it will curdle.) Whisk the sauce rapidly for 30 seconds to cool it, then pour it through a fine sieve. If using vanilla extract, add it now. Refrigerate this custard base until thoroughly chilled. Freeze in an ice cream maker according to the manufacturer's directions.

 HERB SUBSTITUTIONS

- *To make other herbal ice creams, simply infuse the cream and milk with other herbs in place of the basil and cinnamon, using the chart on page 250 as a guide. This recipe calls for 4 cups milk and cream, so be sure to double the quantities listed in the chart. Some other favorites are bay leaf ice cream (to serve with apple pie), lavender ice cream (with plum tart), rose geranium ice cream (good with chocolate cake), and anise hyssop ice cream (with peach crisp).*

Lemon Verbena Ice Cream

Makes 5 cups, 10 servings

Because lemon verbena loses flavor when heated, this ice cream recipe treats the herb in a different way from the preceding custard-based formula. Here lemon verbena is ground with sugar and stirred into cooled milk that has been infused with fresh ginger. To keep it light and vibrant tasting, it contains no egg yolks, and for extra tang, sour cream or crème fraîche replaces heavy cream. It's not quite as smooth as custard-based ice cream, but it's heavenly when served slightly softened.

> *2 cups whole milk*
> *4 ¼-inch-thick slices fresh ginger*
> *1 cup (gently packed) fresh lemon verbena leaves*
> *1 cup plus 2 tablespoons sugar*
> *2 cups full or low-fat sour cream or crème fraîche*
> *2 tablespoons freshly squeezed lemon juice*
> *⅛ teaspoon salt*

1. Milk. Bring the milk to a simmer in a small (1-quart) saucepan over medium heat. Add the ginger, remove the pan from the heat, and let the milk steep and cool uncovered.

2. Lemon verbena. Process the lemon verbena and sugar in a food processor until the leaves are finely ground, about 1 minute. Stir the lemon verbena sugar into the cooled milk. Strain the mixture through a fine sieve. Refrigerate until chilled.

3. Finishing. Whisk the sour cream in a medium mixing bowl to smooth it out. Gradually whisk in the lemon verbena milk, then whisk in the lemon juice and salt. Immediately freeze the mixture in an ice cream maker according to the manufacturer's directions. Serve the ice cream slightly softened.

DRIED HERB VARIATION

You can make this ice cream with dried lemon verbena leaves if they are very fragrant and not stale. Add ½ cup (lightly packed) dry lemon verbena leaves (if the leaves are finely crushed, use ¼ cup) to the hot milk with the ginger. Cover and let steep for 30 minutes, then strain. Stir the sugar into the warm flavored milk, refrigerate until chilled, and proceed with step 3.

APRICOT AND LEMON VERBENA FOOL

4 servings

Fool is a British dessert that in its traditional guise is a fruit purée folded into whipped cream. It is typically prepared with tart fruit such as red currants or gooseberries, but this version combines summer apricots with the vibrant flavor of fresh lemon verbena. It's a very elegant dessert that requires a very small amount of effort.

> *1 pound fresh ripe apricots (about 8 medium), pitted and diced*
> *7 tablespoons sugar*
> *½ cup (gently packed) fresh lemon verbena leaves, center veins removed*
> *½ cup heavy cream*
> *Garnish: 8 Candied Lemon Verbena Leaves (page 313)*

1. Apricots. Mix the apricots with 3 tablespoons of the sugar in a small saucepan. Cook over medium heat until the apricots melt down to a sauce but still have some shape, 4 to 5 minutes. Transfer the fruit to a medium mixing bowl.

2. Lemon verbena. Process the lemon verbena with the remaining 4 tablespoons sugar in a food processor until very finely ground, about 1 minute. Stir the lemon verbena sugar into the apricot mixture and refrigerate until chilled.

3. Finishing. Whip the cream until it forms soft peaks and gently fold it into the apricot mixture. Spoon the fool into 4 stemmed glasses (martini glasses are especially elegant) or small custard cups. If desired, arrange 2 candied lemon verbena leaves on top of each serving. Serve with plain cookies, such as Lavender Shortbread (page 288).

Bay Leaf Crème Brûlée

8 servings

For this recipe you must put bay's association with stews and stocks out of your mind. The flavor of the fresh leaves is full of sweet spice. When I was dining at a small restaurant in Sussex, England, I had a wonderfully subtle bay leaf custard for dessert, and I learned there is a long history of bay being used to flavor sweet custards or rice pudding before vanilla was widely available. I like to use both. Fresh bay gives the custards a warm comforting flavor with hints of nutmeg and citrus and perfectly complements the crisp caramelized topping. Most important, it's subtle enough to be respectful of this classic dessert's simplicity.

> *2 cups whole milk, plus additional 2 tablespoons if needed, or substitute*
> *low-fat (2%) milk for a slightly less rich custard*
> *2 cups heavy cream*
> *12 fresh bay laurel leaves, cracked (not California bay or dried bay leaves)*
> *½ vanilla bean, split and scraped (page 251), or 1 teaspoon vanilla extract*
> *3 large eggs*
> *5 large egg yolks*
> *¾ cup granulated sugar*
> *⅛ teaspoon salt*
> *About ¼ cup turbinado sugar (Sugar in the Raw)*

1. Molds. Arrange 8 6-ounce ramekins in a shallow baking pan large enough so that they don't touch.

2. Infuse the cream. Pour the milk and cream into a 2-quart saucepan and bring it to a boil over medium-high heat. Add the bay leaves and vanilla bean if using, push them under the surface of the liquid with a spoon, and immediately remove the pan from the heat. Cover the pan and steep for 30 minutes. Strain the liquid through a fine sieve into a large liquid measuring cup, pressing down firmly on the herbs to extract all the liquid from the leaves. Add fresh milk if needed to measure 4 cups.

3. Custard. Preheat the oven to 325°F. In a medium mixing bowl, whisk together the eggs, egg yolks, granulated sugar, salt, and vanilla extract if using until smooth. Stir in the infused cream. Strain the custard through a fine sieve into a large pitcher or liquid measuring cup, then pour it into the ramekins, filling them almost to the top. Set the pan on the center oven rack and pour in enough hot tap water to come about ½ inch up the ramekins. Bake the custards until just set but still jiggly, 30 to 45 minutes. Don't let the custards bubble. The most crucial step is to pull them from the oven at just the right moment, but the baking time can vary greatly depending on the temperature of the custard when it was poured, so check them often. If your oven bakes unevenly, you might need to check each one individually. Refrigerate the custards until chilled, at least 2 hours.

4. Caramelized topping. Preheat your oven broiler to high with the oven rack 4 to 5 inches from the heat source. Just before serving, sprinkle the surface of the custards with a thin layer of turbinado sugar, using about ½ tablespoon for each. Shake the ramekins to even the sugar out. Broil the custards until the sugar caramelizes and turns a deep golden brown, but don't let them blacken. Crème brûlée means burnt cream but don't interpret the name literally.

NOTE

If you have a propane or butane torch, it will give you more control for caramelizing the topping. Hold the nozzle of the torch with a medium flame 2 to 3 inches from the top of each custard so that the tip of the flame touches the sugar and slowly move it in a circular motion until the sugar is evenly caramelized.

VARIATIONS

CLASSIC CRÈME BRÛLÉE

Steep the milk and cream with 1 vanilla bean, split and scraped.

CINNAMON CRÈME BRÛLÉE

Steep the milk and cream with 2 3-inch cinnamon sticks and ½ vanilla bean, split and scraped.

ANISE HYSSOP CRÈME BRÛLÉE

Steep the milk with 6 4-inch sprigs anise hyssop, with flower buds if possible, and ½ vanilla bean, split and scraped.

LAVENDER GINGER CRÈME BRÛLÉE

Steep the milk and cream with 4 teaspoons fresh lavender buds (or 2 teaspoons dried) and 6 ¼-inch-thick slices fresh ginger.

Lavender Ginger Panna Cotta

8 servings

Panna cotta is a simple Italian dessert—really nothing more than sweetened milk and cream set with gelatin. I can't resist flavoring it with fresh herbs, and I especially like this combination of lavender and ginger. It's a seemingly light yet satisfying sweet for any season.

2 teaspoons vegetable or nut oil for the molds
3 cups whole milk, plus an additional ¼ cup if needed
1 cup heavy cream
1 ½ tablespoons fresh lavender buds, or 2 teaspoons dried
6 ¼-inch-thick slices fresh ginger
¼ vanilla bean, split and scraped (page 251), or ½ teaspoon vanilla extract
¼ cup Cognac, kirsch, or additional whole milk
½ ounce unflavored gelatin (2 packages)
½ cup sugar

1. Molds. Very lightly oil 8 4- to 5-ounce molds, such as ramekins, custard cups, or disposable clear plastic cups and set them in a baking dish or cake pan so that you can move them as one.

2. Infuse the cream. Pour the milk and cream into a 2-quart saucepan and bring it to a boil over medium-high heat. Add the lavender, ginger, and vanilla bean if using, push them under the surface of the liquid with a spoon, and immediately remove the pan from the heat. Cover the pan and steep for 30 minutes. Strain the liquid through a fine sieve into a large liquid measuring cup, pressing down firmly on the herbs to extract all of the liquid from the leaves. Add fresh milk if needed to measure 4 cups.

3. Panna cotta. Pour the Cognac, kirsch, or additional milk into a 2-quart saucepan. Sprinkle with the gelatin and let it soften for 5 minutes. Add the sugar and 1 cup of the infused milk. Place the pan over medium heat and cook, stirring constantly, until the gelatin and sugar are dissolved and the mixture is just beginning to simmer. Stir in the remaining infused milk. Ladle the mixture into the prepared molds and refrigerate until set, about 3 hours.

4. Serving. Remove the custards from the refrigerator 30 minutes before you are ready to serve them. To unmold, use your finger to gently pull and release the custard from the side of the mold all around the top. With your finger still pulling in one spot to allow air under the custard, turn the mold upside down over a dessert plate and let the custard slip out.

VARIATIONS

Surround the panna cotta with one of the following:

Fresh berries

2 cups sliced apricots or fresh figs warmed in a small skillet with ¼ cup honey

¾ cup dried tart cherries soaked in 1 cup hot lavender-infused simple syrup (page 249) for 2 hours

Sliced fresh ripe mango

Rose Geranium Bavarian Cream with Berries

12 servings

Bavarian cream is a custard sauce, lightened with beaten egg whites and whipped cream, and set with gelatin. Here is a sensational version flavored with rose geranium and white chocolate and served with fresh berries. The preparation requires many steps that require many mixing bowls, but it is well worth the effort to produce 12 servings of this refined dessert.

It's easiest to unmold Bavarian creams if you form them in some sort of bottomless ring. Chefs often cut rings from PVC pipe (the stiff white plastic pipe used for plumbing), but you can make the perfect size molds from ordinary 12-ounce frozen juice cans, by cutting them into 3 rings with a serrated knife. You'll need to save 4 juice cans for this recipe.

About 2 teaspoons vegetable or nut oil for the molds
2 cups whole milk, plus an additional 2 tablespoons if needed
24 medium-size fresh rose geranium leaves
½ vanilla bean, split and scraped (page 251), or 1 teaspoon vanilla extract
½ ounce unflavored gelatin (2 packages)
¼ cup framboise, kirsch, Cognac, or cold water
½ cup sugar
6 large egg yolks
6 ounces premium white chocolate, such as Callebaut or Tobler, chopped
1 ½ cups heavy cream
6 large egg whites
4 cups fresh raspberries, picked over, or ripe strawberries, washed, hulled, and sliced
Garnish: 12 rose geranium flowers, violas, or candied violets or rose petals

1. Molds. Using a serrated bread knife, saw the bottoms off of 4 clean and dry 12-ounce frozen juice cans, then saw each can into 3 same-size rings. Using your fingers or a pastry brush, coat the interiors very lightly with oil. Set the rings on a parchment-lined baking sheet.

2. Infuse the cream. Pour the milk into a small (1- to 2-quart) saucepan and bring it to a boil over medium-high heat. Add the rose geranium leaves and vanilla bean if using, push them under the surface of the liquid with a spoon, and immediately remove the pan from the heat. Cover the pan and steep for 30 minutes. Strain the liquid through a fine sieve into a large liquid measuring cup, pressing down firmly on the herbs to extract all the liquid from the leaves. Add fresh milk if needed to measure 2 cups. Return the infused milk to the saucepan.

3. Gelatin, milk, and egg yolks. In a small bowl, sprinkle the gelatin onto the liquor or water and let it soften for 5 minutes. Add the sugar to the infused milk and set it over medium heat. Put the egg yolks in a medium stainless-steel mixing bowl and float that bowl in a larger bowl half full of hot tap water. Whisk the yolks until they are lukewarm, 90° to 100°F (it will take less than 1 minute), then lift the bowl out of the water.

4. Custard sauce. The instant the milk mixture comes to a rolling boil and rises in the pan, lift it off the heat. With the whisk in one hand and the saucepan in the other, pour the boiling milk mixture into the egg yolks as you whisk constantly but gently. Continue to stir the custard with the whisk for 1 minute. At this point it should be fully cooked. An instant-read thermometer set in the custard should register 170° to 180°F. It will coat a teaspoon, but it will become much thicker when it cools. (If for some reason the custard did not get hot enough to thicken, you can place the bowl on top of a saucepan of boiling water and stir it with a rubber spatula until it reaches 170°F. Do not overheat the custard or it will curdle.) While the custard is hot, stir in the gelatin until it dissolves, then stir in the white chocolate until completely melted. Add the vanilla extract if using.

5. Finishing. This step must be completed quickly without interruptions. Whip the heavy cream and the egg whites in separate bowls until each forms soft peaks. Place the bowl with the custard mixture inside a larger bowl filled halfway with ice water. Stir the custard constantly with a rubber spatula until it cools and begins to thicken. Immediately remove the bowl from the ice bath and quickly fold in the whipped cream, then gently fold in the whipped whites until they are completely incorporated. Spoon the soft mousselike mixture into the prepared molds, filling them all the way to the top. Refrigerate the Bavarians until thoroughly set, about 2 hours.

6. Unmolding and serving. Slide a small spatula under one of the molds and lift it off the parchment paper. Hold it over a dessert plate. Take away the spatula and the custard should slip right out of its ring onto the plate. If it doesn't, run a thin paring knife carefully around the cream, and it should drop easily onto the plate. If it still doesn't, give it a few shakes from side to side. Surround each cream with some of the fresh berries, and if you have them, garnish with a rose geranium flower, viola, or candied violet or rose petal.

Raspberry, Riesling, and Rose Geranium Gratin

8 servings

In this dish, the flavor of rose geranium is incorporated in a unique way—it's infused into the wine that's then used to make a sabayon, a whipped wine-based custard. The sabayon is spread over raspberries in a shallow baking dish, sprinkled with sugar, and broiled until browned. All the flavors—fragrant ripe berries, floral-scented wine custard, and caramelized crust—combine to make a luscious dessert. You can make the sabayon well ahead of time and finish the dessert at the last moment.

SABAYON

*½ cup medium-sweet Riesling wine (not dry Riesling and not
late-harvest)*
12 medium-size fresh rose geranium leaves
4 large egg yolks
¼ cup granulated sugar
½ cup heavy cream

4 cups raspberries
2 tablespoons turbinado sugar (Sugar in the Raw)

1. Infusing the wine. Bring the wine to a simmer in a small saucepan. Drop in the rose geranium leaves, cover, and remove from the heat. Let the mixture steep for 30 minutes. Strain, pressing on the leaves to extract all the liquid.

2. Setting up the double boiler. Create a double boiler by selecting a medium (10- to 12-inch) stainless-steel mixing bowl that will rest on top of a large (6-quart) pot filled with about 2 inches water. The top of the bowl can extend beyond the rim of the pot, but the bottom of the bowl must not touch the water. Put the pot (without the bowl) over medium heat and bring the water to a boil. Fill a large mixing bowl half full with ice water and set it beside the stove.

3. Sabayon. Whisk together the egg yolks and granulated sugar in the medium mixing bowl, then add the infused wine. Place the bowl over the boiling water and whisk constantly with wide strokes until the mixture is fluffy and very thick and there is no liquid remaining at the bottom of the bowl. It will only take 3 to 4 minutes. An instant-read thermometer inserted in the custard should register 170°F. Immediately remove the bowl from the boiling water and set it in the ice water. Whisk the mixture occasionally until it is cold. Whip the cream until it forms soft peaks and fold it into the cooled wine custard. (The sabayon will keep in a covered container in the refrigerator for up to 3 days.)

4. Gratin. Preheat the broiler to high with the oven rack 6 inches from the heat source. Spread the raspberries in a shallow 1½-quart gratin dish or divide them among 8 individual 6-ounce ramekins. Spread the sabayon over the berries and sprinkle with the turbinado sugar. Broil until speckled brown but not blackened. Serve right away.

ANISE HYSSOP–POACHED PEACHES

6 servings

The showy purple spikes of anise hyssop are at their peak in the herb garden at the same time peaches ripen on the trees, and when brought together the two create a miraculous combination of flavor. Here whole peeled peaches are poached in a Riesling syrup infused with branches of the herb. For an elegant dessert, present the peaches in a large glass bowl with some of the syrup and fresh sprigs of the herb, or in individual compote dishes or bowls. Accompany them with ice cream or sorbet and Lavender Shortbread (page 288), or use them in the Anise Hyssop–Poached Peaches Brûlée recipe that follows.

> *4 quarts water*
> *6 medium-size, unblemished, perfectly ripe freestone peaches or nectarines*
> *1 bottle (750 ml) medium-sweet Riesling wine (not dry Riesling, and not late-harvest)*
> *1 ½ cups sugar*
> *½ vanilla bean, split and scraped (page 251)*
> *4 ¼-inch-thick slices fresh ginger*
> *6 4-inch full sprigs fresh anise hyssop, with flowers or buds if possible*
> *Garnish: 6 small anise hyssop leaves and several flowering sprigs*

1. Peeling the peaches. Bring the water to a boil in a 6-quart nonreactive (stainless-steel or enameled) pot. Set a large bowl of cold water near the stove. Cut a shallow slit about 1 inch long in the skin of each peach or nectarine. Drop them into the water and boil them for 30 seconds. With a slotted spoon or skimmer, transfer them to the cold water. Rub the peaches while they are in the cold water and the skins should slip off easily. If they don't, use a paring knife to help pull the skin off.

2. Poaching the peaches. Pour out the water in the 6-quart pot and pour in the wine. Add the sugar, vanilla bean, ginger, and peaches. If the peaches are not completely submerged in the liquid when you press down on them, add cold water to cover. Put the pot over medium-high heat. As soon as the syrup comes to a simmer, remove the pan from the heat and tuck the anise hyssop sprigs between the peaches. Put a heavy china salad plate on top of the fruit to keep it fully submerged in the syrup. As the peaches cool in the syrup, they will continue to cook. (If you had difficulty peeling the peaches, they were not fully ripe, and you will need to continue to cook them on the stovetop, just under a simmer, until the tip of a paring knife can pierce the flesh with only minor resistance.) The peaches will keep in the syrup at room temperature for up to 1 day or in the refrigerator for up to 3 days. Before serving, remove the pits by holding each peach in your hand and using your fingers to gently pull the pit out through the natural separation. Keep the peaches whole and try not to tear the flesh. Serve the peaches in a glass serving bowl or individual dishes and insert the anise hyssop leaves at their tops so that they look like they are growing out of the stem.

VARIATION
ANISE HYSSOP–POACHED PEACHES BRÛLÉE

6 servings

This is my idea of an irresistible dessert. Fragrant poached peaches and a few raspberries are arranged in shallow bowls of rich custard flavored with anise hyssop, and then the whole dish is sprinkled with sugar and caramelized.

> *2 ½ cups Herb-Infused Custard Sauce (page 252) made with 4 4-inch*
> *sprigs anise hyssop and ½ vanilla bean, split and scraped (page 251),*
> *chilled*
> *6 anise hyssop–poached peaches, pitted but left whole*
> *1 cup fresh raspberries*
> *About ½ cup turbinado sugar (Sugar in the Raw)*

1. **Arranging.** Divide the cold custard sauce evenly among 6 heatproof shallow soup bowls or deep rimmed plates. Put the peaches on a double layer of paper towels to blot up extra moisture, then place the peaches, slit side down, off center on the custard. Arrange a small handful of raspberries around each peach.

2. **The caramel topping.** Sprinkle the custard, peaches, and raspberries with a thin and even layer of the turbinado sugar. Hold a torch with a medium flame several inches above the desserts so that the flame gently touches the sugar and move it slowly in a circular motion to evenly caramelize the sugar over the whole dish. Garnish as directed for the poached peaches. Serve right away.

Lavender–Pistachio Pavlova

12 servings

    This dessert delivers a lot of show for little effort. A pavlova is a large meringue filled with fruit and cream. It originated in New Zealand but is named after Russian ballerina Anna Pavlova. It's supposed to be tutu-shaped and as white as the namesake's skin. My version has lavender buds and pistachios in the meringue, which don't do much to flatter Pavlova's complexion, but add intriguing flavor and texture.

    If you have fresh lavender buds, leave them whole, because the lengthy slow baking allows their flavor to gently infuse throughout the meringue. If you use dried buds, you'll want to chop or grind them so their texture is not intrusive.

LAVENDER WHIPPED CREAM

2 cups heavy cream, not ultrapasteurized (page 254)
4 teaspoons fresh lavender buds, or 2 teaspoons dried
¼ vanilla bean, split and scraped (page 251), or ½ teaspoon vanilla
    extract
¼ cup superfine sugar

MERINGUE

About 2 teaspoons unsalted butter, for the parchment
1 cup unsalted shelled whole pistachios
1 tablespoon cornstarch
1 ½ cups superfine sugar
1 tablespoon fresh lavender buds, separated and left whole, or
    1 ½ teaspoons dried lavender buds, coarsely chopped
6 large egg whites (¾ cup), at room temperature
¼ teaspoon cream of tartar

FRUIT

4 to 6 cups mixed berries and sliced fresh fruit, such as peaches,
    apricots, mango, pineapple, banana, and kiwi

GARNISH

About 12 tiny sprigs mint, anise hyssop, lemon balm, or pineapple sage
About 12 edible flowers, such as violas or violets or borage, or Candied
    Rose Petals (page 312)

1. **Infuse the cream.** Pour the cream into a small (1- to 2-quart) saucepan and bring it to a boil over medium-high heat. Add the lavender buds and vanilla bean if using, poke them under the surface of the liquid with a spoon, and immediately remove the pan from the heat. Cover the pan and steep for 30 minutes. Strain the cream through a fine sieve into a large liquid measuring cup, pressing down firmly on the lavender to extract all the liquid. Stir in the vanilla extract if using. Refrigerate until very well chilled.

2. **Setting up for the meringue.** Preheat the oven to 350°F. Trace a 10-inch circle on a piece of parchment paper, turn it upside down on a cookie sheet, and butter it lightly. Chop ¾ cup of the nuts until medium-fine with a sharp chef's knife, using a rocking motion as if chopping herbs. Stir together the cornstarch and ¼ cup of the sugar until well incorporated, then stir in the lavender buds.

3. **Meringue.** Using an electric mixer, beat the egg whites and cream of tartar on high speed until they form soft peaks. Gradually beat in the remaining 1¼ cups sugar, 1 tablespoon at a time, allowing about 5 minutes to add it all. Continue to beat the meringue for 2 more minutes. The mixture should be extremely stiff. Carefully fold in the lavender mixture and the chopped pistachios.

4. **Forming the pavlova.** Turn the meringue out onto the parchment paper and spread it out with an icing spatula inside the circle you drew. Form it high on the outside and depressed in the center, and keep it shaggy and uneven (think tutu). Press the reserved whole pistachios all around the outside of the meringue.

5. **Baking.** Put the meringue in the oven and immediately reduce the heat to 250°F. Bake for 1½ to 2 hours. It should be crisp on the outside but still like marshmallows inside. Remove it from the oven and let it cool completely. If you're serving the pavlova later the same day, keep it loosely covered with plastic wrap; if you want to serve it the next day, wrap the shell airtight in plastic wrap and store at room temperature.

6. **Filling.** Whip the chilled lavender cream with the ¼ cup sugar until it forms firm peaks. Spread the cream on top of the meringue, leaving a border of about an inch all around. Arrange the fruit on top of the cream in an informal manner. Tuck the garnishes here and there among the pieces of fruit. Serve immediately, or loosely cover and refrigerate for up to 2 hours. Cut it into wedges with a cake knife.

VARIATION

Make individual pavlovas by spreading the meringue in 12 4-inch circles on 2 cookie sheets lined with parchment paper. Reduce the baking time to 1 to 1¼ hours.

Pear, Maple, and Rosemary Clafouti

8 servings

Clafouti is a French country dessert of fruit, usually cherries, baked in a flour-thickened custard (similar to crêpe batter) and served hot. This version is made with pears that are first cooked in maple syrup with rosemary. The aroma that develops in the kitchen as the pears bake will drive everyone in your home wild with anticipation, and when the dish comes out of the oven puffed, browned, and beckoning, it will not disappoint. This dessert is very quick to put together and likely to become a favorite that you'll make again and again.

About 1 tablespoon unsalted butter, softened, for the pan
4 medium-size ripe pears, such as Bartlett or Comice
1 cup pure maple syrup
4 3-inch sprigs fresh rosemary
2 large eggs
2 tablespoons all-purpose flour
½ teaspoon vanilla extract
⅛ teaspoon salt
½ cup heavy cream
½ cup whole milk

1. Pears. Preheat the oven to 350°F. Generously butter a 9-inch shallow round baking dish with straight sides or a 10-inch glass pie pan with sloping sides. Peel the pears and cut them lengthwise in half. Use a melon baller to scoop out the cores, then use a paring knife to remove the blossom scar, the stem, and the coarse fiber that runs from the stem to the core. Pour the maple syrup into a 10-inch skillet and place it over medium heat. Arrange the pear halves in the pan, rounded side down, and tuck the rosemary sprigs between them. Cook the pears uncovered at a gentle boil for about 5 minutes. Turn them cut side down and gently boil until the pears are very soft and the syrup is slightly thickened, about 5 minutes longer. (If the pears are not quite ripe, cook them covered for 10 minutes on the first side, then cook on the second side, partially covered, until you can insert a paring knife with no resistance.) Leaving the syrup behind in the pan, carefully transfer the pears to the prepared baking dish and arrange them cut side down and stem end facing inward in a circle. Remove and discard the rosemary sprigs. Pour the syrup that's left in the pan into a measuring cup.

There should be about ½ cup. If there is less, top it off with more maple syrup. If there is more than ½ cup, pour it back into the pan and boil it further.

2. Batter and baking. Whisk 1 egg with the flour in a medium mixing bowl until smooth. Whisk in the other egg, then whisk in the syrup, vanilla, salt, cream, and milk. Pour the batter over the pears. Bake the clafouti on the center oven rack until puffed, set in the center, and a golden color around the edges, 25 to 30 minutes. Cool slightly. Cut into wedges and serve warm.

Nectarine, Blueberry, and Anise Basil Shortcake

6 large servings

Here's one of my favorite versions of shortcake for the summer months. The flavors of anise basil add a subtle and intriguing dimension to a can't-miss combination of warm fruit, ice cream, and sweet tender biscuit.

> *½ cup sugar*
> *6 tablespoons water*
> *4 4-inch sprigs fresh anise basil or Thai basil, or 4 4-inch sprigs sweet basil and 1 to 2 tablespoons Pernod or Ricard*
> *1 to 2 tablespoons freshly squeezed lemon juice*
> *4 quarts water*
> *3 large ripe nectarines or peaches (about 1 pound)*
> *6 Sour Cream Shortcake Biscuits (page 275)*
> *2 cups blueberries, picked over and washed*
> *3 tablespoons unsalted butter, softened*
> *1 pint premium vanilla ice cream or Cinnamon Basil Ice Cream (page 256)*

1. Syrup. Combine the sugar and 6 tablespoons water in a small (1-quart) saucepan and bring it to a full boil over medium-high heat. Add the basil sprigs, push them under the surface with a spoon, and immediately remove the pan from the heat. Cover the pan and let the basil steep for at least 30 minutes. Pour the syrup through a fine sieve and press down firmly on the herbs with the back of a spoon to extract all the liquid from the leaves. Add the Pernod if using and 1 tablespoon lemon juice.

2. Prepare the nectarines. Bring 4 quarts water to a boil in a 6-quart pot. Set a large bowl of cold water near the stove. Cut a shallow slit about 1 inch long into the skin of each nectarine. Drop the nectarines into the water and boil them for 30 seconds. With a slotted spoon or skimmer, transfer them to the cold water. Rub the nectarines while they are in the cold water and the skins should slip off easily. If they don't, use a paring knife to help pull the skin off. Cut the nectarines in half, remove the pits, and cut each half into 8 wedges. (If you want to peel and slice the nectarines ahead of time, toss them with 1 tablespoon freshly squeezed lemon juice to prevent them from browning, then store tightly covered in the refrigerator for up to 4 hours.)

3. Biscuits. Split the shortcake biscuits horizontally in half, using a serrated bread knife with a sawing motion. (If they were baked more than 4 hours ahead of time, lay the halves cut side up on a baking sheet and refresh them in a 300°F oven for 8 to 10 minutes.) Place the bottom half of each biscuit cut side up on a large dessert plate.

4. Fruit. Pour the anise basil syrup into a large (10- to 12-inch) skillet and bring it to a boil over medium-high heat. Add the blueberries and cook, gently stirring, until the syrup returns to a boil and the blueberries start to burst. Add the nectarines and toss until the fruit is heated through. Stir in the softened butter until it melts.

5. Assembling. Put a scoop of ice cream on top of each biscuit bottom. Spoon the fruit and sauce over the ice cream, letting it spread out on the plate as it falls. Place the top or each biscuit over each dessert, allowing them to tilt at an angle, and serve immediately.

SOUR CREAM SHORTCAKE BISCUITS

Makes 6 large biscuits

I've tried numerous versions of shortcake biscuits to find one that is rich, moist, tender, and quick to make. This one is the winner.

> *2 cups all-purpose flour (spoon and level; 9 ounces)*
> *1 teaspoon baking powder*
> *½ teaspoon baking soda*
> *¼ teaspoon salt*
> *¼ cup plus 2 tablespoons sugar*
> *4 tablespoons unsalted butter, chilled*
> *1 cup sour cream (not low-fat)*
> *¼ cup whole milk*

Preheat the oven to 425°F. Sift the flour with the baking powder, baking soda, and salt into a medium mixing bowl. Stir in ¼ cup sugar. Cut in the butter with a pastry blender until the mixture resembles coarse meal. (Or process the dry ingredients with the butter in a food processor until it resembles coarse meal, then return it to the bowl.) Stir in the sour cream and milk. Scoop the dough into 6 high mounds evenly spaced on a parchment-lined cookie sheet. Sprinkle with the remaining 2 tablespoons sugar. Bake until lightly browned, about 15 minutes. Transfer the biscuits to a rack to cool slightly before splitting.

Apple, Rosemary, and Caramel Shortcakes

6 large servings

This is a sensational shortcake for winter months. Apple halves are cooked in caramel with whole sprigs of rosemary, so they become almost candied and infused throughout with a deep resonant flavor. The warm fruit is sandwiched with vanilla ice cream between rich tender biscuits, and the caramel from the apples is turned into a sauce that's drizzled over top.

> *3 large cooking apples (about 1 ¼ pounds) such as Golden Delicious,*
> *   Granny Smith, or Jonagold*
> *¾ cup sugar*
> *2 tablespoons unsalted butter*
> *4 3-inch sprigs fresh rosemary*
> *6 Sour Cream Shortcake Biscuits (page 275)*
> *6 tablespoons heavy cream*
> *1 pint premium vanilla ice cream*

1. Apples. Preheat the oven to 375°F. Peel and halve the apples. Scoop out the cores, using a melon baller, then use the tool to nick off the blossom scars at the bottoms of the apple halves and any skin remaining at the stem ends.

2. Caramelizing. Pour the sugar into a 10-inch ovenproof skillet and place it over medium heat. When the sugar begins to melt, stir it with a wooden spoon. It will form big lumps at first, but keep cooking and stirring until all the sugar is dissolved and you have a light amber syrup. As soon as it reaches this stage, remove the pan from the heat and add the butter to prevent the caramel from overcooking. Stir until the butter is melted and incorporated. Arrange the apples cut side up on top of the caramel and tuck the rosemary sprigs between them. Place the skillet in the oven and bake uncovered for 15 minutes. Using tongs, turn the apples over; bake until the apples are softened, about 15 minutes longer.

3. Sauce. Split the shortcake biscuits horizontally in half, using a serrated bread knife with a gentle sawing motion. (If they were baked more than 4 hours ahead of time, lay the halves cut side up on a baking sheet and put them in the oven with the apples for 5 minutes to refresh them.) Place the bottom half of each biscuit cut side up on a large dessert plate. With a small spatula, lift the hot caramelized apple halves from the syrup and place each one cut side down on a biscuit bottom. Remove and discard the stems of rosemary (don't worry if a few of the needles are left behind in the sauce). Return the pan with the caramel to the stovetop and bring it to a simmer over medium heat (keep a towel wrapped around the skillet handle to remind you that it is very hot). Gradually whisk in the cream. When the sauce is smooth, remove the pan from the heat.

4. **Serving.** Top each apple half with a scoop of ice cream. Drizzle the caramel sauce over the top of each dessert, letting it drip onto the plate. Place the biscuit tops over each, allowing them to tilt at an angle, and serve immediately.

WARM CRÊPES WITH FRESH DATE BUTTER AND CHOCOLATE SAUCE

8 to 10 servings

These crêpes make a terrific dinner party dessert because you can stuff them ahead of time and crisp them in the oven at the last minute. The addition of a little bit of fresh thyme to the filling of fresh dates, butter, and orange zest lends an elusive depth of flavor. With a scoop of coffee ice cream to the side and a lavish drizzle of chocolate sauce you'll have an extraordinary dessert.

CRÊPES

¾ cup all-purpose flour (spoon and level; 3 ½ ounces)
2 large eggs
2 tablespoons sugar
½ teaspoon finely chopped orange zest
⅛ teaspoon salt
½ cup milk
½ cup water
2 tablespoons unsalted butter, melted

FILLING

12 ounces fresh dates, such as Black Sphinx or Medjool, pitted
4 tablespoons unsalted butter, softened
2 teaspoons finely chopped fresh orange balsam thyme, English thyme, or
    lemon thyme
Finely chopped zest of 1 large orange

CHOCOLATE SAUCE

½ cup heavy cream
4 ounces premium bittersweet or semisweet chocolate, such as Callebaut,
    Valrhona, or El Rey, coarsely chopped

2 tablespoons unsalted butter, melted
1 pint premium coffee ice cream

1. Crêpe batter. Mix all the ingredients for the crêpes in a blender or food processor until smooth, or whisk them together in a mixing bowl. Strain the batter through a fine sieve and let it rest at room temperature for 30 minutes, or in the refrigerator for up to 24 hours, to allow the flour to absorb the liquid.

2. Crêpes. Place an 8-inch nonstick skillet over medium heat. When the pan is hot, ladle in a little less than 2 tablespoons (1 ounce) of the batter and immediately swirl the pan so that it coats the bottom evenly. Cook until the edges of the crêpe begin to brown, about 30 seconds, the turn it. The easiest way to do this is to loosen and lift the far edge of the crêpe with a thin spatula, then use both hands to quickly lift the whole crêpe and flip it. Cook the other side for 10 to 15 seconds, then slide the crêpe onto a parchment-lined sheet pan. Continue to make crêpes with the remaining batter, adjusting the temperature under the skillet as necessary. Arrange the crêpes 4 to a sheet of parchment and stack the parchment in layers on the baking sheet. Makes 16 to 20 crêpes.

3. Filling. Mash the dates with the butter, thyme, and orange zest in an electric mixer, a food processor, or a mixing bowl with a potato masher. The mixture should not be completely smooth. Measure out level tablespoons of the filling and divide each tablespoon in half. Place 2 lumps of the filling on each crêpe, putting a lump in each of the bottom 2 quadrants. Fold over the top of the crêpe to cover the filling, then fold the crêpe in half again into a quarter circle. Gently press it with your palm to spread the filling. Arrange the crêpes in a single layer on a parchment-lined baking sheet.

4. Sauce. Bring the cream to a boil in a small (1-quart) saucepan. Remove the pan from the heat, add the chocolate, and whisk until it is completely melted and smooth.

5. Assembling. Preheat the oven to 375°F. Brush the tops of the crêpes with the melted butter and bake until they begin to brown further and sizzle around the edges, 10 to 12 minutes. Transfer 2 crêpes to each plate, put a scoop of ice cream between them, and drizzle with the chocolate sauce.

Rose Geranium and Berry Tarts

Makes 2 tarts, 8 servings each

I love the combination of cool rich custard and ripe berries on top of shatteringly flaky pastry, so I make my berry tarts with crisp free-form shells of flaky butter dough. They're filled with rose geranium flavored pastry cream, which seems to intensify the berry flavors and makes the tarts taste especially exciting. This recipe makes 2 thin tarts. If you want just 1 tart, you can freeze the second tart shell unbaked for up to 3 months and store the extra pastry cream covered in the refrigerator for up to 5 days.

> *2 10-inch Free-Form Tart Shells (page 344), prebaked*
> *2½ cups Herb-Infused Pastry Cream (page 255) made with 12 medium-size rose geranium leaves and ¼ vanilla bean, split and scraped (page 251), chilled*
> *6 cups fresh ripe berries, such as raspberries, blackberries, hulled strawberries, marionberries, and/or loganberries, picked over*

Assemble the tarts within 4 hours of serving. Carefully transfer the pastry shells to flat cake plates or round platters. Divide the pastry cream between the 2 shells and spread it out in a thin layer. Pile the berries on top to completely cover the custard. (You can arrange the berries in concentric rows if you want an ordered look and you have a lot of patience.) If the tarts must sit for more than 4 hours, cover them loosely with plastic wrap and refrigerate.

PUMPKIN-BAY TART

Makes 1 tart, 8 servings

Pumpkin desserts are so often flavored with cinnamon, allspice, and nutmeg that we've come to equate this sweet spice combination with the flavor of pumpkin itself. Less aggressive flavorings, on the other hand, allow pumpkin to reveal its own special subtlety. In this tart I infuse the cream for the pumpkin custard with fresh bay laurel, vanilla, and a touch of fresh ginger. If you use fresh pumpkin purée, the custard will be especially light and delicate, but canned pumpkin also works well. The flavor of fresh bay flatters the flavors of pumpkin or squash in both sweet and savory dishes, and this ethereal tart proves the point well.

1 cup heavy cream, plus an additional 2 tablespoons if needed
8 large fresh bay laurel leaves, cracked
½ vanilla bean, split and scraped (page 251), or 1 teaspoon vanilla extract
5 ¼-inch-thick slices fresh ginger
½ cup (packed) dark brown sugar
⅓ cup light corn syrup
2 large eggs
¼ teaspoon salt
1 cup pumpkin purée, homemade (see Note) or canned, or butternut or acorn squash purée
1 9-inch Almond Shortbread Crust (page 346), prebaked

1. Infuse the cream. Pour the cream into a small (1-quart) saucepan and bring it to a boil over medium-high heat. Add the bay leaves, vanilla bean if using, and ginger, push them under the surface of the liquid with a spoon, and immediately remove the pan from the heat. Cover the pan and steep for 30 minutes. Strain the cream through a fine sieve into a large liquid measuring cup, pressing down firmly on the flavorings to extract all the liquid from the leaves. Add fresh cream if needed to measure 1 cup.

2. Pumpkin custard. Preheat the oven to 350°F. Whisk together the brown sugar and corn syrup in a medium mixing bowl until smooth. Add the eggs one at a time and whisk until smooth after each addition. Whisk in the salt and pumpkin purée, then whisk in the infused cream. Transfer the mixture to a pitcher or liquid measuring cup.

3. Filling and baking. Put the prebaked tart shell on a cookie sheet, place it on the center oven rack, and pour in the custard until it reaches the top of the shell. Do not let the filling spill over the edge of the crust; if there is a little too much, bake the extra separately in a ramekin. Bake the tart until it is set in the center, 25 to 30 minutes. Let the tart cool completely before slicing. If you bake the tart more than 4 hours in advance, store it covered in the refrigerator and bring it to room temperature before serving.

NOTE

To make pumpkin purée, cut a sugar pumpkin in half and scrape out the seeds. Place it cut side down in a baking dish and pour in about ¼ inch hot water. Bake in a 400°F oven until the flesh is tender, 40 to 50 minutes. Turn the pumpkin halves cut side up to cool. Scoop the pumpkin flesh from the skin and purée it in a food processor until smooth. Transfer the purée to a large sieve lined with a double layer of cheesecloth and let it drain for 2–3 hours until it is firm enough to hold its shape on a spoon.

Rhubarb and Angelica Pie

12 servings

Many early twentieth century books on herbs suggest combining angelica and rhubarb. They make an intriguing combination because the stems of both have such similarities in flavor that together they taste like one ingredient. Angelica is said to reduce the amount of sugar needed to sweeten the rhubarb—it mellows the tartness while at the same time it seems to intensify its distinct taste.

> *1 ½ pounds rhubarb stalks, without leaves*
> *¾ cup finely diced young angelica stems*
> *1 ⅓ cups sugar*
> *⅓ cup cornstarch*
> *Flaky Pastry for a double-crust 9-inch pie (page 342)*
> *2 tablespoons unsalted butter, softened*

1. Filling. Preheat the oven to 375° F. Wash the rhubarb, trim, and slice ¼ inch thick. Put the rhubarb in a large mixing bowl and toss it with the angelica, sugar, and cornstarch.

2. Forming the pie. Roll half the pastry dough into a 12-inch circle about ⅛-inch thick and line a 9-inch pie pan with it. Trim any dough that extends beyond the rim of the pan. Mound the rhubarb filling in the shell and dot it with the butter. Roll out the remaining pastry dough into another 12-inch circle and center it on top of the filling. Tuck the edge of the top pastry under the edge of the bottom crust, then flute the combined edge by pressing it at intervals between your thumb and forefinger. Cut 5 slits 1 ½ inches long in the top crust in a star pattern.

3. Baking. Bake the pie on a rack placed in the bottom third of the oven until the crust is well browned and the filling is bubbling through the slits on the top, about 1 hour. Cool at least 1 hour before slicing. Serve the pie with vanilla ice cream.

HERB SUBSTITUTION

RHUBARB LAVENDER PIE
- *Omit the angelica and add 4 teaspoons coarsely chopped fresh lavender buds, or 2 teaspoons coarsely chopped dried lavender buds to the filling.*

APPLE-ROSEMARY SOUFFLÉ

8 servings

Nothing ends a meal with as much glamour as a perfectly timed dessert soufflé, and this apple rendition, cooled with a stream of rich custard sauce, is unforgettable. Sweet soufflés are nothing more than beaten egg whites folded into a base, which can be made of pastry cream, chocolate, or fruit purée, and baked. In this soufflé the base is thick caramelized applesauce highlighted subtly with rosemary. Once these soufflés are risen and ready, they must be rushed to the table because they begin to fall immediately.

About 2 tablespoons unsalted butter, softened, for the ramekins
2 tablespoons sugar for the ramekins
2 4-inch sprigs fresh rosemary
¾ cup plus 2 tablespoons sugar
2 tablespoons unsalted butter
2 pounds tart apples (about 6 large), such as Granny Smith, Jonagold, or
*   Braeburn, peeled, cored, and cut into ½-inch dice*
1 2-inch piece cinnamon stick
½ vanilla bean, split and scraped (page 251), or 1 teaspoon vanilla extract
1 tablespoon finely chopped fresh ginger
3 large egg yolks
Optional: 2 tablespoons Calvados or Cognac
6 large egg whites
1 cup Herb-Infused Custard Sauce (page 252) made with fresh bay laurel
*   leaves or rosemary, and vanilla*

1. Preparing the molds. Generously coat the interiors of 8 6-ounce straight-sided ramekins with the softened butter using a pastry brush or your fingers. Pour 2 tablespoons sugar into 1 dish and turn it until all surfaces are coated, then tip the sugar out into the next and repeat the process until all the ramekins have a thorough coating of butter and sugar. Set the prepared molds in a large shallow baking pan or on a half-sheet pan.

2. Applesauce. Tie the rosemary sprigs together with kitchen twine, wrapping the twine in a spiral up the length of the stems to keep the needles from falling off in the sauce. Put ¾ cup sugar in a 4-quart heavy-bottomed saucepan and place it over medium-high heat. When the sugar begins to melt, stir it with a wooden spoon. It will form big lumps at first, but keep cooking and stirring until all the sugar is dissolved and you have a smooth amber syrup. As soon as it reaches this stage, add 2 tablespoons butter and stir until it is melted and incorporated. Add the apples and stir. The caramel will harden and form lumps again, but once the sauce cooks it will dissolve. Add the rosemary bundle, cinnamon stick, vanilla bean if using, and ginger. Cook, stirring often, over medium heat until the liquid from the apples releases and then boils away, about 15 minutes. Remove the rosemary bundle, cinnamon stick, and vanilla bean. Stir in the vanilla extract if using. Purée the mixture with a handheld immersion blender, in a food processor, or by passing it through a food mill. You should have a deep brown sauce that is thick enough to hold its shape in a mound. (This applesauce can be stored covered in the refrigerator up to 1 week. Bring to room temperature before proceeding.)

3. Egg whites. Preheat the oven to 375°F. In a large mixing bowl, whisk the egg yolks and liquor if using into the applesauce. In a separate bowl, beat the egg whites until they form soft peaks, add the remaining 2 tablespoons sugar, and continue to beat until they form stiff peaks. Using a large rubber spatula, fold one-third of the whites into the apple mixture until it is thoroughly incorporated, then gently fold in the remaining whites. Tilt the bowl over the prepared soufflé cups and, using the rubber spatula to carefully guide the mixture, fill the dishes to ½ inch of the top. Wipe up any spills on the sides of the dishes and, using your thumb, wipe off any mixture that is touching the rims. If the soufflé bakes onto any unbuttered surface at the top of dish, it will stick and prevent it from rising straight up. At this point the soufflés can be held for up to 1 hour at room temperature.

4. Baking. Put the baking pan holding the soufflés in the oven and pour about ½ inch hot tap water into the pan. Bake until the soufflés are nicely browned and risen about 1½ inches, 20 to 25 minutes. Using tongs or oven mitts, immediately transfer the hot dishes to individual serving plates and rush them to the table with pitchers of the custard sauce. Each guest should break open their soufflé in the middle and pour in some of the custard.

VARIATION

For a large soufflé, pour the batter into a 1½-quart soufflé dish, generously coated with butter and sugar. Bake the soufflé in a shallow water bath at 375°F until the top is browned and risen about 1½ inches above the rim, 35 to 40 minutes.

CARAMELIZED TANGERINES WITH ROSEMARY-LEMON ICE

6 servings

Vividly colored satsumas and clementines begin to show up in markets in November and are one of the pleasures of the holiday season. Not only is their flesh easy to peel, tangy, and juicy, but the fragrant skin is also thin and less bitter than most other citrus. You can cook with it in its entirety, without removing the pith. This refreshing dessert is made up of the seedless tangerine sections warmed in caramel syrup with crunchy bits of the candied peel, and contrasted with bracing rosemary lemon ice.

ICE

½ cup sugar
1 ¼ cups water
2 3-inch sprigs fresh rosemary
1 teaspoon finely chopped lemon zest (removed with a zester)
6 tablespoons freshly squeezed lemon juice

1 pound seedless tangerines (5 to 8), such as satsumas or clementines
1 cup sugar
½ cup water
6 tablespoons freshly squeezed tangerine or orange juice

1. Ice. Bring the sugar and water to a boil in a small (1-quart) saucepan. Add the rosemary, cover, and steep for 30 minutes. Strain the syrup through a fine sieve into a small stainless-steel bowl or plastic container. Stir in the lemon zest and lemon juice. Freeze the mixture until it is solid, about 3 hours.

2. Tangerines. Peel the tangerines, reserving about one-third the total amount of peel. Cut the reserved peel into very fine strips with a sharp thin knife. Separate the fruit into individual sections and set them aside.

3. Caramel. Put the sugar, water, and sliced peel in a small heavy-bottomed saucepan and bring it to a boil. Wash down any sugar crystals that stick to the sides of the pan with a clean pastry brush dipped in cold water. Boil the syrup without stirring until it begins to turn an amber color around the edges. At this point, gently whisk until all the syrup is a medium amber color. Remove the pan from the heat and put an oven mitt on your hand that holds the whisk. While whisking, pour in the tangerine juice. It will bubble violently and create a great deal of very hot steam, so keep your hands and face away from the top of the pan. Don't panic if some of the syrup seizes (hardens in lumps); put it back over heat and keep stirring until it dissolves into a syrup again. Stir in the tangerine sections and let the mixture cool until it is just slightly warm.

4. Serving. Spoon the tangerine sections and the candied peel with syrup into 6 small serving dishes or stemmed glasses. Scrape the ice by drawing the side of a large spoon across its surface. It should break up into coarse fluffy ice crystals. Spoon some of the ice into each dish and serve immediately.

VARIATION
Instead of the lemon rosemary ice, serve the caramelized tangerine sections and candied peel with premium chocolate or coffee ice cream or Lemon Verbena Ice Cream (page 258).

LAVENDER SHORTBREAD

Makes 24 cookies

This is the purest form of shortbread—just butter, sugar, and flour—but scented subtly with lavender. Even the salt is left out because I think it detracts from the delicate butteriness. These cookies are perfect with tea or as an accompaniment to ice creams, sorbets, or fruit desserts. Be sure not to over-bake them. If you pull them from the oven when they just begin to turn beige but not brown, they will be remarkably tender when they cool.

8 ounces (2 sticks) unsalted butter, chilled
4 teaspoons fresh lavender buds, or 2 teaspoons dried
½ cup sugar
2 cups all-purpose flour (spoon and level; 9 ounces)

1. Lavender sugar. Fifteen minutes before you begin the dough, remove the butter from the refrigerator. Place the lavender buds in a clean spice mill with ¼ cup of the sugar and grind until fine. If you don't have a spice mill, grind the lavender with all the sugar in a blender or small food processor.

2. Mixing the dough. Transfer the lavender sugar to the bowl of a heavy-duty electric mixer fitted with a paddle and add the remaining ¼ cup sugar if you used a spice mill and the butter. Beat on low speed until the mixture is smooth and there are no detectable lumps of butter when you roll a teaspoon of it between your fingers; do not beat it until fluffy. Add all the flour at once and continue to mix on low speed just until it forms a cohesive dough.

3. Rolling and cutting. Turn the dough out onto a lightly floured surface, press it firmly into a smooth rectangular block with no cracks, and dust it lightly with more flour. Using a rolling pin, roll it into a 12 x 9-inch rectangle, ¼ inch thick, rotating the dough a quarter turn each time you roll to make sure it is not sticking to the work surface. You can also roll the dough out between sheets of plastic wrap or parchment paper. Using a straight edge and a pastry wheel or chef's knife, cut the dough into 3 x 1½-inch bars, or cut out other shapes with cookie cutters. Using a spatula, transfer the cookies to a baking sheet lined with parchment paper, leaving ½ inch space between them. Refrigerate the cookies for at least 30 minutes before baking to allow the dough to rest.

4. Baking. Preheat the oven to 300°F. Bake the cookies until they are colored lightly like sand, not browned, 22 to 25 minutes. Lift one with a small spatula to check the color of the underside; it should be just a shade darker than the top. Let the cookies cool completely on the pan (they are soft while hot). Stack the cooled cookies in an airtight container and store at room temperature for up to 1 week.

MIXING VARIATION

If you don't have a heavy-duty electric mixer, you can mix the dough in a large mixing bowl with a wooden spoon, but you'll need to start with butter that is at room temperature. Mix the butter with the lavender sugar until completely smooth, then stir in the flour. Wrap the dough in plastic wrap and refrigerate for about 1 hour before rolling.

HERB SUBSTITUTIONS

- *In place of the lavender, add 4 teaspoons finely chopped fresh rosemary, thyme, or lemon thyme to the butter and sugar.*

SPICE SUBSTITUTIONS

- *Substitute for the lavender 2 teaspoons dried fennel or anise seeds, or ½ teaspoon green cardamom seeds, grinding the seeds with the sugar as directed.*

CHOCOLATE-MINT TRUFFLE TORTE

Makes 1 cake, 12 servings

This torte uses yet one more technique for infusing fresh herbs. This time you steep mint leaves in warm butter, strain them out, and use the scented butter in the cake. Flourless chocolate cakes are familiar to most serious chocolate lovers because they are the most intensely chocolate cakes imaginable. They are, in fact, cooled dense chocolate soufflés and very simple to make. The fresh peppermint flavor in this version gives it a refreshing note.

About 1 tablespoon unsalted butter, softened, for the pan
1 tablespoon all-purpose flour, for the pan
6 ounces (1 ½ sticks) unsalted butter
½ cup (gently packed) fresh chocolate mint or peppermint leaves
12 ounces premium bittersweet chocolate, such as Callebaut, Valrhona, or
  El Rey, chopped
6 large eggs, at room temperature
6 tablespoons granulated sugar
Garnish: powdered sugar

1. Preparing the pan. Generously butter a 9-inch springform pan and lightly dust the interior with the flour. Turn the pan upside down and bang out the excess flour. Wrap a large square of heavy-duty aluminum foil around the bottom of the pan and partially up the sides. Turn the pan right side up and set it in a shallow baking pan or on a half-sheet pan.

2. Infusing the butter. Melt the butter in a small saucepan. Stir in the mint leaves and let the butter sit in a warm place for about 30 minutes to absorb the flavor of the leaves.

3. Butter and chocolate mixture. Preheat the oven to 350°F. Create a double boiler by selecting a medium (10- to 12-inch) stainless-steel mixing bowl that will rest on top of a large (6-quart) pot. The top of the bowl can extend beyond the rim of the pot, but the bottom of the bowl must not touch the water. Put about 2 inches water in the pot and bring it to a simmer. If the butter has cooled, heat it again to thin it. Pour the butter through a fine sieve into the mixing bowl and press the leaves with the back of a spoon to extract all the butter. Add the chocolate to the bowl and place it over the simmering water. Stir until the chocolate is completely melted, then remove the bowl from the water.

4. Eggs. Beat the eggs and granulated sugar with an electric mixer on high speed for a full 10 minutes. They should quadruple in volume and become light colored, very thick, and fluffy. Fold one-quarter of the egg mixture into the chocolate mixture, then very gently fold in the remaining egg mixture until completely incorporated. Pour the batter into the prepared pan.

5. Baking. Put the baking pan with the cake on the center oven rack and pour in enough water to come about ½ inch up the sides of the cake pan. Bake until an instant-read thermometer inserted in the center of the cake registers 155° to 160° F, 25 to 30 minutes. The top of the cake will lose its glossiness and be slightly mounded, but it should not bake so long that it rises and cracks. If you insert a skewer into the center, it should come out gooey. Let the cake cool completely in its pan on a wire rack. Run a thin knife around the edge of the cake and remove the outer ring. The cake will keep tightly covered in the refrigerator for up to 3 days. Bring it to room temperature before serving. Dust the top of the cake with powdered sugar and serve with whipped cream, ice cream, or custard sauce (page 252).

HERB SUBSTITUTION
ROSE-SCENTED CHOCOLATE TRUFFLE TORTE
- *Substitute 8 medium-size rose geranium leaves for the mint leaves.*

HERBAL CHOCOLATE TRUFFLES

Makes about 36 truffles

These chocolate candies contain unique herbal flavors. You'll find them surprisingly simple and fun to make. An assortment of dark and white truffles with various herbal infusions in a well-chosen box makes a spectacular handmade holiday gift.

BITTERSWEET CHOCOLATE MINT TRUFFLES
1¼ cups heavy cream, plus an additional 2 tablespoons if needed
6 3-inch sprigs fresh chocolate mint or peppermint
1 pound premium bittersweet chocolate, such as Callebaut, Valrhona, or
    El Rey
About ½ cup Dutch-processed cocoa

WHITE CHOCOLATE TARRAGON TRUFFLES
¾ cup heavy cream, plus an additional 2 tablespoons if needed
4 3-inch sprigs fresh French tarragon
1 pound premium white chocolate, such as Callebaut or Lindt
About ½ cup finely ground pistachio nuts

1. Infuse the cream. Pour the cream into a small (1-quart) saucepan and bring it to a boil over medium-high heat. Add the herb sprigs, push them under the surface of the liquid with a spoon, and immediately remove the pan from the heat. Cover the pan and steep for 30 minutes. Strain the cream through a fine sieve into a large liquid measuring cup, pressing down firmly on the flavorings to extract all the liquid from the leaves. Check the measurement of the infused cream; it should equal 1¼ cups. Top it off with the additional cream if needed. Return the cream to the saucepan.

2. Ganache. Chop the chocolate so that most of the pieces are less than ½ inch and put it in a food processor. Heat the cream until it comes to a full boil and immediately pour it over the chocolate. Let the mixture sit for 1 minute, then turn on the machine and process until smooth. You now have an herbal ganache. Using a rubber spatula, transfer it to a small container. Let it sit at room temperature until set, about 2 hours.

3. Forming the truffles. Using a tiny ice cream scoop, a melon baller, or a teaspoon, scoop the ganache into ¾-inch balls and put them on a parchment-lined baking sheet. After all the balls are scooped, quickly roll each one between your palms using steady light pressure to form perfect balls. If you have trouble with the chocolate melting in your palms (some people have warmer hands than others), wash your hands, dip them in a bowl of ice water, dry them thoroughly, and try again. If you are working in a warm room, refrigerate the truffles for about 15 minutes before you roll.

4. Coating. Put the cocoa or pistachios in a medium mixing bowl and drop in 6 truffles. Swirl the bowl to coat the truffles evenly. Transfer the coated truffles to a large strainer and bang the side of the strainer with your palm to knock off the excess coating. Place the coated truffles in a plastic storage container. Repeat the process with the remaining truffles. Tightly cover the truffles and store in the refrigerator up to 2 weeks. Let them come to room temperature before serving.

 HERB SUBSTITUTIONS
- *For the bittersweet chocolate truffles, substitute 8 medium-size fresh rose geranium leaves, or 4 3-inch sprigs fresh French tarragon for the mint.*
- *For the white chocolate truffles, substitute 4 3-inch sprigs fresh Mexican tarragon, 6 3-inch sprigs fresh spearmint, 8 medium-size fresh rose geranium leaves, ¼ cup finely chopped young angelica stems, 6 fresh bay laurel leaves, 1 tablespoon fresh lavender buds (or 1½ teaspoons dried), or ½ cup fresh lemon verbena leaves (or ¼ cup slightly crumbled dried) for the tarragon.*

CHAPTER 10

Sorbets

Every multicourse menu we serve at The Herbfarm has an intermezzo, a small course that serves to cleanse the palate in the middle of the meal. Most often, it's a sorbet flavored with herbs, flowers, or even trees (a signature dish is Douglas Fir sorbet, made by steeping the needles of this native Pacific Northwest tree). Sorbets have a brilliant capacity for capturing the essence of botanical flavors, and their cool light texture and balance of sweet and tart refreshes like nothing else. If you aren't preparing a six- or nine-course meal at home, you'll probably want to serve these sorbets as elegant and uncomplicated desserts. The recipes in this chapter are effortless to prepare and the perfect way to end a meal on a light note. Herb and flower sorbets are also lovely served with sliced fresh fruit at a summer brunch.

These sorbets are made from a base of either sugar syrup, fruit purée, or a combination of the two. The first 3 recipes in this chapter use a technique for making the sugar syrup without heat, so that none of the delicate volatile flavors of the herbs or flowers are lost. The leaves or petals are puréed with superfine sugar in a food processor, then water and lemon juice is added and the mixture is frozen in an ice cream maker. The remaining recipes steep the herbs in either hot sugar syrup or sweetened fruit purée.

If you don't have an ice cream maker, you can still make the sorbets in this book. Pour the sorbet mixture into a stainless-steel mixing bowl and put it in the freezer. Every 30 to 60 minutes scrape down the mixture that has frozen next to the sides with a large spoon and stir it up. When it has the consistency of a firm slush, allow it to freeze until firm. For a smoother consistency, put the workbowl and steel blade from your food processor in the freezer. Shortly before you serve the sorbet, scrape it into the cold workbowl and pulse it until it is smooth and fluffy.

LEMON VERBENA SORBET

Makes 1 quart, 8 servings

Nothing but vibrant and refreshing—it's lemon heaven.

1 cup (gently packed) fresh lemon verbena leaves
1 cup superfine sugar
¼ cup freshly squeezed lemon juice
3 cups cold water

Grind the lemon verbena leaves and sugar together in a food processor until the mixture turns into a bright green paste, about 30 seconds; stop to scrape down the sides as necessary. Add the lemon juice and process for 15 seconds longer, then add the water. Strain the resulting liquid through a fine sieve to remove any bits of leaf. Freeze in an ice cream maker according to the manufacturer's directions.

VARIATION
SCENTED GERANIUM SORBET
Substitute 16 medium-size scented geranium leaves, such as old-fashioned rose or Mabel Gray lemon geranium, for the lemon verbena.

 HERB ADDITIONS
- *The pure lemon flavor of the verbena blends well with other herbs. For a compound herb flavor, grind any of the following with the lemon verbena leaves and sugar: 1 cup sweet cicely leaves, 6 rose geranium leaves, ¼ cup French or Mexican tarragon leaves, or ¼ cup mint leaves.*

OLD ROSE AND CHAMPAGNE SORBET

Makes 5 cups, 10 servings

There is nothing more ethereal than sorbet made from fragrant rose petals and Champagne. In addition to lending their heavenly floral perfume, rose petals have a subtle astringency that makes this sorbet especially refreshing despite its sweetness. Deep red flowers produce a gorgeous magenta sorbet, and pink roses yield a soft pastel color. Scoop it into stemmed crystal glasses for a summer brunch in the garden or to end a romantic dinner for two.

The term *old rose* does not mean the flowers have been in a vase too long but refers instead to old-fashioned types of roses that have heady fragrance and thin delicate petals. These include Gallica, Damask, Bourbon, and Musk roses (some have been in cultivation since medieval times) as well as many new varieties of roses bred with similar characteristics, particularly those developed in England by rose breeder David Austin. Modern varieties that have mild fragrance and thick petals—like many hybrid teas—will be bitter and lacking the flavor needed for this sorbet. Never use roses purchased from a florist because the shrubs they grow on are heavily treated with toxic chemicals. Even if you use homegrown roses, you must be certain they haven't been sprayed with chemicals or grown with systemic pest controls.

> *2 cups (gently packed) rose petals from fragrant thin-petaled roses*
>   *(pesticide free)*
> *1 cup plus 2 tablespoons superfine sugar*
> *3 cups cold water*
> *3 tablespoons freshly squeezed lemon juice*
> *1 cup brut or extra-dry Champagne or sparkling wine*
> *Optional: 1 tablespoon rose water for a more intensely perfumed flavor*

Process the rose petals with the sugar in a food processor until the mixture turns into a smooth paste, about 30 seconds; stop to scrape down the sides as necessary. Add ½ cup of the water and process for about 10 seconds. Add the remaining 2½ cups water, the lemon juice, Champagne, and rose water if using. Pour the liquid through a fine sieve. Freeze the mixture in an ice cream maker according to the manufacturer's directions.

BLACK PANSY SORBET

Makes 1 quart, 8 servings

I first planted black pansies at The Herbfarm to have appropriate garnishes for a Halloween dinner, but I've grown them every season since. Black pansies are members of the viola family whose flowers are colored such a deep purple that they appear black. Some named varieties that you might see in nurseries or seed catalogues include Vulcan, Zorro, and King of the Blacks. Turned into candies, syrups, and sorbets, they not only tint the sweets a startling hot magenta but also have an astonishing flavor, something like minty violet candy. This simple recipe should inspire you to grow them every year in your own garden as well. A half dozen plants will provide enough flowers for many quarts of sorbet over the course of the summer.

When you cook with black pansies, you will witness a magic trick. The mixture of pansy, sugar, and water will be a blue violet, but as soon as you add lemon juice—abracadabra—it turns to hot magenta. When you harvest the pansies, be sure to pick and use the whole flower, not just the petals, for most of the flavor is contained in the green base of the blossom.

> *1 cup (gently packed) black pansy flowers*
> *1 cup superfine sugar*
> *3 cups cold water*
> *3 tablespoons freshly squeezed lemon juice*

Purée the pansy flowers with the sugar in a food processor or blender until they form a smooth paste. Add ½ cup of the water and continue to blend for another minute. Add the remaining 2½ cups water and the lemon juice. Freeze the mixture in an ice cream maker according to the manufacturer's directions.

CHOCOLATE-MINT SORBET

Makes 5 cups, 10 servings

Chocolate sorbet delivers a chocolate hit without the heaviness of most other chocolate desserts. This version, made with best-quality chocolate, has a satisfying chewiness and deep flavor, while the infusion of fresh mint sprigs magnifies the cool and refreshing qualities of the sorbet.

> ¾ *cup sugar*
> *3 cups water*
> *6 4-inch sprigs peppermint, chocolate mint, or spearmint*
> *6 ounces premium bittersweet or semisweet chocolate, such as Callebaut, Valrhona, or El Rey, chopped*
> ¼ *cup unsweetened cocoa*

1. Syrup. Bring the sugar and water to a boil in a medium saucepan. Add the mint, cover, remove from the heat, and steep for 30 minutes. Strain and return the syrup to the saucepan.

2. Sorbet. Return the syrup to a simmer. Add the chocolate and cocoa, remove the pan from the heat, and whisk until smooth. Refrigerate the mixture until thoroughly chilled. Freeze in an ice cream maker according to the manufacturer's directions.

Raspberry and Rose Geranium Sorbet

Makes 1 quart, 8 servings

Raspberry and rose geranium make one of those mystical combinations where you can't tell where one flavor stops and the other begins. Together they create a sorbet that tastes more like raspberries than raspberries alone.

¾ cup sugar
¾ cup water
8 medium-size rose geranium leaves
4 cups fresh raspberries, picked over
2 tablespoons freshly squeezed lemon juice

1. Syrup. Combine the sugar and water in a small (1-quart) saucepan and bring it to a rolling boil over medium-high heat. Add the rose geranium leaves, push them under the surface with a spoon, and immediately remove the pan from the heat. Cover the pan and steep for at least 30 minutes. Pour the syrup through a fine sieve and press down firmly on the leaves with the back of a spoon to extract all the liquid.

2. Sorbet. Purée the raspberries in a food processor. Add the lemon juice and rose geranium syrup. Refrigerate the mixture until chilled. Freeze in an ice cream maker according to the manufacturer's directions.

GRAPE AND ROSEMARY SORBET

Makes 1 quart, 8 servings

Directly behind the site of the original Herbfarm restaurant is a grape arbor that has been there so long nobody knows the names of the grapes that grow on it, but there are three kinds—purple, red, and green—all with large seeds and lots of flavor. Every October when they ripen, I prepare this creamy sorbet. The piney flavor of the rosemary is a terrific match for the mild astringency and tannins in the grapes. When you make this, try to find local grapes with intense flavor or fresh wine grapes—common seedless table grapes will not give the same results.

2 pounds stemmed grapes, such as Concord or Muscat, washed
¾ to 1¼ cups sugar
⅛ teaspoon salt
1 cup water
3 4-inch sprigs fresh rosemary

Put the grapes, ¾ cup sugar, salt, and water in a medium (3-quart) saucepan and cook, stirring often, over medium heat until the grapes collapse and release their juice, 10 to 15 minutes. Taste and add more sugar if needed. Stir the rosemary sprigs into the hot fruit, cover, and steep for 30 minutes. Pass the mixture through a food mill fitted with a fine screen or press the mixture through a fine sieve using the back of a wooden spoon. Refrigerate until thoroughly chilled. Freeze the mixture in an ice cream maker according to the manufacturer's directions.

CRANBERRY AND ORANGE THYME SORBET

Makes 1 quart, 8 servings

Fresh cranberries make a tangy, slightly tannic, and very refreshing sorbet. Infused with the fruity aroma of orange, lemon, or English thyme, the sorbet is a delightfully unique cranberry dish to serve before, during, or after Thanksgiving dinner.

> *12 ounces fresh cranberries, washed*
> *1 cup sugar*
> *1½ cups water*
> *Thinly sliced zest of 2 oranges (removed with a zester)*
> *8 to 12 3-inch sprigs fresh thyme, such as orange balsam, lemon, or English thyme (½ ounce)*
> *1 ½ cups freshly squeezed orange juice*

Bring the cranberries, sugar, water, and orange zest to a boil in a medium (3-quart) saucepan. Partially cover the pan and boil until most of the cranberries pop, about 5 minutes. Stir in the thyme sprigs, remove from the heat, cover tightly, and steep for 30 minutes. Pour the fruit mixture into a fine sieve set on top of a deep bowl. Stir and press down on the fruit with the back of a large spoon to extract as much juice and pulp as you can, leaving the skins and thyme behind in the sieve. Refrigerate the strained mixture until thoroughly chilled. Stir in the orange juice. Freeze in an ice cream maker according to the manufacturer's directions.

CHAPTER 11

The Herbal Pantry: Condiments and Candies

At summer's end when the herb garden is bursting its seams and you feel you have an embarrassment of herbal riches going to waste because you can't possibly cook with all of them, it's time to preserve the abundance for the bleak winter months. Drying and freezing herbs are two options, but this chapter offers many other ways to turn your herbal harvest into a pantry full of vinegars, mustards, chutneys, jellies, and candies to use throughout the year or to give as gifts.

APPLE-THYME JELLY

Makes 3 half-pints, plus about ½ cup

Because of their high pectin content, apples make a superb crystal clear jelly without the need to use packaged pectin. Old-fashioned recipes often call for a leaf or sprig of an herb to be put in the jar to flavor the jelly. I like this tradition but find a single leaf or sprig too subtle. For a more distinct flavor, I steep a small bundle of herb sprigs in the jelly before it is ladled into the canning jars and then place a leaf or sprig in the jar. In this recipe, the combination of apple and thyme gives the jelly a savoriness that makes it an excellent spread for toast to accompany a breakfast with bacon, ham, or a Cheddar cheese omelet. Rosemary, lavender, and sage also make delicious flavorings for apple jelly, but traditionally rose geranium was the most commonly used herb, and it yields a wonderfully fragrant spread for tea time.

> *4 pounds apples (8 to 10 large), any variety*
> *8 cups water*
> *3 cups sugar*
> *8 3-inch sprigs fresh thyme, such as English, lemon, orange balsam, or caraway thyme, tied together with kitchen twine, plus 3 more sprigs for the jars*

1. Apple liquid. Wash the apples. Without peeling or coring them, cut them into eighths. Put the apple pieces in a large (8-quart) pot. Add the water and bring to a boil. Reduce the heat and cook at a steady simmer, partially covered, until the apples are falling apart, about 45 minutes. Set a large very fine sieve, a large coarse sieve lined with a double thickness of cheesecloth, or a jelly bag over a deep bowl or pot. Pour in the apples and liquid and let drain for 4 to 8 hours, undisturbed. Don't press down the apples, but you can rap the side of the sieve or jelly bag frame with your palm from time to time if you want to hurry it along.

2. Boiling the jelly. You should end up with about 6 cups of cloudy liquid. Discard the solids. Pour the liquid into a large (6-quart) heavy-bottomed pot and add the sugar. Bring the mixture to a boil. Use a ladle to skim off any white foam that rises to the top. Continue to boil the jelly uncovered, keeping the heat as high as possible without letting the jelly boil over, until it passes the wrinkle test. It will take 45 to 60 minutes. After about 30 minutes, the jelly will begin to look different, and dense white bubbles will form at the surface. To test for wrinkles, drop ½ teaspoon of the jelly onto a chilled plate and put the plate in the refrigerator for 1 to 2 minutes. When the drop of jelly has cooled, gently push the side of it with your fingertip. Look closely at the drop. If the top wrinkles, it's done; if it stays smooth like a drop of honey would, continue to boil it. When it is at the wrinkle stage, the drop will seem softly jelled, but the jelly will be more firmly set after it sits for 24 hours. Don't boil it longer or the jelly will be rubbery. When the jelly passes the test, drop in the thyme bunch, cover, and remove the pot from the heat. Let the thyme steep in the jelly for 15 minutes.

3. Sterilizing the jars. Meanwhile sterilize 3 half-pint canning jars by submerging them in a large pot of boiling water (make sure they are completely covered by the water) and boiling them for 10 minutes. Leave the jars in the hot water until the jelly is ready. Bring a small saucepan of water to a boil, drop in the bands and 3 new canning lids, and remove the pan from the heat.

4. Canning. Remove the thyme bunch from the jelly and squeeze it between 2 slotted spoons to extract all the liquid. Bring the jelly back to a boil again, then remove it from the heat. Using a jar lifter, grip 1 sterile jar in the hot water, lift, and drain it. Set the jar on a clean towel and put 1 thyme sprig in the jar. Insert a canning funnel if you have one. Ladle in the jelly, filling it to ¼ inch from the top. Wipe off any spills from the rim of the jar with a damp paper towel. Use tongs to lift a lid and band from the hot water. Set the lid on the jar and then screw on the band snugly but not overly tight. Turn the jar upside down on another clean towel. Fill and seal the other 2 jars. Pour the remaining jelly into a small dish or jar, cover and refrigerate it, and you can enjoy it before you open the canned jelly. After 5 minutes turn the jars right side up and let them cool undisturbed. If the jars are properly sealed, the center of the lid will not yield when you press on it. If any jars did not seal, keep them refrigerated.

 HERB SUBSTITUTIONS
- *In place of the thyme, use one of the following tied with twine: 12 rose geranium leaves, 12 flowering lavender sprigs, 3 4-inch sprigs rosemary, 4 4-inch sprigs anise hyssop, or 2 3-inch sprigs sage. Put a leaf or small sprig of the same herb in each jar before you pour in the jelly.*

ORANGE-ROSEMARY MARMALADE

Makes 6 pints

Making your own marmalade is easier than you might think. Because orange rinds contain large amounts of pectin, the conserve will jell firmly without a tedious boiling process or the need to add packaged pectin. The rosemary in this version gives the marmalade a piney flavor that harmonizes perfectly with the bitter orange.

Anytime you make a preserve without packaged pectin you have to pay attention to variables in the ingredients and adjust your recipe accordingly. In this case, the size of the fruit is very important. Smaller citrus with thick skins means there is less orange juice in relation to rind, and larger fruit means there is more. This affects the boiling time, so pay close attention to the wrinkle test.

Because you are using the entire fruit, peel and all, it's best to use organic oranges and lemons for the marmalade. Nonorganic citrus can have chemical residue in the rind.

> 2½ pounds oranges (6 to 8 medium), such as Valencias or blood oranges,
>   preferably organically grown
> 2 large lemons (6 ounces each), preferably organically grown
> 6 cups cold water
> 8 cups sugar
> 6 6-inch sprigs rosemary, wrapped in a single layer of cheesecloth and tied
>   with kitchen twine

1. **Soaking the citrus.** Begin the day before you can the marmalade. Cut the oranges and lemons in half, poke out the seeds with the tip of a paring knife, and slice them about ¹⁄₁₆ inch thick, rind and all. A mandoline or Japanese Benriner slicer will do the job most evenly, but you can use the thin slicing disk of a food processor instead. Put the citrus in a large (6-quart) heavy-bottomed pot, cover it with the water, and let soak at room temperature for 12 to 24 hours. This allows the rind to soften and release its pectin.

2. **Boiling the marmalade.** The next day bring the pot of sliced citrus to a boil and continue to boil it steadily for 30 minutes. Stir in the sugar and rosemary bundle and cook at a steady boil until it passes the wrinkle test, 15 to 30 minutes longer. Keep an

eye on it and adjust the heat so that it doesn't boil over. When it is close to being ready, you will notice the bubbles will get larger and seem thicker. To test for wrinkles, drop a ½ teaspoon of the jelly onto a chilled plate and put the plate in the refrigerator for 1 to 2 minutes. When the drop of jelly has cooled, gently push the side of it with your fingertip. Look closely at the drop. If the top wrinkles, it's done; if it stays smooth like a drop of honey would, continue to boil it. When ready, the drop will seem softly jelled, but the marmalade will be more firmly set after it sits for 24 hours.

3. Sterilizing the jars. Meanwhile sterilize 6 pint canning jars by submerging them in a large pot of boiling water (make sure they are completely covered by the water) and boiling them for 10 minutes. Leave the jars in the hot water until the jelly is ready. Bring a small saucepan of water to a boil, drop in the bands and 6 new canning lids, and remove the pan from the heat.

4. Canning. Remove the rosemary bundle from the hot marmalade and squeeze it between 2 slotted spoons to extract all the liquid. Using a jar lifter, grip 1 sterile jar in the hot water, lift, and drain it. Set the jar upright on a clean towel. Insert a canning funnel if you have one. Ladle in the marmalade, filling it to ¼ inch from the top. Wipe off any spills from the rim of the jar with a damp paper towel. Use tongs to lift a lid and band from the hot water. Set the lid on the jar and then screw on the band snugly but not overly tight. Turn the jar upside down on another clean towel. Fill and seal the remaining 5 jars in the same manner. After 5 minutes turn the jars right side up and let them cool undisturbed. If the jars are properly sealed, the center of the lid will not yield when you press on it. If any jars did not seal, keep them refrigerated.

Dill and Apricot Mustard

Makes 3 cups

This spicy, grainy mustard, sweetened with apricot and laced with dill, couldn't be simpler to prepare. It makes a terrific homemade gift, but remember to tell the receiver that it must be refrigerated. Serve it with leftover roast pork or lamb or on a cheese sandwich.

> *¼ cup dried yellow mustard*
> *⅔ cup yellow mustard seeds*
> *⅓ cup brown mustard seeds*
> *1 cup warm water*
> *¾ cup coarsely chopped dried apricots*
> *1¼ cups apple cider vinegar*
> *1 tablespoon salt*
> *½ cup coarsely chopped fresh dill*

1. Soaking the mustards. Stir the mustard powder and seeds, the water, and apricots together in a mixing bowl. Let sit for at least 2 hours or overnight to allow the ingredients to absorb the water.

2. Finishing the mustard. Put the mustard mixture in a food processor along with the vinegar, salt, and dill. Process until the seeds begin to break down and the mustard looks like a spreadable paste; add more water if necessary. Some of the seeds should remain whole. Transfer the mustard to glass jars, cover, and allow the mustard to ripen in the refrigerator for about 5 days before using. The mustard will keep refrigerated for up to 1 month.

PLUM AND LAVENDER CHUTNEY

Makes 4 half-pints

The winning combination of lavender and plums makes a lovely piquant chutney. Try it layered on a turkey sandwich or spread on crackers with Stilton cheese.

> 2 ½ pounds almost ripe red or purple plums, such as
>   Santa Rosa or Friar
> 1 medium onion (about 8 ounces), finely chopped
> Finely chopped zest (removed with a zester) and juice of 1 lemon
> 2 tablespoons finely chopped fresh ginger
> 1 tablespoon yellow mustard seeds
> ¼ teaspoon dried red pepper flakes
> 6 tablespoons red wine vinegar
> 1 cup (packed) dark brown sugar
> ¾ teaspoon salt
> 1 ½ tablespoons chopped fresh lavender buds, or 2 teaspoons dried

1. Chutney. Cut the plums in half, remove the pits, and cut them into ½-inch wedges. Put them in a large (4-quart) heavy-bottomed saucepan and stir in the onion, lemon zest and juice, ginger, mustard, red pepper flakes, vinegar, brown sugar, and salt. Bring the mixture to a boil. Reduce the heat to low and simmer, stirring often, until it has a jamlike consistency, 35 to 45 minutes. Stir in the lavender. Taste and season with additional salt or red pepper flakes if desired.

2. Sterilizing the jars. Meanwhile sterilize 4 half-pint canning jars by submerging them in a large pot of boiling water (make sure they are completely covered by the water) and boiling them for 10 minutes. Leave the jars in the hot water until the chutney is ready. Bring a small saucepan of water to a boil, drop in the bands and 4 new canning lids, and remove the pan from the heat.

3. Canning. Using a jar lifter, grip 1 sterile jar in the hot water, lift, and drain it. Set the jar on a clean towel. Ladle in the chutney, filling it to ¼ inch from the top. Use a canning funnel if you have one. Wipe off any spills from the rim of the jar with a damp paper towel. Use tongs to lift a lid and band from the hot water. Set the lid on the jar and then screw on the band snugly but not overly tight. Fill and seal the remaining jars in the same manner. Process the jars by boiling them in a canning kettle for 10 minutes according to the instructions that come with the lids or jars. Let the jars cool right side up on a clean towel. If the jars are properly sealed, the center of the lid will not yield when you press on it. If any jars did not seal, keep them refrigerated.

Nasturtium Capers

Makes ½ cup

A real caper is the flower bud of a caper plant, *Capparis spinosa,* and its large seedpod is called a caper berry. The seedpods of nasturtiums look just like the caper plant's buds, and when pickled they taste remarkably similar. Nasturtiums usually don't start forming seedpods until late in the summer and you have to search for them. You'll find them attached to the stems underneath the foliage, where they develop in clusters of three. Pick only young pods that are still green and soft. When they mature, they turn yellowish and the seed inside the pod is very hard and unpalatable.

2 tablespoons salt
1 cup water
½ cup green nasturtium seedpods
¾ cup white wine vinegar
2 teaspoons sugar
2 fresh bay laurel leaves, or 1 dried
2 3-inch sprigs fresh thyme

1. Brining. Bring the salt and water to a boil in a small saucepan. Put the nasturtium seedpods in a half-pint glass jar and pour the boiling brine over them. Cover and let them soak at room temperature for 3 days.

2. Pickling. Drain the nasturtium seedpods in a fine sieve and return them to the jar. Bring the vinegar, sugar, bay leaves, and thyme to a boil in a small (1-quart) saucepan. Pour the boiling vinegar mixture over the seedpods and let cool. Cover the jar and refrigerate for 3 days before using. They'll keep for 6 months in the refrigerator if covered in the vinegar.

Tarragon Vinegar

Makes 3 cups

Making flavored vinegar is an easy and rewarding way to preserve a bumper crop of fresh herbs. I find tarragon vinegar to be the most useful and flavorful of all the herbal vinegars. It's wonderful in all sorts of salad dressings and sauces from a simple vinaigrette to béarnaise sauce. The key to flavorful herb vinegar is steeping it with a large quantity of herbs before it is bottled. The sprigs that you see inside the bottles are just a garnish.

> *4 cups (gently packed) fresh French tarragon sprigs (about 2 ounces)*
> *3 cups white wine vinegar or champagne vinegar*
> *3 4-inch sprigs fresh French tarragon*

Pack the 4 cups tarragon into a 1-quart canning jar and pour the vinegar over it. Cover and let sit in a cool place for 3 to 4 weeks. Put 3 fresh sprigs in a clean 1-quart bottle. Insert a funnel into the top of the bottle and set a tea strainer over the mouth of the funnel. Strain the vinegar into the bottle and cork it. It will keep its flavor at room temperature for 6 months.

CANDIED ROSE PETALS

What could be more elegant than candied rose petals to garnish a dessert, decorate a cake, or offer as an after-dinner nibble? They are sublimely light and crisp, with a delicate sweet floral flavor, a graceful curve, and a range of soft pastel colors. Because rose petals are large and easy to handle, they are the easiest flowers to candy. It still takes a little patience, but the result is so fine that it's worth the effort.

For success the roses must be very fresh and just the right kind. First make certain that they are grown without any chemical pesticides and never use roses from a florist. There are thousands of varieties of roses. Some have thick heavy petals and some have flimsy tissuelike petals. Roses that are best suited for candying have petals somewhere in between—thick enough that they do not wither and collapse under the weight of the coating, but not so thick that they have a bitter flavor and are slow to dry. The more highly perfumed the flower is on the bush, the tastier it will be when candied. The first time you candy rose petals, try as many varieties as you can and see which you like best. The varieties that I use from my own garden are the Bourbon rose Madame Isaac Perrier (considered to be one of the world's most fragrant), the English roses Othello and Graham Stuart Thomas, and the Gallica rose Rosa Mundi (a striped rose in cultivation since the sixteenth century). Pick the blossoms early in the morning or in the evening, and choose ones that are beyond the bud stage but just beginning to open. To remove the petals without tearing them, cup the blossom firmly in your hand and twist and tug out the calyx and base of the blossom. It will pop out with the stamens and pistil attached, and all the petals will fall free.

2 large egg whites
4 teaspoons cold water
1 cup superfine sugar
Very fresh rose petals (pesticide free)

1. Setting up. Lightly whisk the egg whites with the water in a small bowl. Pass the egg whites through a very fine tea strainer or sieve into another small bowl or cup. Assemble your tools: a pair of tweezers, a soft, good-quality watercolor brush, a flat white plate, a baking sheet lined with parchment paper, a small shallow bowl filled with the superfine sugar, and a flatware teaspoon. It's best to candy flowers on a dry day in a cool room.

2. Candying the petals. Using the tweezers, pick up a petal at the base and rest it on top of the plate. While still holding it with the tweezers, brush the top of the petal with a thin but even coat of egg white. Turn it over and coat the other side. Still using the tweezers, rest the petal in the bowl of sugar and spoon some of the sugar over the top to lightly bury it. Lift it from the sugar and tap the tweezers with the teaspoon to knock extra sugar off the petal. Place it on the parchment paper. Continue to candy the rose petals, laying them on the baking sheet in a single layer with plenty of room between them. If the first tray becomes full, start a new tray. A few minutes after you candy a petal, nudge and shift its position slightly on the parchment to make sure it is not sticking. Let the petals dry for 1 to 2 hours, then turn them over with your fingers and transfer them to a fresh sheet of parchment paper so that the other side can dry. Allow a total of 4 to 8 hours for them to dry completely. Store the petals in an airtight container at room temperature. They will last for up to 3 months.

VARIATIONS
OTHER CANDIED FLOWERS
Some other edible flowers that are suitable for candying include pansies and violas, violets, gem marigolds, borage, lilacs, and clove pink petals. For all, proceed as directed for the rose petals.

CANDIED LEMON VERBENA LEAVES
Lemon verbena leaves also candy beautifully and taste like feathery light, crunchy lemon drops. Handle them exactly as directed for the rose petals. They're gorgeous used as a garnish for desserts or to accent candied rose petals as a cake decoration.

CANDIED ANGELICA

Makes about 2 pounds

These slightly chewy green sticks have a complex aromatic flavor, hinting at juniper and vanilla and with an herbaceous edge. Most often I serve them as a unique treat at the end of a meal, but sometimes I chop them and add them to ice cream or a delicate mousse, or slice them into little matchsticks to garnish a fruit dessert.

Choose stems that are bright green, smooth, and of medium thickness. Don't use stems that are old, yellowed, and tough or stems from the flower stalk. The stems that develop at the end of the first season or the spring of the second season will be just right. To harvest, use scissors to cut the entire stem off at ground level, then cut off the leaves. The remaining stalk will look like a three-pronged fork. Cut off the "tines" and snip them and the long hollow stem into 4- to 5-inch pieces. If you have more or less than a pound of angelica, just adjust the amount of sugar, using 2 tablespoons sugar for each ounce of the herb.

1 pound angelica stems, cut into 4- to 5-inch pieces (about 50)
3 ½ cups sugar

1. Saturating the angelica. Bring a large pot of boiling water to a boil. Add the angelica stems and boil them for exactly 8 minutes. Lift them out of the water with a skimmer into a colander to drain. Spread ½ cup of the sugar in a shallow 1 ½-quart baking dish. Arrange the angelica on top in a single layer. Sprinkle with 1 ½ cups of the remaining sugar. Cover with plastic wrap and let sit at room temperature for 24 hours.

2. Syrup. The next day the angelica should be submerged in syrup. Transfer the stems with their liquid and any undissolved sugar to a medium (3-quart) heavy-bottomed saucepan. Bring the syrup to a full boil and continue to boil until it reaches the soft-ball stage, 235° to 240°F on a candy thermometer. Or test by dropping ½ teaspoon of the syrup into a cup of cold water. You should be able to roll the syrup around in your fingers to form a soft ball. Remove the pan from the heat.

3. Final candying. Pour the remaining 1 ½ cups sugar onto a large plate. Line a couple of baking sheets with parchment paper. Lift 1 piece of angelica with tongs, letting it drain briefly over the pot, then set it in the sugar. Turn it to coat both sides evenly and lay it on the parchment. Repeat with the remaining angelica 1 piece at a time. Let them dry in a warm spot overnight, then turn them over and allow them to dry on the other side. The candy may take several days to become completely dry. If you wish, you can speed up the process by placing them in a 150°F oven for several hours. Store the stems in a tightly sealed jar or a resealable freezer bag at room temperature. They will keep for 6 months.

VARIATION
Lovage stems can be candied in exactly the same way. The celerylike flavor is quite unusual and not to everybody's taste, but it's worth trying.

LAVENDER-INFUSED HONEY

Makes 2 cups

In Provence wonderfully fragrant lavender honey is made by bees whose hives are placed in lavender fields, but this is a way to cheat and flavor other types of honey with the delicious fragrance of lavender blossoms. Use the honey in tea, on fruit salads, or as a sweetener for any dessert with dried fruits or nuts.

> **2 cups raw honey, such as clover, blackberry, or orange blossom**
> **24 flowering lavender sprigs, or 1 tablespoon dried lavender buds**

Pour the honey into a small (1-quart) saucepan and stir it over low heat until it is very warm, about 150°F. Stir in the lavender, cover the pan, and remove it from heat. Let the lavender infuse the honey at room temperature for 24 hours. Warm the honey again until it is thin enough to pour freely. Strain the honey into a clean jar, cover, and store at room temperature for up to 6 months.

HERB SUBSTITUTIONS

- *In place of the lavender, steep the honey with one of the following:*
  6 4-inch sprigs anise hyssop, 1 tablespoon green fennel seeds, 2 3-inch sprigs hyssop, 6 4-inch sprigs mint, 3 3-inch sprigs sage, 12 medium-size scented geranium leaves, or 12 3-inch sprigs English, lemon, or orange balsam thyme.

CHAPTER 12

Beverages

Steeping fresh herbs in water, syrup, wine, or other liquids is an effective way to capture their vibrant essence. This makes it easy to add their flavor to all sorts of beverages, from a steaming pot of fresh lemon verbena tisane to elegant Champagne cocktails to a sparkling cooler with lavender and mint. Here are a few recipes for inspiration.

Herbfarm Champagne Cocktails

These cocktails are served at the beginning of all Herbfarm dinners. We arrange fresh herb leaves or sprigs on a tray and ask each guest to choose one. It's crushed into their glass and then filled with Champagne. The herb gives off more of a subtle perfume than a flavor, and unlike cocktails with sugar cubes or syrup, it doesn't mask the wine's qualities.

Platter of beautifully arranged small herb leaves and sprigs, such as mint, lemon verbena, pineapple sage, fresh bay laurel, flowering lavender, scented geranium, lemon balm, and/or anise hyssop
Good bottle(s) of chilled Champagne or sparkling wine

Allow your guests to choose an herb leaf or sprig. Crush it between your fingers, drop it in an empty champagne flute, and slowly fill it with Champagne or sparkling wine.

May Wine

8 servings

This German beverage is so named because it is made with sweet woodruff when it blooms in May. Sprigs of this shade-loving ground cover with its dainty pure-white flowers are steeped in Riesling wine, infusing it with a grassy vanilla and honey flavor. The chilled wine poured into wineglasses and garnished simply makes a wonderful aperitif. If you serve it in a festive punch bowl, float some wild strawberries on top, and surround it with spring flowers, you have a May bowl.

1 bottle (750 ml) medium-sweet Riesling wine (not dry Riesling and not late-harvest)
24 2-inch flowering sweet woodruff sprigs
Garnish: 8 tiny flowering sweet woodruff sprigs and 8 small ripe cultivated or wild strawberries, with stems if possible

Pour about ¼ cup wine out of the bottle to make room for the herbs. Stuff the herbs into the bottle, cork it, and shake it gently. Let it steep in the refrigerator for 24 hours. Strain the wine into a carafe. Pour the chilled wine into glasses and garnish each one with a tiny sprig of sweet woodruff and a strawberry.

Rosemary Lemonade

Makes about 1 ½ quarts

We serve this refreshing drink at summer festivals at The Herbfarm. I make the rosemary syrup in huge stockpots and mix it up with lemon juice and water in giant 5-gallon bottles. The piney astringency of rosemary accents the lemon flavor and makes this lemonade especially thirst quenching. Here's how to make a small batch.

½ cup sugar
6 cups water
6 4-inch sprigs fresh rosemary
½ to ¾ cup freshly squeezed lemon juice

1. Syrup. Bring the sugar and 2 cups of the water to a boil in a small (1-quart) saucepan. Add the rosemary sprigs, cover, and remove from the heat. Let the syrup steep for at least 30 minutes.

2. Finishing. Strain the syrup into a pitcher. Stir in ½ cup lemon juice and the remaining 4 cups water. Taste and add more lemon juice to taste. Refrigerate until thoroughly chilled.

HERB SUBSTITUTIONS
- *In place of the rosemary, use 2 tablespoons fresh lavender buds, 8 scented geranium leaves, ½ cup fresh mint sprigs, or ½ cup fresh basil leaves.*

The Herbfarm's Switchel

Makes 1½ quarts

In its first years, The Herbfarm Restaurant served this beverage as a luncheon accompaniment. It's very loosely based on a Shaker recipe for hay-maker's switchel, a ginger drink made to quench thirsts in the hay fields. It's refreshing any time of day and terrific to have on hand in hot weather. When it's time to cut back your mint and lemon balm plants, make a large batch of the syrup base, store it in small batches in the freezer, and add the sparkling water whenever you want to mix up a pitcher.

> *¼ cup sugar*
> *¼ cup honey*
> *2 cups water*
> *½ cup coarsely grated fresh ginger (no need to peel)*
> *1 4-inch sprig fresh rosemary*
> *2 cups (gently packed) fresh lemon balm sprigs*
> *1 cup (gently packed) fresh spearmint sprigs*
> *¼ cup freshly squeezed lemon juice*
> *½ cup frozen orange juice concentrate*
> *1 quart sparkling mineral water or club soda, chilled*
> *Garnish: small lemon balm or mint sprigs*

1. Syrup. Bring the sugar, honey, 2 cups water, the ginger, and rosemary to a boil in a medium (2-quart) saucepan. Add the lemon balm and mint sprigs, cover, and remove from the heat. Let the mixture steep for 30 minutes.

2. Finishing. Strain the syrup into a pitcher and stir in the lemon juice and orange juice concentrate. Refrigerate until thoroughly chilled. Right before serving, stir in the sparkling water or club soda. Garnish each glass with a sprig of lemon balm or mint.

SPARKLING HERB SODAS

The same herb-infused syrups used to make exciting sorbets (pages 294–301) can also be used to prepare refreshing herbal sparkling beverages. Keep several herb-infused syrups on hand and you can offer guests a choice of flavors any time.

FOR EACH 12-OUNCE GLASS

Ice cubes
2 tablespoons Herb-Infused Simple Syrup (page 249)
1 tablespoon freshly squeezed lemon juice
Sparkling mineral water or club soda
Garnish: 1 fresh herb leaf or sprig

Fill the glass two-thirds full with ice cubes. Pour in the syrup and lemon juice and half fill the glass with sparkling water. Stir well, then fill to the top with more sparkling water and stir again. Garnish with the herb leaf or sprig.

THREE-FRESH-HERB TISANE

4 servings

Tea is made by steeping the leaves of the shrub *Camilia sinensis*, but beverages made from steeping parts of any other herbs are technically called tisanes, or infusions, though we usually refer to them as herb teas. Dried herbs are most often used for tisanes, but many fresh herbs and combinations of fresh herbs can also be used to wonderful effect. Here is a favorite that's especially beautiful when brewed in a glass teapot.

3 4-inch sprigs fresh lemon verbena
5 4-inch sprigs fresh spearmint
1 2-inch sprig fresh rosemary
3 cups boiling water

Put the herbs in a warmed teapot (glass if possible) and pour in the boiling water. Cover and let steep for 5 to 10 minutes. Pour through a strainer into teacups.

 HERB SUBSTITUTIONS

- *Lemon verbena and spearmint make wonderful tisanes when brewed alone. Other good choices for fresh herb tisanes are anise hyssop, fresh fennel seeds, lemon balm, lemon thyme, peppermint or other mints, lavender, scented geranium, and sweet cicely root.*

CHAPTER 13

Sauces and Other Basic Recipes

With a small repertoire of basic herb sauces you can flatter almost any food. A sautéed salmon fillet becomes an elegant course when it sits on a pool of blended chervil butter sauce. Broiled skewers of shrimp turn into a Mediterranean feast when there's piquant salsa verde to dip them in. Tender filet mignon is twice as luxurious when it's served with béarnaise sauce, and tender chicken breast with a few varied greens becomes a brilliant composed salad when napped with green goddess dressing. Many sauces can be found throughout this book, but this chapter has more, both old classics and new inventions, for further inspiration. They are invaluable to any herb-gardening cook.

Blended Herb and Butter Sauce

Makes ½ to ¾ cup

This sauce vividly captures the bright flavor and color of many different leafy herbs, so that by learning the basic recipe, you can prepare at least a dozen different herb sauces. All are particularly delicious served with simply prepared fish and shellfish, but I also serve them as sauce for savory soufflés and on steamed vegetables. You begin by making a light beurre blanc, a classic French sauce made by whisking butter into white wine that's been boiled with shallots and vinegar or lemon juice. You then fill a blender with the fresh green herb(s) of your choice, pour the hot sauce in, and purée until smooth and brightly colored. The beurre blanc base can be made up to an hour ahead of time and kept warm, but you must do the final blending at the last minute.

4 tablespoons unsalted butter
1 small shallot, finely chopped (3 tablespoons)
¾ cup dry white wine
1 tablespoon freshly squeezed lemon juice
¼ teaspoon salt

ONE OF THE FOLLOWING, GENTLY PACKED, OR A COMBINATION
½ cup fresh chervil leaves
½ cup coarsely chopped fresh chives
½ cup fresh cilantro leaves
½ cup fresh fennel leaves
½ cup fresh flat-leaf parsley leaves
½ cup fresh spearmint leaves
½ cup fresh dill leaves
¼ cup fresh young lovage leaves
¼ cup French or Mexican tarragon leaves
¾ cup fresh basil leaves
¾ cup arugula leaves
¾ cup coarsely chopped young mustard greens
¾ cup coarsely chopped sorrel leaves
¾ cup watercress or peppercress leaves

1. Beurre blanc. Melt 2 teaspoons of the butter in a small (1-quart) saucepan over medium-low heat. Add the shallot and cook, stirring constantly, until it is softened but not browned, about 1 minute. Add the wine, lemon juice, and salt, increase the heat to medium-high, and boil until the mixture is reduced to ⅓ cup. Until you've made this recipe many times and can judge the correct consistency at a glance, measure the reduced wine mixture in a measuring cup, then return it to the pan. Reduce the heat to low and rapidly whisk in the remaining butter, 1 tablespoon at a time, allowing each addition to melt before the next is added. The sauce should be the consistency of light cream and emulsified, meaning the butter does not separate and rise to the surface. You can hold the sauce at this stage for up to 1 hour if you pour it in the top of a double boiler or another pan that is set in a larger pan of barely simmering water. Keep the sauce uncovered. Don't worry if it separates slightly—it will come together again when it is blended.

2. Herbs. Put the herbs in the container of an electric blender. Fill the blender container half full of hot tap water, then pour it out, holding the herbs back with your hand. This warms the container and the herbs so they don't cool the sauce when it's poured in. Bring the sauce to a simmer and immediately pour it over the herbs. Cover the blender container and blend on high speed until the sauce is very smooth and bright green, about 30 seconds. It should be thin enough to spread into a pool when spooned on a plate but not runny. If it is too thick, blend in hot tap water, 1 tablespoon at a time. Taste and add additional salt if needed.

BÉARNAISE SAUCE

Makes 1½ cups, 8 servings

Velvety, tangy, and imbued with the elegant and focused flavor of tarragon, this sauce is as rich as they come. A cousin to hollandaise, it involves making a flavored reduction of vinegar and wine, then whipping that with egg yolks over heat to make a very thick sabayon. Finally, loads of melted butter and fresh tarragon are whisked in. The sauce is traditionally served with beef tenderloin, but it's also delicious on poached salmon and steamed vegetables. After you make this sauce once or twice, you'll be able to confidently prepare it in a few minutes.

> 8 4-inch sprigs fresh French tarragon
> ¼ cup tarragon white wine vinegar (page 311), white wine vinegar, or champagne vinegar, plus an additional 1 to 2 tablespoons if needed
> ¼ cup dry vermouth or dry white wine
> ½ small shallot, finely chopped (about 1½ tablespoons)
> ½ teaspoon salt
> ½ teaspoon crushed or coarsely ground black peppercorns
> 8 ounces (2 sticks) unsalted butter, melted and lukewarm
> 4 large egg yolks

1. Tarragon. Remove the tarragon leaves from the stems and put the stems in a small (1-quart) saucepan. Finely chop the leaves—you should have 4 to 6 tablespoons—and set them aside.

2. Reduction. Add ¼ cup vinegar, the vermouth, shallot, salt, and peppercorns to the tarragon stems and bring it to a simmer. Reduce the heat and simmer slowly until the liquid is reduced by half, about 5 minutes. Strain this reduction into a measuring cup. Add cold water if needed to measure ¼ cup.

3. Sabayon. Create a double boiler by selecting a medium (8-inch) stainless-steel mixing bowl that will rest on top of a medium (3-quart) saucepan filled with about 2 inches water. The top of the bowl can extend beyond the rim of the pot, but the bottom of the bowl must not touch the water. Put the pot (without the bowl) over medium heat and bring the water to a boil. Pour the lukewarm melted butter into a liquid measuring cup or pitcher and set it next to a damp kitchen towel, spread out on the counter, that you will use to anchor the mixing bowl when you whisk the butter into the sauce. Drop the egg yolks into the mixing bowl and whisk vigorously until they are very smooth. Whisk in the vinegar reduction and beat until very frothy and about tripled in volume, about 1 minute. Now place the bowl over the boiling water and whisk vigorously and constantly until the mixture becomes very frothy, then thickens to the consistency of thick mayonnaise as it falls slightly. This will happen very quickly, in 1 to 1½ minutes. Do not stop whisking during the entire cooking time. Remove the bowl from the heat and set it on the damp towel. Continue to whisk for about 15 seconds to smooth out any lumps.

4. Adding the butter. Pour in about ¼ cup of the butter and whisk until incorporated. Continue to pour in the butter in a moderate stream as you whisk. You don't have to dribble the butter in but don't pour it faster than it can be incorporated at a steady rate. When all the butter is added, the sauce should be thick and light enough to mound on a spoon, yet fluid enough to pour from it. Whisk in the chopped tarragon leaves. Taste and season with additional salt if needed; if you prefer the sauce tangier, whisk in additional vinegar to taste. Covered loosely with plastic wrap, the sauce will hold in a warm spot, like in an oven with a pilot light or set over a saucepan of hot but not simmering water, for up to 1 hour. Whisk it again before serving. Do not let this sauce cool and then try to reheat it, for it will separate.

Cilantro and Pumpkin Seed Pesto

Makes 1 cup

Cilantro pesto is a new invention—a fusion of Mexican and Italian sauces—that's delicious on grilled or broiled fish, beef, pork, or vegetables. Like true nuts, pumpkin seeds have a rich oil content and give the sauce a warm, deep, and slightly bitter flavor. Be sure to buy dark green hulled seeds, not the beige seeds that look as if they came from a jack-o'-lantern.

¼ cup hulled pumpkin seeds
2 cups (gently packed) fresh cilantro leaves and tender sprigs
2 cloves garlic, peeled
1 tablespoon freshly squeezed lemon juice
1 teaspoon seeded and coarsely chopped jalapeño pepper
½ teaspoon salt
½ cup extra-virgin olive oil

1. Toast the pumpkin seeds. Pour the pumpkin seeds into a small dry skillet and place it over medium heat. When you hear a seed pop, shake the pan continuously until most of the seeds are puffed instead of flat. Pour the seeds onto a paper towel to cool.

2. Pesto. Process the cooled pumpkin seeds with the remaining ingredients except the oil in a food processor until the mixture is finely ground. Stop the machine and scrape down the sides. With the machine running, pour in the oil in a steady stream and continue to process until the mixture is slightly creamy and fairly smooth. Taste and season with additional salt or jalapeño if needed.

Oregano and Roasted Garlic Pesto

Makes scant 1 cup

There's no basil in this pesto. Greek oregano and aromatic marjoram deliver spiciness and fragrance, while roasted garlic and walnuts offer nuttiness and sweetness. Use it as you would traditional pesto—tossed with pasta, spooned on a baked potato, spread on pizza, or to sauce grilled fish. It's also fabulous as a dip for steamed artichokes.

2 tablespoons (gently packed) fresh Greek oregano leaves
¼ cup (gently packed) fresh marjoram or Italian oregano leaves
1 cup (gently packed) fresh flat-leaf parsley leaves and tender sprigs
1 ½ tablespoons Roasted Garlic Paste (page 341)
¼ cup walnut pieces, untoasted
1 teaspoon balsamic vinegar
½ teaspoon salt
6 tablespoons extra-virgin olive oil

Put all the ingredients except the oil in a food processor and pulse until the mixture is finely ground. With the machine running, pour in the olive oil in a steady stream. Stop and scrape down the sides, then continue to process until the sauce is smooth and slightly creamy. Taste and add additional salt if needed. Store tightly covered in the refrigerator for up to 1 week.

Salsa Verde (Green Herb and Caper Sauce)

Makes 1 cup

Like pesto, this is a pounded Italian herb sauce. It has a piquant, salty flavor and is traditionally served with red meats, but I find it's also delicious with broiled seafood and chicken.

1½ cups (gently packed) fresh flat-leaf parsley leaves and tender sprigs
½ cup (gently packed) fresh spearmint leaves
½ cup coarsely snipped fresh chives or green parts of green onions
1 clove garlic, peeled
2 teaspoons Dijon mustard
4 anchovy fillets
2 tablespoons capers, drained
Thinly sliced zest of ½ lemon (removed with a zester)
1 tablespoon freshly squeezed lemon juice
¼ teaspoon freshly ground black pepper
6 tablespoons olive oil

Process all the ingredients except the oil in a food processor until they are finely chopped. Scrape down the sides. With the machine running, pour in the oil in a steady stream and continue to process until the sauce is slightly creamy but not completely smooth.

RED PEPPER AND HAZELNUT SAUCE

Makes 1½ cups

This is a version of romesco sauce, a Spanish pounded sauce made with romesco peppers, almonds, garlic, olive oil, and sometimes tomato. It's tangy and very full flavored. You'll find it a fabulous sauce for all sorts of foods, particularly those from the grill—lamb, chicken, eggplant, shrimp, and fresh tuna—or as a spread for sandwiches in place of mustard or mayonnaise. It also accompanies Pork Tenderloin Crusted with Mediterranean Herbs (page 222).

> *2 large red bell peppers, roasted, peeled, and seeded (see Note), or*
> *1½ cups drained bottled roasted red peppers*
> *¼ cup hazelnuts, roasted and skinned*
> *2 cloves garlic, peeled*
> *2 tablespoons sherry vinegar*
> *1 tablespoon coarsely chopped fresh rosemary*
> *1 tablespoon fresh marjoram or Italian oregano leaves*
> *1 teaspoon sugar*
> *1 teaspoon salt*
> *Scant ⅛ teaspoon cayenne pepper*
> *½ cup extra-virgin olive oil*

Process all the ingredients except the oil in a food processor or blender until the hazelnuts are finely ground. Stop the machine and scrape down the sides. With the machine running, pour in the olive oil in a steady stream. The sauce should have the consistency of thick salad dressing. Taste and add more salt or cayenne if desired. The sauce can be stored covered in the refrigerator for up to 1 week. Bring it to room temperature before serving or warm the sauce gently by stirring it in a stainless-steel bowl set over simmering water. Don't overheat the sauce or the oil will separate.

NOTE

To roast peppers, rub the peppers lightly with extra-virgin olive oil and poke them in several places with the tip of a knife. Bake on a baking sheet in a preheated 400°F oven until they start to brown, about 20 minutes. Using tongs, turn the peppers over and roast until the skin has blistered over much of the surface, about 5 minutes more. Place the peppers in a bowl, cover tightly with plastic wrap, and cool. Peel the peppers under cool running water. Split them open and rinse out the seeds. Discard the stems.

HERBFARM VINAIGRETTE

Makes generous 1 cup

When you compose a gorgeous salad brimming with the freshest greens, herbs, and flowers, the best choice of dressing is a simple vinaigrette with a fairly neutral flavor that gently blends with the flavors of the salad ingredients instead of overriding them. The key is to use good-quality vinegar and olive oil. I use two kinds of vinegar: a good red wine vinegar or aged sherry vinegar for crispness, and a smaller amount of balsamic for its full body and touch of sweetness. You don't need to use a precious old *balsamico tradizionale*, but it's best to stay away from the very low priced brands. This recipe has a slightly higher than average proportion of vinegar to oil to help balance assertively flavored greens. When it comes to choosing the right oil, try to find a first-rate extra-virgin olive oil with a mild flavor, not a brand that's powerfully fruity. You don't want the oil to jump out as the predominant flavor. The exception is when many of your greens are very bitter or hot, like mustard, radicchio, peppercress, or endive, in which case a very fruity oil will balance and tone down their aggressiveness.

If you're using this vinaigrette on a salad of many varied and distinctively flavored greens and herbs, like The Herbfarm Garden Salad (page 45), I suggest you not add more herbs to the dressing. However, if you are making the vinaigrette for a simpler salad of lettuces and other greens or vegetables, try blending in one of the herbs listed in the variations that follow. The vinaigrette also presents an excellent opportunity to use an herb-infused vinegar.

> *¼ cup red wine vinegar or aged sherry vinegar*
> *2 tablespoons balsamic vinegar*
> *1 tablespoon coarsely chopped shallot*
> *2 teaspoons Dijon mustard*
> *½ teaspoon salt*
> *Freshly ground black pepper to taste*
> *¾ cup mild extra-virgin olive oil*

Purée all the ingredients except the oil in a blender or food processor or with a hand-held immersion blender. With the machine running, pour in the olive oil in a steady stream. If you are not going to use the dressing within a few hours, store it tightly covered in the refrigerator; it will keep for several weeks. Bring it to room temperature and shake or whisk it well before you dress the salad.

VARIATIONS
Use an herb-infused vinegar (page 311) in place of the red wine vinegar.

Substitute ¼ cup walnut oil for the same amount of olive oil.

HERB SUBSTITUTIONS
- *Blend any of the following into the dressing: 1 to 2 tablespoons coarsely chopped English or lemon thyme, lovage, mint, oregano, marjoram, or French tarragon; 2 to 4 tablespoons coarsely chopped basil, dill, chervil, or chives; or 2 teaspoons fresh fennel seeds.*

GREEN GODDESS DRESSING

Makes 2 cups

This dressing was invented at the Palace Hotel in San Francisco at the turn of the nineteenth century. The original is a mayonnaise-based dressing, but mine is a lighter version with sour cream or yogurt. Loads of herbs make it fresh and vibrant tasting, and a bit of anchovy lends depth, but the dressing is wonderfully balanced and not overpowering. In addition to the dressing for Green Goddess Grilled Chicken Salad (page 66), it makes a fabulous dip for a platter of crudités.

> ¾ cup (gently packed) fresh French tarragon leaves
> ¾ cup snipped fresh chives
> ¾ cup (gently packed) fresh flat-leaf parsley leaves
> 6 anchovy fillets
> ¼ cup freshly squeezed lemon juice
> ½ teaspoon salt
> 6 tablespoons extra-virgin olive oil
> ¾ cup full or low-fat sour cream or plain whole-milk or low-fat yogurt
> Freshly ground black pepper to taste

Purée the herbs, anchovies, lemon juice, and salt in a food processor or blender. With the machine running, add the oil in a slow stream. Scrape down the sides. Add the sour cream and pepper; process until smooth. Store tightly covered in the refrigerator for up to 3 days.

Herbed Aïoli

Makes 1 ¼ cups

Aïoli is garlic mayonnaise from Provence, which is used as an enrichment for fish soups or as a sauce. This gutsy herbed version is particularly delicious with fish, shellfish, cold chicken, and raw vegetables, or to spread on a sandwich with roasted peppers, chicken, and arugula. This sauce contains raw egg yolks, so don't prepare it if you are not comfortable eating raw eggs, and don't store it for more than 2 days.

2 cloves garlic, peeled
½ teaspoon salt
2 large egg yolks
1 to 2 tablespoons freshly squeezed lemon juice
Dash Tabasco sauce
1 cup extra-virgin olive oil
2 tablespoons finely chopped fresh parsley
1 tablespoon finely chopped fresh marjoram or oregano
1 teaspoon finely chopped fresh rosemary

Finely chop the garlic and sprinkle with the salt. Work the garlic and salt into a paste by alternately pressing it with the side of the knife and mincing it. Scrape up the garlic paste and put it in a medium mixing bowl. Anchor the mixing bowl on the counter by setting it on top of a damp towel. Whisk the egg yolks, 1 tablespoon lemon juice, and the Tabasco into the garlic. Pour the olive oil into a liquid measuring cup or pitcher. While whisking constantly, begin to add the oil in a very slow trickle. After about ¼ cup is added and the sauce begins to thicken, continue to whisk in the rest of the oil at a faster rate but not so fast that it pools up before it has a chance to be incorporated. The sauce should be thinner than commercial mayonnaise but able to form soft mounds when dropped from a spoon. Whisk in the herbs. Taste and season with additional salt, lemon juice, and/or Tabasco. Store tightly covered in the refrigerator for no longer than 2 days.

FRESH MINT CHUTNEY

Makes 1 cup

Though also used as a condiment, this fresh chutney is very different from the thick jammy chutney that comes in a jar. It has the consistency of a light-bodied pesto and a fiery, tangy flavor bursting with fresh mint. For an appetizer or snack, serve this refreshing chutney with pappadam (thin, crisp lentil wafers that you can buy in Indian groceries to fry at home) as you would corn chips and salsa, or serve it on grilled steak, lamb, or fish.

> *2 cups fresh spearmint leaves*
> *2 green onions, coarsely chopped*
> *2 tablespoons coarsely chopped fresh ginger*
> *3 tablespoons freshly squeezed lime juice*
> *1 ½ teaspoons sugar*
> *½ teaspoon salt*
> *1 to 3 teaspoons seeded and coarsely chopped jalapeño pepper to taste*
> *3 to 4 tablespoons cold water*

Process all the ingredients except the water in a food processor until finely chopped. Add 3 tablespoons water and purée until smooth, adding additional water as needed for a thick sauce consistency. Taste and add additional salt, jalapeño and/or sugar if needed. The chutney has the brightest flavor if it is served when freshly made.

CHIVE OIL

Makes ½ cup

This exquisite oil has an intensely deep emerald green color and a fresh sharp chive flavor. It's used in the Grilled Fish with Herb Salad (page 176) and is good drizzled on all kinds of simply prepared seafood, particularly on shellfish salads or smoked salmon.

1 cup coarsely snipped fresh chives
¾ cup extra-virgin olive oil

1. Blending. Put the chives and oil in a blender and purée until the oil begins to warm, 2 to 3 minutes.

2. Straining. Pour the oil into a very fine strainer, or a coarse strainer lined with a double layer of cheesecloth, set over a bowl. The oil that drips out can be used immediately, but let it continue to drip for about 1 hour to extract as much as possible. Let the oil drip undisturbed at its own pace for the clearest oil. Discard the contents of the strainer and store the oil in a covered container in the refrigerator. It will keep for up to 1 month.

Basil Oil

Makes 1 cup

Like the chive oil on page 337, this is a vividly colored green oil but with a concentrated basil flavor. Drizzle it on fish and shellfish, fresh tomatoes, or steamed vegetables, blend it into salad dressings, or dip crusty bread into it in place of butter.

8 cups water
2 teaspoons salt
3 cups (gently packed) fresh basil leaves (about 3 ounces)
1 ½ cups extra-virgin olive oil

1. Blanching the basil. Fill a medium pot with the water, add the salt, and bring it to a boil. Add the basil leaves and boil for 15 seconds. Immediately drain the leaves and transfer them to a large bowl of cold water. Drain again and use your hands to squeeze out as much moisture as you can.

2. Blending. Purée the blanched leaves with the oil in a blender on high speed until the mixture is very green and smooth and begins to warm, 2 to 3 minutes.

3. Straining. Pour the oil into a very fine strainer, or a coarse strainer lined with a double layer of cheesecloth, set over a bowl. The oil that drips out can be used immediately, but let it continue to drip for about 1 hour to extract as much as possible. Let the oil drip undisturbed at its own pace for the clearest oil. Discard the contents of the strainer and store the oil in a covered container in the refrigerator. It will keep for up to 1 month.

HERB BUTTER COINS

Makes 1 8-ounce log

Butter, like oil, has great capacity to capture and absorb the essential oils of herbs and, therefore, preserve the herbs' fresh flavors for long periods of time. These coins of herb butter can be served at the table to spread on bread, or they can be melted on top of hot cooked fish or bowls of vegetables. They're also handy for whisking into sauces, both enriching them and adding herbal flavor.

8 ounces (2 sticks) unsalted butter, at room temperature
¼ to ½ cup finely chopped fresh herbs, such as parsley, tarragon, chervil,
chives, basil, mint, lovage, dill, fennel, oregano, marjoram, or thyme
Optional: ½ teaspoon salt and 2 teaspoons freshly squeezed lemon juice

1. Butter. Beat the butter in a medium mixing bowl with a wooden spoon or with an electric mixer until smooth. Add the herbs, and salt and lemon juice if using, and mix until evenly incorporated. Taste and adjust the seasonings if needed.

2. Forming the log. Lay a 12-inch square of plastic wrap on a work surface. Spoon the butter out in a band about 1 inch wide on the bottom third of the plastic. Tightly roll up the butter in the plastic to form a log. Grab hold of the excess plastic at both ends of the log and twist the ends in opposite directions, like a hard candy wrapper, until it is very taut and the butter forms an evenly round cylinder. Refrigerate until hard. To store the butter, wrap the plastic-covered log tightly in heavy-duty aluminum foil and refrigerate for up to 1 week or freeze for up to 3 months. To form coins, unwrap the cold butter log and slice it ¼ to ⅜ inch thick with a sharp thin knife.

VARIATIONS
For a more homogeneous butter, process the ingredients in a food processor until the butter turns green throughout and the specks of herb are barely visible.

NASTURTIUM BUTTER
Follow the directions for the herb butter (you can add green herbs or omit them if you wish). Coarsely tear 24 brightly colored nasturtium flowers and mix them into the butter so that they remain in large pieces. Shape the butter into a log as directed. When you slice the log, the flowers make a beautiful confetti pattern in the coins and add a mild peppery flavor. You can do the same thing with ¼ cup calendula petals.

SLOW-ROASTED TOMATOES

Makes 24 to 28 tomato halves

This recipe magically transforms the flavor of hard insipid winter tomatoes into something sweet, tangy, and concentrated. If you begin with ripe summer tomatoes, the flavor will soar off the scale. They are used in the Tomato and Basil Crostini (page 73) and the Fish Fillets en Papillote, Many Ways (page 158). Layered between slices of fresh mozzarella with arugula or basil leaves, they make a terrific salad, and coarsely chopped, they turn into a splendid quick pasta sauce.

> *2 pounds plum tomatoes (12 to 14)*
> *2 tablespoons olive oil*
> *¼ teaspoon salt*
> *2 teaspoons sugar*
> *2 teaspoons fresh English thyme leaves*

Preheat the oven to 250°F. Cut the tomatoes lengthwise in half and remove the seeds by poking them out with your fingertip. Toss the tomato halves with the oil, salt, sugar, and thyme in a bowl. Spread them out cut side up on a baking sheet. Bake the tomatoes until they are slightly browned on the edges, the skins have wrinkled, and they have the texture of a soft prune, 2 to 3 hours. The baking time varies greatly depending on the ripeness and juiciness of the tomatoes.

Roasted Garlic Paste

Makes about ½ cup

The flavor of roasted garlic is far removed from the hot bite of raw garlic. It's sweet, nutty, and mild enough to spread on bread. The nut-brown paste is an invaluable ingredient to have on hand to add to cream sauce, pesto, bean dip, mashed potatoes, and a thousand other dishes where the rich mellow taste will add wonderful savoriness.

6 heads garlic
1 tablespoon extra-virgin olive oil

Preheat the oven to 400°F. Cut the top quarter off of each garlic head exposing the tops of the cloves. Put the heads in the middle of a large sheet of heavy-duty aluminum foil and drizzle the oil over the cut surfaces. Loosely wrap the foil around the garlic to cover the heads but don't seal the foil tightly. Bake until the heads yield to pressure when squeezed and the cut surfaces at the top are nut brown, about 1 hour. Let cool until they can be handled, then squeeze out the garlic pulp from each head. Mash the garlic into a paste with a fork. Store tightly covered in the refrigerator for up to 1 week.

FLAKY PASTRY

Makes enough dough for 2 10-inch or 4 7-inch tart shells

Every serious home baker eventually develops her or his own signature pastry dough. My Hungarian grandmother, Kate Luckman, made her dough with butter and sour cream, and her lekvars and rugelach would shatter as you bit into them and then melt in your mouth. My friend Bette Stuart, who has been making flawless fruit pies for 50 years, now makes her thin delicate crusts with butter-flavored Crisco. This is my all-purpose pastry dough. It's an all-butter dough that bakes crisp, tender, and very flaky—good for both sweet and savory pastries.

Although this is a simple dough, there are several very important steps to success. First, measure the flour carefully, preferably with a scale. If you don't have a scale, remember to spoon the flour into the cup and then level; don't scoop up the flour because it will compact and you will end up with more by weight. I like to use brand-name bleached all-purpose flours for their consistency, and because their gluten content is slightly lower than that of unbleached flour, making the dough more tender. Second, pay close attention to the size of the pieces of butter when you process it with the flour. In my dough, I look for butter pieces that are the size of raw grains of barley or short-grain rice. If the pieces are as large as peas, I find the butter sweats out of the pastry when it bakes and makes it seem greasy. If the butter and flour is processed too much—to the point it looks like cornmeal—the pastry will not be flaky enough. Finally, be careful with the amount of water you add. Too much liquid will toughen the dough; add just enough to make the dough malleable but not enough to make it soft or sticky. To have the most control, I don't add the water in the food processor but rather transfer the mixture to a mixing bowl and stir it in with my hand.

> *2 cups bleached all-purpose flour (spoon and level; 9 ounces)*
> *8 ounces (2 sticks) unsalted butter, chilled and cut into ½-inch cubes*
> *½ teaspoon salt*
> *6 to 8 tablespoons ice water*

Place the flour, butter, and salt in a food processor fitted with the steel blade. Pulse about 24 times, then open the machine and lift a handful of the crumbs. The largest pieces of butter should be the size of raw grains of rice or barley. If there are larger pieces, continue to pulse the mixture. When the butter pieces are the correct size, transfer the mixture to a large mixing bowl. Sprinkle 6 tablespoons of ice water onto the dough. Spread the fingers of one hand as if you were about to grab a large ball, and using your rigid fingertips as if they were a large fork, stir the dough quickly and briefly until the liquid is incorporated. Squeeze a handful of the dough in your palm. The dough should have just enough moisture to stay together. Break the piece in half. If it seems dry and crumbly, cautiously add more water a few teaspoons at a time until you can squeeze it into a ball that will not crumble when broken apart. If your kitchen is reasonably cool, the butter was cold, and you used ice water, the dough should be at just the right stage of malleability for rolling out, and it will be easiest to work with immediately. If your kitchen is very warm, wrap the dough in plastic wrap and refrigerate it for about 15 minutes, then take out only as much of the dough as you will work with at once, and roll and form it as quickly as you can.

VARIATION

To make a double crust for a 9-inch pie, make the dough using 1½ cups bleached all-purpose flour (spoon and level; 6¾ ounces), 6 ounces unsalted butter (1½ sticks), ⅜ teaspoon salt, and 5 to 6 tablespoons ice water.

Free-Form Tart Shells

Makes 2 10-inch or 4 7-inch tart shells

I use these prebaked tart shells (also called galettes) for a wide variety of fillings, both sweet and savory. Because you bake them directly on baking sheets, you don't need a cupboard full of tart pans to make any size tart you want. You don't need to weight the tarts as they bake to prevent the sides from caving in, and they always turn out very crisp and delicate throughout because there is nothing to get in the way of the oven's heat flow.

You can prebake the shells up to 24 hours in advance. Store the shells in large resealable plastic bags or in a large, flat airtight container until ready to fill. If the tarts have a filling that does not require further baking, refresh the shells by putting them in a 350°F oven for 5 minutes, then allow them to cool again. This will ensure crispness. Always fill the tart shells as close to serving time as possible. No matter what you do to prevent it, it will take no more than a few hours for a moist filling to turn a crisp pastry soggy.

Flaky Pastry (recipe precedes)
Egg wash made with 1 egg yolk and 2 teaspoons water

1. Rolling the dough. Turn the pastry dough out on a lightly floured board and divide it into quarters for small 7-inch tart shells or in half for large 10-inch shells. Shape 1 piece into a disk and dust the top lightly with flour. Begin to roll out the dough, using quick but gentle strokes with the pin. Start with the pin in the middle of the round and roll to the top, then to the bottom. Rotate the dough ¼ turn each time you roll to be sure the dough is not sticking and use additional flour as necessary. When the round is larger than 9 inches for a small tart, or 12 inches for a large tart, and about ⅛ inch thick, turn a 9- or 12-inch plate or bowl upside down on the dough as a template and cut around it with a sharp knife. Remove the plate or bowl.

2. Forming the edge. Fold ½-inch edge of dough all around to form a decorative rim. Begin by folding a 1-inch-long section over by ½ inch, then overlap the fold by half and roll another piece of dough over, pinching it firmly in place. Continue to roll and pinch, and a twisted rope pattern will form. Roll out the remaining dough and crimp the edges in the same manner. Transfer the pastry shells to baking sheets lined with parchment paper and poke the interior of the shells all over with the tines of a fork. Refrigerate the pastry for at least 30 minutes or up to 24 hours. If you wish, you can freeze the shells on the baking sheets, and when they are frozen, stack them inside freezer bags. Bake the shells without defrosting first.

3. Prebaking. Preheat the oven to 375°F. Brush the rims of the tarts with egg wash. Bake the tart shells (1 baking sheet at a time) for 15 minutes, then reduce the heat to 350°F and continue to bake until they are an even golden brown, 8 to 12 minutes longer. Lift a shell with a spatula and check that the underside is evenly brown. If the tart shells puff up during baking, press down the center of the pastry with the back of a large spoon. Let cool on the baking sheet.

ALMOND SHORTBREAD CRUST

Makes 1 9-inch tart shell

This is a tender, crisp, and buttery tart shell that does not require rolling, making it especially quick and easy. The dough crumbs are turned out into the tart pan and firmly pressed with fingers to form an even crust.

¼ cup sugar
⅓ cup raw almonds, whole or sliced
¾ cup all-purpose flour (spoon and level; 3 ½ ounces)
¼ teaspoon salt
5 tablespoons unsalted butter, chilled, cut into ½-inch cubes
1 large egg yolk
2 teaspoons unsalted butter, softened, for the parchment paper

1. Dough. Process the sugar and almonds in a food processor until very finely ground. Add the flour and salt and process briefly until incorporated. Add the butter and pulse until the mixture is the consistency of coarse cornmeal. Add the egg yolk and pulse just until it is incorporated but the dough does not come together in a ball.

2. Forming the shell. Place a 9-inch tart pan with a removable bottom on a baking sheet. Transfer the dough crumbs to the tart pan and spread them out evenly. Begin to form the crust by pressing the crumbs firmly against the sides of the pan to create an even layer. Be sure the crust is as thick at the top of the side as it is at the bottom by pressing down on the top of the crust with your forefinger while you press it sideways with your other hand. When the sides are complete, even the remaining crumbs out over the bottom of the pan and press them down firmly. If the dough begins to stick to your fingers, refrigerate it for 5 to 10 minutes. When the dough is evenly and firmly pressed in the pan, refrigerate the shell for at least 1 hour.

3. Baking. Preheat the oven to 400°F. Butter a 12-inch square of parchment paper and press it butter side down into the shell, creasing it into the corners. Fill the shell with dried beans, raw rice, or pie weights. Bake until the top edge of the crust is lightly browned, 16 to 18 minutes. Reduce the oven heat to 350°F. Remove the tart shell from the oven and let it cool for 10 minutes. Scoop out most of the beans, then carefully lift out the paper with the remaining beans. If there are any holes, the crust will still be soft enough at this point to repair them by pressing them closed. Bake the shell until the bottom is lightly browned, 8 to 10 minutes longer.

CHAPTER 14

Herbs at the Kitchen Door: The Basics of Growing Your Own

Whether you have a few pots of herbs on a tiny balcony or an elaborate *potager* (kitchen garden), growing and cooking with fresh herbs brings incomparable vibrancy to the food you make. Herbs are easy to grow—they're undemanding and practically take care of themselves. If you love to cook and have any sort of sunny outdoor space—balcony, deck, yard, or acreage—there is no reason not to plant at least a few. When newly cut, herbs have vividly fresh flavors, full of both strength and subtlety and noticeably more intense than the fresh herbs in supermarkets. And then there's the satisfaction of knowing you raised that herb yourself.

From a gardener's perspective, herbs are worth growing just for the simple delights of what they are. They are beautiful plants: from sprawling gnarled thyme, to anise hyssop crowned with furry royal purple spikes, to towering angelica with strapping leaves and great umbels of chartreuse seeds. Both ornamental and useful, they're at home in the flower border, vegetable garden, and window box. And just as a perfumed rose has ten times the charm of a scentless blossom, herbs captivate because they add fragrance to the garden. Lemon verbena permeates the air with piercing lemon scent each time you brush by it. The silvered deep green needles of a rosemary shrub send out a clean and bracing piney fragrance that you can smell from yards away. Lavender charms not just with graceful flower spikes but also with its sweet, alluring perfume. Herbs are the great seducers of the garden.

From a cook's perspective, the herb garden is a source of endless culinary inspiration. When you rub and sniff your way down the paths, the fragrances whet your appetite and you soon have the itch to cook. Run your hand over the lush variegated mounds of lemon thyme edging a path, and the provocative scent they release might have you thinking of a marinade for fresh tuna. Pinch off a bit of the lacy yellow fennel blossom, chew it for a moment, and it will suggest just the right touch of anise flavor for sprinkling over broiled shrimp or a grilled peach. Rub the fuzzy rose-geranium leaf, and you'll remember last summer's crisp raspberry tart scented with its floral leaves.

The ultimate pleasure of having your own herb garden is its proximity to your kitchen. You have the luxury of being able to run out to pick herbs as the inspiration comes to you. If you need a few sprigs of thyme for the stock, a shower of basil for your pasta, or a tablespoon of rosemary for the foccacia, it's right outside the door. And when you shop for recipe ingredients, you won't have to search all over town for the tablespoon of fresh oregano that's called for and end up paying a fortune for a bunch of tired sprigs.

The flavor in a freshly picked herb comes from the concentration of essential oils. Some of the oils are contained in the leaf itself, but much of them are held in little sacs (glands) on the surfaces of the leaves and stems. These oils are volatile, meaning they evaporate into the air. As soon as you pick herbs, their fragrant oils begin to dissipate, so the longer they sit after being harvested, the weaker their flavor. This is the reason the taste of dried herbs only vaguely resembles that of fresh. Some herbs are more vulnerable to losing essential oils than others. Lemon thyme, tarragon, and lemon verbena will be noticeably less intense after a couple of days, while in rosemary, sage, and thyme the difference will be subtle. Fresh herbs in the supermarket are often more than a week old when you buy them.

And then, even if the herbs in your market are harvested daily, many kinds will be nearly impossible to find unless you grow them yourself. Most of the time, you can find fresh rosemary, sage, basil, and thyme, but chervil, lovage, rose geranium, lemon verbena, fresh lavender, and fresh bay leaves rarely make it to markets—there's simply not enough public demand.

As a bonus, when you grow your own herbs, you will discover they offer more than just their leaves. Sage bursts into bloom each spring with delicious-tasting, vivid purple blossoms that are superb sprinkled on pasta or over a salad. Fennel produces copious amounts of potent aniselike seeds at summer's end that add fabulous flavor to seafood and vegetable dishes, and their bamboolike stalks make an aromatic bed on which to cook a whole fish. Basil withers away in October, but you can gather and dry its sturdy stems and use them as fuel in a stovetop smoker.

A BIT OF BOTANY

What Is an Herb?   We all have a vague idea of what an herb is, but a precise definition is harder to peg down. The botanical definition of an herb—a seed-bearing plant that doesn't produce woody stems—is too strict for it would leave out rosemary and sage, and include petunias and cabbages. The layman's definition is more meaningful. An herb is a useful plant, whether it's used for seasoning food, as a medicine or tonic, for fragrance, or even in cosmetics, cleaners, or fabric dye. In this book I talk only about the herbs we cook with, and it is a selective list at that.

What is or is not a culinary herb is itself difficult to establish because some plants that we use for seasoning are called herbs and some spices. There are two implied differences. First, if you use the leaves of the plant, it's usually considered an herb, and if you use the root, bark, buds, seeds, or stems, it's a spice. But, that's not a hard and fast rule. We consider lavender an herb even though we use its buds, and likewise fennel, dill, and angelica though we use their seeds. This reflects the second distinguishing criterion: Herbs are usually grown in temperate climates and spices in tropical climates. Thyme, oregano, mint, and all the other herbs that appear in the following pages can grow in most North American gardens, even though they may not survive the entire year out-of-doors, but spices like cinnamon, allspice, and cardamom can only be grown where the weather stays warm year-round.

Further muddying this definition of a culinary herb is a group of leafy plants that can be thought of as either herbs or vegetables. They are called potherbs, a term that goes back to medieval times and literally means herbs that are cooked in the pot as greens, although they also were, and still are, used fresh in salads. Arugula, burnet, borage, cress, lamb's quarters, mâche, mustard, purslane, nettles, and sorrel all fall in this category. Even though they are used as vegetables instead of as flavorings for other foods, they are often called herbs.

Annual or Perennial Before choosing the herbs to plant in your garden, you need to understand their life cycles. All herbs can be divided into three categories: annual, biennial, and perennial. Annuals, such as basil and dill, grow, bloom, and set seeds in one growing season. Once this cycle is complete, they're like salmon that have just spawned. They have nothing more to live for and they die. Biennials, like angelica and parsley, do the same but over two years instead of one. They grow foliage the first year, bloom and set seed the second year, and then die.

Perennials, such as mint and sage, can live for many years but only if conditions suit them. Perennial herbs have different degrees of tolerance to cold. Tender perennials, like lemon verbena, marjoram, pineapple sage, and scented geranium, are easily killed by frost and must be brought indoors for the winter in all but the mildest climates. Many gardeners treat these sensitive plants like annuals and buy new plants each spring. Other herbs can withstand some frost but will only survive in a mild winter. For instance, rosemary will easily make it through a winter in USDA Zone 8 (lows of 10° to 20°F, see chart on page 359), but it's marginal in Zone 7 and must be protected when temperatures approach 10°F. Fortunately, most other perennial herbs are quite hardy. Plants like chives, mint, oregano, sage, sorrel, and thyme will keep coming back year after year in most parts of the United States, though eventually they may decline and need to be replaced.

Perennial herbs are further divided into two groups—woody and herbaceous—based on the way they grow. Woody perennials develop a framework of branches that remains above ground in the garden through the winter like a small shrub. Lavender, rosemary, sage, thyme, and winter savory all fit this category. Although they won't put out new growth in the cold months, you can harvest the leaves of these plants for the kitchen throughout the year. Herbaceous perennials, on the other hand, die back to the ground in autumn and disappear from the garden, but their roots stay alive. They include chives, fennel, lovage, mint, oregano, sorrel, and tarragon. All begin growth from ground level each spring.

Classifying Herbs When we identify an herb as "sage" or "oregano," we are using the common names. Common names are like people's first names, they're sufficient when it's understood which "Kathy" you're referring to, but there are other Kathys in the world. There are many kinds of sage and bay, but if a plant is labeled *Salvia officinalis* 'Berggarten' or *Origanum vulgare* subsp. *hirtum,* you know exactly what it is. This universal system for classifying and naming plants is based on Latin, and it is useful to become familiar with it. Not only will it help you to select the correct plants at the nursery, but by also recognizing the families of plants you will better understand their growing requirements.

Plant Families The entire plant world is first grouped in broad divisions, classes, and orders according to various criteria, such as if they flower or not and how many seed leaves they have. Then they are separated into families. Surprisingly, even though there are more than three hundred plant families, most culinary herbs fall into just two.

The first is the mint family, or, in Latin, the Labiatae family. Labiate herbs have flowers shaped like lips. They have square stems, leaves that form in pairs opposite each other on the stem, and a branching growth habit. Herbal members of this family include anise hyssop, basil, lavender, lemon balm, marjoram, mint, oregano, perilla, rosemary, sage, savory, and thyme.

The second is the parsley, or Umbelliferae, family. Umbelliferas are best identified by their flower clusters, shaped like upside-down umbrellas with flat tops. They have hollow stems and a circular growth habit that emanates at the base of the plant. Members include angelica, chervil, cilantro, dill, fennel, parsley, lovage, and sweet cicely.

Then there are some strays. Tarragon is a member of the Compositae, or daisy, family; chives, the Liliaceae, or lily, family; scented geranium, the Geraniaceae family; bay, the Lauraceae family; lemon verbena, the Verbenaceae family; and sorrel, the Rumex family. Many potherbs belong to the mustard, or Cruciferae, family.

Genus and Species   After being identified as a family member, plants are given a two-part name. The first is the genus, or generic name, which is capitalized, and the second is the species, or specific name, which is always in lower case. Lavender serves as a good example. All lavender plants are in the genus Lavandula, but there are many different types. *Lavandula angustifolia* is English lavender, *L. stoechas* is Spanish lavender, and *L. latifolia* is spike lavender. (In the text, if multiple species in the same genus are referred to, the genus is abbreviated with its first letter after the first time it is mentioned.) If a plant is a hybrid, meaning a cross of two species, it's indicated by an *x,* so lavenders that are a cross between *L. angustifolia* and *L. latifolia* are named *L.* x *intermedia.*

Varieties and Cultivars   Finally, there are variations in plants within a species. If the variation is naturally occurring, for instance if a species from one geographic area looks slightly different from the same species in another geographic area, it is given an additional subspecies name, such as *L. stoechas* subsp. *pendunculata.* If the variation occurs in cultivation and the plant is propagated to reproduce the same superior or distinguishing characteristics, it is known as a cultivar or selected variety, and it is given a name written in single quotes after the species name. *L. angustifolia* 'Munstead' is a lavender cultivar with a neat, mounding growing habit and brightly colored, strongly scented flowers. It was discovered by the famous Victorian gardener Gertrude Jekyll and is named after her garden, Munstead Wood. In order to reproduce the cultivar, it must be propagated vegetatively (meaning from cuttings or divisions), so that all plants bearing that name should have originated from a cutting that can be traced back to the single plant that Gertrude Jekyll herself selected. Some cultivars, however, can be grown from seed if they are stable, meaning that the seedlings will not vary. *L. angustifolia* 'Lady' is a seed-grown cultivar that was developed to bloom in its first season, and all seedlings with that name should have the same flower color and leaf shape and grow to the same height.

BASIC NEEDS

Herbs are easy to please, and the forty or so culinary herbs I focus on in this book share more likes than dislikes. This is why you can grow many different herbs in one tiny garden. What is disparate are the many types of climates across North America. Herbs that flourish in a Seattle garden with southern exposure may only stand a small chance of surviving a Texas summer if they're given dappled afternoon shade and plenty of mulch. For success in your own area, follow the general advice I give here but back it up with your own experiences and seek the advice of experts at your local nursery, your agricultural extension agency, or from your herb-growing neighbors.

Sun and Soil   Herbs like nothing more than to bask in the sun most of the day. There are exceptions: chervil, sweet cicely, and sweet woodruff like a shady spot, and sorrel, lovage, angelica, and lemon balm are content in part shade. Otherwise culinary herbs require at least half-a-day's sun—six hours—and most appreciate more. When they don't get enough light, they'll be slow growing, spindly, weak in flavor, prone to pests, and generally unhappy. When you choose a site for your herbs, think about the amount of sun it will get throughout the season. If it's in full sun in June, will it still be when the sun is lower in the sky in September? Are there any plants or trees nearby that will grow during the season and shade your herbs out, or will vigorous neighbors overtake them?

Soil is next in importance. In a perfect world, all gardens would have soil that is loamy, sweet, and well drained, often described as "like chocolate cake." Of course, in the real world we're sometimes given stale bread—soil that is either too sandy and dry, or too heavy and mucky. But soil can be improved and herbs are not that fussy. Your delphiniums or rare Himalayan blue poppies may wither in less-than-ideal conditions, but most herbs are fairly easygoing.

However, it is paramount that herbs have good drainage no matter what type of soil you have or what the climate is like. Herbs feel tortured if they have to live in heavy or swampy soil with standing water constantly around their roots. They will be more susceptible to disease and eventually the roots will rot and the plants will perish, particularly if you live where summers are hot and humid. Poor drainage is also responsible for many winter fatalities. When herbs don't come up the next spring in areas where they should be winter hardy, the problem is usually either wet roots in soggy soil or sporadic freezing and thawing. If the ground remained frozen under the insulation of a layer of snow, many plants would have a better chance.

If the poor drainage problem in your garden is caused from heavy clay soil, you can improve its structure by digging in organic matter, sand, or gravel. However, if the water is sitting because of a high water table or a serious layer of hardpan beneath the topsoil, the easiest solution is to garden in containers or to raise the soil level by building a raised bed. Any method you use to hold the soil above ground level will help the situation. You can build a wooden frame, a brick or stone wall, or even just mound the soil up about a foot higher than the surrounding land.

On the other extreme, some gardens have soil that is so sandy and rocky that it won't hold enough water to keep the plants healthy. It's true that many herbs, like oregano, lavender, sage, and thyme are indigenous to rocky hillsides with poor dry soil, and they are remarkably tolerant of these conditions. It's misleading, though, to say that herbs really like poor sandy soil. Herbs thrive in light soil that holds some water but drains well, and if they are moderately nourished.

The cure for improving poor soil structure is the same whether it's too sandy or too heavy. You must add what gardeners call amendments or organic matter. The best is home-made compost, but well-rotted manure, peat moss, and leaf mold will all work. These materials not only add nutrients but also improve the structure by aerating it and increasing the friability (crumbliness). The soil will become crumbly, easier to turn, and will warm earlier in the spring. Improving soil structure is not an overnight process. It can take years to reach the "chocolate cake" stage, but if you keep adding more organic material each season, the soil will steadily improve. Since many plants in the herb garden are perennials, you can't turn all the soil over each spring like you do in a vegetable garden. Whenever you plant something new, use it as an opportunity to dig one or two inches of organic material into the soil. To help the soil structure under established perennial herbs, apply organic material as a top dressing each spring; it will eventually work its way into the soil beneath.

Frankly, I've never paid much attention to the soil pH (concentration of hydrogen ions) of my own garden's soil, but if you're having problems raising herbs and are following all other advice, a soil test is a good place to look for answers. You can send your soil off to be tested in an agricultural lab or buy an inexpensive test kit. The pH of your soil is represented with a number from 0 to 14. Seven represents neutral soil, anything lower means your soil is acidic and anything higher means it's alkaline. Herbs do best in soil ranging from pH 6.5 to pH 7.5. In soil that's too acidic plants have trouble absorbing nutrients, and applying lime to the soil (follow package directions) can correct the problem within a season. Soil that is too alkaline is harder to correct, but digging in iron sulfate or peat moss, or applying acidic mulches like pine needles or bark over a few seasons will eventually bring it in balance.

Water, Food, and Mulch   Many herbs, like fennel, lavender, rosemary, sage, and thyme, can survive periods of drought once they are well established with a good root system, but all herbs do better with occasional watering. When rain is scarce, don't let these herbs die of thirst. Give them a deep drink at least once a week but allow them to dry out partially between waterings. Herbs that are newly planted should never be allowed to dry out completely. Some herbs like a little more water than others. As long as their soil is well drained, mint, sorrel, basil, parsley, and chervil will grow best if kept evenly moist.

On the whole, herbs are not heavy feeders. If the soil is moderately fertile to begin with, a dose of organic all-purpose fertilizer each spring is appreciated, followed by another application when the herbs are cut back after they flower. Fast-growing annuals, like basil, chives, coriander, and dill, need a bit more food. A drink of fish fertilizer or other balanced plant food about once a month will keep these plants growing rapidly.

Mulching your herb garden is usually a great benefit, though it can harbor pests and diseases, and in the Northwest, slugs and snails. If you live in a hot climate, mulching will help your herbs through the summer by keeping the soil cool and moist, and it can be crucial to your herbs' survival in very hot, humid climates. If you live in a cold climate, a thick layer of mulch applied in the fall will help your perennial herbs live through the winter by warming the soil. Mulches also cut down on weeds and improve the soil as they break down. The availability of mulching materials varies regionally, but finely chipped bark, hay, straw, pine straw, compost, shredded leaves, or hulls from cocoa, buckwheat, or cottonseed are all good choices.

Starting from Seeds or Plants   Certain herbs are best acquired as rooted plants, while others are best started from seed. Sometimes both options are good.

For the small-scale herb gardener, I always recommend buying woody herbs like bay, lavender, lemon verbena, rosemary, sage, thyme, and winter savory in pots. These plants can be difficult to start from seed, and they take a long time to grow to a reasonable size. Unless you are a very patient and frugal gardener, it's worth the investment of a few dollars to have the head start of a rooted herb plant. For a home garden, you'll rarely want more than half a dozen of any one plant, and in the case of rosemary or sage, one or two is enough. Unless you're supplying the neighborhood, a whole packet of seeds produces many more seedlings than you really need. Also keep in mind that specific cultivars like Tuscan Blue rosemary, Holts Mammoth sage, and most scented geraniums can't be grown from seed but must be started from cuttings. If you want the true selection, you must either buy the plant or start a cutting yourself. The same holds for both French tarragon and peppermint, which don't produce seeds. I also recommend buying oreganos as rooted plants because seedlings can vary quite a bit in their quality and intensity of flavor. When you buy a plant, you know what you're getting because you can rub and smell the leaves.

Herb plants are most commonly available in pots that are four inches in diameter, although sometimes you can buy perennials like rosemary, tarragon, and thyme in gallon-size containers and annual herbs like basil and cilantro in multipacks. If you can't find the plants you want locally, there are many mail-order nurseries that specialize in herbs. When you are selecting plants to purchase, the most important thing to look for is that they are healthy. They should have bushy foliage and no sign of pests or diseases. Don't buy herbs with spindly stems and yellow leaves—signs of stress from not enough light and water and being in the pot too long. When you pop the plant out of the container, you should see white or light-colored roots. Avoid plants that have a thick overgrown mat of roots. Be sure that you rub the leaves and smell them to be certain that they have a good strength of fragrance, especially if you're buying oregano, marjoram, tarragon, and lemon thyme.

If you buy your plants in the spring and the weather is still cool, ask the nursery man or woman if the plants were hardened off. When plants are gradually acclimated to the outdoors, they will not be startled at suddenly being taken from the greenhouse and plopped in the ground. You might want to take the precaution of hardening them off yourself. To do this, keep the plants in a protected spot, like a garage or porch, and bring them out in the garden for a little longer each day. Begin with a few hours in the shade the first day, and half a day the second, then gradually give them a little more sun each day. In about a week they will be ready to be planted outside with no risk of shock.

There are only a handful of herbs that are easier to grow from seed than from transplants, namely dill, chervil, and cilantro—all members of the parsley family. These herbs have delicate taproots, and they tend to be very fickle about being yanked out of a pot and shoveled into a new home. It will trigger them to bolt (send up their flowering stalks) prematurely at the expense of producing a good crop of leaves. Sow these particular herbs directly in the ground where you want them to grow while the weather is still cool. Always use fresh seed, since seeds from umbelliferous herbs lose their viability quickly.

Many other herbs like basil, dill, sorrel, summer savory, parsley, and marjoram, are readily available as seedlings but are not difficult to start from seed. Growing herbs from seed is economical and rewarding, and in many cases, specific strains are available as seed that you cannot find in local nurseries. You can either sow them in the garden when the weather is warm enough (see the package directions) or start the seeds in small pots on a sunny windowsill or under cool white fluorescent tubes inside the house, then plant them in the garden when they have developed root systems. Be sure to harden them off first.

Harvesting and Pruning   Novice gardeners sometimes seem reluctant to cut their herbs, as if they're expecting the plant to say "ouch." The truth is the plants actually like to be trimmed, and they will grow back fuller and healthier. Deciding where to snip is sometimes puzzling to cooks who aren't experienced gardeners. If you're already an experienced gardener, gathering herbs will be second nature, no different from the tasks you do regularly like pruning, pinching, and cutting back. Beginners need to learn just a few simple principles.

You probably already have the essential tool for harvesting your herbs—an ordinary pair of sharp stainless-steel household scissors. They should be comfortable to use, easy to wash, durable, inexpensive, and sharp enough to cut easily through most herb stems. For the extremely thick woody stems you might encounter in a mature rosemary or sage plant, a pair of good garden pruners is useful as well.

I've often read that you should collect herbs early in the morning, just as the sun is rising and the dew is drying on their leaves. This makes sense if you are cooking in the morning, but otherwise it's not practical. It's really best to harvest herbs just before you're going to cook with them. Set on a kitchen counter or in the refrigerator, herbs lose their freshness and flavor, and the point of growing herbs yourself—to reap their full freshness and aroma—is lost.

Another precept you often hear is that you should harvest herbs right before they flower when they have their highest concentrations of essential oils. If you are harvesting your herbs for drying or other means of preserving, it is certainly the ideal time to gather them, but herbs exist at this stage for only about two weeks of the year. If you want to cook with the fresh herb throughout the season, ignore the advice.

There are a few general rules for harvesting herbs. The first is that you should not cut your herbs back by more than one-third of their total bulk at one time. Herbs, like other plants in your garden, derive strength from the photosynthesis that takes place in their leaves. If you cut back a plant too severely at the wrong stage in its growing cycle, it will lose vigor and have a difficult time recovering. There are many exceptions: Chives, which store energy in underground bulbs, can be cut to the ground, and oregano and mint like a severe pruning after they bloom. But if you are unsure, it's worth following the no-more-than-one-third rule.

Second, it's better to harvest sprigs than individual leaves. Pinching back or cutting off a stem encourages the plant to put out new growth, but stripping leaves from the stems simply weakens the plant. Think of harvesting as a way of pruning your plants—your goal is to keep the plant bushy and attractive. Always keep in mind the shape of the plant. If one side is shorter than the other, cut off sprigs in a way that will even it out. If there are branches growing out into a path or interfering with a neighboring plant, cut those off first.

Herbs in the mint (Labiatae) and parsley (Umbelliferae) families have their own distinctly different ways of growing and, therefore, should be harvested distinctly differently.

Labiate herbs have a branching growth habit with opposite forming leaves that emanate in pairs all along the stems. When you make a cut in the middle of one of these stems or pinch off its growing tip, it will form a fork, sprouting two new branches from the junction of the last set of leaves, and this will make the plant bushier than it was before. Cutting the top of the branch will also often force lateral shoots to sprout from above leaf joints all along the stem. The more growing tips you cut off, the fuller the plant will eventually be. Always snip a stem directly above a set of leaves and usually one-third to one-half of the stem.

Umbelliferous herbs have stems that radiate from a central growing point at soil level. Think of a bunch of parsley or dill. It consists of stems that begin at the base of the plant and branch into thinner terminal stems that hold the leaves at their tops. If you snip one of the stems in half, it will not continue to grow above that point, like members of the mint family. New growth starts only at the center of the plant. The rule is to cut stems off at ground level, the outer stems first. This will encourage vigorous growth to continue from the center of the plant.

Herbs that are not in these two families have their own needs. Tarragon and lemon verbena should be cut midstem just like a labiate. Chives should be snipped all the way to within an inch of the soil, so they can renew themselves from their bulbs. Bay laurel is best harvested leaf by leaf, not with scissors, but by tugging downward on the leaf. Scented geraniums can be harvested by snipping leaves one by one or by clipping whole sprigs from the tips of the stems.

To keep your herbs healthy and vigorous, it's often necessary to prune them even when you have no use for the fresh sprigs. Most herbs benefit from being cut back after they flower but before they go to seed, particularly herbs in the mint family like thyme, oregano, lavender, sage, and marjoram. Once the flowers start to fade, uniformly cut the entire plant back to about one-third of its height, below the point where the flowers began to grow. This will ensure the plants will put forth fresh growth, and often they will bloom again in the same season. Annuals in the mint family, such as basil and perilla, should not be allowed to flower at all. Pinch the flower buds off as soon as they appear to prolong their lives and promote bushiness.

*Harvesting mint
(Labiatae family)*

*Harvesting dill
(Umbelliferae family)*

*Cutting back oregano
after it has flowered*

Woody perennials, such as rosemary, sage, thyme, winter savory, and lavender, are really shrubs. They don't die back to the ground in the winter and start their growth from roots in the spring but instead develop a framework that carries over from season to season. If you don't prune them, they will become leggy, but they're still sensitive to being cut back too hard. The key is to always cut above leaves. If you prune a woody branch below where there is any new growth, it might not have a place to break new stems, and that area of the plant will die out. Also, don't prune these woody perennials back in autumn, since pruning encourages new tender growth that is very susceptible to cold. If you harvest just very lightly before fall sets in, they will have a chance to toughen up in preparation for the frost.

Pinching flower buds off basil

Umbelliferas send up their flowers on tall stalks from the center of the plant. If the leaves of the plant are what you want to harvest, not the flowers or seeds, it's beneficial to cut the flowering stalk off before it has a chance to develop. This treatment will prolong the life of annuals in this family, like dill, cilantro, and chervil. If you cut off the flower stalks of angelica, a biennial, it will sometimes live for three years, and if you do it to lovage, a perennial, it will reward you with a new crop of more tender and less bitter green leaves.

Cutting back sage

Choosing a Home for Your Herbs

The Herb Garden   If you're lucky enough to have a small sunny plot of land not far from your kitchen, think about devoting it solely to herbs. Since many herbs like nearly the same conditions, it makes sense to give them their own garden, and it's handy having them all in one spot so that you can harvest everything you need for the kitchen at once. In a space as small as a few square yards you can grow quite a variety of plants. If you have one or two hundred square feet to set aside, you can create a cook's fantasy garden.

The simplest herb garden can be a little bed by the kitchen steps with a dozen or so plants. The hardest thing will be deciding which herbs to plant. Think about not only which herbs you cook with most often but also which are hard to find at the supermarket or farmers' market, which are better freshly picked, and

Cutting the flower stalk off a lovage plant

which you can continue to harvest from over a long season. For instance, with a limited amount of room, I would pass by parsley and cilantro, because they're easy to buy in the markets, but I'd raise chervil because it's rarely available cut, and tarragon because the quality of homegrown is superior. I'd also grow thyme, sage, and rosemary because they're useful in so many dishes and you can harvest from them all year. I'd have to have marjoram because it's a favorite. Other cooks have their own lists of five or ten essential herbs, and it's up to you to make one for yourself.

One step beyond digging up a little corner of the garden is to build a raised bed devoted to herbs. Raised beds make particularly good herb gardens because they have excellent drainage and you can access them from all sides. You can pack quite a few plants into a small space and let the herbs spill out in all directions. The most common way of creating a raised bed is to build a large wooden frame of railroad ties or lumber, at least four inches high but twelve is best. Think of it as a giant bottomless flowerpot that you can fill with the best soil you can find. If your own garden's soil is not ideal, purchase good topsoil or a mixture of topsoil and compost for the project.

If you have a level plot of land ten or twenty feet square and have had success with herbs on a small scale, why not create a formal herb garden? First visit herb gardens at herb nurseries or botanical gardens to study how they are designed and to familiarize yourself with how the plants grow. Visit them in different seasons so you can see how they change. Then start work on your own. Surround the plot with some sort of a boundary—a rustic woven fence, white pickets, or a hedge—then lay out beds. Traditional herb gardens are geometric and symmetrical and often divided into four quadrants intersected with paths of gravel, brick, or stone. If you wish, each section can be a raised bed. Add romantic touches like a small bench, an arbor, a birdbath, a sculpture, or a giant urn. Fill the beds with herbs, taking into consideration the ultimate height of the plants and whether they are annual or perennial. Contrast leaf textures and colors, and always include edible flowers like old-fashioned roses, nasturtiums, and pinks. The very ambitious can add manicured lavender hedges, ribbons of gold and silver thyme woven into knot designs, and bay laurel topiaries.

Herbs in the Border   A garden with nothing but herbs is certainly a delight, but the other, much freer approach is to let herbs mingle here and there throughout the garden. Plant them as if they were ornamental plants and harvest them like herbs.

At my own house on a small city lot, I have a very practical eight- by four-foot raised herb bed behind my garage that I tightly plant with the necessities for cooking. But in the sanctuary of my private back garden, I integrate culinary herbs into wide borders of mixed plantings. Chives and oregano grow beneath shrub roses, lemon verbena and lavender flourish next to purple petunias and columbine, and red perilla weaves with paisley-leafed coleus. Lemon thyme and nasturtiums spill over rocks that edge a gravel path, and huge clumps of fennel and angelica stand between a weeping pear and a fig tree. Underneath my Japanese maples there is a sea of sweet woodruff, and a gnarled four-foot rosemary stands guard by the gate. They all get along just fine.

All gardens, no matter what the size, have microclimates, giving you the opportunity to find the perfect spot for each plant. A bed in front of a south-facing wall is the best place for plants that need extra warmth and sun in the winter, like rosemary and bay. A plot at a low elevation in the garden that stays moist is best for mints and sorrel. Chervil might do best planted underneath the lacy canopy of an ash. Remember that gardens are never static, and you can always move your herbs around until you find just the right home for them.

Herbs in the Vegetable Garden   If you have a traditional vegetable garden, you can grow herbs like any other crop. Devote whole rows to individual herbs or interplant the herbs among the vegetables. A row of basil will happily produce pesto for the year, or you can interplant the basil between tomato cages, where it's said to keep pests away. A row of thyme will ensure you'll have enough for the kitchen. Short-lived herbs, like dill, cilantro, and chervil, can be planted in succession so that you always have some at their peak—sow a fourth of the row every two or three weeks. Place perennial herbs like sage, rosemary, and lovage out of the way of beds that are tilled each year. Fierce spreaders, like oregano and mint, should be given isolated spaces where they can roam without invading other crops. Be sure to include a few flowers, like nasturtiums, borage, and calendula. They require almost no effort and, tucked here and there, will brighten the garden immeasurably.

Herbs in Containers   If you don't have a yard but do have a sunny deck, patio, or balcony, you can still have your own herb garden, since most herbs love to grow in containers. They provide excellent drainage and you can move them where the herbs can get the sun they need. Use simple clay or plastic pots, big terra-cotta urns, whiskey barrels, or window boxes—anything that has ample holes at the bottom to allow water to drain. A six-inch pot will support a small thyme or marjoram plant, but it's best to put them in larger pots so that they don't dry out as quickly and their roots have room to spread.

Fill the pots with commercial potting mix but be particular about what you purchase. In essence, any dirt can be bagged and sold as potting soil, and I've had very poor results with the inexpensive potting soil sold at warehouse stores. A soilless mix, made from peat moss, perlite, and vermiculite is a sound choice. Even better: Ask a local nursery to sell you the mix they formulate for their own plants, or ask gardening friends what they've had success with. If you have some homemade compost, mix in a few handfuls, and if you are using soilless mix that doesn't contain fertilizer, add some all-purpose organic fertilizer. Plant the containers densely. You can put several types of herbs in the same pot and even mix annual and perennial herbs, but keep aggressive spreaders, like mint and Greek oregano, isolated to their own pots. Keep in mind how large the plants will grow, but herbs can be planted much closer in containers than if they were in the ground and they will spill out over the sides.

Give potted herbs as much sun as you can. Never let them dry out completely. If the drainage is excellent, you shouldn't need to worry about overwatering, and in hot weather they'll likely need a drink daily. Not only do potted herb plants need more water than if they were in the ground but they also need more food because nutrients are washed away each time you water. Fertilize the pots once a month with a water-soluble plant food.

Herbs Indoors   Kitchen windowsills filled with thriving herb plants in little clay pots always look so healthy on television or in magazines, but growing herbs indoors is tricky. Herbs don't like to live in the same sort of indoor environment as people do. Nevertheless, if you're willing to invest the time and energy, you can grow herbs in your house or apartment with success. First, be aware that indoor herb gardens will not yield much. Herbs on a winter windowsill grow much slower than outdoors in the summer. Once you harvest enough leaves from your little thyme or savory plant to give you two tablespoons for a recipe, it will take many weeks for the plant to replenish those sprigs. If you cook often with fresh herbs, you'll have to grow many plants of each variety to produce the amount of leaves you will want to have.

Herbs rarely get enough light indoors, especially in winter. Always put them in the sunniest window you have, and for really healthy plants it's best to grow them under fluorescent or other artificial lights or use grow lights to supplement the light on the windowsill. Second, houses are usually too warm and dry. The best indoor environment for your plants, aside from a greenhouse, is an enclosed sun porch or a windowsill in an unheated spare room with southern exposure. They'll be much happier there than if forced to live in a warm kitchen. Set the pots on saucers of moist gravel to increase the humidity but don't let the bottoms of the pots sit in water. A daily misting from a spray bottle will also help. Allow the soil to partially dry out between waterings but never let them get so dry that they wilt.

All that said, it is delightful to have living herb plants in the kitchen, especially if you are an apartment dweller. The easiest herbs to grow inside are parsley, chives, thyme, chervil, Cretan oregano, African blue basil, French lavender, scented geraniums, Mexican tarragon, pineapple sage, and marjoram.

The other reason to bring pots of herbs indoors is if they will not survive the winter outdoors in your climate. Most often this applies to bay and rosemary and gardening in Zone 6 or colder, and sometimes Zone 7 (see below). First grow the plants in large containers that can stay outdoors in warmer weather, then when temperatures dip into the 20s at night, gradually acclimate them to their indoor environment by bringing them in the house for a little longer each day until they are inside full time. Remember, a cool, sunny room will suit them best. Keep them on the dry side but don't let them dry out completely. Other tender herbs that need protection in the house from heavy frost are pineapple sage, French and Spanish lavenders, African blue and African cinnamon basils, Mexican tarragon, and scented geraniums.

Scented geraniums do particularly well on windowsills. In fall, dig them up, shake off the rootball, and pot them in fresh soil, or repot them if they were already in containers. Cut them back to about a third of their size. Put them in the sun and they will soon bush out and give off their scent all winter. They may even bloom.

USDA Hardiness Zones

The average lowest temperature that can be expected in a year determines what Zone you garden in.

Zone 1: below −50°F	Zone 5: −20° to −10°F	Zone 9: 20° to 30°F
Zone 2: −50° to −40°F	Zone 6: −10° to 0°F	Zone 10: 30° to 40°F
Zone 3: −40° to −30°F	Zone 7: 0° to 10°F	Zone 11: above 40°F
Zone 4: −30° to −20°F	Zone 8: 10° to 20°F	

Growing Requirements

HERB	LATIN NAME	FAMILY	LIFE CYCLE	HARDY TO	HEIGHT
Angelica	*Angelica archangelica*	Umbelliferae	Biennial	Zone 4	5 to 7 feet
Anise hyssop	*Agastache foeniculum*	Labiatae	Perennial	Zone 6	4 feet
Basil, sweet	*Ocimum basilicum*	Labiatae	Annual	n/a	2 to 3 feet
Bay laurel	*Laurus nobilis*	Lauraceae	Long-lived tree	Zone 8	5 to 60 feet
Chervil	*Anthriscus cerefolium*	Umbelliferae	Annual	n/a	½ to 1½ feet
Chives	*Allium schoenoprasum*	Liliaceae	Perennial	Zone 4	1 to 1½ feet
Cilantro (coriander)	*Coriandrum sativum*	Umbelliferae	Annual	n/a	1 to 3 feet
Dill	*Anethum graveolens*	Umbelliferae	Annual	n/a	2 to 4 feet
Fennel	*Foeniculum vulgare*	Umbelliferae	Perennial	Zone 6	4 to 7 feet
Hyssop	*Hyssopus officinalis*	Labiatae	Perennial	Zone 4	1½ to 2 feet
Lavender, English	*Lavandula angustifolia*	Labiatae	Perennial	Zone 5	2 to 3 feet
Lemon balm	*Melissa officinalis*	Labiatae	Perennial	Zone 4	2 to 3 feet
Lemon verbena	*Aloysia triphylla*	Verbenaceae	Tender perennial	Zone 9	3 to 10 feet
Lovage	*Levisticum officinale*	Umbelliferae	Perennial	Zone 5	4 to 6 feet
Marjoram	*Origanum majorana*	Labiatae	Tender perennial	Zone 9	½ to 1 foot

PRUNING	NUMBER TO PLANT FOR AN AVERAGE KITCHEN	SPECIAL GROWING REQUIREMENTS
Cut off flower stalks to promote promote stem production.	1	Transplant when young. Germinates best when seeds are fresh. Likes cool weather and semishade.
Cut back by one-third after flowering	2	Full sun, moderately rich, moist soil.
Pinch off all flower buds.	12	Don't plant out in the garden until the soil warms. Likes heat and moderately rich, moist soil.
Harvest leaves by tugging downward downward.	1	Likes fertile, moist, but well-drained soil. Bring indoors when temperatures fall below 20°F. Watch for pests like scale and wooly aphid.
Cut flower stalks off to encourage leaf growth.	12	Does best in cool temperatures and semishade. Dislikes transplanting.
Harvest stalks all the way to ground; cut back to ground after flowering.	3	Keep well fertilized if you harvest often.
Cut flower stalks off to encourage leaf growth.	6	Sow every 3 weeks. Dislikes transplanting.
Cut flower stalks off to encourage leaf growth.	6	Sow every 3 weeks. Dislikes transplanting.
Cut stalks back to the ground in fall or spring.	1	Likes excellent drainage.
Cut back by one-third after flowering.	1	Likes good drainage.
Cut back by one-third after flowering.	2	Likes excellent drainage.
Cut back by one-half or to the ground after flowering.	1	Rampant self-seeder.
Pinch off flowers.	1	Likes sandy but moist soil.
Cut flower stalks off at ground level to encourage foliage.	1	In southern climates, plant in partial shade.
Cut off flower heads after they form.	6	Grown as an annual in most climates. Likes heat. Keep on the dry side.

GROWING REQUIREMENTS (CONTINUED)

HERB	LATIN NAME	FAMILY	LIFE CYCLE	HARDY TO	HEIGHT
Meadowsweet	*Filipendula ulmaria*	Rosaceae	Perennial	Zone 4	3 to 4 feet
Mexican tarragon (mint marigold)	*Tegetes lucida*	Compositae	Perennial	Zone 8 to 9	2 feet
Mint (spearmint)	*Mentha spicata*	Labiatae	Perennial	Zone 4	2 to 3 feet
Oregano, Greek	*Origanum Vulgare* subsp. *hirtum*	Labiatae	Perennial	Zone 5	1½ to 2 feet
Parsley	*Petroselinum crispum*	Umbelliferae	Biennial	Zone 6	1 to 2 feet
Perilla	*Perilla frutescens*	Labiatae	Annual	n/a	2 to 3 feet
Rosemary	*Rosmarinus officinalis*	Labiatae	Perennial shrub	Zone 7 to 8	3 to 6 feet
Sage	*Salvia officinalis*	Labiatae	Perennial	Zone 5	2 to 3 feet
Savory, summer	*Satureja hortensis*	Labiatae	Annual	n/a	1½ feet
Savory, winter	*Satureja montana*	Labiatae	Perennial	Zone 5	1 foot
Scented geranium, rose	*Pelargonium graveolens*	Geraniaceae	Tender perennial	Zone 9	2 to 6 feet
Sorrel, garden	*Rumex acetosa*	Polygonaceae	Perennial	Zone 5	2 to 3 feet
Sweet cicely	*Myrhhis odorata*	Umbelliferae	Perennial	Zone 4	2 to 4 feet
Tarragon, French	*Artemesia dracunculus* var. *sativa*	Compositae	Perennial	Zone 5	1 to 3 feet
Thyme, English	*Thymus vulgaris*	Labiatae	Perennial	Zone 4	1 foot
Woodruff, sweet	*Galium odoratum* (*Asperula odorata*)	Rubiaceae	Perennial	Zone 4	½ foot

PRUNING	NUMBER TO PLANT FOR AN AVERAGE KITCHEN	SPECIAL GROWING REQUIREMENTS
	1	Likes moist soil.
	3	Likes warm weather. Does well if dug up in fall and grown on a windowsill.
Cut back hard during or after flowering.	3	Grows most vigorously with adequate water. Rapid spreader.
Cut back hard after flowering.	3	Likes sun and well-drained soil. Rapid spreader.
Harvest outer stems first.	6	Often grown as an annual.
Pinch off all flower buds.	3	Likes full sun and warm weather.
Does not require cutting back after flowering.	1	Likes full sun and well-drained soil. Mulch in humid climates.
Cut back after flowering.	2	Likes full sun and very well-drained soil. Mulch in humid climates.
Cut back to prevent flowering.	6	Likes full sun and well-drained soil.
Cut back after flowering.	3	Likes full sun and well-drained soil.
Cut back in spring.	1	Does well indoors.
Cut off flower stalks.	3	Likes moist soil, partial shade, and cool weather.
Cut back after flowering.	1	Likes partial shade, moist soil, and cool weather.
Pinch to keep bushy.	3	Likes full sun and well-drained soil.
Cut back after flowering.	6	Likes full sun and well-drained soil.
	3	Likes shade.

CHAPTER 15

Herbs in the Kitchen: Buying, Handling, and Cooking with Them

FRESH HERBS FROM THE MARKET

Not all cooks can grow fresh herbs, and even those who do will need to buy cut sprigs of those not in the garden or out of season. The increasing availability of cut fresh herbs is heartening. Alongside parsley and cilantro, bunches of fresh rosemary, thyme, sage, basil, mint, dill, and oregano now appear on produce shelves in supermarkets across the country. As more cooks demand them, fresh herbs will be considered less of a specialty product. Their quality and freshness will continue to improve, prices will drop, and more varieties will be offered.

If there is a farmers' market near where you live, make it your first source for fresh herbs. Bunches are usually generous and of good quality because they are harvested the same morning they are sold. At the market you can meet and commend the people who plant and tend the herbs and ask them questions about their harvest. You can sniff or even nibble on the leaves to become familiar with them and be sure they have good flavor.

Fresh herbs in the supermarket are displayed in one of two ways. Some stores put them out in open bunches because a public that is just learning about herbs is more likely to buy them if they can smell and touch them. This is a great idea if the herbs are sold within hours of being put on the shelf, but herbs left out in the open wilt. To stop them from wilting, supermarkets put them under automatic misters along with all the other produce. As the water collects on the leaves and near the base of the stems, they start to decay. If you buy herbs in open bunches, always check the bottoms for signs of deterioration. The same rule applies if their stems are set in a shallow tray of water, like cut flowers.

Herbs that are sold in sealed plastic bags or plastic containers will usually be in better condition. You can still open the bag or plastic box in the store to rub and smell the leaves to check that they have good strength of flavor. Look for herbs that have robust green leaves growing densely from the stems. Avoid herbs with pale leaves or with stems that are stretched, thin, and weak—a sign that they were probably grown in a greenhouse with too much fertilizer and not enough sun. These herbs will be weak in flavor. If you see leaves that are badly wilted or turning yellow, brown, or black, talk to the produce manager. Supermarkets often have fresher bunches in their coolers that they are reluctant to put out until their older batch is sold. When fresh herbs are sold in small bunches, you will be paying more per pound for them than any other produce on the shelves, even more than the most expensive meat or fish in the store, so you have a right to demand herbs of the highest quality. Try to shop at a store where the fresh herb inventory is turned often. And compare prices—in my area one large chain supermarket sells half-ounce bunches, while another sells two-ounce bunches of better quality for the same price.

CLEANING AND STORING FRESH HERBS

If you've just harvested herbs from your own garden and you know they haven't been exposed to pesticides or other contaminants, simply give them a quick inspection for bugs or dirt. If they have neither, there's no need to wash them. Leaves of fresh herbs are much easier to handle and chop when they are completely dry. If you plan to store them in the refrigerator, know that extra moisture on the leaves promotes decay.

If you buy herbs from a supermarket or you can see or feel dirt on the herbs from your own garden (especially if they were harvested close to the ground), you'll have to wash them. When you only have a few sprigs to wash, hold them under the tap for a rinse, then shake them off and pat them dry between paper towels. With larger bunches of herbs it's more effective to submerge them in water the way you would wash salad greens. Fill the bucket of a salad spinner or a large bowl with cold water. Drop in the herbs and swish them around so that the dirt releases and can sink to the bottom. Then lift them out of the water and dry them either in the salad spinner or by patting them dry between paper towels or in a clean dishtowel. If you have a large bunch of herbs with all the stems at the bottom, the way parsley and cilantro are usually sold, the process is even easier. Hold the herb bunch by the stems and plunge it up and down in the water. Still holding it by the stems, remove it from the water and shake it over the sink or out the backdoor, snapping your wrist as if you were shaking down a thermometer. If they're still not dry, spin them or pat dry with paper towels.

The best way to store fresh herbs is to put them into a resealable plastic freezer bag, and keep it at 40° to 45°F, the temperature in a refrigerator's crisper. Don't wash them before you store them—the drier the leaves are the longer and fresher they will keep. When I have several varieties, I put them in separate bags and loosely pack them in a tightly sealed large plastic container, and then keep it in the vegetable crisper or on a refrigerator shelf, but I avoid cold spots like the rear of the lower shelf. Some tender-leafed herbs, most notably basil and lemon verbena, will turn black at temperatures below 40°F. I try to keep the container loosely packed so the herbs don't crush. If just harvested, most herbs should remain in good shape for well over a week, although their intensity of flavor diminishes as time goes on. Herbs with tough leaves like rosemary, thyme, sage, and bay will keep for two weeks or longer, but herbs with delicate leaves, like chervil or lemon verbena, will last only a few days. Some cooks like to wrap the herbs in damp paper towels and then put them in plastic bags, but the extra moisture only invites decay. The resealable produce bags that have tiny holes for air circulation are effective if the leaves are wet and moisture needs to escape, but herbs with dry leaves will last much longer if sealed airtight.

The conventional wisdom that advises storing cut herbs as if they were cut flowers, standing up in a glass or pitcher of water either on the counter on in the refrigerator, makes sense if you are keeping herbs a day or two, but like cut flowers, their stems soon begin to rot and the water becomes rank. Even if you change the water, I find the herbs suffer. And if the glass is placed in the refrigerator, it inevitably gets knocked over, spilling the water onto everything below. The only time I stand herb sprigs in water is when I want to hold them at room temperature for more than an hour. Basil, cilantro, and parsley are three that keep particularly well for a few days with their stems in water on a cool kitchen counter.

REMOVING STEMS

When a recipe calls for a tablespoon of a chopped fresh herb, it really means a tablespoon of the leaf of that particular herb, culled from the stem. There's nothing toxic or foul tasting about the stems of herbs—most have a flavor similar to the leaf—but their texture is an annoyance. Other than the very tender new growth at the tips, most herb stems are coarse or woody and should not be added to a dish unless they're to be strained out later on. Of course there are exceptions: Cilantro and chervil have very soft stems throughout, chives have no stems at all, and the stem of angelica is often the only part you use. But most other herbs have a stem that needs to be removed before you chop them.

Stripping the leaves off an oregano sprig

I'll admit that the simple chore of separating leaf from stem is a bit tedious, but there are ways to accomplish the task quickly and without trying your patience. Suppose you have a sprig of oregano. If you use your fingers as if they were tweezers to pull off each leaf individually, the process will take forever. Instead, hold the bottom of the stem in one hand and use the thumb and first two fingers of the other hand to strip the leaves off from the bottom up in one stroke. There will often be a point toward the top of the sprig where it will break because the stem gets softer the further up the stem you go. The stem above the break is usually tender enough that you can just

Removing the stem from a sage sprig

chop it up with the leaves. To confirm this, roll the stem between your fingers to feel its resistance—it should feel supple and not stiff. Or nibble on a small piece—if it feels like you're chewing on a twig, remove it, but if these terminal pieces of stem are tender they will be unnoticeable in the finished dish. Any herb with leaves evenly spaced along the stems—thyme, tarragon, marjoram, and savory—can be handled in exactly the same way, but with some herbs you'll find that the leaves strip off easier from the top down. I find this to be true of rosemary, mint, and lemon verbena, but try traveling the stem in both directions to see which is easier for you.

Both basil and sage have groupings of leaves at the tops of their stems and they need slightly different handling. Grab the top leaves of the herb sprig in a bundle like you would grab a handlebar, and use the other hand to grab the stem where it meets the leaves. Twist the top off in one motion. Pick through the resulting pile of leaves to make sure that no prominent stems are left, then strip or pick off any leaves from the remaining stems.

Feathery herbs like fennel and dill are even easier to handle. They have a network of branches with extremely thin, soft leaves. Grab the sprig at the bottom by the thick stem and strip upward letting the herb fall onto a cutting board. Pick out any sprigs that still have a prominent stem and strip them individually in the same way. The very small stems will vanish when the herb is chopped.

Parsley and cilantro are especially easy to prepare. In some cases you might want to pick the leaf clusters off the stems one by one, such as for a salad, garnish, or for an extremely fine chop, but in most other instances, you can take a shortcut. Simply keep the washed herb in a bunch and lop off the stems where they meet the leaves. Quickly pull out any substantial stems that are left in the pile and strip the leaves off. The remaining narrow and tender stems will blend in with the leaves when the herb is chopped.

Removing the stem from a dill sprig

Chopped, Torn, Snipped, or Puréed

Cutting the stems off a bunch of curly parsley

It's midsummer, the herb garden is in full force, and you're inspired to make fettuccine sauced only with herbs and extra-virgin olive oil. Ask five cooks to make this dish, and you will end up with five very different results because of the way each cook treats the herbs. They can be pounded to a fine paste with the oil, minced to a powdery sprinkle, given a few coarse chops, cut into shreds with scissors, torn into ragged pieces, or tossed in whole. Each of these treatments will affect the flavor and character of the final dish.

As a first criterion for whether to chop, tear, or purée, consider the style of the dish. A rustic, robust dish, like a garlicky bread soup, calls for generous handfuls of coarsely chopped herbs, while a more refined dish, let's say a seafood mousseline, would be better with a restrained and finely minced sprinkle. And just as a dish has a personality, so does the cook. Some are bold and impulsive, while others are painstaking and measured. It's these differences in approach that make cooking a form of self-expression.

The way an herb flavors a dish subtly changes with the way it's cut. The finer an herb is chopped the more surface area is exposed, the faster its essential oils blend into the food, and the faster they will dissipate as the dish cooks. This means you get a strong and more immediate stroke of flavor but less impact in a long-cooked dish. A fine chop integrates the herbs with other ingredients, both visually and texturally, while a coarse chop makes the herbs more prominent, lends more flavor contrast, and allows the herbs to hold up better in the cooking process.

Let's say you choose oregano, parsley, chives, and sage for your fettuccine. At one extreme, you could make a pesto sauce and purée the herbs with the oil in a food processor. The individual herb flavors will all meld, but they will lose their distinction and will be perceived on the tongue as very strong tasting. The fine purée will accentuate the bitter resinous flavors of the sage, the heat of the oregano, and the acrid onion flavor of the chives. Once it's tossed with the pasta, the flavor will be powerful, sharp, and without nuance. (This combination of herbs is not suited for this treatment, but less aggressive herbs will work superbly, particularly the classic—fresh basil.)

At the other end of the spectrum, you could remove the leaves from their stems, give them a very coarse chop, and then toss them with the fettuccine as is. In this dish the leaves of the herbs will look attractive and will slowly release their flavor into the oil, but the large pieces will distract from the texture of the delicate fresh noodles, stick in your teeth, and be overly strong and unpleasant when chewed.

Clearly the dish will be most appealing with an approach somewhere in between. My own tendency would be to give the herbs a coarse chop. The more I cook with fresh herbs, the more I like to allow their individual shapes and personalities to make a statement in the dish. Coarse pieces of nearly raw sage, however, would be strong tasting and rough textured, so I would lightly toast that particular herb in the olive oil over low heat, then toss it with the carefully cooked pasta and the freshly and casually chopped oregano, parsley, and chives.

When you are chopping fresh herbs and are wondering when to stop, remember this: Coarsely chopped, the herbs will be visually exciting and their individual flavors will come forth distinctly and individually, but they will blend with other flavors more slowly and might distract from a smooth-textured dish. Finely chopped, the herbs will blend in quickly to achieve an integrated taste and unobtrusive texture, but they will lose some of their fresh appeal and identity.

*Chopping fresh herbs
with a chef's knife*

Chopping Fresh Herbs   The essential tool for chopping fresh herbs is a sharp chef's knife. If your knife is dull, you'll end up smashing and bruising the leaves instead of cutting them cleanly. They oxidize quickly, which means they discolor and the flavor will not be as clear. Take a few sprigs of lemon thyme and pound half of them with a mallet or the back of a knife to bruise the leaves. After ten minutes compare the scents. You'll notice the unbruised sprigs smell clean and bright, while the smashed sprigs have a muddier grassy scent.

Be sure your knife is free of a concave bow, which is caused by a poor sharpening job. Choose a large cutting board, either wood or plastic, so you don't need to worry about the herbs falling off the edge, and make sure the board is not warped. If there is not perfect contact between the knife and the board, some leaves will be scored rather than cut all the way through. If the cutting board slides on the counter, lay a damp cloth underneath to anchor it. Grasp the knife firmly with one hand, choking up and gripping the lower blade with your thumb and the top of your index finger for extra control, and place the extended fingers of your other hand over the front end of the blade to act as a pivot. Use the knife in a rocking motion, traveling with the blade to and fro. Don't be afraid to use a good amount of pressure and determination. The herbs will naturally spread out across the cutting board. Every once in a while, after a dozen chops or so, stop and use the side of the knife to scrape the material back into a pile.

Some cooks prefer to use a mezzaluna, or half-moon chopper, to chop herbs. This tool is specifically designed for chopping with its curved blade and vertical handles at either end. You hold both handles and rock the blade back and forth over the herbs. They work beautifully if they are sharp, but most aren't. It's very difficult to keep a good edge on these knives because you can't use a sharpening steel on the rounded blade. Once the blade is dull, you have the same problems of bruising instead of slicing that you have with a dull chef's knife, but if you're good with a sharpening stone or diligent about taking it to a skilled knife sharpener, a mezzaluna is a worthwhile tool.

Yes, you can use a food processor to chop fresh herbs, but it will never do as good a job as you can with a knife and board. You have little control over how fine the herbs are chopped, the pieces of leaf will end up in very uneven sizes, and they will often be smashed and halfway to pesto instead of cleanly cut. Unless you're chopping a huge quantity of herbs, mini processors are the preferred choice. The key is to keep a sharp blade. It's best to buy a second blade and reserve it exclusively for chopping herbs.

The type of cut that delivers large-leafed herbs, like basil, sorrel, or mint, into very thin strips is called chiffonade, and it's a good way to treat the herbs if you want an elegant cut where the leaf is still prominent, such as in salads, stirred into a light soup or sauce, or to sprinkle over a dish as a finishing touch. Remove the leaves from the stems and stack four to six leaves in a pile. Fold the pile in half, or if the leaves are large, roll them tightly in a bundle. Using a very sharp, thin-bladed knife, slice the leaves as thin as possible. If the leaves have thick center veins, as sorrel often does, cut them out with the tip of a paring knife

Cutting basil into chiffonade (thin strips)

before you stack them. You can also cut the leaves into thicker strips, about one-quarter inch wide, as I often do with sage before I toast it in butter or olive oil, or with basil for a tomato sauce.

If your knife skills are not yet at an accomplished level, use a pair of sharp scissors to cut strips from the leaves. Scissors are also handy for snipping chives—just hold a bunch that's about half an inch thick in your hand and cut them to whatever length you like.

To treat soft-leafed herbs in a very casual way, you can simply tear the leaves into large pieces. This works particularly well with basil, whose tender leaves are similar to lettuce and easily discolor, but you can treat other large-leafed herbs, like sorrel, perilla, dill, fennel, or mint, this way. It's perhaps the most satisfying way of handling a fresh herb; you just gently rip away—right into the dish if you like—and enjoy the fragrance.

Always chop, cut, snip, or tear your herbs just before using them. All those newly cut surfaces exposed to the air are likely to brown and the flavor will begin to dissipate, especially with herbs like lemon thyme, tarragon, and marjoram. If you end up chopping more than you can use, refrigerate the leftovers in a small cup tightly covered with plastic wrap and use them within a day. Or keep a jar of olive oil in the refrigerator and every time you have leftover robustly flavored herbs, like rosemary, thyme, sage, savory, or oregano, add them to the jar. You'll soon have a flavorful oil that's especially good for grilling.

MEASURING FRESH HERBS

To measure whole herbs, remove the stems, chop the leaves, then scoop the chopped leaves into the measuring spoon or cup and level the top. If you are measuring whole leaves or very coarsely chopped herbs, press them down gently. Because the strength of any particular herb varies, a little more or a little less will rarely hurt. If there's a pinch left on the cutting board after you measure, add it as well; if you end up with a fraction shy of the two tablespoons called for, just leave it out.

The finer you chop herb leaves, the less fluffy they will be, so that you will need to begin with more herb leaves to yield a finely chopped tablespoon than a coarsely chopped tablespoon.

- **Whole leaves**
  The herb leaves are stripped off the stem but left whole.

- **Very coarsely chopped**
  The herb leaves are not whole, yet they are in very large recognizable pieces. A mint or sage leaf might be cut into six, a tarragon leaf in three. The average-size piece of leaf will be one-half inch long.

- **Coarsely chopped**
  This is a medium chop—appropriate when you want the herbs to be prominent in the finished dish—and the way I most often chop herbs. An average-size piece of leaf will be between one-eighth and three-eighths inch long. Tiny leaves like thyme should be chopped just to the point where they are no longer whole.

- **Finely chopped**
  The leaves should be small enough that they can be easily sprinkled and will not be prominent in the dish or on your tongue. An average-size piece of leaf will be less than one-eighth inch long.

- **Very finely chopped**
  The herbs are as finely chopped as is possible with a knife.

- **Torn leaves**

  This is good for herbs with large leaves like basil, sorrel, and mint. Remove the stems and tear the leaves with your fingers into rough pieces about one-half inch square. Tear feathery herbs, like dill, fennel, and chervil, into bite-size pieces as you take them off the thick stems.

- **Snipped**

  This is most often done to chives. Hold a group of the grasslike leaves in one hand and use a pair of scissors to cut them into lengths about one-quarter inch long.

- **Fine strips (chiffonade)**

  This is another way to cut herbs with large leaves. First remove any thick center veins. Stack the leaves and roll them tightly in a bundle or fold the stack in half. Slice as thinly as you can with a sharp, thin-bladed knife.

- **Whole sprigs**

  The recipe should specify the approximate length of the sprigs. Use full, healthy sprigs. If the herbs are sparse and spindly, increase the quantity or length of the sprigs.

- **Small bunch**

  A small handful of sprigs, a little less than an inch in diameter, three to four inches long and about one-half ounce by weight.

- **Large bunch**

  A medium-size handful of sprigs, about 1½ inches in diameter and one ounce by weight.

ADJUSTING FOR STRENGTH

Fresh herbs vary in strength of flavor depending on their genetics, growing conditions, and freshness. A Greek oregano plant might have a fiery pungency or a mild bite depending on the stock plant it was propagated from. Winter tarragon grown in a greenhouse and fed high-nitrogen fertilizers will be very tame compared to a sprig picked in midsummer from a sun-baked plant grown in rocky soil. Lemon thyme snipped minutes ago from a pot on your deck will be bursting with perfume, while the lemon thyme from a package that's been in the supermarket for two weeks will have only a faint odor. So when a recipe calls for two tablespoons of chopped fresh oregano, tarragon, or lemon thyme, the impact of that amount of herb can vary drastically.

The measurements for the fresh herbs in the recipes that follow are for herbs that fall in the middle of this spectrum—neither particularly strong nor particularly weak. Sometimes you will need to adjust the quantity of a fresh herb specified in a recipe, not only to compensate for the variability of the herb itself but also for variables in other ingredients in the dish and for your own palate. Smell the herbs, nibble on their leaves, taste the food you're cooking. If you think an herb you are using smells especially powerful, don't hesitate to begin with less. If you prepare a recipe and the herbal flavors are not pronounced enough, add more.

When to Add Herbs

When you cook with dried herbs, you always add them at the beginning of the cooking process so that their flavor can release and blend into a dish. But cooking with fresh herbs is different. Much of the flavor in fresh herbs is carried by essential oils, which are volatile, meaning they dissipate into the air. When heated, these oils evaporate rapidly and with them some of the flavor. To capture their full vibrancy and subtlety, many fresh herbs need to be added at the last minute. There are some simple rules for knowing which herbs to add at what stage.

Robust-flavored herbs with tough-textured leaves that stay evergreen in the winter—rosemary, thyme, sage, and winter savory—can be added at any stage in the cooking. Their flavors are strong and stable enough to keep their character through long periods on the stovetop and grill, or in the oven, and it's no coincidence that these are the herbs that keep their flavor best when dried. Add to this short list the flower buds of lavender and green seeds of fennel and dill. When you introduce these herbs early on in a simmered dish, like a soup, sauce, or braise, the herbs will meld and mingle with the other ingredients and their flavors will become softer and less pronounced and blend into the background of the dish. But if you stir in the chopped leaves late in the cooking process, these same herbs will release intense, bright, or sharp flavors that come to the forefront, and their texture will be more noticeable. In the recipe for Braised Chicken with Leeks and Porcini (page 200), I toss bundles of fresh herb sprigs into the pot just before the long simmering, then when the chicken has finished cooking, I stir in handfuls of chopped herbs to finish the sauce. This builds layers of herb flavor, some in the background and some prominent.

These tough-leafed herbs also take well to cooking in oil or butter. In the recipe for Delicata Squash with Rosemary, Sage, and Cider Glaze (page 143), rosemary and sage are cooked in butter until they crisp, before the squash and cider are added to the pan. The herbs lose their toughness while they become toasty and nutty. The same thing happens to sage leaves when they are deep-fried as in the topping for Roasted Asparagus Salad with Fried Sage (page 54). In the Herb-Crusted Rack of Lamb (page 227), a heavy coat of chopped robust herbs is pressed onto the meat before it is seared in a very hot skillet with olive oil. The herbs take on a deeper aromatic quality while losing much of their astringency and fierceness. The herbs that are tossed with oil and baked on top of the Herbed Focaccia (page 234) also respond this way.

At the opposite end of the spectrum are herbs with soft leaves containing flavors that are very sensitive to heat. They include basil, chervil, chives, coriander, dill, lemon balm, lemon verbena, parsley, perilla, sorrel, and tarragon. In any soup, sauce, or simmered dish, these herbs are best stirred in at the last minute. Brief heating brings out their flavors, but as they cook longer, they become limp and lose color as well as their flavor and vitality. In the Lettuce and Tarragon Soup (page 20) the bright flavor of tarragon is captured by adding it to the soup after it's finished cooking and just before it is puréed in a blender. In the Fusilli Carbonara with Fines Herbes (page 106) the combination of parsley, tarragon, chervil, and chives is tossed with the hot pasta in a mixing bowl without any additional heat. The herbs in the Dilled Chicken Piccata (page 206) keep their prominent flavor because they are swirled in the sauce just before it's poured over the sautéed breast.

What remains are the herbs that are neither tough-leafed nor delicate but fall somewhere in between—lemon thyme, lovage, marjoram, mint, oregano, and summer savory. These herbs can take some degree of cooking and still keep flavor, but in very long-cooked dishes their essence comes through more clearly if they are added near the end. Simmered in a sauce for half an hour, their flavor will be integrated but still pronounced. Stirred in at the last minute, they will be bright and prominent. In Halibut Baked with Leeks, Apple, and Lovage (page 162), lovage is stirred into the ragout just before it is baked in the oven for ten minutes, allowing the celery flavor to permeate the mild fish. In the Asparagus and Mushroom Risotto with Lemon Thyme (page 122), the chopped lemon thyme is stirred in when the rice is fully cooked. A few moments in the steaming risotto are all that's needed to release its citrus intensity.

INFUSIONS

To capture the essence of the full, bright flavors of fresh herbs, I often steep the sprigs in a hot liquid. This technique is called infusion, and if you've ever brewed a cup of tea, you've already done it. The only difference is that instead of pouring the liquid over the herbs, I add the herbs to the liquid, which can be milk, cream, stock, juice, syrup, sauce, soup, even thick fruit purée. Bring the liquid to a simmer or boil, stir in the whole sprigs (washed but still on the stem), cover the pot, and remove it from the heat. Most of the flavor from the herbs will be extracted in the first ten minutes, but to get as much flavor as possible let the herbs steep for thirty minutes. Unlike tea, longer steeping will not bring out extra tannins or bitter and astringent flavors, so if you are not able to tend to it in time, the infusion can sit longer without changing the flavor. When the steeping time is up, pass the liquid through a strainer, or in the case of a thicker mixture like applesauce, put it through a food mill or push it through a sieve. The only herbs that don't transfer their flavor well in an infusion are the Umbelliferas like chervil, cilantro, dill, and fennel leaf.

Infusing is a great time-saving technique because virtually no effort is required to prepare the herbs, which are used in whole sprigs and strained out later. The herb flavors come through distinctly without being overbearing, and since none of the leaf texture remains, it's the most effective way to introduce herbal flavors into a dish with a completely smooth consistency. I'm especially fond of using herb-infused milk, cream, or sugar syrups in desserts, and you'll find many recipes in the dessert chapter, beginning on page 247.

CHOOSING AN HERB

The first house I grew up in had herb wallpaper in the kitchen. Bold fifties-style graphics spelled out the names of all the herbs that could be found in the kitchen cupboard, and below each name were listed the foods that the herb could be used in—marjoram for omelets, pot roast, and peas; sage for stuffing, meat loaf, and gravies; and tarragon for chicken fricassee, mushroom soup, and chowder. Quaintly retro, yes, but it was a very handy reference. After all, the question I'm most often asked is, "How do you know which herb to use in what dish?"

As in all pursuits, it's best to start with the classics. Take a look at familiar combinations of herbs and foods in cuisines worldwide. Tomatoes and basil from Italy, salmon and dill from Scandinavia, chicken and tarragon from France, lamb and mint from Great Britain, epazote and beans from Mexico, and cilantro and chiles from many parts of Asia are a few of these classic pairings. Each of these unions has become an integral part of their particular cuisine because the flavors make sense with each other and the two together transcend the individual elements. They are yours to borrow and integrate into your own cooking.

The key to successfully pairing herbs with other ingredients is to match and balance robust and delicate flavors. Unless the herbs are the focus of the dish, such as pasta with pesto sauce or a parsley salad, the flavor of the herbs should complement the other flavors in the recipe, not overpower them or disappear. The mild fresh flavor of poached halibut fillet will be smothered by a handful of rosemary, while a shower of tender chervil will exalt it. On the other hand, the gentle flavor of the chervil will be lost in a boldly flavored braise of lamb shanks, but rosemary will contribute a harmonious astringency and spice. Once you develop a sensitivity to how the intensities of flavor interact in a dish, it will be hard to make a mistake.

The recipes in this book, and the herbal options that follow them, will give you a basis with which to explore what herbs go best with what flavors, as well as the best techniques for incorporating them. In no time, you'll get a feel for how these flavors work together and how much of the herb to use. Not long thereafter you'll gain the knowledge and confidence to cook with herbs from your garden with as much ease as you add salt to a stew or spread mustard on a sandwich. The chart on pages 376–79 is an overview, just like my mother's wallpaper, that will help introduce fresh herbs to your kitchen.

DRYING HERBS

Some herbs keep a good deal of their flavor and personality when dried, but others don't. Forget trying to dry herbs that have soft leaves and elusive flavors, like basil, chervil, tarragon, and marjoram. Freeze them instead or preserve them in pestos or vinegars. Robust herbs with tough leaves, such as rosemary, sage, thyme, winter savory, and bay laurel, are the best candidates for drying, along with Greek oregano, lemon verbena, mint, and lavender buds. Although the flavors of these herbs change when they are dried, they remain strong and distinct. It's worth drying the harvest from your own garden because the herbs will be much fresher than the dried herbs you buy in the store and therefore more aromatic and flavorful.

Herbs will dry if you just leave them on the kitchen counter for a few days, but the best place to dry bunches of fresh herbs is a dark, well-ventilated, dry place, like an attic (the heat helps them dry faster) or shed. For the best flavor, harvest the herbs just before they bloom, while they are still in bud, because this is when they have the highest concentration of essential oils. Cut them in the cool of the day, early morning or late in the evening. Tie them in small bunches with kitchen twine and hang them upside down from rafters or any sort of hook. It will take just a few days to a week for them to become brittle, at which time you should strip the leaves and put them in airtight jars or canisters. Light will rob the herbs of flavor, so if you are storing them in jars, use dark glass if possible. If you use clear glass jars, keep them in a dark cupboard. Be sure to label and date the container. Dry herbs have the best flavor when used within 3 months. Always throw them away after 1 year.

FREEZING HERBS

Freezing is a good alternative to drying, especially for soft herbs that don't dry well, like tarragon and basil. If you simply put fresh herbs in a bag and throw them in the freezer, their flavor and texture will suffer terribly, but if you freeze the leaves in cubes of ice or purée them with oil to make a sort of pesto, they keep their flavor quite well. To freeze herbs in ice, stem and coarsely chop the leaves, then gently pack them in ice cube trays. Fill the trays with cold water and freeze. Store the cubes in freezer bags, where they'll keep their flavor for about 3 months. When making a sauce, soup, or braised dish, drop the cubes into the hot liquid just as you would add freshly chopped herbs, but take into account the extra water they add to the dish.

For freezing herbs I prefer to make an herb and oil purée—a sort of pesto without nuts, garlic, or cheese. I think it preserves a truer flavor than ice, and it's more versatile because it lends a stronger intensity of flavor to dishes without the extra water. It's also easier to prepare because you purée the herbs in a food processor instead of having to chop them by hand. To make the purée, stem the herbs and put the leaves in a food processor with about ¼ cup extra-virgin olive oil for each gently packed cup of the herb. Pulse until it forms a rough paste, then pack it into small resealable freezer bags and freeze. If you want to cook with only a small portion of the bag, it's easy to cut a piece from the frozen block. Stir the herb pastes into sauces, soups, or braised dishes, or blend them into dressings, marinades, dips, or spreads. The herbs that are most useful handled this way are basil, tarragon, marjoram, oregano, dill, and lovage.

Cooking with Fresh Herbs

FRESH HERB	PARTS USED	FLAVOR CHARACTERISTICS	AVERAGE AMOUNT OF CHOPPED LEAF FOR 6 SERVINGS
Angelica	stems, leaves	juniper, vanilla, celery	2 tablespoons, stem
Anise hyssop	leaves, flowers	sweet anise, mint	2 tablespoons
Basil, sweet	leaves, dried stems for smoking	cloves, mint, anise, cinnamon	½ cup
Bay laurel	leaves, stems for skewers	nutmeg, cardamom, vanilla	2 whole leaves
Chervil	leaves, flowers	mild anise	½ cup
Chives	leaves, flowers	onion	½ cup
Cilantro (coriander)	leaves, seeds	pungent, green, citrus.	½ cup
Dill	leaves, flowers, seeds	caraway, parsley	¼ cup
Fennel	leaves, flowers, seeds, stems for grilling or smoking	anise	¼ cup leaves, 1 teaspoon fresh seeds
Hyssop	leaves, flowers	astringent, camphor, thyme,	1 teaspoon
Lemon balm	leaves	lemon	¼ cup
Lemon verbena	leaves, stems for smoking	intense lemon	¼ cup
Lovage	leaves, stems	intense celery	1 tablespoon
Marjoram (and Italian oregano)	leaves, flower heads (knots)	mint, spice	2 tablespoons
Meadowsweet	flowers	honey	1 cup infused
Mexican tarragon	leaves, flowers	sweet anise	2 tablespoons

GOES WELL WITH	BEST HERBAL PARTNERS
rhubarb, oranges, ginger, almonds	lavender, rose geranium
peaches, nectarines, berries, apricots, melons	mint
tomatoes and other summer vegetables, fish, meat, poultry, potatoes, cheeses, garlic, summer fruits	chives, cilantro, fennel, lemon verbena, marjoram, mint, oregano, parsley, rosemary
meat, poultry, winter squashes, pumpkins, potatoes, dried beans, apples, pears, custards, dried fruits	parsley, rosemary, sage, thyme
fish, shellfish, chicken, peas, carrots, squashes, fresh tomatoes, eggs	chives, parsley
all vegetables, eggs, chicken, potatoes, cheeses	chervil, dill, marjoram, parsley, sorrel, tarragon
seafood, meat, chicken, carrots, avocadoes, corn, cucumbers, tomatoes, chiles, citrus	basil, chives, lemon verbena, mint, parsley
chicken, fish, beef, asparagus, beans, beets, carrots, cabbages, corn, cucumbers, mushrooms, onions, tomatoes, breads, eggs, cheeses	chives, lemon balm, lemon thyme, lovage
seafood, chicken, lamb, pork, beets, carrots, tomatoes, eggplants, peppers, onions, garlic, peaches	lavender, mint, parsley, rosemary, thyme
beans, beef, lamb, cabbages, carrots, beets, tomatoes	parsley, rosemary, thyme
fish, carrots, beets, peas, cucumbers, asparagus, citrus, ginger, fruits, berries	basil, chives, dill, mint, parsley
fish, carrots, beets, chiles, ginger, citrus, fruits, berries	basil, cilantro, lavender, mint, rose geranium
fish, clams, mussels, chicken, spinach and other greens, carrots, corn, tomatoes	chives, dill, lemon balm, mint, parsley, sorrel
fish, shellfish, meat, poultry, eggs, beans, carrots, beets, corn, eggplants, garlic, mushrooms, spinach, summer squashes, tomatoes	basil, chives, mint, parsley, rosemary, sage, savory, thyme
custard, honey, vanilla, apricots, cherries, peaches, figs	
fish, shellfish, peaches, berries, melons, apricots	lemon verbena

FRESH HERB	PARTS USED	FLAVOR CHARACTERISTICS	AVERAGE AMOUNT OF CHOPPED LEAF FOR 6 SERVINGS
Mint (spearmint)	leaves	menthol, fruit	¼ cup
Oregano (Greek)	leaves	pepper and spice	2 tablespoons
Parsley	leaves	pungent green	¼ cup
Perilla	leaves	parsley, cumin, cinnamon	2 tablespoons
Rosemary	leaves, flowers, stems for smoking and skewers	pine, pungent spice	2 tablespoons
Sage	leaves, flowers, stems for skewers	spice, astringent	2 tablespoons
Savory	leaves	pepper, spice	2 tablespoons
Scented geranium, rose	leaves, flowers	strong rose	8 leaves infused
Sorrel	leaves	sour, green	½ cup
Sweet cicely	leaves, flowers, seeds, roots	mild anise, green	¼ cup leaves
Tarragon, French	leaves	peppery anise	2 tablespoons
Thyme, English	leaves, flowers	pungent spice, fruit, pear	2 tablespoons
Thyme, lemon	leaves, flowers	pungent lemon	2 tablespoons

GOES WELL WITH	BEST HERBAL PARTNERS
fish, shellfish, meat, poultry, beets, carrots, cucumbers, eggplants, garlic, lettuces, peas, potatoes, summer squashes, chiles, tomatoes, fruits, ginger, chocolate	all other herbs
tomatoes, summer squashes, eggplants, peppers, beef, lamb, oily fish, squid, garlic, citrus, olives, capers, anchovies	basil, chives, mint, parsley, rosemary, sage, savory, thyme
all vegetables, meat, seafood, eggs, cheeses	basil, chervil, chives, dill, fennel, hyssop, lavender, lemon balm, lovage, marjoram, mint, oregano, rosemary, sage, savory, sorrel, tarragon, thyme
salads, seafood, apples, pears	chives, lemon balm, lemon verbena
meat, poultry, shrimp, mussels, tuna, swordfish, eggplants, tomatoes, peppers, onions, garlic, beans, potatoes, breads, citrus, apples, pears	basil, chives, fennel, hyssop, lavender, lemon verbena, marjoram, mint, oregano, parsley, sage, savory, thyme
meat, poultry, shellfish, oily fish, asparagus, beans, corn, onions, garlic, potatoes, winter squashes, mushrooms, pumpkin, citrus, garlic, apples, cherries, blueberries	fennel, lavender, lemon balm, lemon thyme, lemon verbena, lovage, mint, oregano, parsley, rosemary, savory, thyme
meat, poultry, beans, cabbages, beets eggplants, peppers, onions, potatoes, kale, summer squashes	chives, fennel, mint, parsley, rosemary, sage, thyme
berries, apples, cherries, peaches, apricots, plums, rhubarb, custard and ice cream, chocolate, ginger, citrus	lavender, lemon verbena, mint
fish, shellfish, salads, eggs, spinach and other greens	chives, dill, lemon thyme, lemon verbena, lovage, mint, parsley, tarragon
most fruits	lemon verbena, mint
all seafood, meat, poultry, eggs, asparagus, beans, beets, carrots, fennel bulb, peas, summer squashes, tomatoes	chervil, chives, lemon balm, lemon thyme, mint, parsley, sorrel
all seafood, meat, poultry, eggs, vegetables, apples, pears, cranberries, dried fruits	bay, basil, chives, dill, fennel, hyssop, lavender, lemon verbena, lovage, marjoram, mint, oregano, parsley, rosemary, sage, savory
all seafood, meat, poultry, eggs, vegetables, fruits	bay, basil, chives, dill, fennel, hyssop, lavender, lemon verbena, lovage, marjoram, mint, oregano, parsley, rosemary, sage, savory

CHAPTER 16

The Herbs: A Roll Call

ANGELICA

A giant of the herb garden, this biennial in the parsley family starts as a well-behaved clump of long tubular stalks that branch out near their tops into forks of smaller branches holding flat deep green leaves. In winter it withers away, but it comes back the next spring with boundless vigor, quickly taking the same shape it had the previous fall. Then in late spring or early summer, out shoot great purple-tinged flower stalks that reach seven feet without effort and are riveting focal points of the herb garden. Large flat clusters of greenish yellow flowers, arranged like exploding fireworks, open at the top, and they in turn become umbels of small green seeds. Once angelica sets its seed, the mighty plant will turn brown and die, but the seeds will likely germinate at its feet, and the new generation might be ready to bloom the following year.

Cooking with Angelica All parts of this plant—root, stem, leaf, and seed—have uses, from cosmetic to culinary to medicinal, but the stems are the most useful for cooking. They have a unique smell, very green and musky, with elements of sweet vanilla, juniper, anise, and celery, and an underlying bitter edge. Most common are the candied stems. When homemade, they turn out as slightly fibrous sticks of sparkling green confection with a distinct and strangely enticing flavor (see recipe, page 314). They can be eaten as a candy at the end of a meal, cut into shapes to garnish desserts, or chopped and added to ice creams or mousses. Commercial candied angelica has little to recommend it, so if that's all you've tasted, try the homemade. The thick taproots of angelica can be candied as well, but they are bittersweet and an acquired taste.

Angelica stems and leaves can be steeped in milk or cream and the strained flavored milk or cream turned into ice cream or custard. I especially like steeping angelica with a few coins of fresh ginger for added flavor. It's traditional to add angelica when cooking tart fruits because it lessens the amount of sugar needed to sweeten them. Rhubarb and angelica is a classic combination—the two strange plants have an uncanny affinity. When cooked together, the flavors have so much in common that you can't really distinguish the angelica flavor, but the rhubarb will seem less tart and astringent and somehow taste more intensely of rhubarb (see Rhubarb and Angelica Pie, page 283).

Growing Angelica Angelica is native to northern regions, including Iceland and Scandinavia. In a hot climate, growing angelica will be a struggle, but in places where the summers are mild, angelica will thrive. All it will require in addition is well-drained soil and plenty of room to spread and soar. Angelica seeds lose their viability very quickly.

They sprout easily when they have just fallen from their mother plant but often will not germinate if you sow them the following spring. It's a good idea to buy your first plant in a pot. It will grow in sun or part shade and in dry or moist soil.

Harvesting Angelica Cut off the hollow stems all the way down to ground level. Tender young stems and leaves with bright green color have the best flavor; yellowed stems tend to be tough. Those that form in the late summer of the first season or the spring of the second season, before the plant blooms, are the best to use for candied angelica stems. If you cut off the flower stalks at the base of the plant before the flowers open, the plant will sometimes live for a third year.

Storing Angelica Keep angelica stems and leaves in a resealable plastic bag in the vegetable crisper of your refrigerator. They will stay fresh for over one week. (Candied angelica stems can be stored up to six months.)

ANISE HYSSOP

Even if anise hyssop were odorless and inedible, it would be worth growing just for its maroon-tinged spear-shaped leaves and its stunning spikes of feathery vivid purple-blue blossoms. But it smells like heaven and tastes like candy. Rub the sprigs between your fingers and smell the fruity perfume that is like a cross between licorice and mint. The real surprise comes with nibbling a leaf. Many herbs are like unsweetened chocolate; they smell sweet, but eaten on their own, the leaves taste strong and bitter. Anise hyssop is an exception—it has a distinct and almost startling natural sweetness.

Anise hyssop, *Agastache foeniculum,* is always a cause of confusion because it belongs to a separate genus from both anise and hyssop, although it does smell like the former and its flower resembles that of the latter. This perennial belonging to the mint family has an upright habit with slender square stems growing to three feet or taller, and reaches its peak of bloom in midsummer. The most delicious parts of the plant are the tender leaf tips just as they begin to form tiny purple buds in the center, but all parts of the plant are flavorful.

Cooking with Anise Hyssop Because anise hyssop is so sweet, it's most useful in desserts or beverages. By steeping it in milk or cream, it lends an out-of-this-world flavor to ice creams and custards (page 260), and it's a natural partner for summer fruits, especially peaches, nectarines, apricots, and berries. For a real treat, serve custard sauce or whipped cream flavored with anise hyssop with fresh raspberries or warm peach crisp. Macerate fresh fruit or sweeten fruit sorbet with sugar syrup steeped with the herb (page 249). Anise hyssop in full flower will tinge the syrup a delicate pink. Toss the sprigs into the poaching syrup for stone fruit like peaches (page 268) or apricots. In place of a mint sprig garnish for a dessert, use a small purple-topped sprig or leaf of anise hyssop; it not only looks more interesting but also tastes better.

Anise hyssop can add a vibrant flavor to salads. Tuck a few tips into a mixed green salad or add the chopped leaves to a dressing for fennel bulb and orange salad. Blend the chopped leaves into a citrusy dressing for mixed fruit salad, or steep the leaves in warm honey and drizzle it over fresh fruit or berries.

Growing Anise Hyssop   Grow anise hyssop in rich, moist, well-drained soil and give it full sun. Pinch back leaf tips when plants are young to encourage branching. Once the plants finish blooming, cut them back by half to try for a second late-season bloom. Anise hyssop dies back to the ground in winter and should remain perennial to Zone 6 (winter low of −10°F). An overly wet winter can cause the roots to rot so that you may have to replant it in the spring.

Harvesting Anise Hyssop   Cut anise hyssop sprigs right above a leaf joint, no more than halfway down the stem. They have the strongest flavor when they are in bud or in the early stages of blooming.

Storing Anise Hyssop   Keep anise hyssop sprigs in a resealable plastic bag in the vegetable crisper of your refrigerator. They will stay fresh for up to one week.

Anise Hyssop Relatives   *Agastache rugosa,* or Korean mint, is a related plant with smaller leaves, a bushier habit, and lipstick-pink blossoms held more sparsely on the stem. Its flavor leans a little more toward mint than anise hyssop's but the two can be used interchangeably.

Other varieties of *Agastache,* such as Firebird, Apricot Sunrise, and Tutti-Frutti, are grown mainly as ornamentals. Though still edible, their flavor is less aniselike and more minty. There is another species called Mexican giant hyssop—a tender plant that grows to seven feet—which can be lemon or mint scented.

BASIL

It's hard to imagine summer without fresh basil, for its spicy, vibrant scent captures the season. Sweet basil is the bestseller on The Herbfarm's plant list and would come in at the top on any herb popularity contest.

There are more than 150 species of basil and many individual strains and hybrids, but most culinary basils are varieties of the species *Ocimum basilicum.* These vary in form from six-inch mounds of globe basil with tiny half-inch leaves to varieties with giant six-inch leaves. The foliage can be light green, deep green, burgundy red, or a combination. The type we mean when we say simply "basil" is called sweet basil. It's a tender, heat-loving annual, happy in the vegetable or herb garden, that grows two to three feet tall and about one and one-half feet wide with oval leaves one to two inches long. When the plant matures, it sends out flower spikes that carry rows of tiny white flowers. Sweet basil's fragrance is complex, sweet, and spicy. Each time you sniff or nibble, different elements will reveal themselves. First you might smell clove, then anise, cinnamon, citrus, a good dose of mint, and underneath it all a camphor or resinous fragrance that is common to Mediterranean herbs such as rosemary and marjoram. In special varieties of basil like cinnamon basil, licorice basil, lemon basil, and camphor basil one of these elements is predominant.

Cooking with Basil   Basil is so versatile with so many facets to its flavor that it's the only herb The Herbfarm Restaurant honors with its own menu. Each summer we present the

Basil Banquet, where each of the nine courses is prepared with some variety of the herb. We toss it in salads and chowders, use the leaves for fritters and wrappers, pound it for pesto, bake it in bread, poach it with peaches, burn it in the smoker, and steep it in cream for ice cream and white chocolate truffles.

Basil rarely overpowers, so use it generously and casually. Most important to keep in mind is because it loses flavor as it cooks, it's always best to add it near the end of the cooking process. Start by exploring how basil flavors summer vegetables. Toss the torn leaves into sautéed zucchini, glazed carrots, steamed green beans, roasted red pepper salad, eggplant ragout, or corn chowder. For an unforgettable summer treat, slather corn on the cob with basil butter. Small basil leaves make delightful accents in mixed green salads, and you can whisk chopped basil into vinaigrettes or creamy salad dressings.

Basil's spicy anise and clove flavors marry perfectly with a ripe tomato's tangy smack. The two make a venerable flavor combination. Tear basil leaves into a barely cooked tomato sauce for pasta and infuse them in fresh tomato soup. Make a salad of ripe tomatoes layered with fresh mozzarella and whole basil leaves, and stir the leaves into a marinade for a grilled or roasted tomato. Stir chopped basil into tomato-based braises, stews, and ratatouille just before serving for a fresh kick of flavor.

Depending on what it is paired with and how much is used, basil's flavor can be delicate or bold. It can be mild enough for an omelet or butter sauce for poached fish, or bold enough to ally with hot chiles, ginger, and citrus as it does in many Asian dishes. Add whole leaves to sandwiches, instead of sprouts or lettuce; layer them on a roasted vegetable or submarine sandwich or melt them with the cheese in a grilled cheese sandwich. Basil combines well with a long list of other herbs—chives, cilantro, fennel, lemon verbena, marjoram, mint, parsley, oregano, rosemary—and its pungent fragrance is always a good match with garlic.

Pounded with garlic, olive oil, Parmesan or pecorino cheese, and pine nuts, basil turns into pesto, the most sublime of all herb sauces (page 102). This mixture is not only a peerless combination of ingredients but also the best way to preserve the complex flavor of the herb, because it will keep for a month in the refrigerator or up to six months in the freezer. Pesto has many uses beyond pasta sauce; it can sauce a grilled fish, top a baked potato, enrich a bean soup, or replace tomato sauce on pizza.

In desserts, basil's clove and mint flavors pair well with summer fruits like peaches, apricots, raspberries, or blueberries. Infuse sugar syrup with basil to macerate fruit, or steep milk or cream with the herb to make a custard sauce or ice cream to accompany a fruit tart or shortcake. Add chopped basil leaves to a fruit filling for turnovers or to a fruit crisp or cobbler. A small amount of fresh ginger, cinnamon, or anise added to any of these desserts will further amplify basil's own sweet spice.

Basil leaves are very sensitive to bruising and they turn black easily. To prevent this, you'll sometimes hear that you must tear the leaves rather than touch them with the blade of a knife, in the same way lettuce is usually torn for salads instead of cut. I feel both are appropriate. Tearing is best if you want larger pieces of the leaves in your dish, as in a salad or a rustic tomato sauce. If you want smaller pieces of leaf, chop it with a very sharp stainless-steel chef's knife (carbon steel will discolor it). First gather all the leaves in a tight bundle—they don't have to face the same direction—and slice them into strips. Then use the knife with a rocking motion and chop the strips. Basil is rarely chopped very fine because it ends up looking like pesto. For a chiffonade (thin strips), stack about 6 leaves, roll the pile up tightly, and cut very fine strips with a sharp thin knife. Whether you tear basil or chop it with a stainless-steel knife, it will blacken as it sits, but once added to your dish, the off-color is rarely noticeable.

Basil Varieties   Sweet basil is the generic name for *Ocimum basilicum,* but there are many seed strains with subtle differences in flavor or growth. Most garden centers or commercial growers don't specify exactly what strain they grow, but if you start your own basil from seed, you'll find packets for distinct strains in specialty seed catalogues, many of which are imported from Italy. Genovese has smooth medium-small leaves, a clove scent, and is excellent for pesto. Neopoletano and Italian Large Leaf have sweetly flavored, large, crinkled leaves.

You will always want to grow plenty of sweet basil in your garden, but if you have room, try some of the other varieties with their own distinct characteristics.

Opal and Purple Ruffles Basil   Sometimes grown for their ornamental qualities alone, these varieties of basil have beautiful mahogany-colored leaves and a flavor similar to green sweet basil. They are most useful in the kitchen for their color in salads, as a garnish, or to turn a vinegar dusty pink. The leaves turn dark green when exposed to heat. Opal basil has smooth leaves about one inch long, and purple ruffled basil has larger leaves with crinkled edges.

Lettuce Leaf and Mammoth Basil   These varieties produce huge leaves up to six inches long. Their flavor is not always as spicy as the smaller-leafed varieties, but they offer all kinds of possibilities for stuffing or wrapping. Because the leaves are so big, it's often thought that the yield from these types of basil is greater; however, I find it turns out to be about the same because smaller leafed varieties produce many more leaves. In any case, it takes half the time to remove their stems, which can be an advantage when you are making quantities of pesto.

Cinnamon Basil   This is a beautiful plant with red stems, showy red flower bracts, and pointy green leaves that have a distinct spicy cinnamon scent. It's good with tomatoes and poultry and infused in custards and ice cream (page 256) or desserts with summer fruits like peaches or blueberries.

Thai Basil   Sometimes called licorice or anise basil, this plant is similar to cinnamon basil with red stems and slender leaves, but it has a pronounced anise flavor that works well with seafood. It's used extensively in the cooking of Southeast Asia.

Lemon Basil   Lemon basil looks quite different from all its cousins. It bears small slender leaves on less vigorous, low-growing plants. Its subtle basil flavor underscores a pronounced lemon bouquet. Use it with seafood or in desserts with berries or apricots.

Bush or Globe Basil   Also called Fino Verde or Piccolo, these varieties grow into compact mounds about six to twelve inches tall with very fine, closely placed leaves. The flavor varies according to variety; some are very much like sweet basil and some have more pronounced clove or anise flavors.

Anise Hyssop
(Agastache foeniculum)

Sweet Basil
(Ocimum basilicum)

Cinnamon Basil
(Ocimum basilicum
'Cinnamon')

Purple Ruffles Basil
(Ocimum basilicum
'Purple Ruffles')

Bay Laurel
(Laurus nobilis)

Chives
(*Allium schoenoprasum*)

Fennel
(Foeniculum vulgare)

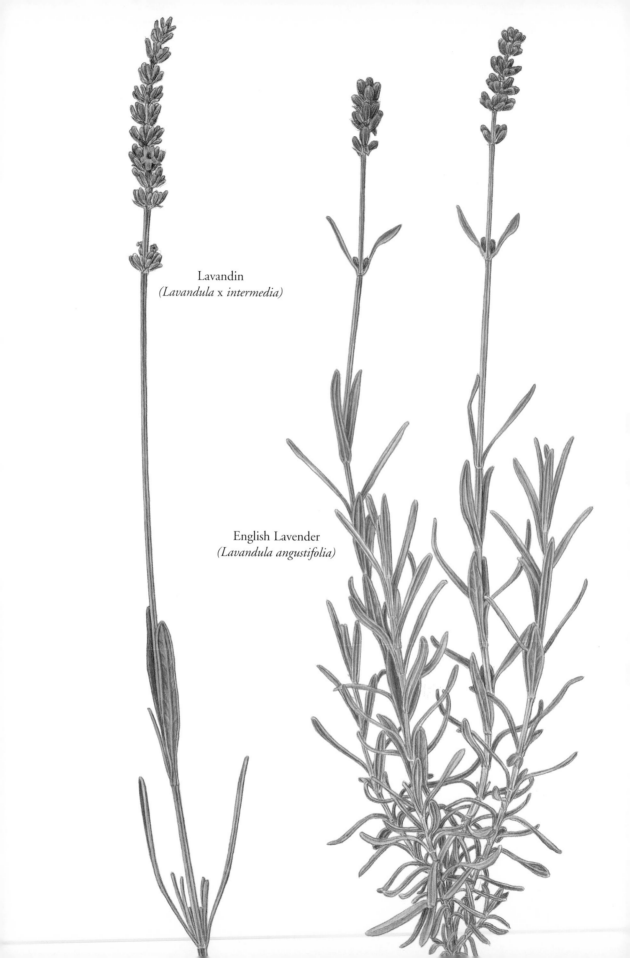

Lavandin
(Lavandula x *intermedia)*

English Lavender
(Lavandula angustifolia)

Lemon Verbena
(Aloysia triphylla)

Lovage
(Levisticum officinale)

Apple Mint
(Mentha suaveolens)

Chocolate Mint
(Mentha x *piperita piperita)*

Spearmint
(Mentha spicata)

Greek Oregano
(Origanum vulgare subsp. *hirtum)*

Sweet Marjoram
Origanum majorana

Red Perilla
(Perilla frutescens 'Atropurpurea'*)*

Perilla
(Perilla frutescens)

Rosemary
(Rosmarinus officinalis)

Garden Sage
(Salvia officinalis)

Garden Sorrel
(Rumex acetosa)

Buckler Sorrel
(Rumex scutatus)

French Tarragon
(Artemesia dracunculus var. *sativa)*

English Thyme
(Thymus vulgaris)

Lemon Thyme
(Thymus x *citriodorus)*

Holy Basil   The original basil from India, this fine-leafed tender perennial has a strong camphoric quality and is rarely used in the kitchen.

African Blue Basil   This vividly marked purple and green plant is a cross between opal basil and the nonculinary African camphor basil. It's a tender perennial with beautiful flower spikes and one of the best basil candidates to grow indoors in the winter. Its flavor is okay for cooking if that's all you have, but it retains some camphoric flavors. Use it as you would opal basil, especially as a garnish. African cinnamon basil is similar, but it has light green leaves and a strong but pleasant cinnamon flavor.

Growing Basil   Basil is widely planted in home gardens because it's fast growing, high yielding, and very rewarding. You can start it from seed outside once the soil warms or get a headstart and sow the seeds indoors in small pots or paper cups on a sunny windowsill. Easiest of all, you can buy seedlings or young plants at a garden center. Six basil plants will be enough for a small family, but plant more if you want to make big batches of pesto to freeze.

Basil loves heat. Wait until the nighttime temperatures stay above 50°F before you transplant it outdoors. In the Pacific Northwest, with our cool wet springs, anxious herb gardeners often plant basil too early, which sets the plants back so much that they never recover, even when the weather finally warms. Give it average soil, plenty of water, and as much sun as you can. Basil differs from other Mediterranean herbs in that it dislikes poor dry conditions. Soil that is too rich, however, will result in fewer essential oils and a weaker flavor and fragrance.

Although basil is generally disease free, a serious fungus disease called fusarium wilt has become a problem in North America. Though the disease is associated with tomatoes, this new strain specifically attacks basil. The pathogen turns the leaves black and will kill an otherwise healthy basil crop in weeks. We had an entire field wiped out by it at The Herbfarm several years ago. The disease infects the soil that the basil grows in, but it is usually transmitted through the seed. New varieties are being bred with resistance to the disease, but until they are available, the best protection is to purchase seeds that have been tested to be free of contamination (it will say on the package). If your plants do become infected, pull them up and throw them in the trash, not the compost heap, and plant your next crop of basil as far from that spot as you can.

Harvesting Basil   When you harvest basil, don't cut more than half the plant at once and always cut right above a leaf pair. It's better to cut short stems off the whole plant than to cut one or two long stems. Even if you don't need them for the kitchen, keep pinching the tips of the basil to promote bushiness. To prolong the life of the plant through the growing season, don't let your basil flower. As it forms flower spikes it will grow lanky, and once it sets seed it will begin to die off. As soon as you see buds start to form at the tips of the leaves, snip off the top of the stem at the leaf junction just below them. Although basil buds and flowers are edible, they are coarse textured and not as aromatic as the leaves.

Storing Basil   Basil can be tricky to store because it blackens if too cold and wilts if too warm. The ideal temperature is about 50°F, which is warmer than your refrigerator and cooler than most kitchens. I always have success if I pack the sprigs loosely in heavy resealable plastic bags and keep them in the vegetable crisper in my refrigerator. If the basil was just picked and the leaves were dry, it keeps for about a week. If you plan on using the basil within a day or two, you can treat the sprigs like cut flowers and stand them in a pitcher of water on the counter.

When the weather turns chilly, your basil will be the first thing in the garden to turn black and wither. As soon as this happens, gather the stems and hang them in a protected spot to dry. The hardened aromatic stems can be used in place of wood chips in a smoker or on the barbecue (see the recipe for Herb-Smoked Salmon, page 181). They give off an incomparable savory smoke flavor that is much subtler than hardwood.

BAY

If you've never smelled a fresh bay leaf, your first sniff will be a revelation. Tear the leathery green leaf in half, crush it in your hand, and take in its fragrance. It has a surprisingly sweet and refreshing pungency, heavy with the scent of nutmeg and cardamom and punctuated by layers of vanilla, lemon, and pine. It's very different from the vague flavor of the brittle dried bay leaves in nearly every cook's cupboard. When bay leaves dry, their ethereal characteristics are lost, leaving behind only a one-dimensional ghost of the flavor. You can always substitute the fresh leaves for dried, but you can't necessarily substitute dried for fresh.

Seasonings that come from trees are usually tagged as spices, but bay leaves are an exception, coming from laurel trees but most often considered an herb. Culinary bay, *Laurus nobilis,* is a broadleaf evergreen that looks something like a camellia bush with its shiny deep green leaves. In a mild climate, like that of the Pacific Northwest, they're marginally hardy and can grow to ten feet or more outdoors, but in subtropical areas they might grow to sixty feet. In any case, one mature plant will provide more bay leaves than you can ever dream of using. If you live where you can't winter over rosemary, the bay tree, too, will perish outside, but you can keep it as a potted plant and give it shelter through the cold months.

The bay we are talking about, *Laurus nobilis,* is often called bay laurel and sometimes Turkish bay or sweet bay (although sweet bay can also refer to a species of magnolia). When purchasing fresh bay, you must be aware of another plant belonging to a different genus called California bay, *Umbellularia californica.* The leaves of this very large tree are similar but skinnier and grayer, and their smell is strong and camphoric with little sweetness. Leaves of California bay are often erroneously sold as a culinary herb, but they should not be eaten, for apart from their severe flavor, they contain umbellulone, a serious toxin. Bay leaf wreaths are often made of California bay.

Cooking with Fresh Bay Leaves   Most cooks already know how to use bay laurel leaves in stews, soups, and braises. The leaves release their flavor slowly, and two or three thrown into a pot will gradually contribute their background flavor to the dish. Too many dried leaves will make food taste acrid and unpleasant, but fresh bay leaves can be added in greater quantities, depending on how distinctly you want their flavor to come through. Before using them, crack the leaves open by holding a small stack with both hands and twisting in two or three places. This allows them to release their scent more effectively. If you wish, you can crush them further by rolling them between your palms. But as with the dried leaves, you don't want to eat the leaf itself—remove them after they have imparted their flavor. The exception is when the leaves are ground very fine in a spice mill as in the herb rub for duck (page 211).

One of my favorite ways to use fresh bay leaves is to stuff them under the skin of chicken, pheasant, or turkey before roasting. You loosen the skin of the bird, crack the leaves, and insert eight or ten between skin and flesh, then roast the bird as usual. They'll infuse the meat inside and out with their distinct and sublime flavor (the recipe is on page 196). Likewise you can insert fresh bay leaves into slits cut in pork, veal, or lamb roasts before they go in the oven. If you have a large bay tree, cut whole branches and use them as a bed on which to rest the meat as it roasts or grills. For skewers, spear the leaves between chunks of swordfish, tuna, chicken, or pork on kabobs, or use the stiff branches themselves as skewers. Bay leaves are essential in any stock, stew, or braise and are an important element in a bouquet garni. When you use fresh leaves, you can double the quantity you would normally use of dry.

Also try the sweet spice of bay leaves with vegetables. To roast a winter squash or pumpkin, cut it open, brush it with butter, and lay broken fresh bay leaves on the flesh before it goes in the oven. Add several cracked fresh bay leaves to the milk for a simple white sauce for cauliflower, creamed spinach, or old-fashioned macaroni and cheese, or add them to the water for making polenta, steaming summer squash, or boiling corn or potatoes.

Most of all, fresh bay leaves are a fabulous flavoring for desserts. This seemingly offbeat use of the herb is not a trendy experiment; in Europe bay leaves were long used to flavor custards and other sweets before vanilla beans were commonplace and are still often used in rice pudding. They add a warm sweet spice. Try Bay Leaf Crème Brûlée (page 260) or make bay-flavored ice cream or custard sauce to accompany desserts with caramel, nuts, fall fruits like apples or pears, and dried prunes, dates, or figs. Add the leaves directly to a simmering applesauce, the poaching liquid for pears, or the syrup for a fall fruit compote, then remove them before serving.

Fresh bay leaves have another confectionery use. The leathery foliage is ideal for molding chocolate leaves. Apply two coats of tempered chocolate with a paintbrush to the leaf's undersides, chill, and then peel off the green leaf. Use the chocolate leaves to garnish cakes, tarts and other desserts.

Growing Bay Laurel Bay trees are notoriously hard to propagate and grow very slowly when young, so potted plants for sale in nurseries are more expensive than other herbs and usually very small. If you live in a Mediterranean-like climate, such as the California coast, you can plant your tree directly in the ground. If you garden in Zone 8 (low to 10°F), it's best to grow the plant in a clay pot until it gets about two feet high and forms woody stems that can withstand cold weather. Until then, shelter it when the temperature dips into the 20s. When you keep it in a pot for the first year or two it will give you a chance to move it around and discover a spot where it will thrive. Bay trees like sun, but their leaves can burn if it's too fierce. Good drainage is essential, but they like fertile moist soil. Never let the plant dry out completely. Once you plant the tree in the ground and it establishes a good root system, it can withstand some frost damage and still recuperate.

If you live where the thermometer is likely to drop below 10°F in the winter, you'll have to keep your tree in a permanent container and bring it indoors in the winter. Like a rosemary plant, it will do best in a cool sun porch or near a well-ventilated window with plenty of bright sun. Gradually acclimate it to the outside again as soon as night temperatures stay above 32°F. Bay is very susceptible to scale, mealy bugs, and aphids while living indoors. Inspect the plants often and remove pests by hand.

Harvesting Bay Laurel   The best way to harvest individual leaves is to pull them off one by one with a sharp downward tug. You'll see a little growth tip where the leaf stem meets the branch that will form a new leaf or branch after the leaf is pulled. Only harvest leaves that have matured and turned leathery; the softer young leaves are not as flavorful. If you have a mature bay tree that needs pruning, harvest whole branches, shaping the plant as you wish.

Storing Bay Laurel   You can occasionally find fresh bay leaves sold in farmers' markets or with other fresh herbs in produce sections, but it's a shame that they are not more widely available because they keep longer than any other fresh herb I know of. Stored in a resealable plastic bag in the vegetable crisper, they'll literally last for months with little flavor loss. You can freeze them sealed in a bag, like kaffir lime leaves are frozen, but I find they lose flavor and it's pointless since they last so long in the refrigerator.

If you want to dry the leaves for longer storage, remove them from the stems and spread them on a screen in a dark and well-ventilated spot. As soon as they are crisp, store them in a tightly covered jar. Dried bay leaves are good in stocks, stews, and braises, but they lose much of their flavor in six months to a year, at which point they should be discarded.

CHERVIL

Everything about chervil is delicate. Its flavor is subtle and only hints at anise and parsley; its leaves are thin, soft, and a gentle green color; and it's very frail—in the garden it's temperamental about climate, and once cut, it wilts at the slightest suggestion of discomfort.

Resembling its parsley cousin, chervil, *Anthriscus cerefolium,* is a short-lived annual that looks like a small lacy fern, growing from six to eighteen inches tall in cool dappled shade. Chervil's flavor is a cross between tarragon and parsley, but much more subdued than either, with a sweet, fresh, light quality, making it the quintessential spring herb. Unfortunately, unless you grow this dainty plant yourself, it will be very hard to get hold of. Because it's so perishable after it's cut, you very rarely see chervil in supermarkets except in a dried form that has less flavor than a peat pot. If you can't grow it outdoors, it's worth trying to grow it on a cool, bright windowsill.

Cooking with Chervil   Naturally, this delicate herb is best paired with delicate foods. It provides the perfect subtle complement to seafood like lobster, crab, oysters, scallops, sole, and halibut, white-fleshed birds, such as young chicken and guinea fowl, and delicate vegetables, such as peas and young carrots. Instead of parsley, garnish a dish with chervil. In place of parsley sprigs, pinch off small bunches of chervil sprigs. As a substitute for chopped parsley, hold a bunch of chervil over the dish and snip it in small pieces with a pair of scissors, letting it fall in a casual way. Shower it over salads, steamed beets, and freshly picked asparagus. Pack it in a blender and whirl it up with a salad dressing or a hot butter sauce. Its soft flavor and texture is especially good with eggs; add a tablespoon or so of chopped leaves to softly scrambled eggs or a simple omelet.

Chervil's lacy white flowers have a delicate texture and flavor similar to the leaves. You can chop these blossoms with the leaves, add them to a salad, or toss them on a finished dish as garnish.

Use chervil with abandon, for a finely minced teaspoon will get you nowhere. From two tablespoons to one-quarter cup is a good starting point for six servings. However, chervil exposed to heat for any length of time will turn drab and flavorless, so always add the leaves to foods at the very last minute. Fragile chervil cannot stand the heat—in the garden or in the saucepan.

Chervil Varieties   You usually won't find anything more specific than plants or seeds labeled Chervil, but sometimes you find seeds offered for a variety called Curled Chervil, whose leaves are slightly more frilled, like those of curly parsley.

Growing Chervil   Chervil is very easy to grow from seed, and because it has delicate taproots that are difficult to transplant, it's best sown where you want it to grow. You can begin planting several weeks before the last frost. It likes rich, moist, and well-drained soil in partial shade, and prefers the cool weather of spring and autumn. In summer, try sowing it in among taller herbs or vegetables that will provide shade. Chervil has a rather short life span. It matures in six to eight weeks, but once it flowers its days are numbered. When the plant is old or stressed, its leaves turn purple or yellow and toughen and lose flavor. Cut off the flowering stems to prolong productivity. If you want a constant supply of chervil, you should sow it successively—a little every three weeks through the season. When it's very happy with its home, it might self-sow, and you can have it year after year if you're not an obsessive weeder. It's an herb you'll want to use freely, so don't just put a few plants in the garden, grow a small bed of it, at minimum twelve plants.

For indoor plants, sow seeds in early autumn in the container you want to grow the plants in and keep them well watered in a cool sunny window. Thin the plants to about five for each four-inch pot and cut off flowering stalks when they appear. You should have fresh chervil to snip all winter. If you don't have an outdoor garden, replant indoors in early spring.

Harvesting Chervil   To harvest chervil, gather a bunch of sprigs together in your hand and cut them off about one or two inches from the ground. Cut the older leaves from the outside of the plant to encourage fresh growth from the center, and don't harvest more than one-third of the plant at once. Cut off flower stems to prolong the plant's life.

Storing Chervil   Keep chervil sprigs in a resealable plastic bag in the vegetable crisper of your refrigerator. They will stay fresh for up to three days.

CHIVES

In 1974, when Herbfarm founder Lola Zimmerman divided her chives and found that she had more plants than she could grow or give to friends, she potted them and set them in a wheelbarrow by the road with a jar of coins for making change. Chives are the little herb that started The Herbfarm.

Chives, *Allium schoenoprasum,* have several particularities in the herb garden. First, they're the only allium, or onion family member, grown specifically for its edible leaves, and so the only allium generally considered an herb. Second, chives are also the only herb always referred to in the plural. That's because they grow in tight clumps, like tufts of grass. A singular chive plant has only a few hollow grasslike leaves and is never seen growing without neighbors. The clumps will grow as much as a foot across and eight to eighteen inches tall, depending on how pampered they are. In spring your chives will bloom. Stiff stems support minaret-shaped buds that burst into pink balls about an inch across. These spheres are composed of small florets, also with a strong onion flavor, that can be separated and sprinkled on salads or soups. If you cut the plants down to an inch or two above ground level after they bloom, they will quickly grow back. Chives are perennial; plant them once and if they are minimally cared for, you should have them always.

Cooking with Chives   Chives have a distinct onion flavor, not necessarily delicate but mild and pleasant with less bite in their raw state than other allium cousins, such as onions or garlic. They're a very simple herb; use them wherever an onion flavor is appropriate, but always add them at the end of the cooking process, for heat renders them flavorless, slimy, and drab. Snip chives over cooked vegetables, stir them into mashed potatoes, whisk them at the last minute into a fish sauce, or sprinkle them on a soup. They're particularly good in simple cheese and egg dishes, from an omelet to a soft cheese spread. Like parsley, chives blend with almost any other herb in a savory dish, and they're a good addition to herb mixtures, as in Green Risotto, Herbal Chicken Noodle Soup, and Grilled Fish with Herb Salad (pages 118, 30, and 176).

Chives can be chopped with a knife or snipped with scissors. To chop chives, line them all up like a ponytail and lay them on the cutting board. Use a very sharp knife (a dull knife will bruise them) and cut them as fine as you like. When you snip them, hold the bundle in your hand and let them fall into the dish as they are cut. If you cut chives one to two inches long, the matchstick shapes will create an angular and attractive garnish.

At the Herbfarm, chives are often put to use as edible string. A single chive can tie up a little bundle of green beans, secure a crêpe that's been gathered into a beggar's purse, or fasten an herb leaf that's bundled around a little piece of fish. For tying, choose long, thick chives. First, blanch them by holding a small bunch with tongs and dipping them into a pot of boiling water for no more than five seconds. Immediately plunge them into a bowl of cold water to stop the cooking. It takes a gentle touch and some patience to tie a chive in a knot or bow. Pulled too tightly, they will break, particularly if they're thin.

Chive blossoms have a flavor that is similar to the leaves but stronger. A whole blossom is too powerful to use on its own, but you can break it up into individual florets and sprinkle them lightly on a soup or salad. Before they show color, the beautifully shaped flower buds can be harvested and pickled. Cut the stems of the buds about two inches long and put them in a shallow bowl. Cover them with boiling seasoned rice wine vinegar and let them pickle overnight in the refrigerator, then add them to salads. The mature chive flower added to an herbal vinegar (page 311) will turn it a rosy hue. The stems that carry the flowers should always be discarded, for they're very tough.

Growing Chives In a sunny spot in the garden, chives will survive most any conditions, but they'll be happiest if grown in rich, well-drained soil and kept well watered. If you harvest from them often, fertilize them often so they have the energy to keep growing.

Harvesting Chives Snip chive leaves to just above ground level, don't cut just the tips. If the clump is in bud or bloom, remove the tough flower stems before you use the chives. Always cut back chives to an inch above ground level after the blooms are past their prime; they will grow back again and might bloom a second time. For a continuous harvest from one clump, cut about one-quarter of it every week; by the time the last part of the clump is cut, the first part will have grown back.

Storing Chives Keep chives in a resealable plastic bag in the vegetable crisper of your refrigerator. They will stay fresh for up to one week.

CILANTRO (CORIANDER)

Cilantro and coriander are the same plant. Not only does it have two common names but it also yields two ingredients—leaves and seeds—and has two shapes of leaves. The Spanish name, cilantro, is most often used to refer to the leaves, and the English name, coriander, to specify the seed, and that's how I'll refer to them in this book. *Coriandrum sativum* is the most universal of all culinary herbs and one of the oldest, dating back to ancient India, Egypt, Greece, and China. We think of it as a staple seasoning in Mexican cooking, but it didn't reach the Americas until brought here by Spanish explorers, relatively recently in its culinary history. The name coriander is derived from the Latin *korris,* which means bedbug. Some say it was so named because the green seeds look like the pest, and others say because they smell like them. Since I'm very fond of coriander's fragrance, let's just say they look alike.

This annual in the parsley family starts out as a six- to nine-inch-tall mound of very thin green leaves that are shaped like flat-leaf (Italian) parsley. After a month or two, when it gets ready to flower, it shoots up stems bearing much thinner lacier leaves. Since you never see it at this stage of growth at the market, many people familiar with cilantro will not recognize it by sight, but the fragrance is unmistakably the same, maybe even a little stronger than the wider leaves. These fine-leafed stalks grow to two to three feet and top themselves with delicate umbrella-shaped clusters of tiny white flowers. The flowers soon turn into umbels of small bright green seeds, usually called coriander. Green coriander seeds are pervasively fragrant; when the plants in your garden are at this stage of ripening, you can smell them from fifty feet away, especially so after a rain. Soon after the seeds form, the plants begin to turn yellow. As they continue to mature, the seeds turn brown and their flavor mellows and becomes nutty, and it's at this stage that the seeds are harvested for drying.

Cooking with Cilantro The distinct flavor of cilantro leaves is cooling, citrusy, and complex. It pairs particularly well with the cooling flavor of fresh mint, the citrus flavors of lemon grass and lemon verbena, and as a contrast to hot flavors like chiles and ginger. Its affinity for fiery dishes makes cilantro a staple in Latin American, Indian, and

Southeast Asian cuisines. Except in a few instances when the leaves are blended into a sauce or herb paste, cilantro is always added at the very end of cooking or just before serving, sprinkled on top. Although the flavor is powerful when raw, the thin leaves quickly lose their character when exposed to high heat. Cilantro's flavor goes well with nearly any type of seafood and meat and with vegetables like carrots, cucumbers, and corn. Pair it with mint, parsley, chives, lemon verbena, and basil, but keep it away from robust herbs like rosemary, oregano, thyme, and savory because the flavors clash with each other. Bunches of cilantro are now as common as parsley in most supermarkets.

To wash the leaves, hold the bunch by the stems and submerge it in a basin of cold water, then shake the bunch dry over the sink or spin it in a salad spinner. If you are going to chop the leaves right away, blot the sprigs dry on paper towels. Cilantro stems are very soft, and there's no need to remove all of them before you chop. Cut off the thicker lower stems just below where the leaves begin, then chop the top of the bunch using a sharp chef's knife with a rocking motion. Because they are so thin, cilantro leaves are usually chopped coarse.

When mature and dry, coriander seeds have a penetrating, nutty, orange-peel smell. If you purchase the seeds, always buy them whole and grind them yourself in a spice mill or blender shortly before using them. The coriander that is sold already ground has little flavor in comparison. Most cooks are familiar with using coriander in a wide range of spice mixtures and herb pastes, particularly those with cumin, chiles, mint, and citrus peel, and in many curries and Latin American dishes. What may surprise is how delicious the seeds are in sweets. They give pastries a warm flavor and seem to intensify their butteriness. There is a long tradition of spicing gingerbread, Danish pastries, pound cakes, muffins, and biscuits with coriander. Earlier in the century, hard candies with a coriander seed in the center were popular, as were sugar-coated coriander seeds called Scotch candies. Coriander was often used instead of nutmeg in rice pudding, and recently the renowned French pastry chef Pierre Hermé created pastries combining coriander seeds with coconut. One teaspoon to one tablespoon of freshly ground seeds is enough for most average recipes.

If you grow coriander in your garden, you'll be able to harvest the seeds while they are still green and soft. At this stage they are exceptionally pungent with a flavor that has elements of both the leaf and dried seed. They can easily overpower other foods, so you have to use them with restraint, but they're a unique and useful ingredient, especially in bold spice rubs and marinades and in fresh chutneys. A teaspoon or two is plenty. I also like to pickle the green seeds by covering them with boiling seasoned rice wine vinegar and letting them sit overnight, during which the flavor mellows somewhat. They make an exciting garnish for oysters on the half-shell, smoked salmon, gravlax, and tomato salad.

Growing Cilantro Cilantro is a quick-growing annual. It's a greedy plant that likes rich soil, plenty of moisture, and sun. Because cilantro doesn't like to be transplanted, it's best to sow the seeds where you want them to grow. For a continuous supply of leaves, sow it in succession, which means plant a small amount every three weeks instead of all the seeds at once. Despite its association with tropical climates, cilantro grows best in cool weather, so the best time to sow it is in the early spring and fall. In hot weather, young plants often bloom and go to seed before they have a chance to develop a good crop of foliage.

Harvesting Cilantro To harvest cilantro, gather a bunch of sprigs together in your hand and cut them off about one or two inches from the ground. Harvest green seeds when they are the size of peppercorns. If you wish to dry the seeds, allow them to mature and turn brown before harvesting.

Storing Cilantro Keep cilantro sprigs in a resealable plastic bag in the vegetable crisper of your refrigerator. They will stay fresh for up to three days.

DILL

I've always thought of dill's flavor as comforting. It's not bold or spicy nor delicate and rarefied; it is savory, down-to-earth, and friendly with many foods. Dill is in the parsley family and the flavor of the leaves has more in common with parsley than anything else—they have the same unmistakable green pungency—but dill also has strong caraway overtones and a hint of citrus.

Dill, *Anethum graveolens,* is a short-lived annual native to southern Europe. Mounds of pretty, deep green, fernlike leaves grow easily from seeds. About two months after sprouting, the plants send up stalks holding yellow flower heads shaped like upside-down umbrellas, which in turn develop quantities of seed. The plants top out at one and one-half to four feet tall depending on the variety, and all parts of the plant can be used for cooking.

Cooking with Dill Dill is very versatile, but its notoriety stems from its use as a pickling herb. Dill pickles are flavored with dill seeds. If you pack homemade pickles with whole heads of fresh dill seed, the flavor will be incomparable to what you can buy. The mild-tasting leaves, called dillweed, are also good in many types of pickled or marinated vegetables, like onions, beets, carrots, cabbage, cauliflower, or beans. Gravlax, Scandinavia's cured salmon, gets its distinctive flavor from lavish amounts of dill pressed between the salted and sugared fish fillets. Also try dillweed in fresh salads, from homey tuna or potato salad to elegant composed salads with shrimp, chicken, or avocado.

On the stovetop, a sprinkle of dillweed adds fresh green flavor to cauliflower and cabbage and root crops such as carrots, beets, and onions. It's also suited to a wide range of dishes with potatoes, mushrooms, onions, egg, and cheese. Toss the leaves with buttered steamed new potatoes, in the filling of a Cheddar omelet, or with braised chicken and mushrooms. Begin with two tablespoons for six servings, then add more depending on its strength. Dill is also delicious with mild-tasting fish like sole, halibut, and trout and is especially good with salmon. Add dill to an onion pudding, a celery root gratin, or an onion tart. Use large branches of the herb as a bed for roasting a whole fish. Dill is one of the best herbs for incorporating in breads, especially biscuits or rye breads—use the leaves or fresh seeds.

Dill is very easy to handle, for the leaves strip easily from the thick central stem. Small soft stems can remain because they will be unnoticeable when the herb is chopped. Once the large stems are removed, gather the fronds in a bunch and chop the soft feathery leaves with a chef's knife. To keep the character of the herb, a coarse chop is usually best. Unless you're baking with it, add it to cooked foods at the last minute. Dill is best paired with other herbs in the parsley family like fennel, lovage, and chervil, but it is also successful with chives, mint, lemon balm, and lemon verbena.

If you have dill that's flowering, try using the yellow blossoms in your cooking. Snip the soft yellow tips off, chop them lightly, and use them wherever you would use the leaves. They have a stronger caraway flavor and are lovely as a garnish. The soft green seeds can be used in the same way but are even stronger tasting.

Dill Varieties   Many varieties of dill are available from seed. They range in height from compact Fernleaf dill that grows only eighteen inches tall to Bouquet at three feet and Mammoth Long Island soaring to four feet. Some like Dukat are stronger flavored, and others like Tetra Leaf are slower to bolt. Surva (*Anethum sowa*) is the Asian Indian variety of dill with especially pungent leaves.

Growing Dill   Because dill likes fertile soil and lots of sun, it grows well with garden vegetables. It's best to sow seeds where you want them to grow because it has a taproot and doesn't like to be transplanted. The move might make it flower prematurely at the expense of leaf production. For a continuous dill supply, sow seeds every few weeks through midsummer. This plant has a short life span; once it bolts and goes to seed, its days are numbered.

Harvesting Dill   When the plants are young, cut off dill sprigs at ground level. As the plants grow, cut off sprigs at the point where they meet the stalks. If you are going to dry the seeds, harvest after they have matured and turned brown.

Storing Dill   Keep dill sprigs in a resealable plastic bag in the vegetable crisper of your refrigerator. They will stay fresh for up to three days.

FENNEL

There are two kinds of fennel—one is used as a vegetable and the other as an herb. Both are named *Foeniculum vulgare* and are members of the parsley family with distinct anise flavor, feathery leaves, and yellow flowers borne on umbels. The vegetable type is called Florence fennel, finocchio, or bulbing fennel; supermarkets often erroneously label it anise. The vegetable is formed in a rounded layered bulb at the base of the plant, like white celery in the shape of an onion.

The herb fennel, a huge plant whose stems shoot up from the ground without a bulb, is grown mostly for its seeds, although its leaves have flavor as well. There are both green and bronze varieties. Bronze fennel has striking coppery foliage and a slightly hardier nature than the green, but otherwise the two are nearly identical. Green fennel grows wild in many warmer parts of the United States from Florida to California. In the San Francisco Bay Area wild fennel grows in vacant lots and along roadsides everywhere. In your own garden, the stature of your fennel plant depends on what region of the country you live in and how old the plant is. In Zone 7 (low of 0°F) and higher, fennel is a perennial, and it will come back bigger and bigger each year, eventually forming a clump up to a yard across and seven feet tall. In colder climates you must grow fennel as an annual, and your plants will reach three to four feet in a season, about the size of a tall dill plant.

Cooking with Fennel   When you grow fennel in your garden, you'll discover that many parts of the plant have uses at different times in the season. If your fennel lives through the winter, its lush, dense fronds are one of the first things to pop up in the garden in spring. At this point the leaves have an intense sweetness and concentrated flavor, and it's the best time to use fennel sprigs in salads, sauces, or stuffings. As the stalks grow, the leaves become more open and lacy and the flavor milder and less sweet, but they still add a pleasant anise flavor and make an especially dramatic garnish.

The parts of the fennel plant I find most exciting to cook with are the flowers and seeds. They can be harvested in any stage of their development, beginning when the buds turn yellow. At this stage the blossoms have a wonderful anise flavor that's even stronger than the leaves. Snip off the golden tips at the ends of the umbels with scissors and sprinkle them over anything that would be flattered by a hint of licorice—a piece of grilled fish, a tomato salad, or cold cucumber soup. In a week or two, as the yellow fades, little green seeds will form and the licorice flavor begins to intensify. By the time the green seeds are full size, they have a very powerful flavor and a pronounced resinous quality. Chop the seeds, young or mature, and add them to vegetable soups, fresh pickles, or salad dressings. They'll perk up shrimp or mussel dishes, fish stews or sauces, summer vegetable dishes with bell peppers, zucchini, or eggplant, or marinades and spice rubs for lamb, pork, tuna, or swordfish. A little will go a very long way, so it's best to begin with a conservative one-half teaspoon for six servings, then add more if you wish.

When fully mature, the seeds will turn dark and dry and the flavor will mellow a bit. They're a favorite snack of songbirds, so you'll have some competition if you want to harvest them for dry seed. One happy mature plant will provide you with an enormous quantity of blooms, but fortunately, not all the flowers will mature at once. Young yellow buds may share the same plant with spent black umbels, giving you a very long season in which to use fresh fennel seeds in the kitchen.

Don't ignore the fennel stalks, which can grow as thick as bamboo. They're especially useful as a bed to roast or grill whole fish (page 179). Cut fresh stalks to a length that will fit in the roasting pan or on the rack and place the prepared fish on top. They'll slowly give off a subtle flavor as the fish cooks. The dried stalks make terrific smoking material for the grill or any type of smoker (see the directions on pages 179–80).

Growing Fennel   Don't pamper fennel. It thrives in sandy poor soil with lots of sun, and it likes to be kept on the dry side. Too much water will cause it to rot at the base. It can have a tough time surviving humid southern summers; in such climates it grows best in spring and fall. Like other members of the parsley family, fennel has a taproot and is hard to transplant once it is past the seedling stage. Give it lots of room to grow and leave it alone. Sometimes fennel will attract aphids—they don't seem to do it much damage—but they are hard to spot in the lacy foliage. You might want to inspect the leaves when you harvest to avoid adding unexpected ingredients to your salad. If you let the seeds mature and fall to the ground, you're likely to have lots of baby fennel plants the next year. It's best to grow your fennel far away from your dill, so that they do not cross-pollinate and produce seedlings of inferior hybrids.

Harvesting Fennel   Cut feathery fennel leaves off at ground level when very young. As the plants grow, cut off sprigs where they meet the stalks. Harvest blossoms after they show yellow, and the green seeds at any point. If you wish to dry the seeds, harvest them after they have matured and turned brown.

Storing Fennel   Keep fennel leaves, blossoms, or green seeds in a resealable plastic bag in the vegetable crisper of your refrigerator. They will stay fresh for up to a week.

HYSSOP

This is a gardener's herb. You'll cook with it infrequently or not at all, but you'll be glad to grow it. Hyssop, *Hyssopus officinalis,* is an entirely different plant from the herb called anise hyssop, *Agastache foeniculum,* though both are members of the mint family. Hyssop forms lovely orderly clumps of healthy deep green foliage, about twelve to eighteen inches tall, topped with colorful stems of small blue (or sometimes pink or white) flowers. Bees and butterflies love it. The leaves are highly aromatic, and though the scent is somewhat camphoric, it has a fragrant appeal when you brush against it.

Cooking with Hyssop   Hyssop's flavor is very strong and strident, slightly reminiscent of thyme or sage but with a bitter resinous edge. Small quantities are the rule. Like sage, hyssop is said to help in the digestion of fats and is most often used with meats. Add small amounts to herb rubs for pork, lamb, or venison or to braised beef or lamb dishes. A tiny bit is also good on green beans, with cabbage, in glazed carrots or beets, and in tomato sauce or soup. The flowers have a similar flavor but with a touch of sweetness; sprinkle small amounts on salads or vegetable dishes for a robust accent.

Growing Hyssop   Give hyssop full sun or it will become leggy. It will grow lushly in fairly fertile, moist, and well-drained soil, but its flavor will be much stronger in poor gravelly soil. Hyssop's most winning quality is that if it's cut back after blooming, it will send up more flowers. Hyssop should be hardy to Zone 4 (winter lows of −30°F).

Harvesting Hyssop   Cut off hyssop sprigs one-third to halfway down the length of the stem. Cut the entire plant back by one-third after it blooms.

Storing Hyssop   Keep hyssop in a resealable plastic bag in the vegetable crisper of your refrigerator. It will stay fresh for up to a week.

LAVENDER

I'm addicted to it. I find it nearly impossible to walk by a lavender plant in full bloom without bending over to pick a stem, roll it around in my fingers, and inhale the heady scent. The gauzy gray-green foliage, graceful violet spikes, and, above all, unequaled perfume make lavender a shameless seducer. Its fragrance is both invigorating and sedating and one of the great pleasures of the herb garden.

Even without scent lavender would be a stunning hardy garden plant. It's a bushy perennial whose woody framework, along with most of its leaves, remain in the garden all winter. The variety we see most often is known as English lavender, *Lavandula angustifolia*, and it's the one that's best to cook with. It grows to two to three feet with one-and-one-half-inch flower spikes on eight-inch stems.

A different type of lavender is most often grown for commercial oil production. Called lavandin, *Lavandula* x *intermedia*, it's hybrid between English and Spike lavender. It grows taller, three to four feet, and produces a dramatic though slightly less colorful display of eighteen-inch-long sturdy stems topped with large buds that are very easy to strip off. Its flavor is sharper and more powerful than the English varieties, with a strong resinous quality, but it's still suitable for cooking.

Cooking with Lavender Unfortunately, lavender is still a stranger to most kitchens, although it's appearing on cooking magazine "in" lists and creeping onto menus in city restaurants. Still eyebrows are inevitably raised when lavender is mentioned with cooking. I think it's difficult for people to get past the perfume and potpourri association, but once they sample a few dishes, sweet or savory, lavender's role as a flavoring is an easy sell.

All parts of lavender, including the leaves and stems have fragrance and flavor, but the flowers and buds are best for cooking. The ideal time to harvest is when the flower buds show their full color but have not quite opened. If you are going to steep the lavender, just snip off the entire flower cluster and use it whole, but if you are going to chop or grind the buds, strip them from the stems with your fingers.

Lavender's sweet fragrance is especially appealing in desserts, and there are several ways to introduce its flavor. First, you can steep the flower spikes or buds in hot milk, cream, or sugar syrup, then use the infused liquid as an ingredient in custard, ice cream, or sorbet. Second, you can chop the buds with a knife and add them to cake batter, meringue, or fruit compote. Lastly you can grind the buds with sugar in a spice mill or blender until they become a fine powder. This last method is especially effective because the sugar helps break down the texture of the buds as it absorbs the essential oils. You can use the lavender sugar in nearly any baked good, and it's especially captivating in buttery shortbread and pound cake. Lavender's flavor goes well with ginger, walnuts, almonds, pistachios, berries, cherries, and plums. Always remember that lavender requires a sensitive hand—too much can be off-putting. It's best to add it as a background flavor in the way that you would add vanilla—you know it is there but it is subtle. Start with two teaspoons of fresh buds for an average-size recipe, then increase it if you find the flavor too faint.

Most surprising is the way lavender works in savory dishes. Lavender has an underlying astringency and camphor quality much like rosemary, but if it is used judiciously, it can add a haunting flavor to robust foods, especially lamb. Add the chopped buds to an herb crust for lamb rack, a spice rub for leg of lamb, or a marinade for lamb chops. Lavender is also good with chicken, game birds like quail and pheasant, and some pork dishes. Potatoes and lavender are an unlikely pair, but somehow the earthiness of the vegetable is amplified by the resinous quality in the lavender, making an exquisite combination that you have to taste to appreciate. You can add the flower spikes to the water when boiling potatoes or toss the chopped buds on steamed new potatoes (page 147) or roasted potatoes (page 146). Lavender is good paired with thyme, rosemary, and savory—the French herb mixture known as herbes de Provence often contains all four of these herbs—and it's also delicious with spearmint.

Lavender Varieties   You can buy plants or seeds simply labeled as English lavender, but many named cultivars of English lavender are available. A cultivar is a selected plant with specific traits and all plants with its name should be identical. The two most common are Munstead and Hidcote, named after the famous turn-of-the-century English gardens of Gertrude Jekyll and Lawrence Johnston respectively. Munstead is pale lavender colored, but Hidcote, my favorite, is a gorgeous deep violet. Both stay under two feet tall. Other cultivars include Twickle Purple which grows taller, Gray Lady with silver foliage, and Jean Davis, which has pink flowers. Named garden varieties of lavandin include Grosso, Provence, and Vera, and all have powerful scents.

Many other species of lavender, including French lavender, *L. dentata,* Spanish lavender, *L. stoechas,* and fringed-leaf lavender, *L. multifida,* will grow into beautiful plants that add interest to your garden, but because they have less sweet, somewhat medicinal fragrances, they're not as suitable for cooking. These more exotic lavenders are also very tender; unless you live in a frost-free climate, they need to be brought indoors for the winter. They do, however, make excellent houseplants for a cool window.

Growing Lavender   Lavender is another Mediterranean native that requires full sun and well-drained soil. In fact, it will be happy in conditions that range from a well-tended fertile flower bed to a neglected hill of poor sandy soil with very little water. It does not like very hot, humid, and stagnant weather, though; if you must grow it in such conditions, mulch it well and make sure it has good air circulation. The English varieties are hardy to Zone 5 (lows to –20°F) and will survive a cold winter with a good mulch and dry feet. Lavandin is slightly less hardy. Be sure to give lavender plenty of room to grow, since a tiny plant in a four-inch pot will take over a two-foot square of garden space by the end of the season.

Harvesting Lavender   Lavender sprigs are most fragrant just before the flowers open, but you can gather them at any stage of bloom once they show purple color. Cut off the whole spike, stem and all, at foliage level.

Once the plant has its main flush of bloom in June, cut it back to an inch or two below where the spikes started, and it might reward you with a second bloom in late summer. This pruning is most important to keep the plants from getting lanky. Don't cut your lavender very far back in the autumn, however, or you will promote new growth that is more susceptible to frost damage and the plants might not survive the winter. Prune the plants again in the spring just as the green leaf nodes begin to appear.

Storing Lavender   Keep fresh lavender in a resealable plastic bag in the vegetable crisper of your refrigerator, where it will stay fresh for over a week. Or keep the flowering stems in a glass of water on the kitchen counter like cut flowers, where they will last for four to five days.

If you don't have fresh lavender buds or flowers on hand, dried lavender buds are an excellent substitution. As a matter of fact, they're one of the few dried herbs I use regularly. To dry your own, harvest the flower stalks at their peak and hang them upside down in small bunches in a dark place with good air circulation. After a few weeks, strip the buds from the stem and store them in a tightly sealed jar in a dark cupboard. Use about one teaspoon dried for two teaspoons fresh. Dried lavender buds are also available in stores, often where herbs are sold in bulk, and by mail order (see

Sources, page 434). They are very light, so a few ounces will fill a large jar. Be sure you buy buds that are food grade and not treated with oils for use in potpourris.

Lemon Balm

If an herb can be cheerful, lemon balm is just that. It's an exuberant grower that loves to live wherever you plant it, and its perky golden green leaves have a delightful lemon scent. *Melissa officinalis* is a mint relative that looks like it could be a mint itself. Its two- to three-foot stems grow in rapidly spreading clumps that hold crinkled leaves with pinked edges and produce tiny inconspicuous flowers at the top. The fragrance is gentle and pleasantly lemony, not powerful and bracing like the scent of lemon verbena or a (lemon-scented) geranium.

Cooking with Lemon Balm Lemon balm is most commonly used in beverages, particularly to make a tisane (herbal tea) or for a garnish in iced tea or lemonade, but it's also good in many summery foods, particularly with vegetables. Finely shred or coarsely chop the leaves and shower them on beets, carrots, summer squash, or garden peas. Add a few lemon balm leaves to a green salad or blend them in a dressing for fennel bulb or green beans. Combined with dill, parsley, or lovage, lemon balm adds an understated citrus accent to delicate fish or chicken dishes. Finely shredded leaves are excellent in fruit salads or strewn on melon. And to make a refreshing sorbet, steep the sprigs of the herb in simple syrup with mint and ginger.

Growing Lemon Balm Lemon balm is among the easiest and most adaptable herbs. Its first choice is a semishaded spot with rich, well-drained, moist soil, but it will grow with vigor practically anywhere. When grown in full sun, the leaves will pick up a golden hue and may wilt in extreme heat. If lemon balm is happy, it will spread rapidly, especially if you let it go to seed.

Harvesting Lemon Balm Cut sprigs of lemon balm anywhere along the stem. It is so vigorous that if the entire plant is cut to ground level, it will soon grow back. Young leaves harvested in cool weather are best for salads. Older leaves are good for infusing, but they can be tough and bitter. When the plant blooms, cut it back by at least one-half to encourage new growth and to prevent it from seeding and colonizing your entire garden.

Storing Lemon Balm Keep lemon balm sprigs in a resealable plastic bag in the vegetable crisper of your refrigerator, where they will stay fresh for up to a week; or keep the flowering stems in a glass of water on the kitchen counter like cut flowers, where they will last for two to three days. Dried lemon balm makes an excellent tisane (herb tea); hang small bunches upside down in a well-ventilated spot. When crisp, remove the stems and store the leaves in a tightly sealed container in a dark cupboard.

Lemon Verbena

If you have any sort of outdoor garden, lemon verbena is a plant you must grow. Its scent is glorious and intoxicating, like a truckload of lemon drops distilled into a leaf.

Place it near a doorway, by a well-traveled path, or next to your favorite chair on the patio, so you brush against it often. Even if you never cook with it, you'll want to pet it and indulge in its fragrance.

Lemon verbena, *Aloysia triphylla,* is a rather scraggly tender perennial that grows to about three feet in a season. In frost-free climates its woody framework will eventually reach ten feet or more. It has lance-shaped leaves with a rough texture, like a cat's tongue, that grow anywhere from one to four inches long and are always arranged in whorls of three around the stem. Beginning in midsummer, the thin branches bear sprays of tiny white flowers at their ends.

Cooking with Lemon Verbena   If you're a fan of lemon desserts, lemon verbena will be a star. Use it in sorbets and ice creams, custards and curds, tarts and cakes, fruit salads and compotes. It tastes more lemony than a lemon but has no sourness. Its flavor is brightest when you pair it with tangy ingredients that make up for its own lack of acidity; otherwise you might find the flavor flat. I like to match it with apricots, gooseberries, and red currants and often add it to lemon curd and lemon sorbet to intensify the citrus taste.

This herb's flavor markedly diminishes as it cooks and stays clearest when it is added to a recipe without heating at all. Its very tough leaves are unpleasant on the tongue if not chopped fine enough or strained out. The easiest way to skirt both these problems is to make a sort of sweet pesto, called a conserve in eighteenth-century cookbooks, by grinding the leaves with sugar. Put one part sugar and two parts lightly packed lemon verbena leaves in the food processor and purée for a full minute or two until you have a smooth green paste. Add the resulting paste to water to make a syrup or sorbet (page 295) or cooled milk to make ice cream (page 258). Or stir a tablespoon or two into any kind of dessert sauce, custard, fruit purée, or icing. Be sure to adjust the sugar in the recipe to account for the amount used to grind the leaves. To preserve lemon verbena for winter desserts, freeze the herb paste in resealable freezer bags. Because of the high sugar content, it will remain soft and easy to spoon out as you need it.

If you brush the lemon verbena leaves with egg white and sprinkle them with sugar, they will become crisp and candied (page 313). In fact its leaves are the only ones I find truly easy to candy because their rough surface grabs on to the coating and they dry quickly. They are absolutely delicious and make a knockout cake decoration, especially with other candied flowers. They'll keep in an airtight container for months.

Lemon verbena's flavor can also be extracted by infusing it in milk or cream or a sugar syrup (pages 248 and 249). You don't get quite as much flavor as you do with the sugar paste method, but you avoid the green color and use less sugar.

Lemon verbena is wonderfully refreshing in beverages. Whole leaves can serve as a garnish for cold drinks like lemonade, or they can be floated in glasses of mineral water. To make a fresh lemon verbena tisane (herb tea), fill a teapot half full with loosely packed sprigs and cover them with boiling water. Let it steep for ten minutes, then pour. For an even fuller flavor, steep a couple of teaspoons of green tea leaves with the herb.

In savory foods, lemon verbena can take the place of lemon grass, a tough reed-shaped herb that shares a similar citrus flavor and is often added to spicy Asian dishes, like Thai tom yam gung soup. As a stand-in, use an equal quantity of coarsely torn lemon verbena leaves and stir them in at the last minute. Chopped fine or infused in stock or wine, lemon verbena is good in any dish flavored with combinations of ginger, chiles, garlic, green onion, cilantro, and mint.

In hot weather when lemon verbena grows rapidly, its leaves become quite large, and the central vein of each leaf becomes tough and more prominent. If you cook with the herb at this stage in a recipe where the leaves will not be strained out, you must first remove these veins. This is easiest to accomplish while you are removing the leaves from the stem. With one hand, grasp the thick vein at the base of the leaf where it meets the stem and use the other hand to gently strip the leaf free. The leaf will be split in two and the vein will remain behind, still attached to the stem.

Growing Lemon Verbena   Grow lemon verbena in full sun and in well-drained soil. The plants are naturally lanky and grow into odd unsymmetrical shapes, but frequent cutting will make them bushier. To keep the plant vigorous, cut off flower sprays when they appear. Temperatures in the low 20s will kill lemon verbena, and it rarely survives a Zone 8 winter (lows of 10° to 20°F). If your plant is in a pot, you can bring it indoors before the first frost and set it by a cool window. It will go dormant and lose all its leaves in most environments, inside or out. Cut it back by two-thirds in late winter and set it outside again when the weather warms. To avoid the bother of this overwintering process, treat lemon verbena like an annual and buy a new plant each spring. It grows very fast once the weather warms.

Harvesting Lemon Verbena   Harvest lemon verbena sprigs from any part of the plant, snipping above a leaf joint and remembering not to cut more than one-third of the entire plant at once.

Storing Lemon Verbena   Cook with lemon verbena as soon as possible after it's harvested. Keep sprigs in resealable bags in the vegetable crisper of the refrigerator for up to two days, but expect them to lose some fragrance and to discolor. Like basil sprigs, they will also hold for up to one day if you treat them like cut flowers, with their stems in a tall glass of water on the kitchen counter. (Lemon verbena and sugar paste will last for six months if stored tightly covered in the freezer.)

To dry lemon verbena, hang the branches in a dark well-ventilated spot until the leaves are crisp. Then strip the leaves off the stems and store them in a tightly sealed container in a dark cupboard. Save the dried branches for a fragrant smoking material to use in a stovetop smoker or kettle barbecue in place of wood chips (see page 182). The scent of the dried leaves does not compare with that of fresh sprigs, but when steeped in a hot liquid, dried leaves will still release a respectable flavor. Unfortunately, the dried lemon verbena that is available commercially is often stale and full of chopped stems. If you buy dried lemon verbena, look for leaves that are fluffy and not finely crushed. They should be dull green, not straw yellow, free of stems, and have a pronounced lemon fragrance. The dried leaves make an excellent tisane (herb tea).

LOVAGE

Lovage (pronounced with the emphasis on *love*), *Levisticum officinale,* tastes like celery tenfold with a strong dose of parsley. It's rarely seen in markets because there is little public demand for it, but it's a rugged plant that's extremely easy to grow in your own garden. This towering perennial herb in the parsley family has been used to season foods since Roman times. Its pungent and concentrated flavor is compatible with a great variety of foods, making it an herb worth getting to know.

You can almost watch the stems of lovage shoot up from the ground in early spring along with the tulips and peony stems. Once the sprouts begin to emerge, they grow rapidly to about two feet, becoming long hollow stems that branch into narrow terminal stems holding flat wedge-shaped leaves. Then in late spring the plant gets a growth spurt to rival any adolescent and rockets its flower stems nearly six feet high.

Cooking with Lovage   You can use lovage in any dish where the flavor of celery or celery seed is appropriate, but I find that there are several foods with which it finds perfect pitch. With spring greens, particularly spinach, chard, and wild nettles, it seems to intensify their greenness, to heighten what they're all about. Small amounts of the herb are an unbeatable complement to delicate fish like skate or halibut, and when clams or mussels are steamed with lovage their liquor takes on a captivating aroma. I have recently discovered the combination of apples and lovage. The pairing might seem contrary to cooking with the seasons, because lovage is a spring herb and apples are a fall crop, but lovage can still be harvested in autumn and apples are stored till spring. Spiked with some tartness from wine or vinegar, the verdant herb mixed with the sweet fruit makes a delectable sauce for seafood or pork.

I hate to encourage anyone to be timid with fresh herbs, but because of the strength and strangeness of lovage, you might want to start out using small amounts until you become more familiar with it. The stems, seeds, and roots all have flavor, but it's the young leaves that you'll want to cook with. Chop the leaves fine and start by adding about two teaspoons for six servings. As with most soft-leafed herbs, you can stir lovage in at the end of the cooking process for a strong forward taste, but the flavor will hold up to heat and when it is cooked longer it will slowly permeate a dish. Use a cluster of leaves in a bouquet garni for a lengthy braise, or slowly simmer the chopped leaves in a rich tomato or Bolognese sauce.

Lovage stems have some uses as well. When cut into ten-inch lengths, they make a perfect straw for a bloody Mary. As the drink passes through, it picks up the distinct celery taste. In past centuries the stems were candied like angelica (page 314). I like the result, but be warned it's not for everyone—the flavor is quite pungent and out of the ordinary.

Growing Lovage   Unless you have a restaurant, you only need one lovage plant. You can give it a home in any out-of-the-way, well-drained spot with half-a-day's sun. It's much more tolerant of shade than most herbs; in hot climates it dislikes baking in the sun all day. I planted one behind my house in a very dry, sandy spot where nothing else would grow. I give it no care, yet it comes back bigger season after season. The plant will stay fairly small the first year you plant it and probably won't bloom, but in a year or two it will form a tidy clump with a tenacious, deep root system that ensures its longevity.

After the plant flowers and sets seed, the leaves will wither away. If you plan to use the greenery through autumn, it's best to sever the flower stalk before it reaches its summit and make the plant live unfulfilled for the season. This will force new leaves to grow from the base.

Like tarragon, lovage requires a period of cold dormancy. Herb gardeners in the extreme southern parts of the United States will have trouble keeping it from year to year and should treat it like an annual.

Harvesting Lovage   Cut off the stalks at their base, harvesting the outer ones first. Don't cut off the tender heart, because it will be your future crop; however, young leaves are best for cooking. As the weather becomes hot and the leaves mature, they tend to get quite bitter, sometimes to the point of being inedible. Taste and use accordingly.

Storing Lovage   Keep lovage in a resealable plastic bag in the vegetable crisper of your refrigerator. It will stay fresh for up to a week.

MARJORAM

I've always known this pungent oregano relative as sweet marjoram, but when I was showing off our kitchen garden to an English visitor, I learned another name. She announced, in a voice like the great English actress Margaret Rutherford, "I see you have a great deal of knotty marjoram." I thought she meant the herbs had misbehaved.

Of course, knotty describes how the plant looks when it flowers. Tight little green balls carrying tiny white blossoms cover its upper stems, making the plant appear macraméd. Knotty marjoram and sweet marjoram are two names for the same plant, *Origanum majorana,* a member of the mint family originating in North Africa and growing six to fourteen inches tall. Although technically a perennial, it hates chilly weather and will not survive a mild frost, so it's nearly always grown as an annual. Marjoram is in the same genus as oregano, but it lacks the hot flavor or bite of many of the other species. That's not to say it's subtle or understated; marjoram's fragrance and flavor are pronounced and quite intoxicating, with complex sweet spice and citrus flavors underlined by a subtle pine aroma.

Cooking with Marjoram   Naturally I can't choose a favorite herb—that would be like choosing a favorite child—but in midsummer when it is abundant, I cook with marjoram more often than any other herb in the garden. Its flavor is distinctive and appealing, but it is not as forceful as its oregano cousins. Toss the chopped leaves into dishes with beets, carrots, zucchini, and green beans or add them to mashed potatoes or a potato gratin. Sprinkle the whole leaves over a vine-ripened tomato salad or blend some into a vinaigrette for mixed greens. The sweetly pungent flavor of marjoram is particularly good with fresh summer corn; add it to corn chowder, corn pudding, corn bread, or stuff the sprigs under the husk for grilled corn on the cob. Blend the leaves into garlic butter for garlic bread or add them to the sauce for old-fashioned macaroni and cheese. I love to stir the leaves into fresh clam sauce for pasta or wild mushroom risotto. Also try marjoram with fish or shrimp, scatter some on an omelet or scrambled eggs, or stuff sprigs under the skin of a roasting chicken.

Marjoram combines well with most of the other herbs in the mint family: rosemary, sage, savory, thyme, mint, and, especially, basil. Use it generously but always taste it first because its intensity varies. The essential oil content, which determines its strength of flavor, is higher if it is grown in dry, sandy soil and it soars in hot weather. Though not fragile, its flavor is less stable than that of other Mediterranean herbs like oregano or rosemary, so it's best to add it near the end of cooking. Remove tough stems—soft ones will be unnoticed—then chop it as fine as you wish or use the leaves whole. The "knots," or little flower buds, have the same flavor and intensity, and you can chop them with the leaves.

Marjoram Varieties   Sweet or knotty marjoram will often be simply labeled as marjoram. It has a relative called Italian oregano (or hardy marjoram), which is a cross between sweet marjoram and Greek oregano. Its taste is nearly the same as sweet marjoram and the two can be used interchangeably, but Italian oregano is much hardier. It will survive a Zone 7 winter (lows of 0°F) and will grow in cool spring and autumn weather, whereas sweet marjoram will sulk. In a mild winter you can harvest from it year-round. Other types of marjoram like golden, curly, and variegated are tolerant of cold weather and attractive garden plants, but they have weak flavor compared to the sweet. If you're growing the plant specifically for cooking, make sure you buy plants labeled sweet marjoram, knotty marjoram, or Italian oregano and give them the smell test—when rubbed, their aroma should be pronounced and pungent.

Growing Marjoram   Marjoram loves the heat. Give it a sunny, well-drained spot, preferably with sandy soil, and keep it on the dry side. Wait until the weather warms before planting because a cool, wet spring will set the plants back. If you like marjoram as much as I do, you'll want to grow at least a half-dozen plants. Sweet or "naughty," there never seems to be enough in the garden.

Marjoram is not easy to grow indoors, but if you want fresh sprigs for clipping in the winter, it is possible. Try potting up young plants in early fall, about three for each four-inch pot. Give them as much full sun as you can. Water them judiciously but don't let the pots dry out completely.

Harvesting Marjoram   Grab a section of the plant in a bunch and cut it off halfway down the stems. It will grow back bushier. Cut off all the "knots" as they develop, or the plants will become lanky and unproductive. If you cut the plants back throughout the season, even if you don't need to cook with them, you will be able to harvest the herb all summer and into the fall.

Storing Marjoram   Keep marjoram in a resealable plastic bag in the vegetable crisper of your refrigerator. It will stay fresh for up to five days.

MINT

When my three-year-old neighbor was prompted by his mother to smell the herbs I have growing in back of my house, he had a reserved interest in the rosemary and thyme and was blasé about the sage, but when he got to the spearmint, his face lit up. He had to have a sprig to take home. Of course, I was delighted to oblige and encourage a budding herb fancier. After all, mint was my first fresh herb. Both of my childhood homes had huge patches of spearmint in the backyard. I remember lingering among their fragrant stems at a very early age, in awe that anything could smell so good.

There are literally hundreds of varieties of mints, originating from about twenty-five different species. Some are tiny-leafed ground covers like Corsican mint, and others like apple mint can grow four to five feet tall. Flavors vary, ranging from very spicy to very fruity, but all contain menthol, which gives them the common underlying fragrance we know of as minty. The primary mint for the kitchen is spearmint, but peppermint and the fruity mints also have uses.

Spearmint, *Mentha spicata,* grows two to three feet tall and is named for the spear shape of its crinkled deep green leaves. It's best to identify the herb by its fragrance and flavor, not its appearance, for mint varieties cross easily and variations often occur in leaf shape and color. Some are rounder, more pointy, more crinkled, or lighter or darker green. As long as it smells and tastes like spearmint, you can cook with it like spearmint. The flavor should be cool and refreshing, fruity and slightly spicy, but without the chilling menthol quality of peppermint. Because spearmint is aromatic and sweet, not numbing, it works in both savory and sweet foods. Fresh mint in the market labeled simply "mint" is almost always a form of spearmint.

Peppermint, *M. piperita vulgaris,* has existed since the 1600s. It's a hybrid mint, not a species, and its seeds are sterile, so it must be propagated through cuttings or divisions. It has reddish stems, and its leaves are rounder and smoother than those of spearmint. Peppermint has a very high menthol content, giving it a forceful bracing coolness that makes it appropriate for some sweets—especially chocolate ones—and for teas. This icy strength, however, makes peppermint too dominant for most savory dishes.

Cooking with Mint   Mint is the most widely cultivated herb in the United States, but most is grown for oil used in breath mints and toothpaste. The culinary uses of this herb are often underestimated. Mint adds a flavorful and unexpected accent to everything from light and summery foods to hearty substantial dishes to many desserts. Next to parsley, it's also the most versatile. It pairs well with spicy Mediterranean herbs like oregano and rosemary, cooling herbs like cilantro and lemon verbena, and even floral herbs like rose geranium and lavender.

The refreshing quality of spearmint complements delicate flavors, as in chilled cucumber soup, minted peas, or new potatoes, and also contrasts and balances spicy hot ingredients, as in a fiery carrot jalapeño salad. The leaves can be chopped coarse or very fine or cut in thin strips. To preserve its full aroma, it's best to stir it into dishes during the last stages of cooking. The flavor will rarely take over, and you can use anywhere from two tablespoons to one-half cup for six servings. For just the essence of the herb's flavor, infuse whole mint sprigs in a hot liquid, then strain them out. Or add the sprigs to the water used for steaming fish or boiling vegetables.

In past decades, lamb chops were often served with cloying, bright green mint jelly, which has its origins in the centuries-old English sauce of fresh mint pounded with vinegar and sugar that helped calm the gamy flavors of the meat. Don't dismiss mint and lamb as cliché—it's a peerless combination that is also found in Mediterranean cuisine. Mint can be used in marinades and rubs not only for lamb but also for chicken and beef and as an ingredient in relishes or salsas that accompany meats. In India, a chutney is made by grinding mint leaves with citrus juice and chiles (page 336). Mint also complements all sorts of fish and shellfish preparations. Add it to a marinade for fresh tuna or sea bass, toss it into a skillet of sautéed shrimp, grind it into a pesto for baked mussels (page 82), or blend it into a sauce for a delicate sautéed skate wing or grilled trout. It also pairs well with salty Mediterranean ingredients—try it in a piquant tomato sauce with capers or mixed into chopped black olive tapenade—and amplifies simple dishes like roasted potatoes and white bean soup.

For most people, mint is the herb that first comes to mind for fruits and sweets. Nearly all varieties are suited. Use finely chopped mint leaves to macerate berries, melon, tropical fruits, or fruit salad, or infuse the sprigs in syrup, milk, or cream (pages 248–55) that will be used in desserts, especially those with citrus, ginger, or lavender. Mint sprigs are a ubiquitous dessert garnish, but for something more elegant and edible, slice the leaves as thinly as possible (chiffonade) and judiciously strew them over the dessert.

As exemplified by a peppermint patty or a bowl of mint chocolate-chip ice cream, mint is the chocolate lover's herb. Here's the chance to use cool peppermint or its cousin chocolate mint, which is a variety that truly smells like a peppermint patty before it even gets close to real chocolate, and is a personal favorite. Infuse a handful of fresh sprigs in milk or cream (page 248), then use this minted milk or cream in your chocolate recipe. Try chocolate mint mousse, soufflé, pot de crème, ice cream, or truffles.

Mint Varieties   Spearmint is so common that it's often just called garden mint. Many other mint varieties share its fruity flavor and can be used interchangeably. Curly mint has large wavy leaves, true mint has smaller leaves and a more branching habit, and silver mint has gray-green leaves, but all have essentially the same spearmint flavor. Moroccan mint is spicier and less sweet than spearmint, and it's one of my favorites to use in bean dishes or with lamb.

There are many mints that faintly mimic fruit flavors. Orange, grapefruit, lemon, and lime mint all smell like mild peppermint mixed with a pinch of their respective namesake flavors. Apple mint, *M. suaveolens,* is a very popular and attractive tall-growing mint with fuzzy silvery leaves. It has a soft scent, like weak spearmint with the subtlest suggestion of a freshly sliced apple. Its smaller cousin pineapple mint has a similar subdued flavor that hints at tropical fruit, and I especially like the beautiful variegated version of this variety. These fruity mints are delightful to have around to rub and sniff, as a garnish for a beverage, or to occasionally flavor fruit desserts, but their fragrance outshines their flavor, which limits their use as culinary herbs.

Growing Mint   There is a gardener's saying, "You don't have mint, mint has you." Mint is pushy and infamous for running amok. The plants spread by vigorous underground stolons (stems) and will quickly overtake more reserved neighbors. The best solution is to give mint its own territory away from other herbs. At The Herbfarm, many mint varieties have found their way into a llama pasture where, well fertilized, they happily grow chest high and spread wherever they please. If you haven't the space to devote to this solution, plant mint in large pots or containers like whiskey barrels or chimney flues that you can leave above ground or bury in the garden and which will keep the roots under control. Mint is such an adventurer that even when grown in raised beds, it often wanders to other parts of the garden.

Mint tolerates most growing conditions. It will survive dry periods but prefers plenty of water, as long as the soil is well drained. Apple mint is the most tolerant of drier conditions. Give mint at least half-a-day's sun and keep the plants well fed. Most mint varieties are hardy anywhere in the United States but overly wet roots can kill the plants during the winter.

Mint's worst enemy is rust, a fungal disease that covers the plants with red-brown spots, ruins its leaves, and stunts its growth. Unfortunately there's little you can do to cure your plants, but you can prevent it by keeping them healthy and well watered. If rust attacks your mint, cut the plants back to ground level and destroy all the infected material. If the problem is very bad, replant uninfected mint plants in a different part of the garden.

Harvesting Mint You can harvest mint however you please. Cut off tips, individual leaves, or whole stems. Even if the entire plant is shaved off at ground level, it will soon grow back enthusiastically. For the best leaf production cut the plants back by half when they bloom.

Storing Mint Keep mint sprigs in a resealable plastic bag in the vegetable crisper of your refrigerator, where they will stay fresh for up to a week; or keep the flowering stems like cut flowers in a glass of water on the kitchen counter, where they will last for two to three days.

To dry mint, harvest the stems just before the flowers open and hang them upside down in bunches in a well-ventilated place. When the leaves crisp, strip them from the stems and store them in tightly covered jars in a dark cupboard.

OREGANO

Greek oregano, *Origanum vulgare* subsp. *hirtum,* is by far the spiciest plant in the herb garden. Belonging to the mint family, this perennial has slightly fuzzy, dark green leaves held on soft stems that grow in clumps to about two feet high. In summer the stems are topped with clusters of tiny white flowers held in green bracts. Its fragrance is pungent and pronounced, but not until you chew into a leaf does it reveal its fierce peppery bite underscored with mint, thyme, and camphor flavors—a bite so strong that a freshly picked leaf will tingle in your mouth like a mild chile pepper.

You might have tasted oregano from your own garden or from the supermarket and think my description of its exuberant flavor is quite overstated. The disparity is due to a popular confusion. There are other types of oregano, and most widely grown is a wild variety that is often called common oregano, *O. vulgare* subsp. *vulgare.* It looks almost the same as the Greek, but it's a more vigorous grower and, instead of all-white flowers, its blossoms range from blush white to deep pink. It may take a trained eye to tell them apart by sight, but a sniff will instantly reveal the difference. Common oregano has a very weak, almost negligible, flavor. It's an attractive, if somewhat invasive, garden plant, but it's simply not a culinary herb. Unfortunately oregano plants sold in garden centers and cut oregano sprigs in the market are rarely labeled specifically or accurately. Often you will end up with the common type. To complicate the issue further, oregano varieties cross easily, and if started from seed, the plants will often range in flavor from the intensity of the true Greek to the blandness of the common. Plants in nurseries should be propagated by cuttings taken from a mother plant with a strong flavor, not from seed. All this leads to one simple rule: Before you buy it, smell it. Let your senses tell you if you're getting the correct herb. Rub the leaves and then smell—they should be heavily perfumed. Better yet, nibble on a leaf—as you chew, it should fill your mouth with heat, as if you bit into a black peppercorn.

Cooking with Greek Oregano   Greek oregano's flavor is hot and lively, and it likes to blare its presence rather than stay in the background. It can easily overpower. Its flavor works best with other "big" flavors, particularly other Mediterranean ingredients like olives, capers, lemon, garlic, and anchovies, and with tangy sweet sauces and hot chiles. Traditionally, oregano is added to tomato sauce (earning it the title of Pizza Herb) and cooked with red meats, particularly lamb, but it's also good with summer vegetables like zucchini, eggplant, and bell peppers, with sturdy seafood like swordfish, squid, and shrimp, and in sharp salad dressings.

Because oregano's flavor is so bold, it's quite durable through most cooking processes. You can toss potatoes with oregano and garlic, then roast them in a blazing oven; the herb will not lose its identity. Likewise you can simmer it in Bolognese sauce for hours and still know it's there. Pair oregano with other strong Mediterranean herbs like rosemary, thyme, and sage, or with the always affable parsley or chives. Keep it away from herbs it would drown out or compete with, like chervil, tarragon, dill, and cilantro.

Oregano Varieties   The flavor we connect with oregano comes from the essential oil cavracol. There are other oregano species with high amounts of this oil, and they can stand in for the true Greek variety. Labels are not always reliable, so if you want the plant for culinary use, always choose it based on smell. Plants labeled Syrian, Turkish, or Turkistan oregano will generally have a flavor somewhere between Greek oregano and sweet marjoram. Dittany of Crete is a low grower with thick fuzzy leaves, a strong flavor, and little sweetness. Pot marjoram is another very strong-tasting oregano. It will not withstand frost, but it's the best choice for growing indoors.

Apart from the *Origanums*, there are completely unrelated plants that contain cavracol and lend the same flavor in cooking. Oregano thyme is a vigorous ground-covering plant that tastes as much like oregano as it does thyme (which it is). Mexican oregano is related to lemon verbena, and its leaves are often found in commercial dried oregano. Cuban oregano is in the coleus family and has pungent fleshy leaves. Any of these, tablespoon for tablespoon, make an acceptable substitute for Greek oregano.

Sweet marjoram (page 404) is a species of oregano usually grown as an annual, but its flavor is so much smoother and its uses are so different that it's essentially a different herb. The same is true of Italian oregano, or hardy sweet marjoram, which is a sterile hybrid between Greek oregano and sweet marjoram. It grows better in cool weather than sweet marjoram does and is hardier—likely to live through a Zone 8 winter (lows to 10°F).

Growing Oregano   Like most Mediterranean herbs, oregano likes well-drained soil and lots of sun. These two simple requirements can please it so much that it will invade your entire herb bed, so keep an eye on it next to less energetic inhabitants. Also, don't grow common oregano anywhere near other oregano varieties. Because it spreads by underground stolons or by seeding itself, it may replace your more flavorful oregano plants without your realizing it. Once it gets out of control, its roaming root system will invade neighboring plantings and it will be difficult to pull out without uprooting everything.

Harvesting Oregano You can harvest oregano sprigs as far down the plant as you like. After the plant flowers, cut the stems back by at least two-thirds to encourage fresh growth from the base. The plants can go through several flowering cycles each season, depending on your climate.

Storing Oregano Keep oregano in a resealable plastic bag in the vegetable crisper of your refrigerator. It will stay fresh for up to five days.

Greek oregano keeps its flavor extremely well when dried, and the dried form is actually preferred by some Mediterranean cooks. Your own freshly dried oregano will have far more flavor than anything you buy in a supermarket as long as you grow a pungent variety. Harvest long stems right before the buds open and hang them in bunches upside down in a well-ventilated spot. When the leaves crisp, strip them from the stems and store in a tightly covered jar.

PARSLEY

Although it's an icon of American cuisine, a parsley sprig garnish does little to advertise this herb's versatility. Parsley is so common that it's often overlooked, yet this verdant herb's flavor should never be underestimated. Pretend you've never tasted it before and take a moment to sample a leaf. It has the essence of fresh green flavor and a distinct pungency that speaks for itself as well as harmonizes with nearly any other herb in the garden.

Parsley, *Petroselinum crispum,* is a biennial that will stay beautifully green all winter, even buried under snow. The first year it grows to about twelve inches, and the second season it sends up flower heads that extend its reach to about two feet. Two different types are commonly available. Curly parsley is the variety we know best. Its fluffy leaf texture makes it an outstanding foliage plant in the garden and an attractive garnish. Vying for popularity, and now available in most markets, is flat-leaf or Italian parsley. It's a taller and more open-growing plant, with compound dark green leaves shaped like small celery leaves. The difference in flavor between Italian or flat-leaf and curly is very subtle, although Italian or flat-leaf parsley is considered to be stronger and better tasting. As with any herb, flavor can vary, but in a blind tasting, it can be hard to tell them apart. The two varieties can be substituted for each other in nearly all instances, but I find the texture of Italian or flat-leaf parsley leaves more pleasing. It's my first choice if the leaves are to be left whole or coarsely chopped.

COOKING WITH PARSLEY

When you stir a handful of chopped parsley into a dish at the end of cooking, the emerald flecks instantly make the dish look livelier while adding an elusive layer of flavor that can only be described as herbal and green. Parsley is appropriate in nearly anything savory—stir it into sauces, stews, braises, and soups and sprinkle it over sautéed vegetables, meat, and seafood. Of course, you have to use some discretion—don't load parsley on everything you cook—but don't ignore it because other herbs seem trendier.

Another reason for parsley's usefulness is its ability to mix with nearly any other savory herb. It blends with delicate herbs like chervil, chives, and tarragon without taking away anything or competing with their flavor. When parsley meets stronger-flavored herbs like rosemary and sage, its fresh green flavor seems to tone down their astringent or camphoric characteristics and prevents their assertive flavors from overpowering. And in instances when you need a large quantity of an herb, as in an herb crust, but don't want too strong a flavor, parsley fills out the herb mixture—it's the herbal equivalent of bread crumbs.

Parsley can also serve as the main ingredient in a salad or a large part of it, as in Herbed Couscous Salad (page 68). Whole bunches can even be cooked like spinach with shallots and butter for a unique side dish.

Fried parsley is a traditional garnish, usually used on fried fish. The glimmering crisp sprigs are a translucent emerald green and have a vegetative seaweedlike flavor. Curly parsley yields a more dramatic garnish than the flat-leaf variety. Before you deep-fry the sprigs, be sure they are completely dry or the oil will splatter violently. Even if dry, they will still seem to explode when you drop them in the oil, so stand back. Fry about one-half cup at a time in one to two inches of vegetable or olive oil heated to 350°F just until they stop making noise, about fifteen seconds. Drain the sprigs on paper towels and sprinkle with salt.

To wash parsley, hold a bunch by the stems, dunk it vigorously in a basin of cold water, and swish it around, then pull it out and shake it dry. If you want a sprinkle of chopped parsley, it will need to be very dry—use a salad spinner or pat it between clean towels. Still holding the bunch by the stems, use a sharp knife and cut right below where the leaves begin, releasing most of the greenery from the thick lower stems. (Save the stems for bouquet garni for stocks or braises.) Strip out any thick stems that were left behind with the leaves, but you don't need to pick out every tiny stem, since they're soft enough to blend in once the herb is chopped. Gather the sprigs with your fingers into a tight bunch and chop them coarsely in one direction. Then use the knife with a rocking motion to achieve the degree of fineness you're after. Often a coarse chop is best for lively color and texture, but a very fine chop is in order if you want to sprinkle it on an elegant dish or blend it into the mixture for an herb crust on meat or seafood.

In cooking school I was taught that the way to make parsley easier to sprinkle is to put the chopped leaves in a towel and twist it to squeeze out every drop of juice you can. The problem is you also end up removing every remnant of flavor and freshness. This idea makes me cringe. Just be sure the herb is dry before you chop it.

Growing Parsley Grow parsley in full sun under the same conditions most vegetables like. Give it good drainage, decent soil, and keep it well watered and fed. Parsley is easy to grow from its large seeds, but you need plenty of patience. They can take over a month to germinate.

Parsley is a biennial, meaning it grows leaves the first year, blooms the second year and then dies. Because its leaves can be tougher and a bit bitter in its second season, it's often grown as an annual. You can plant it in early spring for a summer crop or plant it in late summer so that it lives through the winter and gives you a generous crop in the spring. Parsley is as easy to grow in pots as in the ground. It's one of the few herbs that grow well indoors, but because it's so easily purchased as a cut herb, I'd have a hard time giving it valuable window space. If you choose to grow it inside, give it lots of sun and water.

Harvesting Parsley Cut parsley stems all the way down to ground level, harvesting those on the outside of the plant first.

Storing Parsley Keep parsley in a resealable plastic bag in the vegetable crisper of your refrigerator. It will stay fresh for up to one week.

PERILLA

This herb is often used in sushi, so many Americans know it best by its Japanese name, shiso, but its Latin name is *Perilla frutescens* and its English name is perilla. Native to Asia, from India to Japan, it has been cultivated in European gardens since the eighteenth century. It first showed up in America in the mid-nineteenth century but then escaped the gardens to grow wild throughout the Southeast United States. Sometimes it is called rattlesnake weed, a reference to its rattling stems of seed pods.

Perilla is an annual in the mint family with a branching two- to three-foot growth habit, very much like that of sweet basil. It holds beautifully textured bumpy leaves, three to five inches long, which have toothed and frilled edges. Like basil, it sends up six-inch spikes of white or pale pink flowers, and once the seeds ripen, the plants wither. There are two types of perilla: purple (sometimes called red) and green. The purple—nicknamed beefsteak plant for its raw-meat hue—ranges from sanguine to so deep a purple that in bright sunlight it can look black. After the plant blooms, the color turns paler and greener. Green perilla's leaves are rounder and smoother, although there is a variety called Crispa with leaves that are very frilled and evoke a paisley pattern.

Cooking with Perilla Perilla's flavor is best described as a cross between cumin and parsley with a hint of cinnamon. The leaves are strong tasting with a flavor quite different from any other plant in the herb garden—savory but somehow refreshing. Perilla is often used raw in salads, relishes, and cold marinated dishes, and it's especially good with cold seafood like crab and shrimp. I like to shred the leaves into very fine strips and either toss them into the dish or strew them on top. Dipped in tempura batter and fried, the leaves make terrific fritters to serve as appetizers or alongside fish dishes. In Korea the pickled leaves are added to rice. Perilla's penetrating flavor is good with marinated onion, avocado, and particularly raw apple and pear. If you soak the chopped leaves of the purple variety in vinegar, wine, or lemon juice, it will turn the liquid a vivid magenta color.

Growing Perilla Grow perilla just as you grow basil. Give it lots of sun, warmth, moderately good soil, and moisture. Pinch off the buds whenever they appear; this will not only keep it bushy and long lived but also stop it from overtaking your yard. In warm climates perilla will self-sow with great determination.

Harvesting Perilla   Cut sprigs above a leaf joint, remembering not to harvest more than one-third of the entire plant at one time.

Storing Perilla   Keep perilla in a resealable plastic bag in the vegetable crisper of your refrigerator. It will stay fresh for up to five days.

ROSEMARY

Rosemary is an herb of the hearth. It loves the licking flames of a grill, the steady heat of a baker's oven, or hours slowly simmering with braised meats. Wafting from a pot on the stove or a plant in the field, its sweet pinelike fragrance travels far and lingers in the air, on your fingers, and in your thoughts. Historically, this unfading quality has made it the plant of remembrance and constancy, and so it's played a symbolic role in both funerals and weddings. But the memories it brings to mind are those of great food.

The plant is native to the Mediterranean seacoast, and its Latin name, *rosmarinus,* means dew of the sea. Rosemary is a woody evergreen shrub in the mint family, well designed for a windy coastal hillside. Its narrow leaves, emanating from stiff branches, are leathery, needlelike, and a deep pine green with silvery undersides. In climates mild enough for it to live through the winter (the hardiest rosemary cannot survive temperatures below 10°F), it will grow into an impressive shrub from three to six feet tall, supported by a gnarled branching framework. Many varieties grow prostrate and trail along the ground or tumble over rockery. In spring rosemary covers itself with tiny blue flowers and follows the show in summer with lush, soft tufts of young growth.

Cooking with Rosemary   Rosemary's flavor is resinous, spicy, uplifting, and forceful. It has a sweet, piney perfume underscored with astringency and bitterness. There's no subtlety about it, so it needs a judicious hand. By no means be afraid of it, for this herb has the potential to enhance a great variety of dishes, but always keep in mind it can be clumsy and overpowering when too much is used on delicate foods.

Use rosemary with other full flavors. It's a top choice for the grill because it's flavor stands up to the intense heat and melds beautifully with smoky flavors. Add the coarsely chopped needles to a grill marinade for chicken, shrimp, swordfish, or eggplant. Poke it around meats before roasting, particularly its classic partner lamb. On the stovetop, add several teaspoons to caramelized onions, glazed carrots, or crispy potatoes. The sprigs can season the liquid used to steam mussels or shrimp or add flavor to hearty braises and stews. Historically it's used to marinate meats, not only for its flavor but also because, like sage and thyme, it has antibacterial and antioxidant agents that prevent fat from turning rancid—it acts as a natural preservative.

Rosemary is also an herb that works remarkably well for baking. It's my first choice to add to yeast breads, and it's delicious in biscuits and muffins. Just stir a tablespoon or two of the chopped leaves into the dough or batter. In desserts, rosemary's piney flavor balances sweetness and adds a sophisticated note. Try adding it to simple buttery sweets like shortbread and pound cake or any dessert with apples or pears, like Pear, Maple, and Rosemary Clafouti (page 272). And sorbet made of Concord grapes flavored with rosemary (page 300) is a refreshing autumn treat.

Because of its sturdiness, you can add rosemary early in the cooking process. For braises, stews, and roasts, coarsely chop the needles and let them cook in the dish from the start. If the herb will be only briefly cooked, as in a quick sauté with shrimp, it's best to chop it fine and use it sparingly. For a garnish or textural accent, deep-fry the sprigs for ten to fifteen seconds to turn the leaves crunchy and much more palatable. Similarly, if rosemary needles are coated with a little oil before they bake, as on top of focaccia or in a pan of roasting potatoes, they crisp up and become a fragrant toasty accent. To add rosemary's flavor to desserts, infuse sprigs in milk, cream, or caramel, then strain them out. A few teaspoons of the very finely chopped leaves lend intrigue when stirred into a cake or quick bread batter, or butter cookie dough.

Rosemary is an herb whose flavor varies drastically depending on variety, how fresh it is, the season in which it's harvested, and where and how it's been grown. If I harvest sprigs from the rosemary shrub in my backyard in January, I'll need to add one-quarter cup of chopped leaves to a pot of white bean soup, but rosemary sprigs harvested from a plant growing in a hot greenhouse will be so strong that less than a tablespoon will provide the same level of flavor. If the sprigs feel sticky with resin, it's a good indication that it will be strong tasting and have more distinct camphoric and bitter flavors. It doesn't mean you can't cook with it, but you should always smell and taste the herb first to evaluate its intensity. If it seems particularly strong, bitter, or tannic, begin with less; if it's on the mild side, add more.

When you grow your own rosemary, you'll find there's more to cook with than just the leaves. The large woody stems make terrific skewers for the grill, and the small woody stems are good for little hors-d'oeuvre "picks." Leave some needles on the end for looks. When you use a charcoal kettle grill, throw several large branches directly on the hot coals just before you place the food on the rack, then cook with the grill lid on; the food will pick up a haunting smoky flavor. The early spring blossoms are the greatest bonus, for they have the subdued flavor of the leaves with a touch of sweetness and make a beautiful garnish tossed over pasta, salad, or a grilled chop.

All of the strong Mediterranean herbs are very comfortable with rosemary. You can't go wrong using it in combination with oregano, sage, thyme, or parsley, and it's an essential ingredient in the herb mixture called herbes de Provence. Citrus rinds or juices are appropriate partners, and, of course, the bite of garlic is always a good match to rosemary's pungency.

Rosemary Varieties Rosemary is usually propagated from cuttings, and there are many named cultivars that differ in growth habit, leaf and flower color, tolerance to frost, and, in some cases, flavor. One of the hardiest varieties is Arp, which can reportedly survive temperatures as low as −10°F if grown in a sheltered spot, like by a sunny south wall, and mulched. It has a comparatively mild flavor and is a good grower, but it's not the most attractive rosemary—its needles are hard and rather sparse, its growth sprawling, and its flowers a washy light blue color. More fetching and tasty but slightly less hardy are the varieties Tuscan Blue, Logee's Blue, and Shimmering Stars. These three all have lush foliage, upright growth, and deep blue flowers. Golden Rain is a good grower with golden needles that look stunning next to its deep blue blossoms, and it bears a particularly sweet scent. Majorca Pink has pink blossoms, and Alba has white.

Trailing varieties, like Huntington's Carpet and Lockwood, make excellent ground covers or hanging basket specimens, but they are less tolerant of frost. Because they tend to continue growing throughout the winter, rather than going semidormant as most uprights do, they are good varieties to grow as potted plants that spend winters indoors.

Growing Rosemary   Because it's a tender shrub, rosemary must have mild winter temperatures to be able to survive outside year-round. If you live in a mild climate where winter temperatures rarely fall below 20°F (Zone 8), you can plant it in a sunny, sheltered spot and harvest from it all year round, but if you live in Zone 6 or 7, you will be taking a chance of losing it. In Mediterranean-like climates, like much of California, rosemary will grow with no effort at all and will even make a splendidly fragrant and rugged hedge. This herb dislikes muggy weather; in very hot and humid areas, like the Southeast, the shrubs will need some nurturing. Be sure they have perfect drainage, good air circulation, a good thick mulch, and keep them on the dry side.

If you live in colder winter areas, you can grow rosemary either as an annual or plant it in a pot and give it shelter in winter. If you are going to pot it up, choose a container large enough to accommodate growth but not too big, because they like to be slightly potbound and you need to be able to move it easily—a twelve-inch-diameter pot works well. Keep it outside in full sun while the weather is warm. When nights begin to threaten frost, gradually acclimate it to an indoor environment, preferably one with plenty of direct sun, good air circulation, and cool temperatures. An enclosed porch is ideal. Keep it on the dry side but don't let it dry out completely. You can harvest from the plant but be judicious because it grows back slowly. When the weather warms, acclimate it to the outdoors again slowly, setting it out in the shade for a few hours each day at first. An outdoor summer vacation is important for the plant's health, so rosemary is very difficult to grow exclusively as a houseplant.

Harvesting Rosemary   Harvest from your outdoor rosemary as if you were pruning a shrub. You have the choice of clipping tender new growth or taking large pieces of woody branches deep into the plant. Because of its shrubby framework, rosemary is one herb that does not require cutting back after flowering.

Storing Rosemary   Keep rosemary sprigs in a resealable plastic bag in the vegetable crisper of your refrigerator. They will stay fresh for up to two weeks.

If you grow rosemary as a perennial, you can harvest fresh sprigs throughout the year. If you grow it as an annual, you might want to dry some branches before the plant succumbs to frost, because it keeps its flavor well. Harvest it in the late summer and hang the branches upside down in an airy spot until the needles are brittle, then strip the leaves from the stems and store them in a tightly sealed container in a dark cupboard.

SAGE

It's easiest to describe sage's flavor in "wine-speak." Like a great Burgundy, rather than being sweet or fruity, sage is dry and austere; instead of light and clean, it's earthy and weighty. As a result, sage adds a haunting savoriness to foods. Stirred into a pot of roasted garlic soup or stuffed under the skin of a roasting chicken, it produces an extraordinary depth of flavor.

Sage belongs to the enormous group of plants called salvias, which in turn are members of the mint family. Culinary sage is *Salvia officinalis*. Its first year in your garden, a sage plant will be quite compact and have mostly soft stems, then in subsequent years it will develop into a spreading, woody shrub that remains semi-evergreen in mild climates. Most plants will eventually reach two to three feet high and three feet wide, but you can prune them back to a more manageable size. The leaves can be gray green, purple tinged, golden, or variegated, but they are always soft, thick, and irresistible to rub.

Cooking with Sage Sage is traditionally used with fatty meats like pork, goose, and duck. Long considered a medicinal herb that helps with digestion, sage seems to cut through the richness of fats. Fortunately it also adds a delicious flavor. Sage, like rosemary and thyme, is a rugged herb; it will hold up to roasting, stewing, or grilling and still keep its character. In traditional American cooking, we're most familiar with sage as an ingredient in Thanksgiving turkey stuffing, but it can make its way into stuffings for many other foods as well. One of the most delicious is the Italian dish, saltimbocca where whole sage leaves are layered with prosciutto between slices of pounded veal. Sage leaves can also be tied around the outside of a pork or lamb roast before it goes in the oven, or you can insert them into slits in the flesh.

Because of its chewy texture and astringency, sage is more palatable once it's cooked. If you're using it in a briefly cooked dish, either chop it very fine or first cook the leaves in oil or butter. If you flash-fry the leaves in hot oil for ten to fifteen seconds, they become crunchy and delicately flavored and make a delicious garnish or crunchy ingredient in a salad or pasta. Fried leaves of variegated sage are especially beautiful. An inspired Italian technique is to cook sage in plenty of butter in a small skillet until they crisp up and the butter begins to brown slightly. The fragrant crunchy leaves are delicious tossed with pasta and gnocchi and spooned over vegetables like asparagus or green beans.

Shrimp and sturdy fish like tuna or swordfish appreciate the flavor of sage. Either marinate the seafood with the chopped leaves or skewer the seafood with whole sage leaves and lemon slices for the grill. Sage also pairs well with many vegetables—asparagus and peas in the spring, corn or beans in summer, and squash, onions, and root vegetables in fall and winter. Sage combines most successfully with other strong Mediterranean herbs like rosemary, thyme, and bay, and with mint and lemon herbs. For desserts, sage-infused syrup or honey goes well with cherries and blueberries and in sweets with orange, pear, honey, or dried fruit flavors.

Keep in mind it's easy to overdo this herb, especially with delicate foods. You never want its astringent, medicinal side to be noticed. Begin with two teaspoons for six servings and increase from there. Like many other herbs, its strength varies according to the seasons, growing conditions, and the variety of sage you are using. Fresh sage sold in supermarkets is often much weaker than what you clip from your garden. As always, taste as you add, even when following a recipe.

Sage blossoms are an added bonus of growing your own plants. Because they only bloom for several weeks late in the spring, the flowers are a rare ingredient, but one mature plant will provide you with more than you can use during that short time. The violet blue flowers have a very delicate texture, and their flavor is similar to that of the leaf but with a distinct sweetness replacing the astringency. Harvest them by grasping the petals between your thumb and forefinger; gently tug on the blossom, leaving the calyx behind. It takes time to gather them, but it's a good excuse to dawdle among the herbs. Right before serving, sprinkle the azure-colored blooms on salads, pastas, or any other foods that would be good with sage leaves.

Sage Varieties   Many cultivars of culinary sage are available, each with distinct characteristics. Perhaps the biggest difference between varieties is one you don't see when you buy a little four-inch pot off the shelf—some sages are more likely to bloom than others. Common culinary sage, or garden sage, will reliably burst into bloom in late spring sending up twelve-inch spikes covered with sweet-tasting blue purple blossoms (although some special varieties have white or pink flowers). Afterward the exhausted plants become very lanky and require a strong cutting back. Many named cultivars, like Holts Mammoth, Berggarten, and Woodcote Farm have been bred with a more compact habit and larger leaves, but depending on climate and growing conditions, these varieties do not always bloom, and when they do, they are not as floriferous as common sage. Rather than trying to set seed, they spend their energy producing lush foliage so they yield a bigger crop of leaves. I suggest growing several kinds of sage. It would be a shame to miss the profuse bloom of garden sage, yet it's nice to have the abundance and diversity of foliage that other varieties offer.

Most sages are a soft gray green color, but there are many exceptions. Purple sage has the same growth habit and flavor as compact green sages, but it has gorgeous dark burgundy green foliage. Golden, tricolor, and variegated sages all have dazzling leaves with good flavor, but they are less vigorous and much less hardy than green-leafed sages.

Growing Sage   Sage is easy to grow if you give it full sun and very well drained soil. If you can't keep it alive, it's because the roots stay wet and rot. Most varieties will survive very cold winters, down to Zone 5 (low of –20°F), but a good layer of mulch and roots that are not waterlogged will ensure they overwinter. In the heat and humidity of the Southeast United States, sage plants might not live year to year, but they can easily be grown as annuals.

Harvesting Sage   You can harvest leaves individually, but it's better to snip whole sprigs above pairs of leaves. If the plant is mature and has woody branches, the longest and straightest ones make flavorful skewers for the grill.

If your sage plant flowers, always cut it back after it's done. It's not too severe to cut all the stems back by half their height to keep the plants from becoming lanky. If you're lucky, you might even get a second smaller flush of flowers in late summer. Don't cut the plants back in the fall, however, or the new growth will not have time to mature and the plants will be more susceptible to winter damage. If you grow a variety that doesn't bloom, it should be cut back in midspring after it begins to show growth, about the same time as deciduous trees leaf out. Never cut below where new leaves are sprouting, for the plant may not be able to break growth below the cut, killing the branch.

Storing Sage   Keep sage in a resealable plastic bag in the vegetable crisper of your refrigerator. It will stay fresh for up to two weeks.

Sage retains quite a bit of flavor when it's dried. If you can't harvest fresh leaves year-round in your climate, try drying your own because they will have much more flavor than anything you can buy. First remove and discard the stems, which are thick and dry too slowly. Lay out the leaves in a single layer in a shallow box or, better yet, on a screen. Keep it in an airy spot out of direct sunlight and toss the leaves about every day or so. When they are crisp, crush them lightly and store them in a tightly sealed jar in a dark cupboard.

SAVORY

This herb's name tells the whole story. The two culinary savories, summer savory, *Satureja hortensis,* and winter savory, *S. montana,* are deliciously aromatic and definitely not sweet. They both have a delightful deep peppery flavor that perks up roasts and stews, dried beans, and all sorts of vegetable dishes. Don't overlook them for more familiar herbs like thyme, rosemary, and sage.

The underlying flavor of summer savory and winter savory is essentially similar, and they can nearly always be substituted for one another, but there are also big differences between the two. Summer savory is a quick-growing annual, reaching twelve to eighteen inches. It has a lanky habit with soft spindly stems and thin, soft, sparsely spaced gray green leaves. When the plant is mature, very delicate light pink or white flowers appear between the leaves along the upper portions of the stems.

Winter savory is an evergreen or semi-evergreen shrubby perennial with a bushy spreading habit, rarely taller than twelve inches high, but as much as fifteen inches across. Its short, narrow leaves are thick, glossy, very dark green and tightly spaced on woody stems. Its flowers are also on the upper stems, but they are showier. Winter savory's flavor is markedly hotter and more biting than that of summer savory.

Cooking with Savory   It's quite simple: Cook with summer savory in summer and cook with winter savory in the months when summer savory is not in the garden. Both are known as the Bean Herb because savory gives an incomparable flavor to any dish made from dried beans. Tie a bundle of the sprigs together with a bay leaf or two and let it simmer with the beans, or chop the leaves and add them with onions and other flavorings. Savory, especially the summer variety, is also superb on fresh green beans, runner beans, and fresh fava beans. Add a tablespoon or two of the chopped leaves at any point in the cooking or toss them into dressings for bean salads. It's also good with other vegetables like cabbage, Brussels sprouts, onion, kale, summer squash, beets, and tomato, and it's delicious on roasted potatoes or in potato salad. Add it to marinades and herb rubs for beef, lamb, pork, and chicken before they're roasted or grilled. Savory is always a good addition to hearty braised dishes, especially those with red wine.

Growing Savory   Summer savory is very easy to start from seed and can be sown where you want it to grow. It does well in most soils, especially those with very good drainage. It must have plenty of sun and grows best if kept well fertilized and well watered.

Winter savory tolerates poor soil more than the summer variety, but it is essential that drainage be excellent. It should be hardy to Zone 5 (lows of −20°F), but if it has wet roots all winter, it will probably not make it to spring.

Harvesting Savory   Cut sprigs of both summer and winter savory about one-third of the way down the stems. When summer savory starts to bloom, cut the entire plant back by one-third to prolong its life and encourage more foliage. Cut winter savory back after it blooms to keep it bushy and productive.

Storing Savory   Keep savory in a resealable plastic bag in the vegetable crisper of your refrigerator. Summer savory will stay fresh for up to one week and winter savory for up to two weeks.

SCENTED GERANIUMS

These unassuming plants hide big secrets. Like magic lanterns, you only need to rub them to unleash their power. They'll overwhelm you with vibrant fragrance. Some smell intensely lemony, others like a heady rose bush in full bloom, and still others mimic scents of peppermint, apple, coconut, nutmeg, or lime.

Scented geraniums are in the genus *Pelargonium* and are cousins of window-box geraniums, but they should not be confused with true geraniums, which are hardy perennial border plants belonging to the genus *Geranium* and are not edible. Originating in South Africa, scented geraniums have been popular in Europe since the seventeenth century and have been grown in America since the eighteenth. Rose geraniums were especially popular in the Victorian era and were used to scent fingerbowls, potpourris, perfumes, and jellies. Today rose geraniums are an important crop, grown for their oil, which is used extensively in perfumes.

Originating from a handful of species, there are now hundreds of varieties of scented geraniums. Their thick leaves can be smooth, fuzzy, or raspy and range from slightly lobed to deeply serrated. Foliage color ranges from many shades of green to silvery gray, and some are even variegated or striped with gold and burgundy. All are tender perennials, killed by any degree of frost, but they make excellent pot plants, indoors or out. In frost-free climates some varieties will grow three to six feet tall, but in one season you can expect them to develop into a mound two feet high and wide. Just like window-box geraniums, they produce round clusters of brightly colored five-petaled blooms in shades of white, pink, red, and violet, but the flowers of scented geraniums are small and insignificant compared to the foliage. Nevertheless, their blossoms are charming and make tasty and exquisite garnishes for desserts and beverages.

Cooking with Scented Geraniums   It's tempting to grow them all, but there are only two "flavors" of geranium that I think are essential for the culinary herb garden—rose and lemon. There are many individual cultivars with the rose scent. You might find plants in nurseries labeled Old-fashioned Rose, Attar of Roses, Lemon Rose, or just Rose, but they all share an intense rose fragrance that is delightful as a flavoring in a variety of desserts, beverages, and preserves. Steep the leaves in milk or cream to flavor ice cream and custards, or in syrup or honey to flavor sorbets, fruit sauces, and fruit salads. The flavor of rose geranium harmonizes with fruits like apricot, apple, peach, and berries—in particular raspberries—and seems to deepen the essence of the berry flavor. A small dish of ripe fragrant raspberries with a dollop of rose geranium–scented whipped cream (page 264) and garnished with a single rose geranium flower makes a stunning dessert. For an old-fashioned rose geranium pound cake, line a buttered pan with about a dozen of the leaves before filling it with batter. Before serving, you peel the tough leaves off, but the whole cake will be infused with the heavenly rose scent.

Mauny Kaseburg, a Northwest media personality, relayed an amusing story about rose geranium leaves and the food writer M. F. K. Fisher. Mary Frances, in front of a table of guests, constructed a tea sandwich with two slices of crustless white bread, a smear of unsalted butter, and a large rose geranium leaf. She wrapped it in waxed paper and instructed Mauny to sit on it—literally—for ten minutes to release the rose scent into the butter. After sitting on it for the required time, she removed the pressed sandwich and was then informed by M.F.K. that her derrière was not sufficiently warm enough or soft enough to incubate her snack!

My favorite lemon-scented geranium is Mabel Grey. It has roughly textured, star-shaped bright green leaves that are two inches wide and a delightful scent that is so strong it rivals lemon verbena in intensity. Another strongly scented lemon variety is Frensham lemon; its leaves are smaller, about one inch across, and a deeper green. Use lemon geranium leaves exactly as you would lemon verbena. Although you can steep them like rose geranium in hot milk, cream, or syrup, the lemon flavor will be brighter if you don't expose it to heat at all. Like lemon verbena, the best way to incorporate the flavor is to grind the leaves with sugar in a food processor or blender, then dissolve the sugar in liquid and strain it to remove any tough bits of leaf. Handled this way, lemon geranium makes a delicious bright green syrup for sorbet, sparkling drinks, or dressing for fruit salad.

Growing Scented Geraniums   Scented geraniums will flourish in a wide range of climates and require nothing more than rich, well-drained soil and plenty of sun. They should do equally well whether planted in the ground or in a pot. The bigger the pot, the bigger your plant will grow. They'll respond well to a twice monthly feeding of water-soluble food. If your geraniums are in the ground, dig and pot them up in early fall; if they are already potted, knock them out and replant them in fresh soil. After you pot them, cut them back hard—to about one-third of their original height—and put them on a sunny windowsill. They'll brush out again soon and indulge you with their heavenly scent all winter. In fact I find scented geraniums to be the easiest of all herbs to grow indoors.

Harvesting Scented Geraniums   Gather scented geraniums by cutting off individual leaves where they meet the stem or by cutting short sprigs from the branches, above a leaf joint.

Storing Scented Geraniums   Keep geranium leaves in a resealable plastic bag in the vegetable crisper of your refrigerator. They will stay fresh for up to a week. To capture their flavor for longer periods of time, bury about twenty-four leaves in a one-pound jar of sugar and store it in a dark cupboard. The sugar will become permeated with the geranium scent and stay fragrant for about three months. Sprinkle the sugar on fruit, use it to sweeten whipped cream, or stir it into iced tea.

SORREL

Sorrel is an enigma among culinary herbs. It hangs out in the shade and is not the least bit pungent or aromatic. Really it's a potherb, meaning it's used as a green rather than a flavoring. Although it's often described as lemony, I think that attribute is not deserved, for it has none of lemon's sweet citrus perfume, just a common acerbity. Its other name, sour grass, best pinpoints its verdant, tangy character, yet it does little to convey how delicious sorrel is with many foods.

There are two distinctly different types of culinary sorrel. Both are perennials. The variety most often grown in North America is garden sorrel, *Rumex acetosa*. It has deep green leaves with a distinctive, long spearlike shape and a substantial size, often six inches long. The leaves have the same texture as spinach, and they grow upright on short stems, each emanating from the crown of the plant. When the plant flowers, usually in May or June, tall spikes carry the leaves upward, topping out at about three feet. Buckler sorrel, *Rumex scutatus,* looks quite different. Its leaves are much rounder, much smaller (about one inch across), and held on long stems. The flavor is similar to garden sorrel, though slightly milder and less grassy. Both types are referred to as French sorrel, which confuses everyone. Technically buckler's sorrel is the true owner of this title, but for clarity it's best to use the terms garden or buckler's in specifying a type. They both have the same sour flavor and you can substitute one for the other ounce for ounce; however, when a recipe calls for sorrel, it's most likely referring to garden sorrel.

Cooking with Sorrel Add sorrel to dishes where you might use a squeeze of lemon or a dash of vinegar and where its grassy flavor will be an asset rather than a distraction. Traditionally it's used to make sorrel soup and to flavor egg dishes and sauce for delicate fish, particularly salmon. The large leaves of garden sorrel are perfect for cutting into fine chiffonade (thin strips), to fold into a butter sauce for seafood, or to sprinkle over a fish dish as a garnish. Unless the leaves are very young, remove the tough center vein before you cut them. In classic French cuisine, sorrel is used to stuff whole fish with tiny bones, like shad or trout, because the oxalic acid that gives sorrel its tartness softens the fish bones so they are not noticeable when eaten. A few handfuls of chopped sorrel leaves add a tart accent to sautéed greens, like spinach or chard. In salads, sorrel adds a contrast to bitter greens or sweet vegetables—use whole buckler's sorrel leaves or the torn leaves of larger garden sorrel. The delicate tang of shredded sorrel leaves is delicious folded into scrambled eggs or as an omelet filling. If you cook the shredded leaves in butter, they quickly melt into a richly flavored purée that's ideal for poached or baked egg dishes, such as Smoked Salmon and Sorrel Benedict (page 96), and as a fish sauce.

Sorrel has a very particular tendency. When cooked even briefly, it turns a homely gray green, akin to canned asparagus. It's best to use sorrel raw or add it at the very last second of preparation. Another trick is to use it in conjunction with something greener, like spinach or chives, which overrides the drab hue. In some dishes it's best to just ignore the color and enjoy how good it tastes.

Use a minimum of ¼ cup of shredded sorrel leaves for six servings and increase from there. Sorrel is a relatively mild herb so that two cups is not too much for some dishes. It pains me to see it sold in tiny one-ounce bunches for the same price as other herbs because it is so easy to grow and very small quantities are of little use. In hot weather sorrel becomes bitter, so be sure to taste it first. Spring and fall are the best seasons for harvesting.

Sorrel combines nicely with chives, parsley, tarragon, chervil, dill, and the other lemony herbs like lemon verbena and lemon thyme.

Growing Sorrel   Garden sorrel is a long-lived and spreading perennial that prefers cool weather, plenty of moisture, and a partly shady spot. Snails and slugs adore sorrel, and even though a few holes in the leaves won't affect the flavor, you'll probably need to control the pests if you garden where they're a problem; that is, the Pacific Northwest.

If you live in a hot climate, you might have better luck growing buckler's sorrel. It likes more sun and can tolerate drier conditions but still prefers rich, moist soil. It also tends to make a better roommate for other herbs. There is also a silver buckler's sorrel with beautifully marked leaves.

Harvesting Sorrel   Sorrel is one of the first herbs of spring, eager to burst out of the ground when trees are budding. Harvest the leaves freely at this time, for they're at their most tender and flavorful stage. Later in the spring, flower stalks will bolt upward. Cut them off at ground level to encourage the plant to produce more leaves from the crown, unless, that is, you want it to spread rapidly. Sorrel is an enthusiastic self-sower; if you let it go to seed, it will quickly take over more territory.

Storing Sorrel   Keep sorrel leaves in a resealable plastic bag in the vegetable crisper of your refrigerator. They will stay fresh for up to five days.

SWEET CICELY

If you garden where summers are very hot and humid, you can turn the page because you will have quite a struggle getting sweet cicely to grow in your garden. But in the Pacific Northwest or other northern areas with mild summer temperatures, sweet cicely is about the easiest thing you can grow, and you might even find yourself cursing its vigor.

Those not familiar with this plant always think it's a fern. Sweet cicely, *Myrrhis odorata,* sometimes called sweet chervil, is a perennial in the parsley family that likes to grow in the shade. Its leaves are not tough like a fern's but soft and slightly fuzzy, and if it's grown in a climate that suits it, they are one of the first things to appear from the ground in early spring. The emerald green foliage quickly grows two to four feet tall, then in midspring it's topped with sweetly scented clusters of lacy white flowers, followed by tasty little green seeds that turn brown a week or two later. The lush foliage remains in the garden late into the fall, even after tree branches are bare. All parts of the plant are edible and have an anise scent. The leaves have a very mild taste, the flowers and seeds have the strength of fennel, and the enormous thick plunging taproots that form when the herb matures have a powerful licorice fragrance.

Cooking with Sweet Cicely I will occasionally add small tips of the leaves to salads, but primarily I like to use sweet cicely's ferny leaves as liners, like natural green doilies. If I'm serving a shallow bowl of soup or a stemmed crystal glass of sorbet, I'll put one of the flat graceful sprigs on the plate underneath. Not intended to be eaten, they prevent the plate from slipping when it is served and bring color and texture from the garden to the table.

Like angelica, sweet cicely leaves are said to reduce the amount of sugar needed to sweeten tart fruits. I can't say I find this to be true, but the chopped leaves lend a pleasant, though green, anise flavor to fruit salad and pies.

When the flowers are just open and before they form seeds, small pieces of the blossoms can be added to salads or used as a garnish for vegetables like steamed carrots or peas. The whole flower clusters can be dipped in tempura batter and fried (page 72), then generously dusted with powdered sugar and served for dessert with ice cream or custard sauce.

You can make a sort of homemade licorice from the intensely flavored roots by peeling, slicing, and candying them in sugar syrup. The remaining slightly bitter syrup can then be used to make sorbets or to flavor beverages.

Growing Sweet Cicely Sweet cicely seeds itself freely in the garden, yet it can be slow to germinate when you plant seed, so buy a potted seedling to begin with. It will grow in any well-drained soil but sandy soil is best. Though it can take full sun, it will look healthiest if grown in partial shade in an open wooded spot. Cut back the flowering stalks right after they form seeds to keep it producing more foliage and to prevent it from seeding all over the garden. The tenacious roots are a struggle to dig up once they become established.

Harvesting Sweet Cicely Cut the leaves from any part of the plant at any time. Harvest the flowers when they first open and the fresh seeds when they first turn green and are still tender. The roots are best dug in the fall.

Storing Sweet Cicely Keep sweet cicely leaves and seeds in a resealable plastic bag in the vegetable crisper of your refrigerator. They will stay fresh for up to five days. (Candied sweet cicely root will keep for over three months.)

Tarragon

If you've never tasted fresh tarragon, nibble on a leaf and you're in for quite a surprise. It bears absolutely no resemblance to the grassy dried flakes of the same name found in cupboards or to the subtle hint of flavor in a tarragon vinegar or mustard. Instead, it is powerful and sweet with a pronounced aniselike flavor and a pungent bite. Freshly picked tarragon will fill your mouth with a strong minty heat and release a peppery sensation in your throat that lingers for quite some time. The predominant flavor in tarragon comes from the identical essential oil that's found in anise, but rather than having a cloying licorice quality, it has citrus and green herb characteristics that, combined with its spiciness, produce a delicious savoriness.

French tarragon (*Artemesia dracunculus* var. *sativa*) is a hardy perennial, and the only common culinary herb in the daisy family. Growing one to three feet tall with a sprawling habit, it has long, tough, wiry stems covered with narrow deep green one- to two-inch leaves that give it a rangy, shaggy appearance. Actually French tarragon looks somewhat awkward and lacks the vigor of most of its herb garden neighbors, but it makes up for its scruffiness with unique refined flavor.

There are two types of tarragon, French and Russian, and they are sometimes mislabeled. The flavor of French tarragon is far superior, and it's the only type you should use in the kitchen or plant in the garden. Because it is slow growing and doesn't set seed (it must be propagated by cuttings or root divisions), it's expensive for nurseries to produce. Russian tarragon, on the other hand, can be grown from seed and is much more vigorous in growth but far weaker in taste. Russian tarragon has lighter-colored and tenderer green leaves—often over two to three inches long—softer, thicker, and straighter stems, and can grow as tall as five feet. It produces tiny clusters of greenish white flowers at the tops of the mature sprigs. Before I knew the difference, I was more than mildly jealous of a good friend who grew a bed of four-foot-high robust tarragon, while the puny plants in my own garden seemed half starved in comparison. I must admit that when I learned hers was the Russian variety and had an inferior flavor, my gardening ego felt better. Be especially wary of packaged herbs or potted plants simply labeled tarragon. If the herb for sale in your market or nursery has tall straight stems, long light green leaves, and flower buds, it's probably Russian. The surest way to tell the difference is to nibble on a leaf. Russian tarragon will have only a faint flavor and scent, but French tarragon's flavor will explode on your tongue.

Cooking with Tarragon   Tarragon's flavor is complex. It doesn't work with everything, but there are a great many foods suited to its sweet and refined taste. The first to come to mind are mild seafood. Stir the chopped leaves into a lemony sauce for poached halibut or sole, add it to a mixture for crabcakes, or sprinkle it over seared sea scallops. In the true version of oysters Rockefeller, tarragon flavors the spinach stuffing. The green anise quality of tarragon also pairs beautifully with vegetables like young carrots, beets, peas, asparagus, and green beans. Use it in salads, tossing in whole leaves or blending it into a vinaigrette. It's excellent with tomatoes, raw or cooked. Classic Green Goddess dressing and sauce rémoulade both rely on tarragon for their distinctive tastes. The leaves perk up egg preparations from omelets to lobster soufflé. Tarragon with chicken is a timeless pairing—a cream sauce laced with fresh tarragon leaves and napped on a juicy chicken breast is hard to improve on. Béarnaise sauce—the traditional accompaniment to Châteaubriand—gets much of its character from fresh tarragon, and tarragon works well in many other dishes with tender cuts of beef, veal, and pork.

On the sweet side, tarragon is good in salads with ripe melon, peaches, or apricot and is particularly intriguing in citrus desserts like grapefruit sorbet or lime tart. Tarragon is also one of the very few herbs that pairs well with chocolate. You can infuse it into the cream for a chocolate truffle or into the butter for gooey flourless chocolate cake.

Despite the versatility of tarragon, you have to acknowledge it can be an herbal prima donna. Depending on the amount used, its flavor can come through subtly or assertively, but it's always distinct. If it's sharing the pot with another herb that might upstage it, like rosemary, Greek oregano, savory, or sage, it will put up a fight. Keep it away from resinous herbs that will clash with and overpower tarragon's more specialized flavor and only pair it with herbs it gets along with. Tarragon is compatible with parsley, chives, and chervil—when you put the four together you have the French herb mixture known as fines herbes—and with mint or lemony herbs. Because fresh tarragon infuses its flavor beautifully into acidic ingredients, it's often used to flavor vinegar and mustard.

Always add fresh tarragon at the very end of the cooking process, since it quickly loses flavor if heated for long. You can chop it fine or purée it, but I like tarragon best when the leaves are coarsely chopped or even left whole. Begin with one tablespoon for six servings and add more as you wish.

Tarragon's intensity can vary wildly. If you are harvesting from your own garden, the flavor will change with the seasons and reach its peak of strength in the heat of midsummer. The packaged sprigs from the supermarket, even if the true French variety, are sometimes disappointing, partly because they're grown quickly with high nitrogen fertilizer, often in hydroponic greenhouses, and partly because they might have been picked weeks ago. Tarragon is particularly susceptible to flavor loss with age, so try to use it as close to the time of harvest as possible. If weakly flavored tarragon is all you can get, use a larger amount.

Growing Tarragon Give tarragon excellent drainage and plenty of sun. Unlike more rugged herbs, like thyme or sage, tarragon grows best in reasonably rich soil. The plants will die down to the ground in the fall and should survive very cold winters as long as the roots aren't waterlogged. Every three or four years it's beneficial to dig and divide the plants in early spring, then replant the pieces with some space between.

A particularity of tarragon is that, like a tulip, it requires a period of cold dormancy. If you live in a frost-free climate, you might have trouble growing it as a perennial. If this is the case, try growing Mexican tarragon, *Tagetes lucida,* an unrelated plant that is actually a marigold (and sometimes called marigold mint) and loves the heat. It has a slightly sweeter and more intense licorice flavor than French tarragon and its leaves are thicker and coarser, but it tastes similar enough that it can be used as a substitute tablespoon for tablespoon. As a bonus, Mexican tarragon produces small edible marigold-like flowers in late summer and fall.

Harvesting Tarragon Clipping from a tarragon plant is very simple: It doesn't really matter where you cut but don't harvest more than half the plant at a time. Leave enough green to provide strength for the plant to grow back.

Storing Tarragon The sooner you cook with tarragon after it is picked, the better, but fresh sprigs will keep in a resealable plastic bag in the vegetable crisper of your refrigerator for up to four days. Don't bother trying to dry the herb; it loses its flavor entirely. If you want to preserve its flavor, make tarragon vinegar (page 311).

THYME

English Thyme If you cook very much with fresh herbs, thyme deserves a place right beside salt and pepper. Its ingratiating flavor works in more dishes than any other plant in the herb garden. Whether it's humming in the background or conspicuously assertive, thyme seems to go with everything.

There are a great many types of thyme, some culinary, some not. In the kitchen, when we say thyme, we usually mean the plant *Thymus vulgaris,* and specifically the variety called English thyme. A garden relative of the wild thyme that grows on Mediterranean hillsides, it's a tiny evergreen shrub in the mint family with highly aromatic, tough little leaves and wiry stems. Its spicy fragrance has subtle tones of pine and camphor and a certain fruitiness that reminds me of ripe pears.

Cooking with Thyme As long as you match the quantity of the herb you use to the robustness of the food, thyme is comfortable with nearly any meat, poultry, fish, or seafood. Likewise, it adds savoriness to most vegetables, from hearty roots and tubers like parsnips and potatoes to summer crops like eggplant and tomatoes. It always goes well with onions and their relatives; imagine it in a caramelized onion soup or a leek tart. It's good with cheeses, particularly goat cheese, and eggs, and at least a hint of thyme is essential when you cook dried beans.

English thyme is indispensable when making stocks. If you leave it out, it's like making a cake without vanilla—it tastes okay but a bit flat, and you know something is missing. Add it to marinades, stews, braises, roasts, and breads. Tie it with parsley and bay leaves and you have a classic bouquet garni, a little herb bag or bundle that simmers in the pot. English thyme even works in some desserts. With a judicious hand, it adds interest to simple pound cake and shortbread, and it's quite good with pears, figs, sweet cheeses or combined with caramel or honey. Most of the other Mediterranean herbs—rosemary, oregano, marjoram, and sage—are easy matches with thyme, as are chives, fennel, bay, lavender, and parsley.

English thyme's agreeable flavor is very sturdy. You can add it at any point in the cooking process from the beginning of a braise to a last-minute sprinkle. For dishes with marinades or long-cooking times you can use the leaves whole. When you don't want the texture to be noticed, chop it very fine or use it in an herb bundle that will be pulled out and not eaten. Be as timid or daring as you wish with the herb, using anywhere from one teaspoon to one-quarter cup for six servings. The larger amount will make a strong statement and is best with something like a grilled leg of lamb or a hearty winter soup.

Thyme Varieties Several other species of *Thymus vulgaris* are interchangeable with English thyme. French thyme, sometimes called summer thyme (English thyme being winter thyme), looks and smells almost identical, but its leaves are slightly narrower. The growers at The Herbfarm are big fans of it because it's less woody and produces more soft lush growth, but the tradeoff is it's not as hardy. Another variety is silver thyme, a lovely garden plant with shimmering grayish leaves and the same habit and flavor as the English.

Lemon Thyme Lemon thyme is a real charmer in the herb garden. It's like English thyme in many ways but has a delightful citrus fragrance on top of its savoriness, making it more food friendly than other lemon herbs.

Two types of lemon thyme, *T. citriodorus,* are commonly grown. The one you're most likely to see in nurseries is a variegated variety whose tiny leaves are a bold vivid gold and bordered with a green stripe. It's a gorgeous plant that provides a glowing foliar contrast to the green leaves of other herbs. But like other variegated plants, the absence of green causes less photosynthesis to occur, resulting in a smaller and slightly less vigorous herb. An all-green variety of lemon thyme with an identical flavor is also available. In exchange for the lack of gilding, it grows larger and faster and is more winter hardy.

The degree of lemon flavor in this herb fluctuates markedly depending on the season, soil conditions, and how recently it was cut. It's always stronger tasting in hot weather and when grown in a sunny, well-drained spot. Before you buy a plant, particularly the nonvariegated type, give it a smell test to be sure it's from good stock. Often you'll buy a plant labeled as lemon thyme to find it smells much more like English thyme or hardly smells at all.

While not as all-purpose as English thyme, lemon thyme is still very versatile. It loves seafood in particular, adding a harmonious savoriness while allowing the sweetness and freshness of fish and shellfish to come through. Let it give a delicate accent to halibut or sole, a haunting fragrance to a seafood consommé, or a lively stroke in a garlicky bouillabaisse. Think of it with any vegetable you would serve with lemon—beets, carrots, asparagus, spinach, or fennel bulb. Add it to all types of poultry dishes or delicate meats like veal or rabbit. It makes terrific shortbread to serve with fruit compotes, and it adds a deep lemon note to poaching syrups, especially for pears or quince.

In contrast to its sturdy cousin, the flavor of lemon thyme is very fleeting. Add it at the end of cooking so that its lemony oils won't evaporate. It's also one of the most sensitive herbs once chopped, quickly losing flavor and blackening, so prepare it just before you add it.

Caraway Thyme   Caraway thyme is a creeping, low-growing plant with the same flavor as the seed of the caraway plant. Its Latin name is *T. herba-barona,* because it was used in medieval times to season baron of beef, the huge mountain of roasted meat (in modern times, the double sirloin) that can still be seen on buffet lines.

Pair caraway thyme with beef, venison, cabbage, potatoes, cucumbers, beets, caramelized onions, and with mushrooms, particularly morels if you're lucky enough to have them.

Orange Balsam Thyme   The fragrance of orange balsam thyme elicits strong reactions. Some people adore it and others think it smells like harsh soap. Even if its pungency doesn't appeal to you, it's attractive to have in the garden for its healthy deep green foliage and its ability to look better through the winter than any other culinary thyme.

This thyme's powerful and astringent bitter orange taste makes it a difficult herb to use successfully in cooking, but it does have its uses. Most of all I like it with cranberries—in a sauce, bread, or candy. It can add a distinct citrus accent to pork or rabbit, and in sweets with nuts, dates, bananas, pears, and apples. Remember to begin with a tiny amount and add more a little at a time.

Growing Thyme   Thyme is perennial, very hardy, and carefree. It should flourish in any part of the country, but the key to growing it well is a sunny spot and well-drained soil. Thyme hates to grow in a water-saturated bed; its flavor will be weaker, its growth stunted, and the wetness, not the cold will most likely kill it off in the winter. Since it doesn't take up much room, you can tuck thyme plants here and there in the flower border. It's an easy plant for growing in pots, either by itself or sharing a planter with other herbs and flowers. You'll want at least a half-dozen plants to provide you with a constant supply.

It's a good idea to give your thyme plants an annual spring pruning to keep them vigorous and to prevent them from getting woody and lanky. When new growth starts, usually about the time of the last frost, trim the plants back by about a third of their total height, but don't cut back below where there are any leaves.

In late spring or early summer your thyme will cover itself in bloom, and the quarter-inch clusters of white or pale pink blossoms will have all the flavor of the leaves. You can chop them with the green leaves or use them as a garnish to sprinkle on any dish you like. Be aware that their texture can be a bit coarse, so use them sparingly on a creamy potato soup or a smooth salmon mousse, and reserve the generous toss for tomato bruschetta or white bean salad. After the plants flower and you've enjoyed their blossoms, cut them back again by about a third to encourage fresh growth and another bloom later in the season.

Harvesting Thyme   There are two ways to harvest thyme. The most common method is to simply grab a handful of sprigs and snip them about halfway down the stem, remembering not to cut more than a third of the total plant at once. But if you harvest when the plants have a nice flush of soft new growth, you might want to give the plants a little haircut instead. Take your scissors and trim about one-half inch evenly off the top of the plants, letting it fall into a bowl or basket below. Trimmed this way, the stems will all be soft, and when you bring the cuttings into the kitchen, you can chop the whole lot without having to first remove tough stems. The buzz-cut (trim) keeps the plants nicely manicured and bushy, and they'll soon produce another flush of growth.

Storing Thyme   Keep fresh thyme sprigs in a resealable plastic bag in the vegetable crisper of your refrigerator. They will stay fresh for up to two weeks with little flavor loss.

Because thyme keeps its flavor so well, it is one of the best herbs for drying. Harvest thyme when in bud, hang it upside down in bunches until dry, and then store it on or off the stem in a tightly sealed jar in a dark cupboard. For the next six months you can substitute it for fresh, especially in stocks and stews, using one teaspoon in place of one tablespoon of fresh leaves.

CHAPTER 17

Cooking with Flowers

An herb garden is filled with more than sprigs of green leaves. You'll find tiny pale pink blossoms topping the mint and thyme, brilliant sky blue stars among the rosemary needles, and azure buds held above the sage leaves. Elegant purple spikes rise from silvery lavender, violet globes are held aloft above slender chives, and lacy yellow umbels tower over dill and fennel. With the exception of French tarragon, all herbs bloom. Most have flavor characteristics that are similar to the leaves of the plant, often with a bit of extra sweetness. Some herb blossoms are milder tasting than the foliage, like thyme, sage, and oregano, and some are stronger, like chives and lavender. All make lovely garnishes when used with restraint.

Apart from the blooms of culinary herbs that have aromatic leaves, there are many other edible flowers that have been used in cooking for hundreds of years and are an integral part of a traditional herb garden. These include calendula, nasturtium, borage, clove pinks (dianthus), old-fashioned roses, pansies, violas, and violets. Others are less traditional but nevertheless tasty, like some varieties of tulips, tuberose begonias, and certain vegetable flowers like mustard, kale, pea, and runner-bean blossoms.

Please keep in mind that because a flower is edible does not mean it tastes good. Fuchsia blossoms and African marigolds are not poisonous, but they don't belong on your dinner plate. And even flowers that are pleasant in small amounts can be unpalatable in quantity. A few florets of chive blossom floating in a bowl of soup are elegant and delicious, but the entire blossom is so strong it is impossible to eat in one bite without grimacing. A sliver of red tulip petal in a salad will taste like a raw pea, but an entire tulip flower is like an entire bowl of raw peas. A tiny viola is a charming garnish for a small slice of strawberry tart, but a giant pansy looks tawdry.

Before you eat any flower, or even use it as a garnish for food, pay attention to the following rules. First, you must be able to identify the flower you plan to eat and you must be certain the species is edible—never guess. Many flowers are toxic, some mildly and some seriously. A few of the more common garden flowers that are poisonous are daffodil, delphinium, foxglove, hyacinth, monkshood, and sweet pea, but there is a long list of others. Second, be sure the plants that bear these flowers were grown without toxic pesticides, which means never eat flowers from a florist's shop because the chemicals used on them do not take food safety into consideration. For the same reason, when you purchase ornamental plants from a nursery, like pansies or calendula, allow them a few weeks in your garden before you eat the blossoms because you don't know what they've been treated with. They are often fed growth retardant to prevent them from outgrowing their pots while waiting to be sold.

BORAGE

Some gardeners think borage is coarse and weedy, but I think it is a masterpiece of form, texture, and color. Bold gray green leaves, covered with a bristly fuzz, support graceful two-foot lilting sprays of flowers and buds. The flowers themselves are small, wispy five-pointed stars of clear, silky azure blue with a sharp black point sticking out the middle like a pencil tip. They are held in prominent calyxes, and to harvest you must lightly grab on to the black point and gently coax the blossom out of its holder. They have a mild cucumber flavor, but the flower is so thin and light that the taste is almost unnoticeable. Their splendid color and form, however, make them an invaluable garnish. Picture three casually dropped on a bowl of carrot soup, a tomato salad, or a plate of scallops with saffron sauce.

Traditionally borage, *Borago officinalis,* was considered a potherb, meaning an herb whose leaves are used as greens. Although this practice would displease with most modern palates, the very young tender leaves in small quantity are good in salads. The cucumber flavor is much more noticeable in the greenery than in the flowers.

Borage is an annual and very easy to grow. It dies back very soon after flowering but loves to self-sow, so you can have several crops of it in one season. Incidentally its blue flower is best known as a symbol of courage.

CALENDULA

Calendula officinalis is the plant the English call a marigold or pot marigold (what we call marigolds, they call African marigolds), but in the United States we say calendula. The plant's bright orange or yellow daisylike flowers, each about two inches across, hold from dozens to hundreds of petals. This flower has been used for cooking since Roman times. In the medieval kitchen, where they seemed to be obsessed with coloring their foods, the bright golden petals served as a saffron substitute. I like to sprinkle a few of them on a salad like confetti, let a few petals fall on a bowl of cherry soup or borscht, or add them to an herb butter for a bit of color.

DAYLILY

Both the petals and the buds of daylilies, *Hemerocallis,* have a sweet lettuce flavor. Like roses and tulips, some varieties taste better than others. The most delicious is the early blooming yellow variety called lemon lily, which has a strong citrus scent. A new variety has just been introduced that was bred specifically for eating called Buttercrunch. One or two flower petals are delightful in a salad, and the closed buds can be cooked like a vegetable. Harvest them just before they are about to open and stir-fry them quickly. They are a nice accent with other vegetables like green beans, snap peas, and young carrots. Dried daylily buds, called golden needles, are sold in most Asian groceries. They are soaked in hot water for fifteen minutes and added to Chinese dishes like hot-and-sour soup and moo shu pork.

MEADOWSWEET

Fillipendula ulmaria, or meadowsweet, is a hardy perennial that grows four to five feet tall and blooms in June. When steeped in milk or cream, the lacy white sprays of tiny blossoms give off a summery honey flavor, similar to the scent of alyssum. The herb is often used medicinally because the flowers are a natural source of salicylic acid, or aspirin, which means if you are allergic to aspirin, you should not eat meadowsweet.

MONARDA

Also known as bee balm, Oswego tea, or bergamot (not to be confused with the citrus fruit used in Earl Grey tea), *Monarda didyma* is a three- to four-foot perennial in the mint family with showy, shaggy composite flowers of red, pink, purple, or white. The petals have a flavor very much like oregano. Pull them off the coarse flower center and sprinkle them over salads and steamed or sautéed vegetables, or use them as colorful additions to herb butters.

NASTURTIUMS

If you're skeptical about eating flowers, try a salad with a few nasturtium blossoms and you might become a believer. These bold, cheerful blossoms in brilliant clear shades of yellow, orange, red, and apricot have a delicate and slightly crisp texture and a deliciously hot radishlike bite, underscored with a touch of sweetness. Born on exuberant plants with round bright green leaves (also edible), *Tropaeolum majus* is among the easiest annual to grow from seeds. The species sends out stems six to eight feet long, while selected strains like Gleam, Whirlybird, and the variegated Alaska form compact ten- to fifteen-inch mounds.

When you bring nasturtiums into your kitchen, always check them inside and out for aphids, flea beetles, or any other living creatures and brush any you see off with your finger or a pastry brush. Nasturtiums make a stunning and tasty garnish for salads and other savory dishes, either used whole or torn into multicolored confetti. I also like to toss whole blossoms with greens or vegetables when dressing a salad. Keep in mind that once the flowers are coated with dressing, they wilt rapidly and the salad must be served right away. If you gently mix several dozen whole blossoms of different colors with a half pound of soft butter, then roll it into logs in plastic wrap, chill, and slice it in coins, you'll have kaleidoscopic butter pats (page 339). Stuffed nasturtiums make gorgeous hors d'oeuvres—just pipe a flavored cheese or other spread into their centers and arrange them on a platter lined with nasturtium leaves. You can even pickle the green seed pods and produce something very similar to a homemade caper (page 310).

The other species worth growing in the kitchen garden, *Tropaeolum tuberosum*, is rarely seen in American gardens but it is a food crop in Bolivia, Chile, and Peru, and we grow it at The Herbfarm in great quantity. A tall and ardent climber with deeply lobed, dark green leaves, it sends out slender tubular orange blossoms on long stems very late in the fall. We grow this plant for the underground tubers, which also begin to form when the days grow short. Looking very much like a small fingerling potato, they have a wonderful crispness and a hot bite similar to the flowers of common nasturtiums. When cooked, they lose their peppery quality and become very sweet with a unique nuttiness.

PANSIES, VIOLAS, AND JOHNNY JUMP-UPS

Pansies, violas, and Johnny jump-ups are essentially the same flower in three different sizes, all members of the genus *Viola*. Pansies have the largest blooms, up to two inches across, in all shades except true red; violas have a smaller flower, usually about an inch across; and Johnny jump-ups have even smaller blooms with characteristic whiskered faces of purple and white with yellow highlights. These easy-to-grow annuals reach four to eight inches tall and have a spreading habit; they do well spilling over the sides of containers or weaving among low-growing herbs in the ground. The more you pick them the more they'll bloom, and they are especially floriferous in the cool weather of spring and fall. They can even tolerate mild frosts.

All forms of these flowers have a pleasant flavor—perfumed and slightly sweet, with a floral wintergreen flavor and no bitterness—so rather than pushing them aside as incidental garnish, they are worth a nibble. Most of the flavor is concentrated in the base of the flower where the petals meet the calyx. Scatter a few Johnny jump-ups on a mixed salad or float a small yellow viola on smooth green lettuce soup. Brushed with egg white, sprinkled with sugar, and dried (page 313), they keep indefinitely and make elegant additions to a plate of chocolate truffles or stunning garnish for a special-occasion cake.

My favorite technique for cooking with these flowers is to grind them in a food processor with an equal amount of sugar, then use the resulting paste to make syrup or sorbet (page 297) or as a natural food color. I most often process black pansies and violas in this way (the flowers are such a dark purple they seem black) because they have a particularly delicious violet flavor, and the resulting syrup is a brilliant magenta. Deep purple pansies and violas can also be used.

PINKS

Clove pinks or gillyflowers, *Dianthus caryophyllus,* are related to carnations. They have an intoxicating, powerfully sweet clove scent and have been a favorite flower for turning into syrups, candies, cordials, and other preserves since the sixteenth century. In today's kitchen you can add the individual petals to salads, use them to garnish desserts, candy them (page 313), or steep them in syrup to make sorbet. Before you cook with the petals, cut off the small white base which has a bitter taste.

ROSES

Foods made with rose petals signal romance, and they have been used in cooking since Roman times. Throughout the centuries they were pounded into conserves, steeped in honey and vinegar, and made into syrups, candies, and cordials. If you taste a delicate candied rose petal or a refreshing sorbet made of roses and Champagne, you'll want to revive this tradition in your own kitchen.

These old-fashioned recipes require old-fashioned roses. The modern long-stemmed hybrid tea roses in florists and grown extensively in home gardens were bred for form, and usually have thick bitter petals and, more important, little scent. They are also more susceptible to disease and are often sprayed with pesticides. What you want is a highly fragrant blossom with thin to medium-thin petals. You'll find them on roses classified as Damasks, Bourbons, Gallicas, and Musks—all old varieties with shrubby growth habits. These flowers come in a variety of shapes, but most are rounder and flatter than the high-centered teas and have a color range limited to white, pink, red, and violet. Most bloom only once a year in a great flush of glory in June. Recently rose breeders have been developing roses with the form, scent, and habit of the old-fashioned varieties but that bloom throughout the season and are resistant to disease. Most notable is the group of roses bred by David Austin in Great Britain.

To extract the flavor and color of these fragrant roses, I like to treat them in the same way I handle black pansies or lemon verbena leaves—I put them in a food processor with sugar and grind them to a paste. You can then dissolve this paste in water to make a flavored syrup, as in Old Rose and Champagne Sorbet (page 295). A small delicate petal or two is lovely in a tossed salad, and strips of petals can be added to rice or grain dishes. Rose petals are the easiest and most delicious flowers to candy by painting with egg white and sprinkling with sugar (page 312). Prepared this way, they last for months and make a divine cake decoration, garnish for desserts, or little nibble to end a meal.

Rose water, available in Middle Eastern or Indian groceries, is a clear essence distilled from fresh roses. It has a similar fragrance and flavor as the petals from your own backyard. A tablespoon or two is all you need for an average recipe.

SQUASH BLOSSOMS

These giant golden orange blossoms have a flavor very similar to the squash itself. Zucchini blossoms are most commonly used for cooking, but all varieties of squash blossoms are edible. Taste them first because some, particularly flowers of winter squash, can be bitter. Squash blossoms are either male or female. Males have a spiky calyx and slender stem at the base. Females have a little baby squash attached at the bottom. Both have the same flavor and can be used in the same ways. To encourage squash plants to keep producing blossoms, you must keep harvesting the fruit and not allow any squash to mature. The blossoms are at their peak for one day. They begin in a trumpet shape, open wide like a giant golden five-pointed star, then close again. If you buy squash blossoms at a market, keep in mind that if the petals are wilted and curled shut at the top, the flower is old and dying. Before using the female blossoms, snap off the pistil inside the blossom because it has a disagreeable texture. The stamens in male blossoms can be left alone.

Piles of zucchini blossoms, usually just males, are sold in bundles at produce markets all over Italy. The traditional Italian way to prepare them is to dip the blossoms in batter and deep-fry them. Large blossoms are perfect for stuffing, so before I fry them, I like to put a cube of fresh mozzarella and a teaspoon of pesto inside. As an alternative to frying, I often blanch the blossoms, stuff them, and heat them in a warm oven (page 84), so they keep their vibrant color and fresh flavor. The raw blossoms can be torn into pieces and stirred into risotto, and in Mexico they are often stirred into soups. Torn blossoms are also lovely in salads.

Other Blossoms in the Vegetable Garden   Not all blossoms in the vegetable garden are edible. Never eat those of plants in the nightshade family like tomatoes, eggplant, or peppers. But you can eat flowers of legumes like runner beans and garden peas, brassicas like kale, mustard, and cress, and all squash. They all have a sweet flavor reminiscent of the vegetable they come from. Add them to salads or sprinkle them onto foods as garnish. See Salad Ingredients for The Herbfarm Garden Salad (page 45) for a more detailed list.

Sweet Woodruff

This charming ground cover, *Galium odoratum,* is a rapidly spreading, low-growing shade plant. In mid-May it covers itself with dainty white flowers. The peculiarity of this herb is that it has little fragrance until it's dried or steeped, when it comes forth with a cross between hay, vanilla, and honey. Sweet woodruff is the flavoring for May wine, a German drink of Riesling wine steeped with the flowering sprigs (page 318).

Tuberose Begonia

Tuberose begonias have thick fleshy leaves and stems topped with big, floppy rose-shaped flowers in vibrant clear shades of yellow, orange, pink, and bright red. Their blossoms don't look anything like food, but they are edible with a wonderful tart flavor very similar to sorrel, and a crisp, delicate texture. Don't get them mixed up with wax begonias, which have glossy leaves, small single waxy flowers, and are not edible.

Small pieces of tuberose begonia petal are delightful in green salads or seafood salads. Always tear or snip the petals at the last minute because they bruise easily and discolor quickly. Ron Zimmerman, The Herbfarm's owner and first chef, likes to snip thin strips of the petals into beurre blanc (French wine and butter sauce) for fish. They bleed a little, lend a delicate lemon flavor, and create a gorgeous confetti-like pattern.

Tulip

Yes, tulip petals are edible. Some tulip varieties have petals that taste like sweet fresh peas, while others lack sweetness and are not as tasty. You have to sample each one and make your own judgment. At The Herbfarm, we've found that red Emperor tulip petals always have good flavor, and small pieces of the petals make a striking addition to a mixed green salad.

Violets

Violets are also members of the genus *Viola,* but they are low-growing perennial shade plants with heart-shaped leaves. Their small flowers are most often purple, though yellow and white varieties exist, and they appear in early spring. An individual flower may have only a faint perfume, but a mass of them gives off an elusive heady scent. Treat them as you would other violas—as a salad garnish or for syrup, and they're especially wonderful candied.

Sources

The Cook's Garden
P.O. Box 535
Londonderry, VT 05148
Herb, vegetable, and flower seeds

The Herbfarm
32804 Issaquah-Fall City Road
Fall City, WA 98024
www.theherbfarm.com
*Herbal products and herb plants, dried
lavender buds*

Johnny's Selected Seeds
Foss Hill Road
Albion, ME 04910
www.johnnyseeds.com
Herb, vegetable, and flower seeds

Nichols Garden Nursery
1190 North Pacific Highway
Albany, OR 97321
www.gardennursery.com
*Herb and vegetable plants and seeds, dried
lavender buds*

Richters
357 Highway 47
Goodwood, Ontario
L0C 1A0 Canada
www.richters.com
Herb seeds and plants

Sandy Mush Herb Nursery
316 Surret Cove Road
Leicester, NC 28748
Herb plants

Seeds of Change
P.O. Box 15700
Santa Fe, NM 87506
www.seedsofchange.com
Herb and vegetable seeds

Shepherd's Garden Seeds
30 Irene Street
Torrington, CT 06790
www.shepherdseeds.com
Herb, vegetable, and flower seeds

Territorial Seed Company
P.O. Box 157
Cottage Grove, OR 97424
www.territorial-seed.com
Herb, vegetable, and flower seeds

The Thyme Garden
20546 Alsea Highway
Alsea, OR 97324
Herb plants and seeds

Well-Sweep Herb Farm
205 Mt. Bethel Road
Port Murray, NJ 07865
Herb plants and seeds

Wrenwood
Route 4, Box 25411
Berkeley Springs, WV 25411
www.wrenwood.com
Herb plants

BIBLIOGRAPHY

Beston, Henry. *Herbs and the Earth.* Garden City, New York: Dolphin Books, 1935.

Bown, Deni. *Encyclopedia of Herbs and Their Uses.* London: Dorling Kindersley Limited, 1995.

Boxer, Arabella, and Philippa Back. *The Herb Book.* London: Octopus Books Limited, 1980.

Bremness, Lesley. *The Complete Book of Herbs: A Practical Guide to Growing and Using Herbs.* New York: Viking Penguin, 1988.

Bryan, John E., and Coralie Castle. *The Edible Ornamental Garden.* San Francisco: 101 Productions, 1974.

Child, Julia. *The Way to Cook.* New York: Alfred A. Knopf, 1989.

Clarkson, Rosetta E. *Green Enchantment.* New York: Macmillan Publishing Company, 1940.

———. *Herbs: Their Culture and Uses.* New York: Macmillan Publishing Company, 1942.

Clifton, Claire. *Edible Flowers.* New York: McGraw-Hill Book Company, 1983.

Cutler, Karen Davis. *Burpee—The Complete Vegetable and Herb Gardener: A Guide to Growing Your Garden Organically.* New York: Macmillan, 1997.

Ferrary, Jeanette, and Louise Fiszer. *Season to Taste.* New York: Simon and Schuster, 1988.

Foley, Daniel J., ed. *Herbs for Use and Delight.* New York: Dover Publications, 1974.

Foster, Gertrude B. *Herbs for Every Garden.* New York: E. P. Dutton and Company, 1966.

Foster, Steven. *Herbal Renaissance.* Salt Lake City: Gibbs-Smith Publishers, 1983.

Fox, Helen Morgenthau. *Gardening with Herbs for Flavor and Fragrance.* New York: Macmillan Publishing Company, 1933.

Gayre, Lt. Col. G. R. *Common Herbs as Grown in the Hortyards at Gulval and Their Use.* Gulval, Cornwall: Mead Makers Ltd., 1950.

Grieve, M. *Culinary Herbs and Condiments.* New York: Harcourt Brace and Company, 1934.

Hall, Dorothy. *The Book of Herbs.* Sydney: Angus and Robertson, 1972.

Harrison, S. G., G. B. Masefield, and Michael Wallis. *The Oxford Book of Food Plants.* London: Oxford University Press, 1969.

Hatfield, Audrey Wynne. *Pleasures of Herbs.* London: Museum Press Limited, 1964.

Hayes, Elizabeth S. *Spices and Herbs: Lore and Cookery.* New York: Doubleday and Company, 1961.

Hazan, Marcella. *Essentials of Classic Italian Cooking.* New York: Alfred A. Knopf, 1992.

Hemphill, Rosemary. *Herbs for All Seasons.* London: Cassell Publishers Limited, 1972.

Hess, Karen. *Martha Washington's Booke of Cookery.* New York: Columbia University Press, 1981.

Hill, Madalene, and Gwen Barclay with Jean Hardy. *Southern Herb Growing.* Fredricksburg, TX: Shearer Publishing, 1987.

Hylton, William H., ed. *The Rodale Herb Book.* Emmaus, PA: Rodale Press, 1974.

Kourik, Robert. *The Lavender Garden.* San Francisco: Chronicle Books, 1998.

Krutch, Joseph Wood. *Herbal.* New York: G. P. Putnam's Sons, 1965.

Leyel, C. F. *Herbal Delights: Tisanes, Syrups, Confections, Electuaries, Robs, Juleps, Vinegars, and Conserves.* London: Faber and Faber Limited, 1937.

Masson, Madeleine, and Joan Wolfenden. *The Grand Salad.* Bonchurch, Isle of Wight: Peacock Vane Publishing, 1984.

Miloradovich, Milo. *The Art of Cooking with Herbs and Spices: A Handbook of Flavors and Savors.* Garden City, NY: Doubleday and Company, 1950.

Muenscher, Minnie Worthen. *Minnie Muenscher's Herb Cookbook.* Ithaca: Cornell University Press, 1978.

Muenscher, Walter C., and Myron A. Rice. *Garden Spice and Wild Pot-Herbs.* Ithaca: Comstock Publishing Associates, 1955.

Paston-Williams, Sara. *The National Trust Book of the Country Kitchen Store Cupboard.* London: David and Charles, 1985.

Paterson, Allen. *Herbs in the Garden.* London: J. M. Dent, 1985.

Paterson, Wilma. *A Country Cup.* London: Pelham Books, 1980.

Peck, Paula. *The Art of Fine Baking.* New York: Simon and Schuster, 1961.

Pellegrini, Angelo. *The Food Lover's Garden.* New York: Alfred A. Knopf, 1970.

Phillips, Roger, and Nicky Fox. *The Random House Book of Herbs.* New York: Random House, 1990.

Preus, Mary. *Growing Herbs.* Seattle: Sasquatch Books, 1994.

Rohde, Eleanour Sinclair. *A Garden of Herbs.* Hale, Cushman & Flint, 1936.

Rombauer, Irma S., Marion Rombauer Becker, and Ethan Becker. *Joy of Cooking.* New York: Scribner, 1997.

Root, Waverly. *Food.* New York: Simon and Schuster, 1980.

Saville, Carole. *Exotic Herbs.* New York: Henry Holt and Company, 1997.

Schneider, Elizabeth. *Uncommon Fruits and Vegetables: A Commonsense Guide.* New York: Harper and Row, 1986.

Teubner, Christian. *The Herbs and Spices Cookbook.* New York: Penguin Studio, 1997.

Tillona, Francesca, and Cynthia Strowbridge. *A Feast of Flowers.* New York: Funk and Wagnalls, 1969.

Walter, Eugene. *Hints and Pinches.* Atlanta: Longstreet Press, 1991.

Willan, Anne. *La Varenne Practique.* London: Dorling Kindersley Limited, 1989.

ACKNOWLEDGMENTS

This book is rooted in a place—The Herbfarm—where I have cultivated my love and knowledge of living herbs. The spirit of The Herbfarm will always belong with the founders, Lola and Bill Zimmerman, who planted and nurtured the seeds that began the business and are still watching it grow. Their love of the herbs and the earth, their gardening wisdom, and their gentle warmth guide all of us at The Herbfarm every day.

It is the creative vision and tireless work of their son and daughter-in-law, Ron Zimmerman and Carrie Van Dyck, that has turned an out-of-the-way garage into a world-class restaurant. Their commitment to creating an incomparable dining experience for every person who sits at our tables is responsible for the success of The Herbfarm Restaurant. It is a privilege to be able to work with them and I thank them for the opportunities they have given me.

While this book was just an idea in my head and I was looking for inspiration, I pulled a stack of my favorite cookbooks off my shelf. Most were edited by Maria Guarnaschelli. Maria has told me that I'm lucky in life. The fact that she saw the potential in my proposal and became my editor proves her right. I am deeply grateful for the generous time and expertise she has given to this book. Her enthusiasm, encouragement, and brilliance have guided me through every chapter and I have learned so much from her.

My wonderful agent, Judith Riven, convinced me I could write this book and has been there to follow through in every stage of the process. I thank her for leading me through this unfamiliar territory and making it a pleasant adventure.

I owe much for the support of everyone who has worked at The Herbfarm Restaurant over the years. I'd particularly like to thank Matt Dillon, Lisa Gordanier, Craig Serbousek, Tom Zimmerman, and Jodell Campbell.

I'm grateful to Louise Smith for her exquisite watercolors, Elayne Sears for her wonderful drawings, Jonelle Weaver for her color photographs, and my friend and fellow gardener Virginia Hand for her lovely interior design. Thanks to Barbara Ottenhoff for her meticulous copy editing, M.C. Hald for her tireless effort on behalf of the book through all of its stages, Erich Hobbing for his design expertise, Olga Leonardo for her production skills, Paul Dippolito for his adroit paging, and Fran McCullough for valuable help with the early stages of the manuscript. My appreciation goes to all who tested recipes, including Jon and Kathy Riper, Mary Kay Malinoski, and Heidi Gregory.

I'd like to thank Jon Rowley for teaching me about umami, Jordi Viladas and Carla Leonardi for teaching me about pasta, Greg Atkinson for inspiring me with his writing, Bette Stuart for her overwhelming generosity and those fresh eggs, Mauny Kaseburg for her rose geranium story, and Ernesto Pino, Richard Gray, Carrol Sullivan, Kathy Anderson, Kim Chalupka, Terry and R. Niel-Volstad, and Judy Mahnke for their friendship and support.

I give much love and thanks for the support of all of my family: my parents, Poppy and Irving, who have encouraged me to pursue my love of cooking since I first picked up a whisk at age eleven; my sister, Sue Hardy, and her family; my brother, Jon, and his family; and, most of all, Stephen Hudson, who has shared my life for twenty years and is always there for me.

Index

toasts, thyme honey and gorgonzola, grilled figs with, 78–79

tomato(es):
and basil, slow-roasted, fish fillets en papillote with, 158–60
and basil crostini, 73
and fennel soup, 22–23
and herbs, fresh, fettuccine with, 108–9
and herb salad, fresh, 60
and herb salsa, roasted, 219
roasted cherry, spaghetti with thyme and, 110
salad, herbed, stuffed squash blossoms on, 84–85
slow-roasted, 340
sun-dried, braised lamb shanks with orange, rosemary and, 231–32
tomato sauce, 108–11
torte, mint-chocolate truffle, 290–91

trout:
rainbow, with browned herb butter, 164–65
smoked, and corn puddings, 86–87

truffles, herbal chocolate, 292–93
truffle torte, chocolate-mint, 290–91
tuberose begonia, 50–51, 433
tulip, 50–51, 433
tuna steaks, herb and peppercorn-crusted, with perilla salad, 166–67

U
umami carrot soup with mint, 24–25

V
vanilla bean, in desserts, 251
vegetable blossoms, 432–44
vegetables, 124–56
artichokes stuffed with basil and walnuts, 128
asparagus and mushroom risotto with lemon thyme, 122
balsamic potato salad, 62
braised fennel bulb, 132
carrot and jalapeño salad, 56

vegetables (cont.)
chanterelle and corn chowder with basil, 26
cold borscht with dilled sour cream, 42
delicata squash with rosemary, sage, and cider glaze, 143
fettuccine with fresh tomato and herbs, 108
fettuccine with sage butter and peas, 105
fresh tomato and herb salad, 60
green bean and nasturtium salad with tarragon, 52
green gazpacho, 40
green mashed potatoes, 150
grilled eggplant with rosemary, 140
grilled marjoram-scented corn, 138
herb-roasted potatoes, 146
leek and fennel soup, 23
lettuce and tarragon soup, 20
mashed potatoes with toasted coriander, 151
potatoes in herbed cream, 148
potatoes with lavender and rosemary, 147
pumpkin and shrimp bisque, 28
roasted asparagus salad with fried sage, 54
roasted beet, dill, and frisée salad, 58
roasted beets with chives and lemon balm, 137
roasted Belgian endive salad, 64
roasted parsnips with thyme, 145
roasted ratatouille, 141
runner beans with summer savory and bacon, 130
smoked trout and corn puddings, 86
snap peas with mint and chervil, 125
spaghetti with roasted cherry tomatoes and thyme, 110
spicy red cabbage with apple and cilantro, 144
spinach with sorrel, mint and anchovy, 127

vegetables (cont.)
fish fillets en papillote with, 158–60
stuffed squash blossoms on herbed tomato salad, 84
sweet onion and yogurt salad, 61
Swiss chard gratin, 134
stock, golden, 14–15
umami carrot soup with mint, 25
white bean and squash soup with parsley pistou, 34–35
young carrots with tarragon, 126
zucchini strands with mint, 136
see also specific vegetables

verbena, lemon, see lemon verbena
vinaigrette, Herbfarm, 332–33
vinegar, tarragon, 311
violas, 50–51, 431
violets, 50–51, 433

W
walnut(s):
artichokes stuffed with basil and, 128–29
lavender, and honey slipper breads, 240–41
warm crêpes with fresh date butter and chocolate sauce, 278–79
whipped cream, herb-infused—master recipe, 254
white beans, see bean(s), white
whole fish grilled on fennel stalks, 179–80
wine, May, 318
winter savory, 362–63, 417–18
runner beans with bacon and, 130–31
woodruff, sweet, 362–63
in May wine, 318

Y
yogurt and sweet onion salad, 61
young carrots with tarragon, 126

Z
zucchini strands with mint, 136